Mike Meyers' Certification

Passport

Network+®

Second Edition

Brian Schwarz
Glen E. Clarke

Osborne

New York • Chicago • San Francisco
Lisbon • London • Madrid • Mexico City
Milan • New Delhi • San Juan
Seoul • Singapore • Sydney • Toronto

The McGraw·Hill Companies

McGraw-Hill/Osborne
2100 Powell Street, 10th Floor
Emeryville, California 94608
U.S.A.

To arrange bulk purchase discounts for sales promotions, premiums, or fund-raisers, please contact McGraw-Hill/Osborne at the above address. For information on translations or book distributors outside the U.S.A., please see the International Contact Information page immediately following the index of this book.

Mike Meyers' Network+® Certification Passport, Second Edition

1234567890 DOC DOC 01987654

Book p/n 0-07-225349-5 and CD p/n 0-07-225350-9
parts of
ISBN 0-07-225348-7

Acquisitions Editors
Tim Green
Nancy Maragioglio

Project Editor
LeeAnn Pickrell

Acquisitions Coordinator
Jessica Wilson

Technical Editors
Glen E. Clarke
Dan Lachance

Copy Editor
Bart Reed

Proofreader
Stefany Otis

Indexer
Karin Arrigoni

Composition
Jean Butterfield
Peter F. Hancik
John Patrus
Dick Schwartz

Illustrators
Melinda Lytle
Kathleen Edwards

Series Design
epic, Peter F. Hancik
and Kelly Stanton-Scott

Cover Design
Ted Holladay

This book was composed with Corel VENTURA™ Publisher.

About the Authors

Brian Schwarz is a network operating system specialist who focuses on bringing conflicts between Windows and Linux networks to peaceful resolutions. Since 1994, Brian has been designing and delivering basic and advanced computer training to a wide range of audiences. Brian holds both the CompTIA A+ and Network+ certifications and an MCSE for Windows NT 4.0 certification, and he has built networks with just about every network operating system around, from the "good old days" of Windows for Workgroups and LANtastic to more current operating systems such as Red Hat Linux, Novell NetWare, and Windows 2000. Brian's previous publications include *A+ PC Technician's Pocket Reference, Network+ All in One Certification: Exam Guide (First Edition),* and *MCSE NT4 All-In-One Certification Exam Guide.*

Brian currently lives in Houston, Texas, where he works as an independent network consultant and technical trainer. You can contact Brian at brian@bluecollartech.com, or through his website at http://www.bluecollartech.com.

Glen E. Clarke is a Microsoft Certified Systems Engineer (MCSE), a Microsoft Certified Database Administrator (MCDBA), and a Microsoft Certified Solution Developer (MCSD). Glen also holds a number of Prosoft certifications including the Certified Internet Webmaster Certified Instructor (CIW CI) certification and the Certified Internet Webmaster Security Analyst (CIW SA) certification. Glen is also an A+ Certified Professional, Network+ Certified Professional, and a Security+ Certified Professional. He currently works as a technical trainer and consultant for GigaBlink Technologies Inc., a computer training and consulting company in Nova Scotia, Canada, where he teaches courses on Windows 2000/2003, SQL Server 2000, Exchange Server 2000, A+, Visual Basic, ASP, and security-related topics. Glen has also worked on a number of certification titles, as both a technical editor and an author, including topics such as A+ Certification, Windows 2000/2003 Certification, and Security+ Certification.

When he's not working, Glen loves to spend quality time with his wife, Tanya, and their three children, Sara, Brendon, and Ashlyn. He is an active member of the martial arts community, where he currently holds his first-degree black belt in Tae Kwon Do. You can contact Glen at gleneclarke@hotmail.com.

About the Technical Editor

Dan Lachance is a Master Certified Novell Instructor (MCNI), a Microsoft Certified Systems Engineer (MCSE), and a Certified Lotus Instructor (CLI). Dan also holds the Network+ Certified Professional certification. He works as a technical trainer for Polar Bear Corporate Education Solutions, one of Canada's leading training providers, providing instruction in programming, networking, and security-related topics.

About LearnKey

LearnKey provides self-paced learning content and e-learning solutions to enhance personal skills and business productivity. LearnKey claims the largest library of rich streaming-media training content that engages learners in dynamic media-rich instruction complete with video clips, audio, full motion graphics, and animated illustrations. LearnKey can be found on the Web at www.LearnKey.com.

Dedication

To all of my wonderful friends, but especially Dan and Rachel DiSepio, Scott Jernigan, Cindy Clayton, Brian and Shannen Smith, and Kim Guarino—you know why.

—Brian Schwarz

For my beautiful wife, Tanya, who has shown amazing love and support throughout the long nights of this book. If it were not for your love and understanding, I would not have the inspiration to write.

—Glen E. Clarke

Acknowledgments

We would like to take a moment to acknowledge the many folks who helped make this book possible.

Our families, for their patience and support throughout yet another big project.

The folks at McGraw-Hill/Osborne, for their wonderful input, encouragement, and threats of bodily harm, particularly Nancy Maragioglio and Jessica Wilson.

All of the folks at Total Seminars, who touched this book in ways large and small.

Dan Lachance, who provided invaluable technical feedback.

Dan and Rachel DiSepio, Scott Jernigan, and Cindy Clayton, for special contributions too numerous to be listed here.

—Brian Schwarz

I want to thank the wonderful people at McGraw-Hill/Osborne, especially Nancy Maragioglio and Jessica Wilson for their extreme patience and for creating a great team atmosphere! A special thank you to Nancy who has offered amazing encouragement and who has been a great team leader. You are the best! Thank you to close friend and former coworker, Dan Lachance, for great feedback and encouraging ideas as the technical editor. I would also like to thank another close friend and former coworker, Ed Tetz, who is always around when I need to pick someone's brain! Thanks Ed! Last, but not least, I would like to thank my three children, Sara, Brendon, and Ashlyn, for helping Daddy see the world through the eyes of a child all over again and gain respect for the simple things—running in the grass, watching the stars late at night, and sneaking the OREO cookies from the cupboard before mommy notices! I love the time I spend with all three of you!

—Glen E. Clarke

Contents

Check-In

May I See Your Passport?

What do you mean, you don't have a passport? Why, it's sitting right in your hands, even as you read! This book is your passport to a very special place. You're about to begin a journey, my friend: a journey toward that magical place called certification! You don't need a ticket, you don't need a suitcase—just snuggle up and read this passport. It's all you need to get there. Are you ready? Well then, let's go!

Your Travel Agent: Mike Meyers

Hello! I'm Mike Meyers, president of Total Seminars and author of a number of popular certification books. On any given day, you'll find me stringing network cable, setting up a website, or writing code. I love every aspect of this book you hold in your hands. It's part of a powerful book series called the *Mike Meyers' Certification Passports.* Every book in this series combines easy readability with a condensed format—in other words, the kind of book I always wanted when I went for my own certifications. Putting a large amount of information in an accessible format is certainly a challenge, but I think we've achieved our goal, and I'm confident you'll agree.

I designed this series to do one thing and only one thing: to get you the information you need to achieve your certification. You won't find any fluff in here. Nigel and I packed every page with nothing but the real nitty-gritty of the Network+ Certification exam. Every page has 100 percent pure concentrate of certification knowledge! But we didn't forget to make the book readable, so I hope you also enjoy the casual, friendly style.

My personal e-mail address is mikem@totalsem.com, and Nigel's e-mail address is nkendrick@skillmarque.com. Please feel free to contact either of us directly if you have any questions, complaints, or compliments.

Your Destination: Network+ Certification

This book is your passport to CompTIA's Network+ Certification, the vendor-neutral industry-standard certification for basic networking skills. Network+ Certification can be your ticket to a career in all-around networking or simply an excellent step in your certification pathway. This book is your passport to success on the Network+ Certification exam.

Your Guides: Brian Schwarz, and Glen Clarke

Since 1994, Brian Schwarz has been designing and delivering basic and advanced computer training to a wide range of audiences. Brian holds both the CompTIA A+ and Network+ certifications, and has built networks using just about every network operating system around, from Windows for Workgroups and LANtastic to Red Hat Linux, Novell NetWare, and Windows 2000. Brian's previous publications include *A+ PC Technician's Pocket Reference, Network+ All in One Certification: Exam Guide* (First Edition), and *MCSE NT4 All-In-One Certification Exam Guide.*

Glen E. Clarke (Halifax, NS) holds a number of industry certifications such as Microsoft's MCSE, MCDBA, MCSD, MCSA:Messaging, and MCSA:Security. He also holds a number of Prosoft certifications including the Security Analyst (CIW SA) certification, and CompTIA certifications such as Security+, Network+, and A+. Glen is an experienced trainer, author, and technical editor, and works for GigaBlink Technologies Inc., a training and consulting company located in Dartmouth, Nova Scotia.

Why the Travel Theme?

The steps in gaining a certification parallel closely the steps in planning and taking a trip. All of the elements are the same: preparation, an itinerary, a route, even mishaps along the way. Let me show you how it all works.

This book is divided into 12 chapters. Each chapter begins with an *Itinerary* section that lists the objectives covered in that chapter, and an *ETA* section to give you an idea of the time involved in learning the skills in that chapter. Each chapter is organized by the objectives, which are either drawn from those officially stated by the certifying body, or reflect our expert take on the best way to approach the topics. Also, each chapter contains a number of helpful items to highlight points of interest:

Exam Tip

Points out critical topics you're likely to see on the actual exam.

Travel Assistance

Lists additional sources, such as books and websites, to give you more information.

Local Lingo

Describes special terms in detail in a way you can easily understand.

Travel Advisory

Warns you of common pitfalls, misconceptions, and downright physical peril!

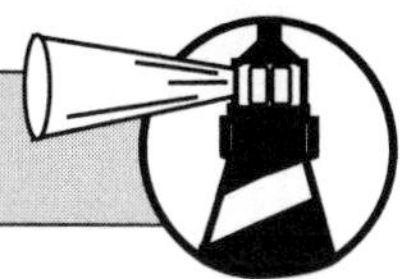

The end of each chapter gives you two handy tools. The *Checkpoint* reviews each objective covered in the chapter with a handy synopsis—a great way to review quickly—and end-of-chapter *Review Questions* (and answers) test your newly acquired skills.

But the fun doesn't stop there! After you've read the book, pull out the CD and take advantage of the free practice questions! Use the full practice exam to hone your skills, and keep the book handy to check your answers.

If you want even more practice, log onto http://www.osborne.com/passport, and for a nominal fee, you can get additional high-quality practice questions.

When you find yourself acing the practice questions, you're ready to take the exam. Go get certified!

The End of the Trail

The IT industry changes and grows constantly, *and so should you.* Finishing one certification is only one step in an ongoing process of gaining more and more certifications to match your constantly changing and growing skills. Read Appendix B, "Career Flight Paths," at the end of the book to find out where this certification fits into your personal certification goals. Remember, in the IT business, if you're not moving forward, you're way behind!

Good luck on your certification! Stay in touch!

Mike Meyers
Series Editor
Mike Meyers' Certification Passport

Network Fundamentals

ITINERARY

- **Objective 1.01** Overview of Network Hardware
- **Objective 1.02** Overview of Network Software
- **Objective 1.03** Data Packets
- **Objective 1.04** The OSI Seven-Layer Model
- **Objective 1.05** Real-World Networking

NEWBIE	SOME EXPERIENCE	EXPERT
4 hours	2 hours	1 hour

This chapter introduces you gently to the world of networking so that you can read the following chapters with some fundamental knowledge already in place. If you think you already have enough basic network experience, you can skip this chapter, but then again, a little refresher on the basics (especially the OSI seven-layer model) may not be a bad idea—and the chapter is not long!

All networks serve the same purpose—to share resources, whether the resources are printers, files, e-mail, web pages, or web services. Networks enable multiple users to access these shared resources simultaneously. Back in the late 1980s, the high cost of printers provided the motivation for many companies to install networks. Being unable to print over the network in 1984 would have generally been inconvenient. Today, networks provide access to a broader range of resources—archives of documents, customer databases, e-mail, and all the information we find on the Internet. Many businesses come to a virtual halt when the network fails because businesses have come to rely on their networks for far more than just printing. Today, computer users assume network connectivity, and our job is to ensure that network resources remain available at all times, or at least 99.999 percent of the time (an expectation commonly referred to as "guaranteeing five 9s.")

Overview of Network Hardware

We need to begin with some hardware on our network (see Figure 1.1), the most obvious example of which is a PC. Let's recognize early on, however, that networks can include a lot more than just the typical Windows 2000 or Windows XP PC that you find on many desks. Your network may include other operating systems, such as Linux, UNIX, Novell NetWare, or BSD. Some of the computers on your network might not even be PCs—you may have mainframe computers, Macintosh computers, maybe even an AS/400 system.

There's usually no problem linking together these seemingly incompatible systems, but recognize that the reason there is no problem is that some network engineer has already done the hard part for us. The networking software and hardware take care of the issues that arise from accessing information stored on one kind of system from a completely different type of computer. As an end user, you just see another drive letter on your computer—maybe W: for word processing. The details of the network remain invisible to the end user.

FIGURE 1.1 A typical pile of networked hardware

Clients and Servers

Networks have two categories of computers: those that access the networked resources (clients) and those that provide the resources (servers).

Clients

Any PC or other computer system that makes use of network resources is a client. In the old days, we might have called them *workstations,* but the modern term is *client.* Some may say *terminal,* but that really refers to a display and keyboard-only setup (no processing power, no Windows!) used for working with mainframes and minicomputers that do all the thinking for you.

Local Lingo

client A computer system that makes use of shared network resources. Network resources include files and printers, but may also include other kinds of resources, such as e-mail, web pages, and other network services.

Almost any PC can be a client, provided that you can attach it to the network and run the software needed to communicate with the network. Networking a PC does not make it more powerful; instead, it allows the PC to use remote resources, either in the same building, or perhaps halfway around the world.

Servers

Servers manage and host the network's shared resources. A small network may have a single server, but even relatively small companies can have dozens, each performing a specific task. One server may hold the network's files, and another may manage printers. A third server may control access to the Internet while acting as a firewall to keep out hackers. Ultimately, the number of servers required for a particular network depends on the workload the network will face. Sometimes a single server can do it all, but in large and medium-sized networks you will generally find multiple specialized servers. Later chapters will discuss how networks behave under load and what can be done to keep things running smoothly.

Local Lingo

server A computer system that provides and manages shared network resources. Shared network resources include files and printers, but may also include other kinds of resources, such as e-mail, web pages, and other network services.

Servers try to protect your resources from unwanted access. Every major network operating system (NOS), such as Microsoft Windows 2003 Server, Novell NetWare, UNIX, Linux, and BSD, will require each user to provide a valid username and password before granting access to its resources. If the user provides the right username and password, the server authenticates them and allows access to the server's resources. Other common features include the ability to restrict a specific user's network access to one or more machines or to certain days or times only.

Client/Server Networks

Most medium-sized and large business networks use dedicated servers, a model of networking referred to as a *client/server* or *server-based* network (see Figure 1.2). The server has a specific role to play (it's a server!) and will be tucked away safely (maybe in a computer room) and left to get on with its job—you won't find someone sitting at the server running Microsoft Word or Half-Life 2. The only time anyone touches the server keyboard will be when an authorized person performs some administrative task, such as updating software or performing a backup. The key benefits of the client/server network model are security, performance, and centralized administration.

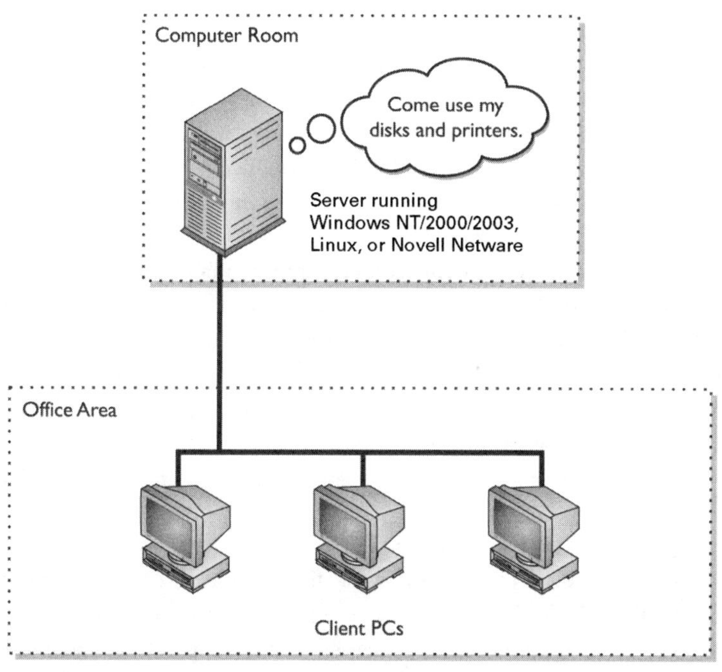

FIGURE 1.2 Some clients and a server

Although any network will offer some security options, a network using the client/server model will host all important resources on dedicated servers using an operating system with robust security features such as Linux or Windows 2003 Server. Some operating systems, such as Windows 98, are not intended for use as a dedicated server and supply relatively weak security options. In a client/server environment, the operating system will be able to authenticate users and provide varying degrees of access to each user according to their needs (as determined by the network administrator, of course).

Using dedicated servers offers performance benefits as well. A dedicated server does not have to divide its computing power between a local user and every client system on the network. Operating systems intended for use on a dedicated server include performance-tuning options that can be used to maximize performance further. The hardware used in dedicated servers also tends to include high-end options such as hardware RAID arrays, high-speed network interfaces, and powerful processors. Certainly you don't have to use high-end hardware, but it makes sense to invest in better hardware for your dedicated servers—if a server fails or performs poorly, many users suffer. Some of the performance benefits of using dedicated servers comes from the use of optimized server operating systems such as Windows 2003 Server and Red Hat Linux Advanced Server, but many of the benefits come from simply knowing where to spend your hardware dollars—by installing high-performance machines for these critical roles, you maximize performance in a way that impacts your end users in a positive way. In the event that performance problems do arise, a network technician can often address the problem by upgrading the server without making any changes to the client.

Using dedicated servers also provides centralized management, reducing the costs associated with the day-to-day operation of the network. Instead of roving across the building backing up every end-user system, the network tech can simply back up the server. If the end users have been properly trained to store their important data on the server, then replacing a failing desktop PC becomes a trivial exercise—just give the end user a spare system so that they can access their data on the server and repair or replace the faulty system at your leisure.

Peer-to-Peer Networks

OK, so you have a PC on your desk; is it a client or a server? Ha, trick question! You can't tell just by looking—it could be either (or both)! Although corporate networks typically employ dedicated servers, modern operating systems (Windows 9*x*/2000/XP, Linux) enable any client system to act as a server. The distinction between clients and servers becomes fuzzy because every machine on a network can be both a client and a server at the same time. Every machine is the same in this respect, and we say that they are all *peers* (equals) because you don't need a dedicated server. If you wish, you can have each PC on the network share its files, printers, and other resources, making each system a de facto server. So is peer-to-peer networking preferable to client/server networking? It depends.

Peer-to-peer networking (see Figure 1.3) is ideal for small offices or groups of people who need to share a printer or two or transfer an occasional file. Peer-to-peer works best for sharing lightly used resources. The poor fellow whose machine serves up the customer database will feel the heat if other users access that database regularly. First, his desktop performance may suffer. Second, every time he reboots his machine, the rest of the employees will feel the impact: lost data, delays in accessing data, reduced productivity. Also end-user machines face all kinds of dangers from which a dedicated server can be protected, such as power outages, e-mail viruses, incompatible applications, and the most dreaded threat of all: user error! Any system where somebody sits down to do their work will be more vulnerable to all these risks. In many small networks, however, the network usage can be light enough to make these risks acceptable.

The other challenge posed by peer-to-peer networks is management. Who is responsible for backing up data on all the peers? Who sets up the access permissions on each system? If you have every peer sharing some resources and the network has more than two or three machines, controlling access and ensuring reliable data backups becomes a daunting task.

Exam Tip

Peer-to-peer networking is ideal for small workgroups, but it offers limited security and is easily disrupted by computer shutdowns.

Local Lingo

peer-to-peer networking Sharing resources among networked client systems, which can also act as servers, so no dedicated server is needed.

The Changing Landscape

Although still useful concepts, the terms *client/server* and *peer-to-peer* cannot fully capture current trends in network technology. Many networks use dedicated servers for the most vital resources (e-mail servers, database servers, and centralized file storage) but use a peer-to-peer model for sharing lower-priority resources such as printers. Client/server and peer-to-peer are useful concepts, but many real-life networks don't fit neatly into these categories.

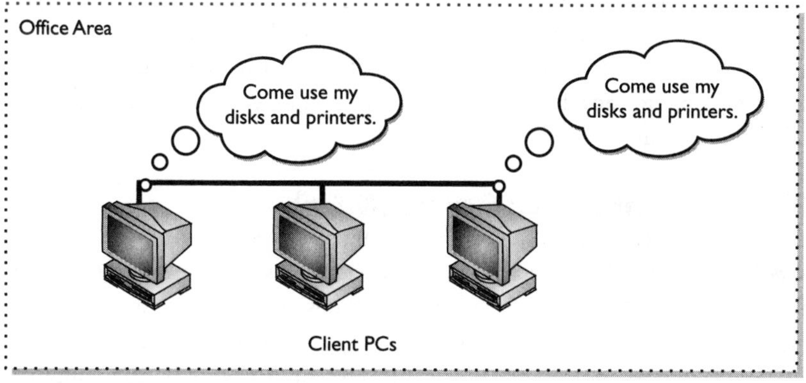

FIGURE 1.3 A peer-to-peer network

Exam Tip

For the Network+ exam, don't overthink the questions. The basic definition of client/server and peer-to-peer, as discussed here, should be sufficient, even if the real-life network with which you work doesn't fit neatly into either category.

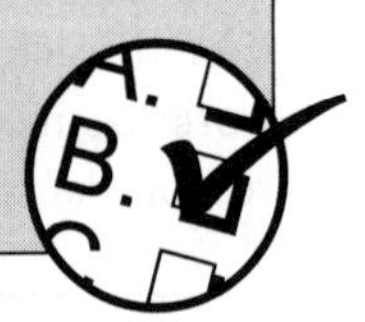

Linking It All Together

Our network will need to transfer data from servers to clients. We need a way to connect our computers to the network. This section discusses the basic network components required to network systems together. Later chapters will elaborate, but here is the basic picture of the hardware and software components that make up a network.

Network Wiring

The vast majority of the network you see will be in the form of copper cabling, snaking from the back of your PC down the back of the desk to a socket in the floor or wall, or perhaps just on into the distance somewhere. There are a number of network wiring types, each with its own characteristics, speed, length limitations, and restrictions. You may find that your network uses one type of wiring in one area and something completely different in another area, depending on the age of the installation and the cable type chosen to match the requirements at the time. Networks can also use other forms of "wiring," such as optical fiber, infrared, and wireless. Clearly, some of these wiring types don't use wire at all, so if we want to be more precise we use the term *network media* to encompass all varieties. Figure 1.4 shows one type of network wiring called *unshielded twisted pair*, or *UTP*. We'll talk in more detail about specific media standards in Chapter 2, but for now let's discuss the basic components common to any type of network media.

Network Interface Cards (NICs)

A NIC is the network interface between your computer system and the network media. Physically, this interface may manifest itself as an expansion card, an integrated part of the PC motherboard, a USB device, or a PC card. Every client and server must have at least one NIC (yes, a system can have more than one under some circumstances), and the NIC must be compatible with your computer hardware (PCI, USB, and so on), the network media, and the way in which the network passes information. If it isn't, your PC isn't going to do much networking! Figure 1.5 shows a typical NIC.

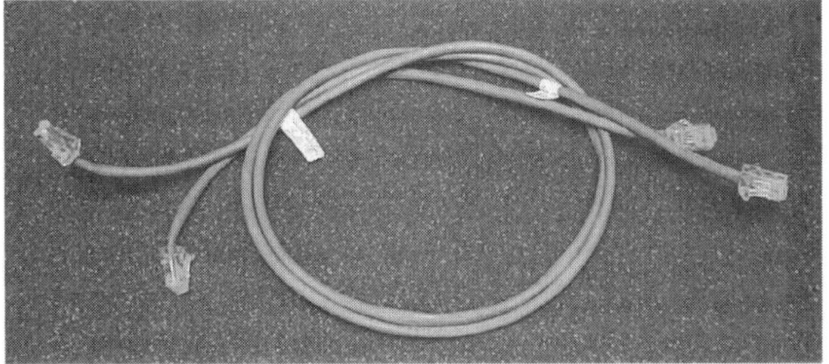

FIGURE 1.4 UTP wiring (patch leads)

Network Equipment

The NICs of each PC on the network will communicate with each other using whatever network technology you choose to employ. When designing a network, you have to take into account a variety of factors, including cable lengths, capacity limits, cost, and reliability. The equipment used to build this *network infrastructure,* the hardware and software your network relies on, includes devices such as repeaters, hubs, switches (see Figure 1.6), bridges, and routers. As you'll see in Chapter 4 when we discuss these devices in more detail, you can have a lot of choices, but generally the needs of your network will drive your choice of equipment.

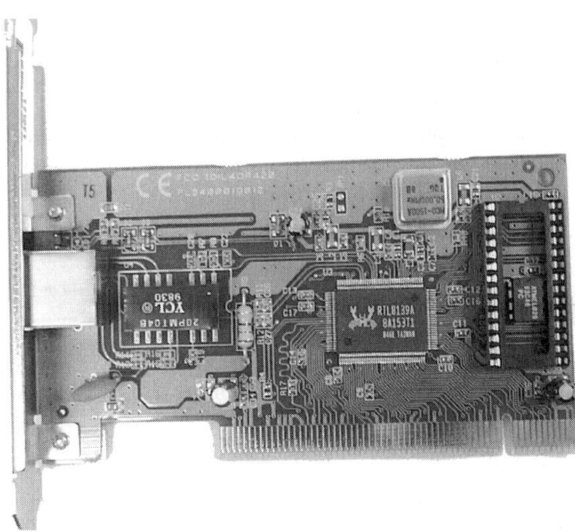

FIGURE 1.5 A typical NIC

FIGURE 1.6 A network hub and switch

Overview of Network Software

Once we select our hardware, we need software to tell that hardware what to do. We've already mentioned the mainstream, server-based networking products such as Microsoft Windows 2003 Server, Linux, and Novell NetWare, and we've told you about the peer-to-peer functionality built into most desktop operating systems. This section expands on these concepts and describes the component parts that must be installed and configured correctly to make your computer system work properly on a network, whether it functions as a client, a server, or a peer-to-peer machine. In many cases, the basic installation of these software components is automatic, and everything you need is actually supplied with your operating system. For example, Windows 9*x*/2000/XP can detect when you add a NIC and install the right drivers—the amount of input required from you may be minimal.

NIC Driver

Nothing happens if you can't send and receive data through the network. The NIC itself can transmit and receive streams of ones and zeros, but it's the NIC driver's job to pass information between the operating system and the NIC. The NIC is connected to the network media, and the server or client operating system probably comes supplied with suitable drivers. If it doesn't, just reach for the disk supplied with the NIC or perhaps visit the manufacturer's website to download a suitable driver. A visit to the website is generally a good idea in any case, just to make sure you are using the latest driver.

Protocol Driver

Once you have the right NIC driver installed, you need to consider the language—or *protocol*—that the network will use to convey the data. Over the years, various protocols have been developed, and you need to ensure that the client and server PCs (yes, and peer-to-peer systems) all speak the same language. If they don't, you won't be able to communicate with some or all the resources potentially available on the network. To complicate matters, you may need to ensure that the systems support more than one protocol—this is true when you have a mix of systems services on the network, and there's no common protocol that fits them all. The main communication protocols referred to on the Network+ exam are NetBEUI, IPX/SPX, and TCP/IP, and you'll find much more about these in Chapter 5.

Local Lingo

protocol A standardized way of performing a specific action, such as communicating across a network or exchanging information.

Client and Server Software

If you're installing one of the major network operating systems (NOSs), then a lot of the files copied from the installation CD represent parts of the core NOS—the *server software.* On the other hand, if you're working on a client PC running, say, Windows XP Home Edition, then the client and server software services are actually just modules that need to be enabled and configured using the Network applet in the Control Panel. And, as we said before, you might find that most of this is done automatically anyway. Did you notice that we mentioned "Windows XP Home Edition" and then "server software"? Surely Windows XP Home Edition is used for *client* PCs and not servers? True, but don't forget that to be a peer-to-peer machine, a client PC also needs to act as a server, so Windows 98 SE (and 95, 2000, Me, XP, and so on) comes with a *file and printer sharing* service module. This module provides the capability to act as a file and print server.

Redirector

One important role played by the client software is to provide an interface between the resources of the network and the functions of the host PC's operating system. This means, for example, enabling a network storage location to appear as a driver letter (say, W:) or a shared network printer to be accessed from a PC by printing to LPT2, even if the PC doesn't actually have a physical second parallel port.

In networking terms, this feature is called *redirection* (Novell also uses the term "requester"). You simply refer to a resource by a drive letter or port that's not alien to the operating system, and before the OS has a chance to realize that W: or LPT2 doesn't actually exist, the client software has already stepped in and redirected the request to the relevant network resource. The redirector also allows a program to treat remote resources as though they were local, even without assigning a local drive letter or port. For example, in Windows 9*x*/2000/XP you can save a file directly to a remote resource simply by navigating through the Network Neighborhood or My Network Places option in the Save dialog box. In either case, the redirector functions as an intermediary, allowing you to use a remote resource the same way you would use a local one.

Exam Tip

Client software is also known as *redirector* or *requestor software.*

Now That We Are Whole...

To summarize, three main software components must be installed and configured correctly to enable a PC to run on a network (see Figure 1.7).

- NIC driver
- Protocol driver(s)
- Client software

Optionally, you can also install server software if you want the PC to function as a server on your network. Remember, you don't have to install the server software just because it's included.

Once you have these core components in place, the operating system and applications can make use of (or provide, in the case of a server) network resources.

If you look at what's been covered to this point, you'll notice that the focus has moved from the media, to the network card, to protocols, to the client/server software, and then to the operating system and applications—a clear progression in layers of functionality.

Strangely enough (almost as if we'd planned it!), there is an industry standard way of describing how networks and their hardware and software function with reference to a model that has seven layers of generic functionality—the OSI seven-layer model, which we will discuss in a moment. But first....

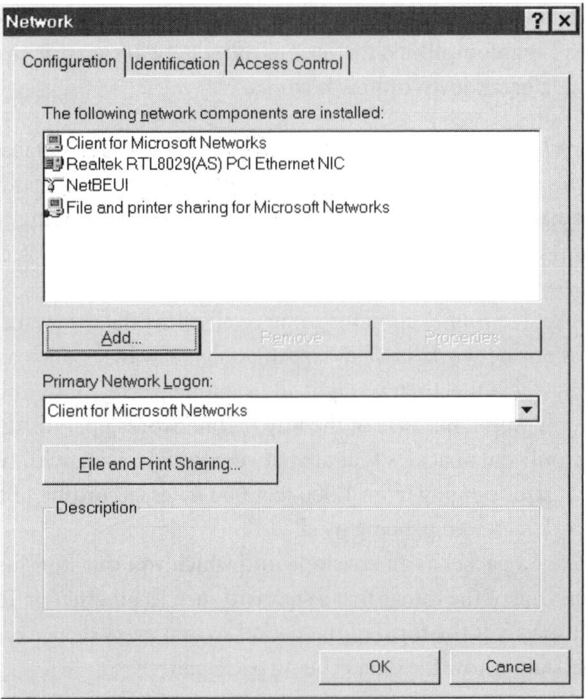

FIGURE 1.7 A Windows 9*x* machine with a client driver, NIC driver, protocol, and file and printer sharing service installed

Objective 1.03 Data Packets

The fundamentals of computing are all about data: moving data, storing data, processing data, transmitting data, and receiving data. Networks rely on data, too, and so, before we move on, we need to talk about the facts of (data) life.

Consider a data file: It can be small, like a 200-byte text file, or big, like a 20MB database. In either case, we want to be confident that when we click Save, our data makes its way safely to the server. In addition to application data, our networked PC is also going to send data codes with special meaning to our servers—instructions such as, "Log me in. My username is.... My password is.... Send this to SALES_LASER02." (In reality, these requests won't be encoded in plain English, but rather in binary data sequences understood by the NOS.)

All this data will travel through our network media, but you need to understand *how* this is accomplished for various other networking principles to make sense. Here is a breakdown of how it works:

- *Networks carry data in packets.* The data in our 20MB database is really a series of binary ones and zeroes. If we just throw all that binary information onto the network, no other machine is going to know what it is, where it came from, or where it needs to go. We need order—we need *packets*!
  A packet (or *frame*) contains some or all of the data we want to send across our network. If we're sending only a few bytes, such as our 200-byte text file, then it might all fit in one packet, but our database certainly won't. Because of the way that networks operate, they can carry only data packets that are between certain sizes, with typical packet sizes ranging from 1,500 to 4,000 bytes, according to the network technology being used.
  Think of a packet as an envelope into which you can stuff just so much paper. One of the things that a standard such as Ethernet or Token Ring must specify is the form of the packet so that every device on a network understands how the data is being packaged.
- *Packets need addresses.* You wouldn't post a letter without writing an address on the front of the envelope, and we certainly won't put a packet of data on a network without stating where it should go. In fact, a data packet contains both the recipient's and the sender's addresses so that the recipient knows where the packet came from (or, in case there's a problem, how to contact the sender).
- *How big is that packet?* A packet can contain any amount of data within the limits defined by the network technology used (Token Ring, Ethernet, and so on). Every data packet includes a note of how much data it actually contains. Among other things, this aids in error checking because the recipient can determine whether the packet that has just been received is complete.
- *What protocol is this packet using?* Every basic network packet includes a protocol ID field to help devices on the network determine how to decode and understand the contents of the packet. We'll talk about these protocols (NetBEUI, IPX/SPX, and TCP/IP) in detail in later chapters. This field allows network devices to determine how to interpret the data when a NIC driver passes the data packet to the operating system.

- *That packet looks unwell!* Your data has a hard slog through all the media from your PC to the destination device, and it may encounter electrical interference, loose connectors, power glitches, and a host of other events. To help detect dodgy data packets, each packet includes a cyclic redundancy check (CRC) value that's computed by the sending device using the data in the packet. The CRC value is the result of a complex binary mathematical calculation on the data that is performed by both the sender and the recipient of the packet. If the CRC in the packet (built by the sender) and the locally generated CRC (calculated by the receiver) don't match, then the data has been altered or corrupted during delivery, and the recipient will ask for the packet to be resent.

Figure 1.8 shows the format of a basic data packet.

Packet Summary

Data packets contain important pieces of information. A typical data packet will contain the following information (the exact structure of the packet will depend on which technology is being used):

- The sender's address
- The recipient's address
- A protocol ID
- A data length field
- The data
- A CRC value

Exam Tip

Data is carried around networks in packets (frames).

Source Address	Dest. Address	Protocol ID	Length	DATA	CRC

FIGURE 1.8 A basic data packet

The OSI Seven-Layer Model

This is the part of the course that strikes fear into many a network technician, but we're pretty confident that when you finish this section, you'll wonder what all the fuss is about! Honest.

The Open Systems Interconnect (OSI) seven-layer model was developed by a standards organization called ISO. Contrary to popular belief, ISO is not an abbreviation—it's derived from the Greek word for "equal."

ISO created a framework into which the major network hardware and software components and protocols could be placed to give every item a common reference point—a means of relating the components and their functionality to each other and a way of standardizing some of the components and protocols.

Exam Tip

The Network+ exam expects you to know the layers by name (especially layers 1 through 4), how they function in relation to each other, and what they represent.

The seven-layer model provides a critical common language that network hardware and software engineers can use to communicate and ensure that their equipment will function together. Each layer of the model represents a particular aspect of network functionality. For example, layer 1—the Physical layer—represents electrical signals, connectors, and media types and the way that data is placed on the network media.

As well as helping to standardize the design elements of network components, the OSI model helps describe the relationships between network protocols. As you'll see, more than one protocol or action is needed to get your data onto a network (or, indeed, to do the reverse and pick up data from a network).

To summarize, the OSI seven-layer model is a theoretical representation of how a networked device functions and helps us understand the interrelationships among hardware, software, protocols, and applications. Many network technicians refer to network devices by their positions in the model; for example, a repeater (a device mentioned earlier) is a layer 1 (Physical layer) device.

The Layers and What They Represent

Let's run through the layers and an overview of their tasks and responsibilities. Figure 1.9 summarizes the layers and their functions.

Layer	Functionality
7. Application	Network services, authentication
6. Presentation	Translation, encryption
5. Session	Connections, sessions
4. Transport	Fragmentation, defragmentation, reliable data delivery, error correction/management, flow control
3. Network	Addressing, routing
2. Data Link	Packets/Frame, CRC generation/checking, network access
1. Physical	Media, connectors, electrical signals

FIGURE 1.9 The OSI seven-layer model

Layer 1: Physical Layer

Layer 1 defines the network standards relating to electrical signals, connectors, and media types and the way that data is placed on the network media.

Layer 2: Data Link Layer

Layer 2 defines the rules for gathering together and completing all the elements that make up a data packet and putting the whole thing together so that it can be passed to a Physical layer device and on to the network. The exact components of the data packet will vary depending on the Data Link protocols being used, but would typically include the data being sent, information, an identifier for the sending machine, an identifier for the receiving machine, and an error correction mechanism such as a cyclic redundancy check. The Data Link layer on the sending machine assembles outgoing packets and calculates the CRC by applying a standard mathematical formula to the contents of the packet. The receiving machine performs the same calculation for incoming packets, allowing the receiving machine to verify the validity of the data by comparing its locally generated CRC value with that sent in the packet. If the values don't match, the packet is discarded and requested again. The Data Link layer also determines whether it is possible or permissible at any instant to try to send data to the network. At any instant, another computer may already be using the network. If you transmit data at the same time, both packets will become corrupted. The Data Link layer also sets rules for addressing network devices within a local area network (LAN).

Layer 3: Network Layer

Layer 3 is responsible for routing and addressing functions. Layer 3 describes internetwork addressing—how to find the ultimate destination address for a data packet across a wide area network (WAN) such as the Internet. The routing of traffic across multiple networks relies on this addressing. Network routing, the process of moving data between distinct networks, is said to occur at the Network layer for this reason.

Layer 4: Transport Layer

If the data being sent is bigger than the packet size allowed by the lower-level protocols, the Transport layer breaks the data into smaller, manageable chunks that will fit inside two or more packets. Breaking up data into smaller chunks is also known as *fragmentation.* The Transport layer is also responsible for confirming whether transmitted packets have reached their destination intact and retransmitting them if they haven't (error correction/management). For incoming packets, the Transport layer reassembles the fragmented data (performs defragmentation), ensuring that received packets are processed in the right order. The Transport layer also manages the flow of data to ensure that packets are sent at a pace that's suitable for the receiving device and for general network conditions. Sending data too quickly is like speaking too fast—you may have to keep repeating yourself to get the message understood, which is actually counterproductive.

Layer 5: Session Layer

Layer 5 sets up, manages, and terminates the data connections (called *sessions*) between networked devices. These sessions enable networked systems to exchange information.

Layer 6: Presentation Layer

Layer 6 is responsible for managing and translating information by catering to differences in the ways some computer systems store and manage their data. Presentation layer protocols are also responsible for data encryption and data compression.

Layer 7: Application Layer

Layer 7 represents the network-related program code and functions running on a computer system. This program code provides network support for the main applications being run, such as the redirector software discussed earlier, allowing a shared network location to appear on a machine as drive W: and providing services such as login authentication. Note that the Application layer does not refer to applications such as Microsoft Outlook or WSFTP. Instead, it refers to the protocols on which those programs rely. For example, POP3 and SMTP are important Application layer protocols, but many different end-user applications use those protocols (Outlook, Eudora, Mozilla Thunderbird).

Using the Seven-Layer Model

The seven-layer model is only a theoretical representation of how networks function. Although knowing it inside out won't change your life, it should help you pass the Network+ exam. The conceptual use of the model assumes that an event on one computer system (for example, a user pressing ENTER on a login screen) creates some data that sets off a chain of events. The data runs down through the layers on the sending machine and then leaves the system in a data packet, which travels across the network and then up through the layers on the receiving machine, until the data arrives intact at the Application layer and is processed by the receiving system. Later chapters in this book point out where certain key protocols and hardware fit into the model, and this can be useful stuff to know for both the Network+ exam and real life. Be prepared for a shock, however, because some network arrangements and protocols don't fit exactly into the model and, under some circumstances, not all the layers are actually used. Does this matter? Well, as long as your data gets from point A to point B successfully, probably not. The folks designing new network protocols need to fully understand this model at a level far beyond what the typical network technician will ever need to implement networks using the latest technologies.

Real-World Networking

Enough theory! Let's get back to the real world. You've a few more terms to absorb before you're ready to be let loose on the next chapter.

Network Size

You may have heard the terms LAN and WAN before, but did you know there's a whole bunch of other *AN abbreviations that also describe the general size of a network (see Figure 1.10)? This section lists the main ones in order of size, with the smallest first.

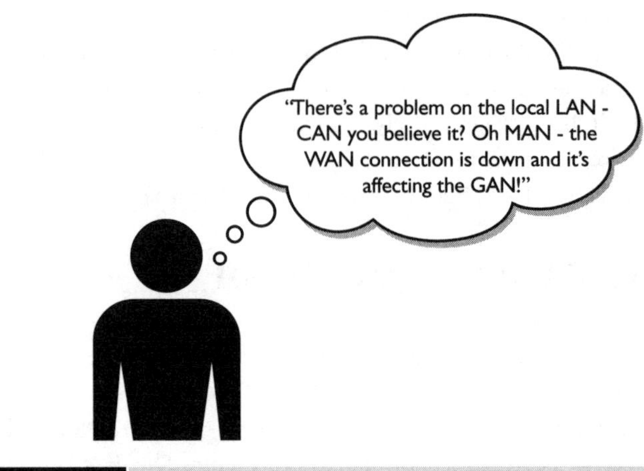

FIGURE 1.10 Terms to describe network sizes

By the way, network technicians often refer to every network they mention as either a LAN or a WAN. In practice this doesn't really matter unless you feel like correcting them just to see how they react.

Local Area Network (LAN) A LAN is a single network confined to one building or area of a building. There may be links to other locations at the same site, but these will be very localized.

Campus Area Network (CAN) CAN is used to describe a group of interconnected LANs within a small geographical area, such as a school campus, university, hospital, or military base.

Metropolitan Area Network (MAN) The term MAN is usually applied to networks that have a sociopolitical boundary, such as a network of district authority offices in a town or city. Sites on a MAN are usually interconnected using fiber-optic cable or some other high-speed digital circuit (rather than standard phone lines, for example), and the MAN itself may well carry voice as well as data traffic.

Wide Area Network (WAN) A WAN is two or more interconnected networks spread over a large geographic area, even on different continents. The Internet is the largest WAN in existence.

Global Area Network (GAN) A GAN is a single network with connection points spread around the world. GANs are used mostly by large corporate organizations and consist of a series of networked, orbiting satellites. Note the subtle difference between a WAN and a GAN: The latter is a single network, not a number of interconnected networks.

Travel Advisory

These terms don't exist as official standards, but their use and definitions have become generally accepted over time.

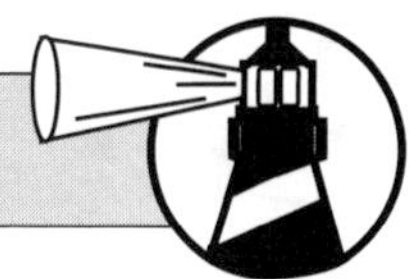

Network Performance

Many factors affect network performance, but here we want to talk about just the basic speed of a standard network, how network speed is measured, and some of the terms related to performance.

Bandwidth

Network data speeds are measured in megabits per second—sometimes abbreviated Mbps. That lowercase *b* is important, because an uppercase *B* would imply mega*bytes*. For a standard corporate network, the speed at which data travels between networked systems will typically range between 4 and 1000 Mbps, depending on the network standard used.

So where does this word *bandwidth* come in? Well, the data signal traveling through the network media (usually some form of copper wire) is an electrical signal that's changing voltage rapidly to represent a string of binary data (remember our packets?). Any signal that changes in this cyclic way has a frequency associated with it—measured in Hertz (Hz)—which is known as its *bandwidth*. Your network media is designed to operate across a certain range of frequencies, or bandwidths, and if you try to push data through the network at a faster rate (exceeding your bandwidth), you will quickly discover that the laws of physics are not negotiable!

The bandwidth of the network is closely related to its maximum theoretical speed. So network technicians will often say things like, "Our network has a bandwidth of 10 megabits per second," when they really mean, "Our network has a top speed of 10 megabits per second" or "the bandwidth of our network provides a throughput of 10 megabits per second." For the purposes of the Network+ exam, all these variations are considered to be correct and to mean the same thing. Also keep in mind that the stated maximum speed is usually a theoretical maximum—the real-world speed is often quite a bit slower. How much slower? That will depend on the technology being used and the details of a specific network implementation. In general, the only way to determine your effective bandwidth is to test the real network.

Local Lingo

bandwidth A term used to refer to the performance (speed) of a network.

✔**Objective 1.01: Overview of Network Hardware** The most obvious pieces of network hardware are the computers on the network. These are divided into client and server systems unless they are desktop systems that are sharing resources, in which case they are known as peer-to-peer systems. Corporate networks generally use dedicated servers because they offer higher performance, greater stability, and better security than peer-to-peer options. Your network won't be complete without some media—such as copper wiring, fiber optics, wireless, or infrared—to interconnect your systems, as well as a Network Interface Card (NIC) to connect your system to the media. Other devices on the network—such as repeaters, hubs, bridges, and routers—enable you to expand the system locally or to other sites.

✔**Objective 1.02: Overview of Network Software** The major software components of a network are the network operating system (NOS), NIC drivers, protocol drivers, and client/server services. Most of the components needed to get a network up and running are supplied as standard with your NOS or as part of your client operating system (Windows NT/9*x*/2000/ME/XP, Linux, and so on).

✔**Objective 1.03: Data Packets** To send a piece of data across a network, it has to be placed in a standard, formatted structure known as a packet or frame. These packets also state the source and destination addresses of the data, the protocol being used, and the amount of data being sent. A cyclic redundancy check (CRC) value is also added to the packet to enable the receiving device to check the packet for errors. If the packet looks faulty, the recipient will ask for it to be resent.

✔**Objective 1.04: The OSI Seven-Layer Model** The OSI seven-layer model describes how data flows from one networked system to another—it's a theoretical model into which many of the standards, components, and functions of a network fit. The model promotes the use of recognized network standards and helps ensure compatibility between network hardware and software from different manufacturers.

✔**Objective 1.05: Real-World Networking** Networks come in all shapes and sizes, and there is a number of de facto abbreviations that can be used to describe different types of networks, from small LANs to worldwide GANs.

One of the key features of a network is its performance at the desktop (that is, the speed at which the client machines can send and receive data), which is usually measured in megabits per second. Accessing data across a network is not necessarily that fast compared to accessing the same data from a local hard disk, but this is far outweighed by the benefits of being able to share data and resources, such as printers, with a large number of clients. The term bandwidth is often used interchangeably with speed, although the two are not quite the same thing.

REVIEW QUESTIONS

1. What name is given to a computer that can act as both a client and a server? (Select one answer.)
   - **A.** A multitasking computer
   - **B.** A mainframe computer
   - **C.** A peer-to-peer computer
   - **D.** A LAN computer
2. Which of the following statements are *not* true? (Select all that apply.)
   - **A.** A peer-to-peer server is the best choice for a large corporate network.
   - **B.** Client/server networks are more robust than peer-to-peer networks.
   - **C.** Novell NetWare is an example of a peer-to-peer NOS.
   - **D.** Windows 98 SE does not support peer-to-peer networking.
3. You have configured a new client PC and connected it to your LAN. You can see some of the servers on the network, but not all of them. What is the most likely cause? (Select one answer.)
   - **A.** A faulty NIC
   - **B.** Faulty media
   - **C.** A faulty OSI layer
   - **D.** A missing protocol driver
4. Which of the following items is *not* part of a data packet? (Select one answer.)
   - **A.** Media identifier
   - **B.** Data length
   - **C.** Protocol ID
   - **D.** CRC

5. Which layer of the OSI model is responsible for addressing and routing? (Select one answer.)
   - **A.** Transport
   - **B.** Network
   - **C.** Session
   - **D.** Application
6. Which layer of the OSI model handles the encryption and decryption of data packets? (Select one answer.)
   - **A.** Application
   - **B.** Presentation
   - **C.** Session
   - **D.** Transport
7. At which layer of the OSI model is CRC error correction performed? (Select one answer.)
   - **A.** Data Link
   - **B.** Transport
   - **C.** Physical
   - **D.** Session
8. Layer 3 is the __________ layer of the OSI model. (Select one answer.)
   - **A.** Session
   - **B.** Application
   - **C.** Data Link
   - **D.** Network
9. Which of the following take place at the Data Link layer? (Select all that apply.)
   - **A.** Packet fragmentation
   - **B.** Routing
   - **C.** CRC checking
   - **D.** Encryption
10. Which of the following are *not* common network protocols? (Select two answers.)
    - **A.** IPBEUI
    - **B.** IPX/SPX
    - **C.** NetBEUI
    - **D.** NET/IP

REVIEW ANSWERS

1. **C** A desktop PC acting as a client and a server is said to be a *peer-to-peer system.*
2. **A** **C** **D** Only statement B is true. Client/server networks are more robust than peer-to-peer networks.
3. **D** You know that you're on the network because you can see *some* resources, so the NIC (A) and media (B) must be okay. Choice C is just meaningless. Because you can't see *some* resources, you probably don't have the required protocol installed (D).
4. **A** There's no such field as "media identifier" in a data packet, but all the others are present.
5. **B** The Network layer provides addressing and routing functionality.
6. **B** The Presentation layer handles the encryption and decryption of data.
7. **A** CRC error correction is performed by the Data Link layer. Note that other kinds of error correction may take place at other layers.
8. **D** Layer 3 is the Network layer.
9. **A** **C** The Data Link layer puts everything together in a packet and checks incoming CRC information. Routing occurs at layer 3 and encryption occurs at layer 6.
10. **A** **D** From the list provided, only IPX/SPX (B) and NetBEUI (C) are true protocols; the others are made-up names.

Network Media

ITINERARY

- **Objective 2.01** Coaxial Cable
- **Objective 2.02** Coaxial Connectors
- **Objective 2.03** UTP and STP Cable
- **Objective 2.04** UTP Connectors
- **Objective 2.05** Optical Fiber
- **Objective 2.06** Optical Fiber Connectors
- **Objective 2.07** Other Media Types

NEWBIE	SOME EXPERIENCE	EXPERT
2 hours	1 hour	30 minutes

Welcome to Chapter 2! Since you've made it this far, we'll assume that either you enjoyed Chapter 1 so much that you've decided to continue, or you skipped the first chapter because you feel you're already comfortable with the basics of networking and network terminology. Well, in either case, here's your first test.

People in the know talk about network *media* rather than *cabling*. How come? Well, of course, as you knew all along, it's because some parts of a network's data highway can be made up of materials other than physical cable or fiber. For example, there might be a laser or microwave link between buildings, and perhaps infrared or wireless devices connecting laptops to your main network. Inside the building, you'll find connectors, adapters, wall ports, and other such parts.

Local Lingo

bounded media Physical network cabling (copper and fiber).

unbounded media Microwave, wireless, and infrared network links.

As you might imagine, there are a number of different network media types. Some are faster than others, some will work over relatively long distances, and some don't require a physical connection to the main network (ideal for mobile executives and their laptops). This chapter covers all the major media types and their characteristics, uses, and key features.

Exam Tip

Network media and connectors and the electrical signals traveling over them are represented by standards at layer 1 (the Physical layer) of the OSI seven-layer model.

Objective 2.01 Coaxial Cable

Coaxial cable is used to bring the signal down from a rooftop antenna to a TV set or radio receiver—or, in this case, to link together networked devices. "Coax" is the granddaddy of all mainstream network media types and is very much associated with the original designs of the popular Ethernet networking standard, developed in 1973, and is still found in some legacy installations.

Coaxial cable has a central conducting core surrounded by a protective, insulating layer, an outer metal screen made of a woven copper mesh, a metal-covered plastic or foil (or both), and an overall insulating jacket (see Figure 2.1). The metal screen helps shield the data traveling down the central core from being corrupted by external signals, such as radio waves, and other sources of electromagnetic interference (EMI), such as high-current power cables, mobile phones, electric motors, fluorescent tubes, and local electrical storms. The screen also reduces the amount of data signal that can radiate from the cable to become another source of EMI and thus cause problems for other data cables and systems. The cable is referred to as *coaxial* (or simply *coax*) because both the center wire and the braided metal shield share a common axis, or centerline.

Local Lingo

crosstalk An unwanted interaction between two electrical signals.

Coax is not used much these days for new local area network installations and is considered old technology. That said, if you want to link a few PCs together in a small office to share data and perhaps a printer or two, coax might do—but there are more modern, sexier ways to set up a network. The remaining niche for new coax LAN installations lies in high-interference environments where unshielded cabling cannot function well, although fiber optic cabling would probably be the more common solution to interference problems today. Coax will also crop up when connecting a LAN to an Internet connection provided by your local cable company.

Coaxial Cable Types

There are a mind-boggling number of different types of coax, each one suitable for a specific purpose, such as audio, video, TV, satellite, cable, radio, and, of course, data. Each coax type has its own characteristics, closely matched to the type of signal that cable is designed to carry. Using the wrong type for a particular

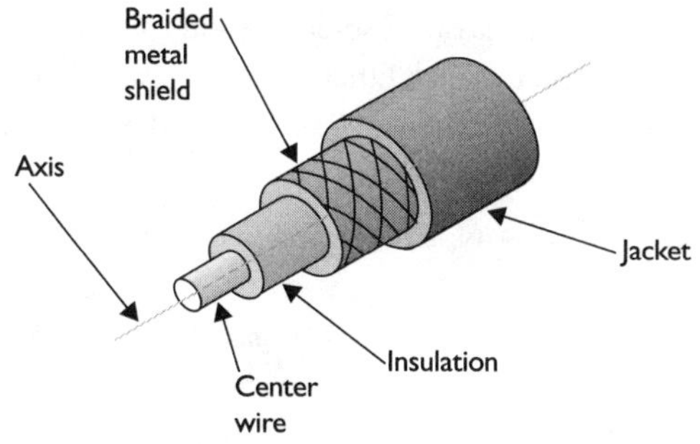

FIGURE 2.1 Coaxial (coax) cable

purpose can mess up the signal traveling down the cable. In the wonderful world of data communications, the two coax types most often mixed up because of their similar physical appearance are those used for networks based on the Ethernet standard and those used for an older standard known as ARCNet. Using even one small length of the wrong coax may cause complete network failure or bizarre problems such as dead spots along the length of the network. There aren't many working ARCNet networks anymore, so unless you've already run into ARCNet you are not likely to do so.

Specific coax types were developed for the Ethernet standard, but a number of radio cables have very similar characteristics, and these so-called *radio-grade (RG)* cables also became associated with Ethernet. Another RG coax type is commonly associated with ARCNet. Table 2.1 shows the RG coax types used for data networking. The nominal impedance, a measure of how much the cable impedes or resists the flow of electric current, is one of the factors that determines the RG type. As you can see, the nominal impedance (the measure of the wire's resistance) of ARCNet coax is different from that of Ethernet coax. This difference is the main reason why the cable types should not be used in conjunction with the wrong technology. The differences between thick and thin Ethernet are explained in the next chapter.

Objective 2.02 Coaxial Connectors

Both Thin Ethernet and ARCNet use BNC connectors, shown in Figure 2.2, to attach the coax to other devices, such as the network interface cards (NICs) inside a computer. These twist-and-lock connectors were originally fitted to the coax using wire strippers, a soldering iron, and a wrench, but it's much quicker and easier to use wire strippers, crimp connectors, and a crimping tool. "Crimping" means to bend or squeeze the metal of the connector around the cable to secure it to the cable, which definitely beats the hassle of soldering and using the wrench.

Network devices connect to Thick Ethernet coax via an adapter box known as a *transceiver.* The transceiver itself clamps directly onto the cable and makes contact

TABLE 2.1 Coaxial Cable Types for Networking

Network Type	Coax Type	Maximum Distance	Nominal Impedance
Thin Ethernet	RG-58	185 meters	50 ohms
Thick Ethernet	RG-8 or RG-11	500 meters	50 ohms
ARCNet	RG-62	Variable	93 ohms

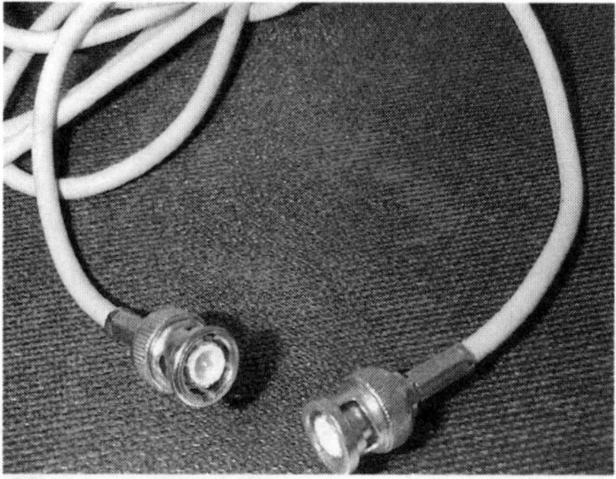

FIGURE 2.2 Coaxial cable fitted with BNC connectors

with the inner conductor and outer braid using a set of sharp spikes known as *bee-sting* or (plastic fangs ready?) *vampire taps.* Occasionally, you will encounter a transceiver that uses connectors that screw on, known as PL-259s, though these are often associated with radio equipment (antennas, radio ham sets, and so on). PL-259 connectors (the PL stands for *plug*) screw into SO-239 (socket) connectors. These connectors may also be found at the ends of the coax to attach the bus terminators (covered later in this chapter). Keep in mind that although the Network+ exam may include questions about Thick Ethernet, you would be hard pressed to find a working Thick Ethernet network today. Even Thin Ethernet has become fairly rare, as faster, cheaper alternatives such as 100BaseT have become available.

Local Lingo

BNC The origins of the acronym BNC have been lost. Various sources call it a bayonet connector, bayonet navy connector, British Naval Connector, Bayonet Neill Concelman, bayonet nut connector, and so on. You need to know only what a BNC connector is and how to use it. Don't worry about what the acronym stands for!

Objective 2.03 UTP and STP Cable

Many modern networks use a telephone-type cable known as *unshielded twisted pair (UTP).* UTP network cables, as shown in Figure 2.3, have four pairs of twisted wires. The twists in the cable pairs reduce crosstalk (remember that?) and also act as a partial shield. As you might have guessed from

FIGURE 2.3 Four-pair UTP cable

the name, UTP has no overall metal screen—just the cable pairs inside the covering. UTP cable is popular because it is relatively cheap and simple to install. Better still, the same wiring infrastructure can be used for data and voice/telephony. That means when you install UTP cable as part of a building's infrastructure (or as part of a refit), the same cabling system can be used for many of the building's services, such as computer networks, security systems, telephones, and so on.

Although UTP cable provides a low-cost solution, it supports some fairly high-tech, high-spec, high-price kits to create very sophisticated, high-performance networks.

As the name implies, shielded twisted pair (STP) cable *does* have a screen covering the wire pairs, and there is also a ground wire (also known as a *drain wire*) running the length of the media. STP is intended for use in electrically noisy environments and is also specified for certain IBM networking requirements, but generally UTP is more widely used, so we won't spend much time on STP cable in this chapter. In most cases, routing network cabling away from interference remains cheaper than installing shielded cabling.

UTP Cable Types

UTP comes in a variety of grades, called *categories,* numbered Category 1 through Category 5, as summarized in Table 2.2. These categories define the maximum supported data speed of the cable, and they have been developed over the years to cater to faster and faster network designs.

Exam Tip

If you do a bit of net surfing, you will probably find references to a proposed CAT 7 standard. Don't worry; this proposed standard is not covered on the exam, in part because the standard has not yet been finalized.

Travel Advisory

Note that CAT 5 cabling is sufficient for both 100BaseT and 1000BaseT, but most new installations will go ahead and use CAT 5e or CAT 6 as a way of "future-proofing" their wiring (preparing for future standards that haven't been defined yet).

It might have caught your eye in Table 2.2 that UTP cable is used for Ethernet networks, but a few paragraphs ago, you learned about Ethernet and *coax* cable. Well, UTP is the way forward, and Ethernet was one of the first networking standards to be reengineered to work on this media type. In addition, most new cabling installations will use Category 5 (CAT 5) cabling because it supports all current (and planned future) data speeds and standards. In fact, although it is typically associated with data rates up to 100 Mbps, some variations of Gigabit Ethernet can use CAT 5 cabling. The category level of a piece of cable will normally be written on the cable itself, as shown in Figure 2.4. All cable accessories, such as the wall- or pillar-mounted data ports, must also match the category of the cable being used. Mixing CAT 5 cable with CAT 3 wall sockets, for example, could cause that part of the network (known as a *segment*) not to work properly. The post-installation network testing should pick up this type of mismatch, but it is better to get things right the first time rather than find out later you need to replace all your data outlets!

TABLE 2.2 UTP Cable Categories

Category	Maximum Rated Speed	Typical Use
Category 1	1 Mbps	Regular analog phone lines; not used for data communications
Category 2	4 Mbps	Telephony and alarm systems
Category 3	16 Mbps	Ethernet over UTP at 10 Mbps (10BaseT)
Category 4	20 Mbps	Token Ring at 16 Mbps
Category 5	100 Mbps	Ethernet over UTP at 100 Mbps (100BaseTX) and Gigabit Ethernet (1000BaseT)
Category 5e	100 Mbps	Ethernet over UTP at 1000 Mbps (1000BaseT)
Category 6	250 Mbps	10 Gigabit Ethernet (10GbE)

FIGURE 2.4 The markings show this to be Category 5e UTP cable.

Patch Cable and Premises Cable

If you've ever picked up a UTP patch lead (the sort of lead that connects a PC to a wall port or that connects pieces of a network kit together in the computer room cabinet) and it felt stiff and inflexible, it's probably made from the wrong type of UTP cable. Just to add yet another twist to the story, there are two types of UTP cable: the stuff that's used for patch leads and the stuff that's used to wire buildings. To make patch leads flexible and easy to route through wiring cabinets, under desks, and the like, the conductive core of each wire is made from fine strands of copper. But to make *premises* wiring cable more robust and able to withstand some heavy handling as it's (professionally) pulled through trunking and plenum space, the cores are made of solid copper. It's very tempting to use UTP premises wiring cable for patch leads—especially if there are reels of the stuff lying around at the end of a job. If you do, though, you're setting yourself up for a fall, because the crimp connectors in UTP plugs (see the next section) are designed for stranded core cable, and if you use the solid stuff, the squeezing action of the crimp procedure compresses the solid copper core enough to make it brittle and prone to cracking. After a few months in service, it may start to do annoying things like failing intermittently.

Local Lingo

horizontal wiring Solid core UTP, also called *premises wiring,* often laid out flat in ducting or in cable trays in the plenum.

plenum A fancy name for the gap between the real ceiling (or the bottom of the next floor up, if you want) and the suspended tiles.

While we're talking about plenums, if you read the instructions for many pieces of networking hardware, you will notice that they specifically exclude plenum areas in their installation notes. This is because the equipment may give off toxic fumes in the event of a fire that could spread quickly through the plenum area, creating a hazard. Plenum cable (copper and fiber types) has a special, low-toxicity jacket specifically for installation in these areas. Don't use regular (PVC) jacketed cables in the plenum.

Objective 2.04 UTP Connectors

UTP network cabling uses an eight-contact connector type known as an RJ45, as shown in Figure 2.5 (the RJ stands for *registered jack*). The pins on the RJ45 are numbered from 1 to 8, as shown in Figure 2.6, and different pin combinations are used with different networking standards, as covered in the next chapter. One feature of this arrangement is that interconnecting the wrong types of networking equipment is unlikely to have a disastrous effect.

Many UTP networking standards use only two of the four UTP cable pairs, but the best practice is always to connect all four pairs at every network connector for compatibility with other, and future, standards. Theoretically, you could use a four-pin connector like the RJ11 jack used in standard phone systems, but in practice it's not done. Instead, the RJ45 connector is used, with all eight wires connected, so that the wiring does not have to change when you switch to a newer networking standard that uses all four pairs.

UTP Wiring Standards

It probably won't come as a surprise to know that UTP connectors and wiring have a color code and wiring scheme associated with them (just something else for you to remember!). Each wire inside a UTP cable must connect to the proper pin on the connector at each end of the cable. The wires are color-coded to assist in properly matching the ends; each pair of wires has a solid-colored wire and a striped wire: blue/blue-white, orange/orange-white, brown/brown-white, and

FIGURE 2.5 An RJ45 connector

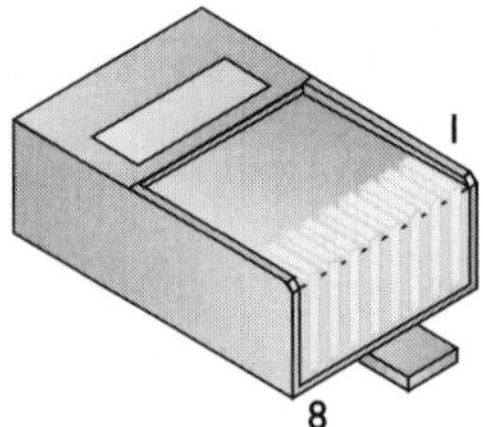

FIGURE 2.6 RJ45 connector pin numbering

green/green-white. Because signals sent down pin 1 on one end of a cable must be received on pin 1 on the other end of the cable (and so on), the same wire must connect to pin 1 on both ends. Industry organizations have developed a variety of standard color codes to facilitate installation. The most common spec in use today is known as EIA/TIA 568B (for Electronics Industry Association/ Telecommunications Industry Association; see Figure 2.7). Using an established color-code scheme ensures that the wires match up correctly at each end of the cable. A standardized color-code also makes specific pairs of wires carry specific signals in a way that minimizes potential problems such as crosstalk. Consistency makes troubleshooting and repair easier.

UTP Testing

Because UTP cable doesn't have shielding, it is much more susceptible to EMI and crosstalk than coax cabling. Because of this vulnerability, the installation of UTP cabling must meet specific requirements. Just like coax, for example, UTP should not be routed near light fittings in the plenum, run parallel to heavy power cables, or run over and squashed on a regular basis by your office chair! But in the case of UTP cable, the way the wires are attached to the wall plates and the number of sharp bends in a horizontal run can adversely affect performance. Professional installers will test every single run (segment) of UTP cabling to satisfy themselves,

Wire	Pin
Orange/White	1
Orange	2
Green/White	3
Blue	4
Blue/White	5
Green	6
Brown/White	7
Brown	8

FIGURE 2.7 The EIA/TIA 568B standard

and their customer, that the job has been done right using a special testing kit that measures the overall length of each segment, checks various electrical characteristics, and detects possible crosstalk (with fancy names such as "near-end crosstalk" and "far-end crosstalk") between the wire pairs. Cable segments that fail to meet the required specs may not work properly at the intended (or future) data speeds and may have to be rejoined to the wall plates or, worse case, rerouted or replaced. Once everything has been sorted out, the printed test results are often presented to the customer as part of the network installation completion sign-off process.

Objective 2.05 Optical Fiber

Optical fiber is relatively expensive to purchase and install because it requires specialist handling and connection techniques. For this reason alone, fiber is not usually installed for desktop network connection unless a special need exists (such as locations with high levels of electromagnetic interference). In general, fiber will be used where one or more of the following apply:

- Long distances need to be covered, up to the maximum segment distance of 2 km (some newer standards cover even greater distances).
- A link is needed between buildings, and other options, such as microwave and laser, are impractical (no line of sight, for example), too expensive, or electrically unworkable.
- High speeds are required (initially, 1000 Mbps Ethernet required fiber optic cabling, but "Gigabit over copper" is available today).
- Security is a concern. Optical fibers don't radiate signals that can be picked up by listening equipment, and it is difficult to tap a fiber without being detected.
- The general environment is electrically unfriendly to data—that is, full of EMI, such as in a factory or in a radio/TV/radar transmitter room.
- Any potential for an electrical spark must be eliminated, such as in a laboratory using flammable gases and other volatile chemicals.

Data can be sent down an optical fiber cable as either infrared or laser light, according to the system in use and the maximum distances involved. Each type of system requires a specific type of media; infrared LED systems use so-called *multimode fiber (MMF)*, whereas laser-diode-based systems (mainly used for high-speed, long-haul data and telecom links) use *single-mode (SMF)* cable.

Travel Advisory

Infrared and laser diode light sources can cause eye damage if stared at directly, so never look down a fiber cable to see if it's working. Professional testing kits use optical sensors and/or cameras. If you don't have the proper equipment available, test for faults by replacing suspect fiber leads with known good ones.

An optical fiber cable has three components: the fiber itself; the cladding, which actually makes the light reflect down the fiber; and the insulating jacket. Fiber cabling is specified by its mode of operation and a two-number designator representing the core and cladding diameter in microns (μm, or millionths of a meter). The most common size used for general networking is multimode 62.5/125 μm, which can be used for cable runs of up to 275 meters. Almost all fiber networking standards require two fibers, and a pair is often connected together as duplex optical fiber cabling (Figure 2.8). Longer cable runs, of up to 70 km, are possible with other types of fiber optic cabling.

Objective 2.06 Optical Fiber Connectors

Because they are optical, rather than electrical, fiber cables have their own series of connector types. You cannot, for example, whack a BNC connector onto a piece of fiber (well, you probably *could*, but it won't impress anyone!). The two most common types of fiber optic connectors are the ST (twist and lock) and SC (push fit) types (see Figure 2.9), but you may also come across an FDDI duplex connector. FDDI (Fiber Distributed Data Interface), can sometimes be found linking servers

FIGURE 2.8 Duplex optical fiber cable

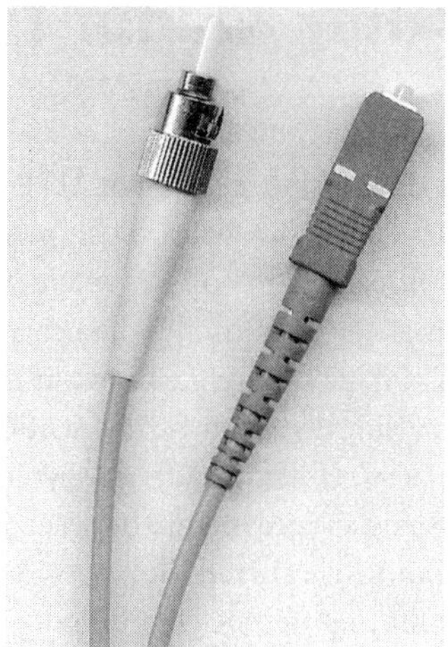

FIGURE 2.9 ST and SC fiber connectors

and other high-performance systems in some data centers; you'll learn more about the FDDI topology in the next chapter. ST connectors *do* look a bit BNC-ish, but be careful. Unlike a BNC connector, which can be impaled on its socket and twisted with total abandon until the locking guides engage with the fixing lugs, ST connectors have a keying mechanism to stop just this kind of youthful exuberance. If you do get carried away, you can snap the ceramic connector body—so easy does it!

Uses for Fiber

Although science programs often delight in telling you how many times a second the entire works of Shakespeare can be transmitted down a single fiber across a transatlantic phone link, that's not the primary use for fiber cable. Most of the fiber you are likely to encounter will be 10BaseFL or 100BaseFX, running at 10 or 100 Mbps, respectively, providing interlocation links on Ethernet-based networks. You will also find fiber cable, using the 100Mb FDDI standard, interconnecting systems in a computer room. Table 2.3 gives descriptions and speeds for the three basic fiber optic standards.

TABLE 2.3 Common Fiber Optic Cabling Standards

Standard	Description	Speed
10BaseFL	Ethernet over fiber	10 Mbps
100BaseFX	Ethernet over fiber	100 Mbps
1000BaseSX	Ethernet over fiber	1000 Mbps
FDDI	Fiber Distributed Data Interface	100 Mbps

Objective 2.07 Other Media Types

Don't even think of using copper (coax or UTP) solutions for links between buildings because differences in the neutral-to-earth voltage (a small voltage that develops at the point where an electrical system is grounded) of two buildings can cause major data corruption problems as well as a possibly dangerous voltage difference between the ends of the medium. The problem in this situation is caused by the ground materials—the water and minerals in the soil between the buildings—which act like the chemicals in a battery. When you string a piece of wire between the two poles of the battery (in this case, the buildings), a current flows between the poles, messing up the data and causing a voltage difference to build up, as shown in Figure 2.10. A few years ago, one member of the Total Seminars writing team encountered such a phenomenon, and the measured voltage between two points on the coax installation was just over 70 volts!

When a common grounding point cannot be established or guaranteed, the only way to link two buildings is by using fiber because it uses photons rather than electrons to carry the signal, providing no electrical connection. You can also use a wireless or laser link between buildings.

Interbuilding Wireless Links

Interbuilding links can extend your network by up to perhaps 1.5 km over a line-of-sight microwave link. Although the unit cost for such a microwave link seems high, it's likely to be a lot cheaper than digging a trench and installing fiber—an option that may not be available in your local business neighborhood

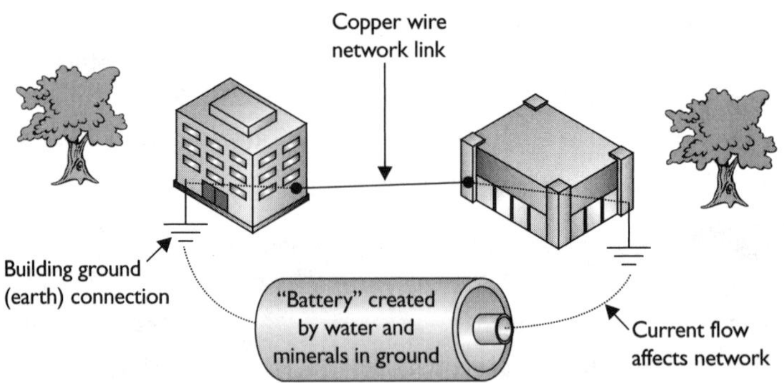

FIGURE 2.10 The use of copper media to link two buildings can create a battery effect.

anyway. As the technology continues to evolve and mature, wireless network links between buildings will increasingly compete with DSL and cable as options for bringing broadband Internet access to buildings.

802.11 Wireless Networks

The IEEE 802.11 committee supports three standards for wireless networking: 802.11a, 802.11b, and 802.11g. Each of these wireless standards use cellular radio links to provide network connectivity to PCs and laptop computers through a transmitter/receiver unit (transceiver), generally known as an *access point (AP)* or *wireless access point (WAP)*, which transmits and receives signals to and from the wireless network adapters (see Figure 2.11). By installing a number of strategically placed transceivers, coverage over a wide area of floor space can be achieved. Table 2.4 summarizes the key features of the main 802.11 networking standards. Keep in mind that the distance limitations specified in the table assume perfect conditions. In the real world, walls, plumbing, and other factors will often limit your wireless network to much smaller coverage areas.

TABLE 2.4 802.11 Wireless Networking Standards

Standard	802.11a	802.11b	802.11g
Maximum throughput	54 Mbps	11 Mbps	54 Mbps
Maximum range	150 feet	300 feet	300 feet
Frequency	5 GHz	2.4 GHz	2.4 GHz
Security	SSID, MAC filtering, industry-standard WEP, WPA	SSID, MAC filtering, industry-standard WEP, WPA	SSID, MAC filtering, industry-standard WEP, WPA
Compatibility	802.11a	802.11b	802.11b, 802.11g
Spread-spectrum method	DSSS	DSSS	DSSS
Communication mode	Ad-hoc or infrastructure	Ad-hoc or infrastructure	Ad-hoc or infrastructure
Description	Products that adhere to this standard are considered "Wi-Fi Certified." Eight available channels. Less prone to interference than 802.11b and 802.11g.	Products that adhere to this standard are considered "Wi-Fi Certified." Fourteen channels available in the 2.4 GHz band (only 11 of which can be used in the U.S. due to FCC regulations). Three non-overlapping channels.	Products that adhere to this standard are considered "Wi-Fi Certified." Improved security enhancements. Fourteen channels available in the 2.4 GHz band (only 11 of which can be used in the U.S. due to FCC regulations). Three non-overlapping channels.

FIGURE 2.11 Wireless networking equipment for the office

Although wireless networks free us from the need to work with cabling and grant us mobility with our portable computers, wireless networks have three main drawbacks: cost, security, and speed. Cost is beginning to disappear as an issue—the price of wireless networking equipment has dropped dramatically as the technology has become more popular. In terms of speed, wireless networks can seem slow compared to their wired equivalents. Consider that mainstream, copper-based network solutions can give you speeds up to 100 Mbps on each PC on a switched network, whereas a wireless network provides shared bandwidth at 11 or 54 Mbps. As for security, stories abound of techno-addicts (and investigative journalists!) driving around with makeshift *Mission Impossible* antennae on their cars (often constructed from an old Pringles can), tapping into corporate wireless networks and surfing the Net for free. Certainly, current wireless standards are evolving as weaknesses in the WEP (Wired Equivalent Privacy) standard have become widely known and widely exploited.

802.11 Networking Security

For ease of configuration, wireless networking devices often ship with none of their security features turned on. Your network's data packets are traveling through the air instead of safely wrapped up inside network cabling. What's to stop an unscrupulous network tech with the right equipment from grabbing those packets out of the air and reading that data?

To address these issues, wireless networks use three methods: Service Set Identification (SSID), MAC address filtering, and data encryption.

The *Service Set Identification (SSID),* sometimes called a *network name,* is a 32-bit identification string used in the header of each 802.11 data packet. When properly configured, only wireless clients whose SSID matches that of the wireless access point can gain access to the wireless network. Data packets that lack the correct SSID in the header are rejected. The SSID, thus, provides some minimal wireless security, and perhaps more importantly provides a method for clients to distinguish between networks whose coverage overlaps.

By default, wireless access points broadcast their SSID to let clients within range know that the network exists. Many techs disable this SSID broadcast to make their networks somewhat more difficult for intruders to find. Wireless access points also use a generic SSID set by the manufacturer by default. For example, the default SSID for Linksys wireless access points is "linksys." Using a default SSID and leaving the SSID broadcast feature turned on is like announcing to the world, "Come hack my network. I haven't bothered to change any of my default settings!"

Most wireless access points support *MAC address filtering* (sometimes called *MAC address reservations*), a feature that enables you to limit access to your wireless network based on the physical, hard-wired addresses of the wireless network adapters you support. MAC address filtering allows you to control who can use your wireless network. A table stored in the wireless access point lists the MAC addresses that may participate in the wireless network. Any data packets that don't contain the MAC address of a node listed in the table are rejected. Specifying the MAC addresses of wireless NICs that may connect to your network is not a perfect solution. A talented hacker can modify the MAC address used by a wireless NIC, but restricting access to your network based on MAC addresses considerably increases the level of difficulty for potential intruders.

To provide real security for your wireless network, you must encrypt your data. Turning off the SSID broadcast and creating MAC address reservations will not stop a truly determined intruder. With *encryption*, data packets are electronically encoded (using an encryption key) before being transmitted onto the wireless network. The receiving network device has to possess the encryption key to unscramble the packet and process the data. Therefore, any data packets surreptitiously grabbed by an intruder out of the air are useless without the encryption key. Enabling wireless encryption through either Wireless Equivalency Privacy (WEP) or Wi-Fi Protected Access (WPA) provides a good level of security to data packets in transit.

Wireless Equivalency Privacy (WEP) encryption uses a 64-bit encryption algorithm to scramble data packets, but most vendors now enable stronger 128-bit algorithms. WEP, however, is a flawed standard that can be cracked using well-known hacker tools such as Airsnort. If your wireless access points and NICs provide no other option, WEP does increase the security of your network by keeping out casual intruders, but you need something better to protect yourself from a motivated intruder.

Wi-Fi Protected Access (WPA) provides a newer encryption standard that addresses the weaknesses of WEP. WPA offers security enhancements such as dynamic encryption key generation (keys are issued on a per-user and per-session basis), an encryption key integrity-checking feature, user authentication through the industry-standard Extensible Authentication Protocol (EAP), and other advanced features that WEP lacks. WPA isn't available on all wireless networking devices, so make certain that all your access points and NICs support WPA before turning it on.

Ad-hoc and Infrastructure

802.11 networks can operate in one of two modes: ad-hoc or infrastructure. In an ad-hoc network, the wireless nodes communicate directly with each other; you would not need to have a wireless access point for two hosts to communicate. Although this might be handy for transferring files between two laptops in the train station, ad-hoc 802.11 networking doesn't help you connect to your corporate network or the Internet. To connect to an existing wired network, you need to use infrastructure mode and send all wireless traffic through a wireless access point. That wireless access point will most likely be connected to either an Internet connection or to a private, wired network, providing access to that wired network for the wireless network nodes.

Laser Links

Lasers are also an option for point-to-point links, but setup is a little trickier, and laser systems can suffer from weather-related problems (bright sun, rain, and fog) as well as loss of signal as the high-power laser emitter ages. In any case, laser (and microwave) systems require a line-of-sight path between the transmitter and receiver, so the possible effect of intermediate obstacles needs to be assessed.

Bluetooth

Bluetooth creates small wireless networks, called *personal area networks (PANs)*, between PCs and peripheral devices such as PDAs and printers, input devices such as keyboards and mice, and consumer electronics such as cell phones, home stereos, televisions, home security systems, and so on. Bluetooth was *not* originally designed to be a full-function networking solution, although many vendors have adopted it for this purpose.

Bluetooth is the basis for the IEEE organization's forthcoming 802.15 standard for wireless PANs. Bluetooth uses the FHSS spread-spectrum broadcasting method, switching among any of the 79 frequencies available in the 2.45-GHz range. Bluetooth hops frequencies some 1,600 times per second, making it highly resistant to interference. The Bluetooth specification allows for transfers of data at rates from 723 Kbps to 1 Mbps, with a maximum range of 10 meters (~33 feet).

Bluetooth devices interoperate in a *master/slave* scheme, in which one master device controls up to seven active slave devices. These roles are designated automatically and do not require any configuration. The personal area network (PAN) created by Bluetooth is sometimes called a *piconet.* More than seven Bluetooth slave devices (up to 255) can participate in a piconet at one time, but only seven of those devices can be active at one time. Inactive slave devices are referred to as *parked* devices.

Bluetooth devices use a four-stage process to find each other and create the PAN, as detailed in Table 2.5.

The services supported by Bluetooth are called *profiles.* Here are the 13 common Bluetooth profiles:

- **Generic Access Profile** Defines how Bluetooth units discover and establish a connection with each other.
- **Service Discovery Profile** Enables the Bluetooth device's Service Discovery User Application to query other Bluetooth devices to determine what services they provide. This profile is dependent on the Generic Access Profile.
- **Cordless Telephony Profile** Defines the Bluetooth wireless phone functionality.
- **Intercom Profile** Defines the Bluetooth wireless intercom functionality.
- **Serial Port Profile** Enables Bluetooth devices to emulate serial port communication using RS232 control signaling, the standard used on ordinary PC serial ports. This profile is dependent on the Generic Access Profile.

TABLE 2.5 Bluetooth Four-Stage Process

Stage	Purpose
Device discovery	The device broadcasts its MAC address and a code identifying the type of device.
Name discovery	The device identifies itself by a "friendly" name, such as *iPAQ Pocket PC.*
Association	The device joins the Bluetooth network.
Service discovery	The device announces the services that it can provide.

- **Headset Profile** Defines the Bluetooth wireless telephone and PC headset functionality.
- **Dial-up Networking Profile** Defines the Bluetooth device's capability to act as, or interact with, a modem.
- **Fax Profile** Defines the Bluetooth device's capability to act as or interact with a fax device.
- **LAN Access Profile** Defines how the Bluetooth device accesses a LAN and the Internet.
- **Generic Object Exchange Profile** Defines how Bluetooth devices exchange data with other devices. This profile is dependent on the Serial Port Profile.
- **Object Push Profile** Bluetooth devices use this profile to exchange small data objects, such as a PDA's Vcard, with other Bluetooth devices.
- **File Transfer Profile** Used to exchange large data objects, such as files, between Bluetooth devices. This profile is dependent on the Generic Object Exchange Profile.
- **Synchronization Profile** Used to synchronize data between Bluetooth PDAs and PCs.

Bluetooth devices have to support identical profiles to communicate; for example, your PDA and PC both have to support the Bluetooth Synchronization Profile if you want them to synch up.

For security, Bluetooth offers proprietary 128-bit encryption and the capability to set per-user passwords to guard against unauthorized access to the Bluetooth network. Bluetooth also supports industry-standard Point-to-Point Tunneling Protocol (PPTP) and Secure Sockets Layer (SSL) security through browser-based remote access. Access to Bluetooth networks can be controlled through MAC address filtering, and Bluetooth devices can be set to non-discovery mode to effectively hide them from other Bluetooth devices. Bluetooth specifications are shown in Table 2.6.

Infrared Wireless Networking

Wireless networking using infrared technology, although slow compared to 802.11 networks, comes standard on many laptop computers and can provide an easy way to transfer files between computers without purchasing additional hardware.

Communication through infrared devices is enabled via the *Infrared Data Association*, or *IrDA*, protocol. The IrDA protocol stack is a widely supported industry standard and has been included in all versions of Windows since Windows 95. Apple computers also support IrDA, as do Linux PCs.

TABLE 2.6 Bluetooth Specifications

Standard	Bluetooth
Maximum throughput	1 Mbps (some devices boast 2 Mbps)
Maximum range	Typically 30 feet, but some high-powered Bluetooth devices have a maximum range of 300 feet
Frequency	2.45 GHz
Security	Proprietary 128-bit encryption, password-protected access, PPTP, SSL (through browser-based remote access client)
Compatibility	Bluetooth
Spread-spectrum method	FHSS
Communication mode	Master/slave: a single master device with up to seven active slave devices
Description	Bluetooth is designed to enable wireless communication between PCs and peripheral components, as well as consumer electronics. Bluetooth is not a full-fledged networking solution, and it is not intended to compete with or replace 802.11-based wireless networking technologies.

Infrared devices transmit data more slowly than most other wired or wireless networking options. Infrared devices can transfer data at up to 4 Mbps. The maximum distance between infrared devices is 1 meter, and connections must be in direct line of sight, making them susceptible to interference. An infrared link can be disrupted by anything that breaks the beam of light—a soda can, a co-worker passing between desks, or even bright sunlight hitting the infrared transceiver can cause interference.

Exam Tip

Infrared devices transfer data at a maximum of 4 Mbps and have a maximum distance of 1 meter.

Infrared is only designed to make a point-to-point connection between two devices in ad-hoc mode—no equivalent to the infrastructure mode or 802.11 exists for infrared. You can, however, use an infrared access point device to enable Ethernet network communication using IrDA. Also, infrared devices operate at half-duplex, so they can't talk and listen at the same time. IrDA has a mode that emulates full-duplex communication, but it's really half-duplex.

In terms of security, the IrDA protocol offers exactly nothing in the way of encryption or authentication. Infrared's main security feature is the fact that you have to be literally within arms' reach to establish a link. Infrared is not the best solution for a dedicated network connection, but for a quick file transfer or print job, it'll do in a pinch. Table 2.7 summarizes the key specifications for IrDA.

TABLE 2.7 IrDA Specifications

Standard	Infrared (IrDA)
Maximum throughput	Up to 4 Mbps
Maximum range	1 meter (39 inches)
Security	None
Compatibility	IrDA
Communication mode	Point-to-point ad-hoc
Description	Infrared is best suited for quick, small transfers, such as zapping business card information from one PDA to another or sending print jobs to an infrared-capable printer.

✔ **Objective 2.01: Coaxial Cable** Coax cable is the classic example of bounded network media. Coax cable consists of an inner core and an overall metal screen, plus layers of insulation. The screen gives the cable a degree of protection against electromagnetic interference, but still, as with most copper-based media, it should be kept away from sources of interference. A wide variety of coax cable types exist, but specific types must be used for networking—not just any coax will do. The two networking standards most closely associated with coax are Ethernet and ARCNet, although other media types have generally superseded coax in network designs, and ARCNet installations, in particular, are now quite rare.

✔ **Objective 2.02: Coaxial Connectors** BNC connectors, used with Thin Ethernet, originally were soldered and bolted to the cable, but now they are almost universally fitted by crimping (compression). Thick Ethernet installations may use PL-259 plugs and SO-239 sockets, a connector type originally developed for radio use.

✔ **Objective 2.03: UTP and STP Cable** The vast majority of new network installations use unshielded twisted pair (UTP) cable, a four-pair cable originally intended for telephone circuits but enhanced to carry data. Over time, various categories of UTP cable have been developed, each capable of operating at faster data rates than its predecessor. There are two general types of UTP wiring: Patch cable uses stranded copper to make the wiring flexible, and premises cable (so-called *horizontal cable*) uses a solid core to give the wiring more strength to withstand rougher handling as it is installed in ducting and cable trays. Mixing the cable types—for example, using horizontal cable for patch leads—can lead to reliability problems.

✔ **Objective 2.04: UTP Connectors** Most UTP installations use RJ45 connectors and wall ports. RJ45 connectors have eight contacts to match the four pairs of wires in the UTP cable. The cable pairs are color-coded to make it easier to follow a standard wiring pattern when connecting media or fitting the cable to wall ports. Various wiring standards stating which pair of wires should be fixed to which connectors have appeared over the years, but the most commonly used standard is EIA/TIA 568B. Because UTP cable is not screened, it must be installed well away from other sources of electrical interference, and most installations are thoroughly tested to make sure they meet basic functional criteria. A screened version of UTP—called *STP*—is available, but it is much more expensive and rarely used unless local conditions demand a high level of screening.

✔ **Objective 2.05: Optical Fiber** Optical fiber cabling is much more expensive to install than copper alternatives, but it offers several advantages, including greater maximum distance and improved security. Fiber can also be used between buildings at different ground (earth) potentials and in electrically noisy or chemically hazardous environments (no danger from sparks). There are two main types of optical fiber: single-mode fiber (SMF) and multimode fiber (MMF), the latter being the most commonly used type for general networking. Optical fiber is specified according to the core (fiber) and cladding diameter (in microns), the most common size being 62.5/125.

✔ **Objective 2.06: Optical Fiber Connectors** Optical fiber has its own set of connectors because it's an optical system, not electrical. The most common connector types are known as ST (a twist-and-lock connector) and SC (a push-fit connector). Optical fiber connectors should always be handled with care because they can be broken fairly easily.

✔ **Objective 2.07: Other Media Types** Wireless networking solutions exist for both point-to-point building links and general intraoffice connectivity. Office-based solutions are becoming increasingly popular, especially since key technical issues have been formalized with the IEEE 802.11 and 802.11b standards, allowing different manufacturers to produce compatible equipment and increasing competition in the marketplace. Wireless networks operate in the office by means of one or more cells, each connecting users to the main network via an access point (AP). Wireless network security remains a concern as new security standards try to address the weaknesses in the WEP encryption protocol. Laser-based systems can also be used for interbuilding links, but they can be relatively expensive, and setup can be a bit more complex compared to a microwave solution.

REVIEW QUESTIONS

1. Which of the following connector types is associated with fiber optic cable? (Select one answer.)
   - **A.** RJ45
   - **B.** BNC
   - **C.** ST
   - **D.** RG-58
2. Which of the following UTP cable categories can support data transmissions at 100 Mbps? (Select one answer.)
   - **A.** CAT 3
   - **B.** CAT 4
   - **C.** CAT 5
   - **D.** All of the above
3. You have been tasked with installing a network link between two buildings approximately 250 meters apart. Which of the following media types is unlikely to be suitable? (Select one answer.)
   - **A.** Microwave
   - **B.** Laser
   - **C.** Fiber
   - **D.** Thick Ethernet
4. Which of the following connector types is associated with UTP cable? (Select one answer.)
   - **A.** RJ45
   - **B.** BNC
   - **C.** SC
   - **D.** NBC
5. What name is given to the problem caused when signals from adjacent cables interfere with each other? (Select one answer.)
   - **A.** Talkback
   - **B.** Crossover
   - **C.** Backchat
   - **D.** Crosstalk

6. Which of the following names describes a type of Thick Ethernet transceiver connection? (Select one answer.)

   A. FDDI clamp
   B. Nettle sting
   C. Vampire tap
   D. TE tap

7. You notice that the computer in your office can't connect to the network when you switch on the room lights, but with the lights off it works fine. What is most likely to be the problem? (Select one answer.)

   A. There is a voltage drop when the lights are turned on.
   B. There is a loose BNC connector.
   C. There is light entering a nearby fiber cable.
   D. The cabling system is faulty.

8. What layer of the OSI model does an RJ45 connector represent? (Select one answer.)

   A. Physical
   B. Data Link
   C. Network
   D. Session

9. Which of the following media types is used for Thin Ethernet–based networks? (Select one answer.)

   A. CAT 3
   B. RG-58
   C. RG-45
   D. 62.5/125

10. You have been tasked with providing network connections for a group of sales reps who regularly bring their laptop computers into the office. Which of the following media types would most likely provide the best solution? (Choose two answers.)

    A. FDDI
    B. UTP
    C. Wireless
    D. 100BaseFX

REVIEW ANSWERS

1. **C** ST connectors are associated with fiber optic cable.
2. **C** CAT 5 (and higher) cabling can support data transmission at 100 Mbps.
3. **D** Using copper-based media for interbuilding links can lead to electrical problems.
4. **A** RJ45 connectors are associated with UTP cable.
5. **D** Crosstalk between adjacent cables causes interference.
6. **C** Vampire taps are used to connect transceivers to Thick Ethernet cable.
7. **D** Because applying power to the lighting circuit seems to cause the problem, it is likely that the network media is located too close to the light fitting or wiring in the plenum.
8. **A** Connectors are Physical layer devices.
9. **B** RG-58 coax is used for Thin Ethernet networks.
10. **B** **C** UTP and wireless are the best choices. Using fiber (answers A and D) would be very expensive.

CHAPTER 3

Network Topologies and Standards

ITINERARY

- **Objective 3.01** The Bus Topology and Ethernet
- **Objective 3.02** The Star Bus Topology
- **Objective 3.03** Ring Topologies
- **Objective 3.04** Wireless Networking
- **Objective 3.05** Distributed Star Topology—ARCNet
- **Objective 3.06** Mesh Topology

NEWBIE	SOME EXPERIENCE	EXPERT
4 hours	2 hours	1 hour

A network *topology* provides a general description of how the devices on the network link to each other, either logically or physically. Topologies do not define specifics about how to implement a network installation. They only provide a very high-level look at how network nodes connect. To move from a theoretical overview to a working solution, you must implement a specific network standard such as Ethernet or Token Ring.

Particular network topologies are generally associated with specific networking standards that provide the specifics that define how the network sends data between devices, the type of media used, the maximum network speed (also known as *bandwidth*), and the number of devices (nodes) that can attach to the network. Questions regarding network topologies and network standards are well represented on the Network+ exam. Pay attention here—there's a lot to take in, and it's all important stuff.

The Bus Topology and Ethernet

If you can imagine your laundry hanging on a long, straight clothes line, you have a pretty good idea of how a bus topology network is constructed. Everything hangs off one long run of cable, as shown in Figure 3.1. The bus topology has been associated with one network standard in particular—Ethernet.

Ethernet Overview

Ethernet, introduced by Xerox in 1973, remained a largely proprietary technology until 1979, when Xerox looked for partners to help promote Ethernet as an industry standard. Working with Digital Equipment Corporation (DEC) and Intel, the company published what became the Digital-Intel-Xerox (DIX) networking standard. The standard described a bus topology network using coaxial cable that enables multiple computing systems and other devices to communicate with each other at 10 Mbps.

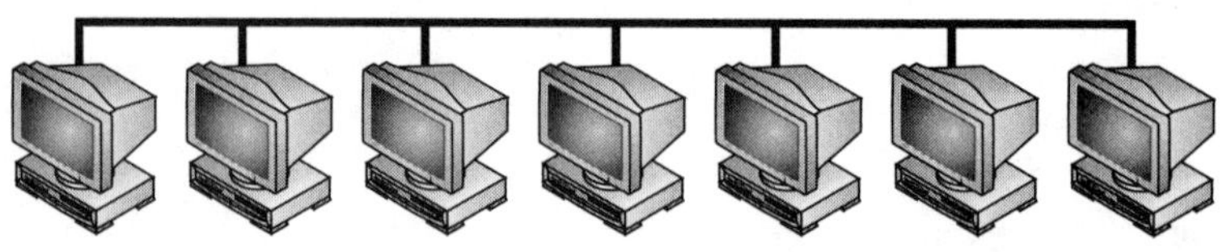

FIGURE 3.1 Bus topology, where everything is attached to the one cable

Local Lingo

segment A run of cable (media) linking one or more nodes on a network.

How Ethernet Works

Any network design must address a number of key elements: the type of media to use, how to send data across the wire, how to identify the sending and receiving computers, and how to determine which computer should use the shared cable next.

In Chapter 2, we discussed the physical cabling used in Ethernet. Ethernet networks can use coaxial cable, UTP, or fiber. Regardless of the physical cabling used, the data moves across the wire in essentially the same way. Any network requires a method for determining which device uses the network media at a given time, and Ethernet uses a technique known as CSMA/CD.

CSMA/CD

Ethernet networks use *Carrier Sense, Multiple Access/Collision Detection (CSMA/CD)* to determine which computer should use the shared media at a given moment. "Carrier Sense" means that each machine on the network, referred to as a *node*, examines the cable before sending a data packet (see Figure 3.2). If another machine is using the network, the node detects traffic and waits until the cable is free. If the node detects no traffic, the node sends its data packet. Carrier sense is analogous to the process you use to get an outside phone line in a large office building. When you have a call to make, you pick up the phone, press a button, and listen. If you hear a dial tone (that is, if the line is free), you make your call. If you hear a busy signal (that is, if someone else is already using the line), you wait your turn.

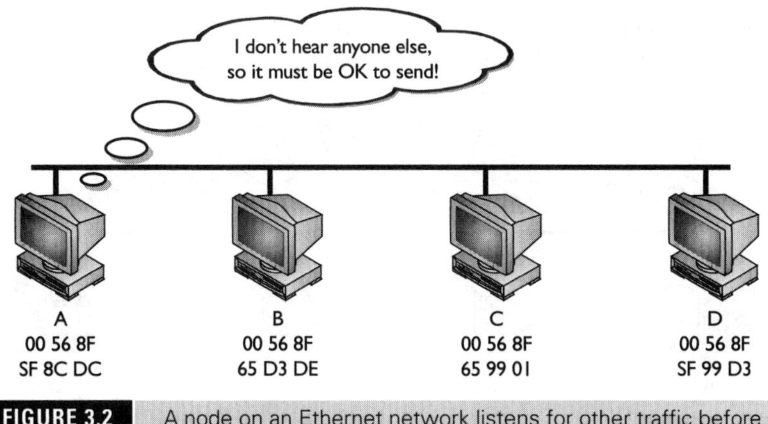

FIGURE 3.2 A node on an Ethernet network listens for other traffic before sending a data packet.

"Multiple Access" means that all machines have equal access to the wire. If the line is free, an Ethernet node does not have to get approval to use the wire—it just uses it. From the point of view of Ethernet, it does not matter what function the node is performing. The node could be a desktop system running Windows 2000 Professional or XP or a high-end file server running Windows 2000 Server, Windows 2003 Server, or Linux. In Ethernet, all nodes are created equal. Access to the cable is determined on a first-come, first-served basis. But what happens when two machines listen to the cable and simultaneously determine that it is free? They both try to send.

When two nodes use the cable simultaneously, a *collision* occurs. Both of the transmissions are lost (see Figure 3.3). Two nodes transmitting at the same time is like two people talking simultaneously. The listener hears the mixture of the two voices and can't understand either voice.

When a collision occurs, both nodes detect the collision by listening to their own transmissions. By comparing their own transmissions with the signal they receive, they can determine whether another node has transmitted at the same time, as shown in Figure 3.4. If the nodes detect a collision, both nodes immediately stop transmitting and wait for a short, random period of time before retrying.

Because CSMA/CD is easy to implement in hardware, Ethernet NICs are relatively cheap. That simplicity comes at a price: an Ethernet node will waste some amount of its time dealing with collisions instead of sending data. As you add more devices to the network and/or increase the amount of traffic—for example, by installing new, data-intensive applications on the network—the number of collisions on the network will increase as the nodes generate more packets. Every Ethernet network wastes some amount of its available bandwidth dealing with these collisions. The typical Ethernet network advertises that it runs at either 10 Mbps or 100 Mbps, but the advertised speed assumes that no collisions ever take place! In reality, collisions are a normal part of the operation of an Ethernet network, and the typical throughput will rarely be greater than about 70 percent of the theoretical maximum bandwidth.

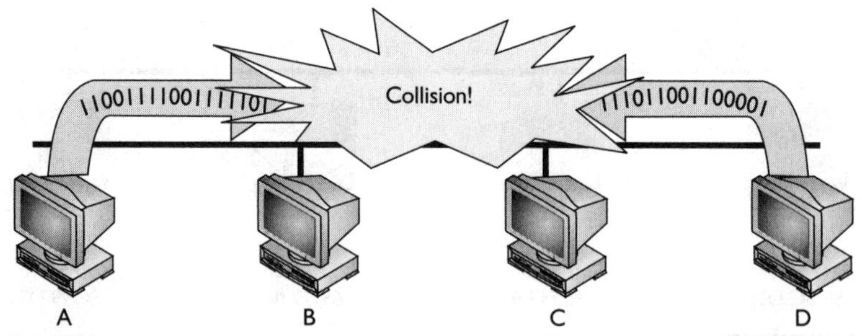

FIGURE 3.3 If two nodes transmit simultaneously, a data collision occurs.

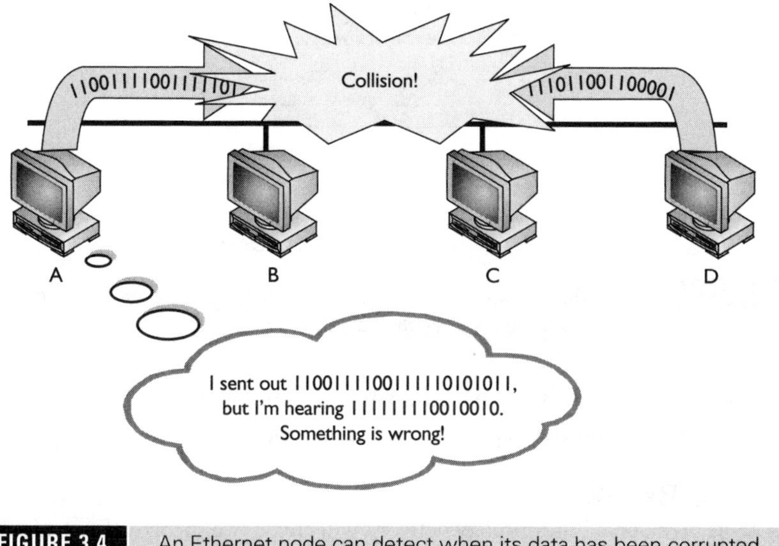

FIGURE 3.4 An Ethernet node can detect when its data has been corrupted by a collision.

The use of CSMA/CD leads to a number of classic conditions familiar to most users of Ethernet networks. When everybody sits down at 9 A.M. to check e-mail, for example, many networks run noticeably slower. Virtually every station on the network contends for the use of the cable at the same time, causing massive collisions and retransmission attempts. Typically, end users will not receive any kind of error message as a result of high levels of traffic. Instead, they will just notice that the network is running slowly. The Ethernet NICs will continue to retry transmission until they eventually send their data packets successfully. Only if the collisions become so severe that a packet cannot be sent after 16 retries will the sending station give up, with an error message sent to the user.

Termination

Ethernet networks using a physical bus topology (such as those using coax cabling) function properly only if both ends of the network bus are fitted with terminating *resistors.* Without one or more of these terminators in place, some of the energy in the electrical signals that make up the data packets bounces back up the wire, a phenomenon known as *reflection,* as shown in Figure 3.5.

To all other nodes on the network, these reflections look like a mass of data and collisions being generated by other devices, so they will wait for the network to become clear before transmitting. The reflections quickly build up to a point where the network looks permanently busy, so very soon all devices enter a permanent

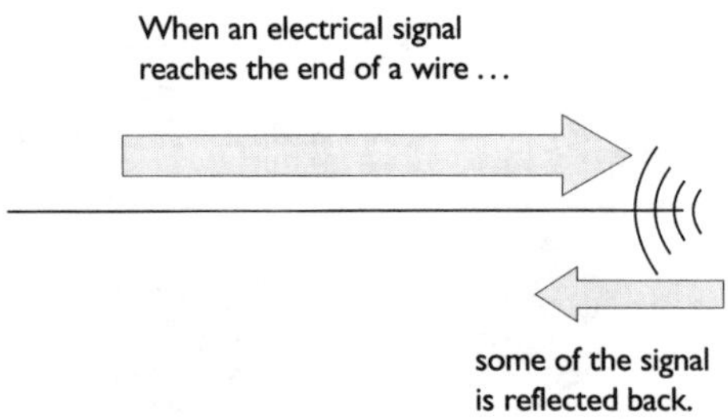

FIGURE 3.5 When a signal hits the end of an unterminated wire, some of its energy reflects back along the wire.

wait mode (see Figure 3.6). The terminating resistor (see Figure 3.7) absorbs the reflections and allows the segment to function properly.

Cable Breaks

A cable break on a bus topology network will create two incorrectly terminated segments, causing multiple reflections in both directions. In this scenario, all stations on the network go into perpetual wait mode (see Figure 3.8). This condition disables all nodes connected to the broken cable. Because a single break can take down the entire segment and all nodes connected to it, bus-based networks are said to have a "single point of failure."

Ethernet Standards

In the early 1980s, the *Institute of Electrical and Electronics Engineers (IEEE)*, an organization that defines industry-wide standards in the fields of electronics and computing, adopted the DIX Ethernet standard as a general standard for networking. The IEEE working group (or committee) responsible for general

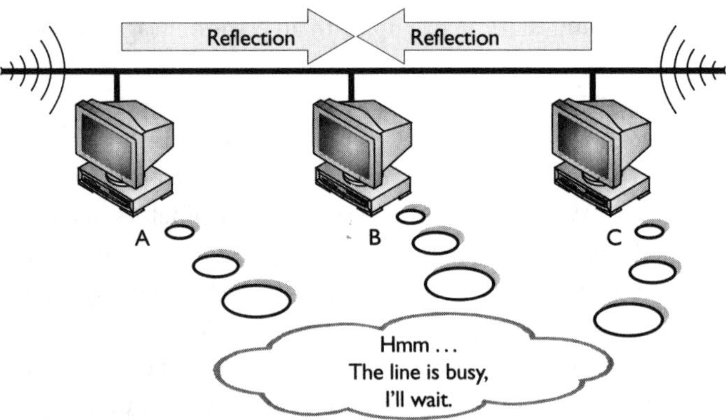

FIGURE 3.6 Reflections cause the network to look permanently busy.

FIGURE 3.7 Thin Ethernet (10Base2) BNC terminators house the terminating resistors.

networking standards is known as the *802 committee,* and Ethernet became IEEE standard 802.3. As you will soon discover, the 802 committee and its subcommittees and working groups are responsible for many of the network standards you will encounter and, thus, many of the facts you have to remember for the Network+ exam!

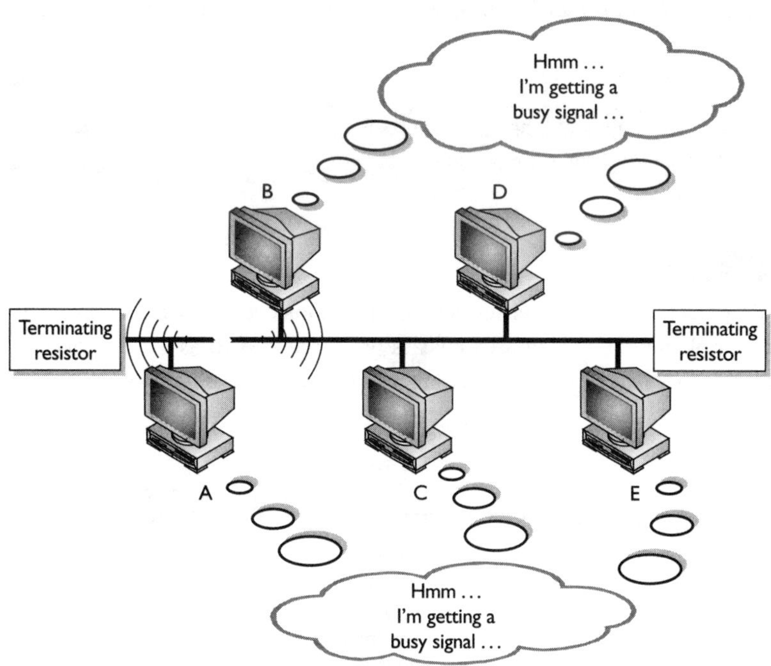

FIGURE 3.8 Reflections caused by a cable break disrupt the entire network.

IEEE 802.3

The term "Ethernet" now refers to any network based on the IEEE 802.3 standard. If you want to be totally accurate, IEEE 802.3 and the original Ethernet spec are not identical—for example, the original Ethernet standard makes reference to the use of only coax cable for the network media, whereas 802.3 allows for the use of other types (which is just as well, with all those UTP installations out there!). In practice, the terms "Ethernet" and "IEEE 802.3" can be used interchangeably.

Ethernet on the Bus

Two main standards exist for creating a bus-based Ethernet network, with wonderfully descriptive names: 10Base5 and 10Base2. The IEEE coined these labels, and they each describe three key features of the network, as shown in Figure 3.9:

- The "10" signifies an Ethernet network that runs at 10 Mbps.
- "Base" signifies that 10Base5 uses *baseband* signaling, meaning that there is just one channel of communication on the cable at any time, as opposed to a broadband system (such as cable TV coax), which can have multiple signals on the cable.
- The "5" indicates that 10Base5 cables may not be longer than 500 meters. The "2" in 10Base2 is the distance rounded up from 185 meters.

Exam Tip

Another key feature of Ethernet networks is that they support a theoretical maximum of 1,024 nodes.

10Base5

10Base5 describes an Ethernet network that looks very much like the original DIX implementation. 10Base5 coax is often referred to as *Thick Ethernet,* or *Thicknet,* because of the large diameter of the cable (see Figure 3.10).

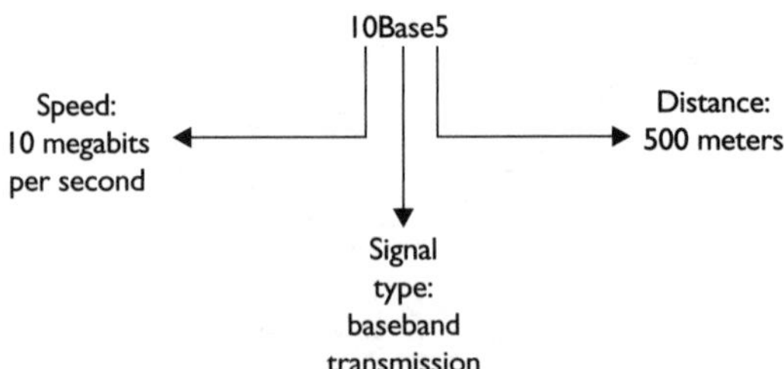

FIGURE 3.9 The term "10Base5" tells us three things about the network.

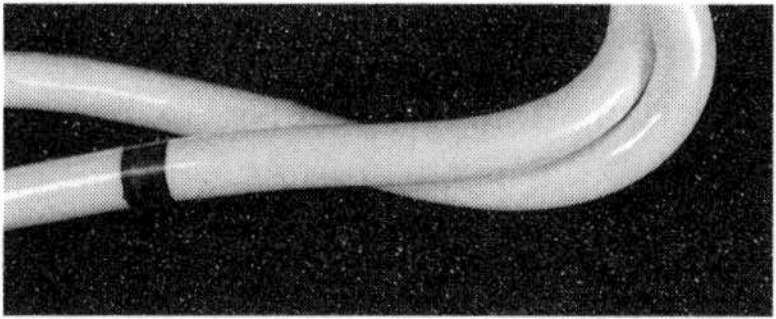

FIGURE 3.10 Thick Ethernet coax—note the black band.

Travel Advisory

AUI connectors on network interface cards are identical to PC joystick/MIDI connectors, so be careful: connecting the wrong device to your network or sound/midi/game card may damage something!

Thicknet has the heaviest shielding of any cabling commonly used for 10 Mbps Ethernet, making it an excellent choice for high-interference environments. The thick copper core also reduces signal degradation over the length of the cable, contributing to the 500-meter maximum segment distance. Although 10Base5 represented a revolutionary cabling system when originally introduced, its high cost and difficult installation limit its use today. New installations incorporate 10Base5 only in situations that require its heavy shielding or generous distance limitation.

Although not mandatory, proper Thicknet cable is almost always yellow, and because of this and its rigidity, it is occasionally referred to as "yellow cable" or "frozen yellow garden hose." Some confusion has also been caused by the availability of *blue* Thicknet coax—some techs are convinced that blue coax is exterior-grade stuff, and that it will quite happily sit in puddles of water on rooftops between networked locations (presumably, someone worked out the idea that blue = water = outside). In reality, *all* forms of standard Ethernet coax are for *interior* use only, and external runs need suitable protection from the elements; otherwise, you'll eventually experience the thrill of water dripping from your coax connectors.

Connecting to the Coax

10Base5 installations use the Thicknet coax as a backbone to carry data around the area covered by the network, but the coax itself is usually hidden away in the ceiling void (plenum) or in trunking, partly because it's quite bulky and stiff and would be a pain to install at desktop level. Devices (nodes) are connected to the coax via a transceiver box. The connection between a node and transceiver uses a multicore cable fitted with 15-pin male DB connectors. These cable assemblies are formally known as *attachment unit interface (AUI)* drop cables and connectors.

Cable Length and Other Limitations

AUI drop cables can be any length up to 50 meters, but the external Thicknet transceivers must be placed an absolute minimum of 2.5 meters apart, as shown in Figure 3.11. In fact, the distance between transceivers must be a multiple of 2.5 meters. Remember that black band in Figure 3.10? Those bands are printed every 2.5 meters along the coax and help technicians space the connections properly when installing the cable. Figure 3.12 shows the connection between a 10Base5 transceiver and a NIC. Up to 100 nodes (transceivers) can be connected to a ThickNet segment.

10Base5 Summary

Here are the key features that distinguish 10Base5 cabling:

- Speed of 10 Mbps (megabits per second)
- Baseband signal type
- Distance of 500 meters per segment
- 100 nodes per segment maximum
- 2.5-meter intervals between nodes
- Cables marked with a black band every 2.5 meters to ease installation
- Expensive cost per foot compared to other cabling systems
- Also known as Thick Ethernet, Thicknet, yellow cable, or frozen yellow garden hose

Although some organizations continue to use 10Base5 cabling, most new 10 Mbps installations use either 10Base2 (discussed next) or 10BaseT (discussed later).

10Base2

10Base2 offers a cheap and quick way to network a small number of computers using coaxial cable and Ethernet. 10Base2 is much easier to install and much less expensive than 10Base5. It uses a thinner coax cable, which limits overall

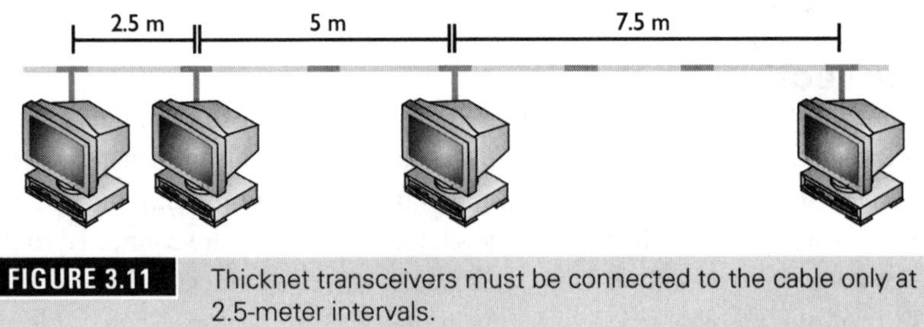

FIGURE 3.11 Thicknet transceivers must be connected to the cable only at 2.5-meter intervals.

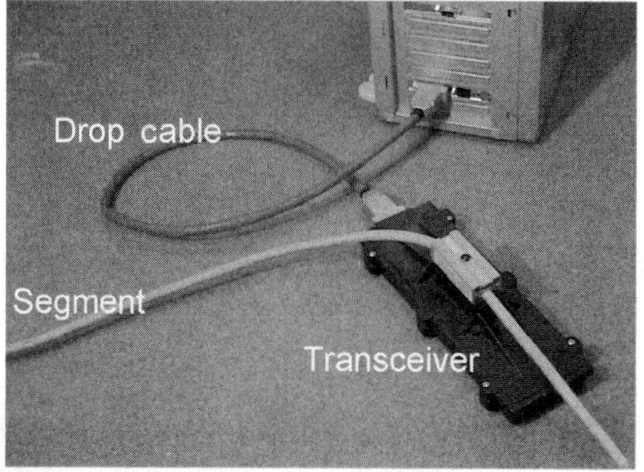

FIGURE 3.12 A 10Base5 transceiver and drop cable

segment length (to 185 meters, remember?), and you can only fit 30 nodes on a single segment, but these limitations can be overcome by extending the network as described later.

10Base2 NICs include an integrated transceiver so there's no external box to clamp to the (much thinner) coax. Instead, the coax arrives and leaves the NIC via a BNC T-connector, as shown in Figure 3.13.

The 10Base2's transceiver spacing requirements are also much simpler. The only rule is that they must be at least 0.5 meter apart, and they don't need to be spaced at specific intervals. Because the transceiver is integrated into the NIC, for "transceiver spacing" you can substitute the words "T-connector spacing" or just "node spacing."

Each end machine on the network has a coax cable arriving at its T-connector (see Figure 3.14) and a BNC terminator taking the place of the other cable (see Figure 3.15).

FIGURE 3.13 A BNC T-connector

FIGURE 3.14 A BNC T-connector on the back of a NIC with two coax cables attached

10Base2 Summary

Here are the key features that distinguish 10Base2 cabling:

- 10 Mbps (megabits per second)
- Baseband signal
- 185 meters per segment
- 30 maximum nodes per segment
- Nodes must be spaced at least 0.5 meter apart
- Inexpensive cost per foot compared to 10Base5
- Known as Thin Ethernet, Thinnet, Cheapernet

FIGURE 3.15 A BNC T-connector with one cable and a terminator attached

Historically, 10Base2 probably once represented the greatest installed base among *all* network types, and there's still a lot of these networks out there, but newer standards, such as 10BaseT and 100BaseTX, offer the same, or better, performance, with greater expansion options and improved reliability, such as no single point of failure. In addition, the cost of 10BaseT and 100BaseT hubs has declined in recent years, to the point that the traditional cost advantages of 10Base2 has largely disappeared.

Objective 3.02 The Star Bus Topology

Newer Ethernet standards use a hybrid topology known as a *star bus.* Star bus networks use a physical star topology that provides improved stability as well as a logical bus that maintains compatibility with existing Ethernet standards.

Physical Star

In a star topology, all nodes connect to a central wiring point, as shown in Figure 3.16. The key advantage of the star topology is that a break in a cable affects only the machine connected to that cable. In Figure 3.17, machine C cannot communicate with any other node, but machines A, B, D, E, and F communicate with each other just fine.

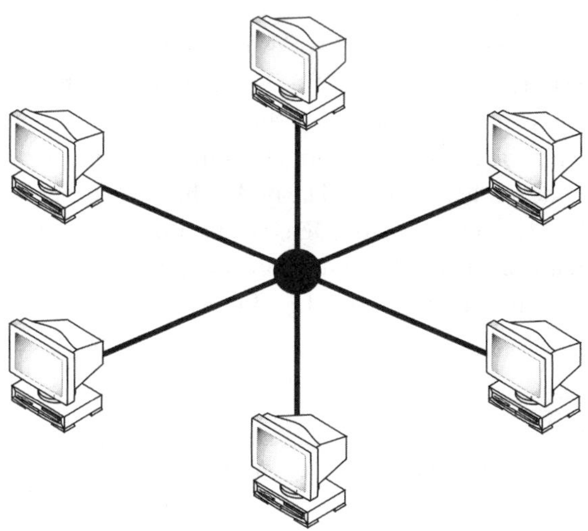

FIGURE 3.16 A star topology

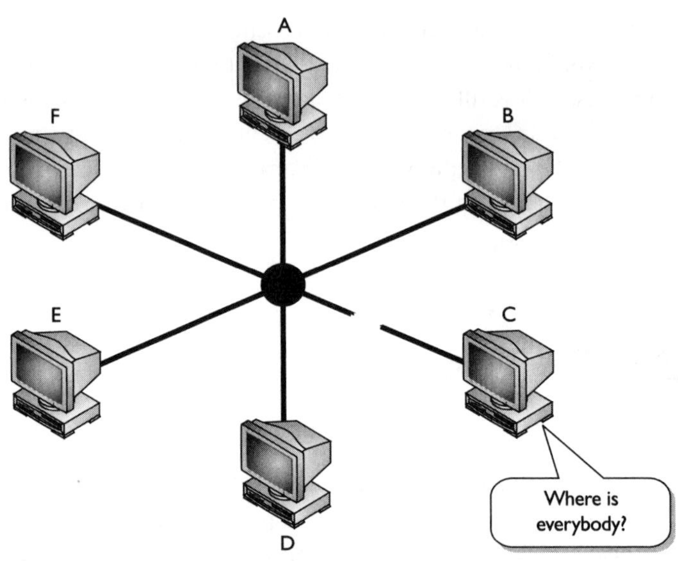

FIGURE 3.17 In a star topology, a broken cable affects only the machine connected to it.

Although the star topology provides a more robust, fault-tolerant cabling system than bus topology, pure star topologies aren't used for modern computer networks.

Logical Bus

In the real world, star topology networks use multiport hubs to link together groups of machines (see Figure 3.18). The way that these hubs pass data between their ports represents the logical (bus) part of the star bus partnership; in effect, each hub behaves like a terminated Ethernet segment, with each port becoming a node on that segment. The nodes share the segment according to the same CSMA/CD rules used for 10Base2 and 10Base5. Using the star bus topology maintains compatibility with previous Ethernet standards, but provides the stability of a star topology; if a cable gets cut, only one node drops off the network.

Exam Tip

10BaseT is a classic example of a star bus topology network.

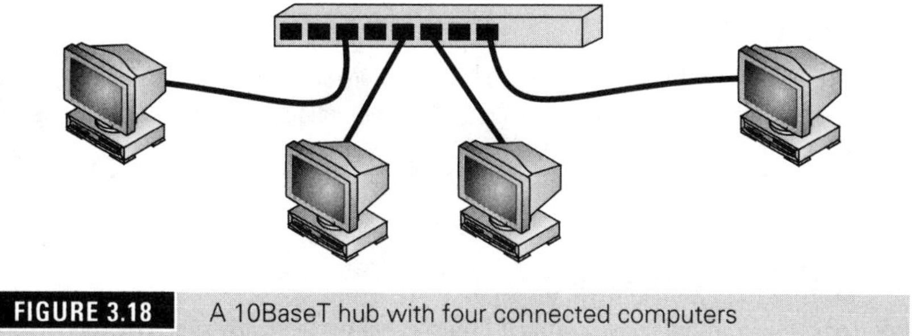

FIGURE 3.18 A 10BaseT hub with four connected computers

10BaseT and 100BaseT

The term "10BaseT" describes an Ethernet cabling system that uses a star bus topology. Unlike 10Base2 and 10Base5, 10BaseT uses UTP cabling rather than coax. Most of the other basic characteristics remain the same—for example, the network operates at the same speed (10 Mbps) and supports a maximum of 1,024 nodes.

The name "10BaseT" doesn't quite follow the naming convention used for earlier Ethernet cabling systems. The "10" still refers to the speed: 10 Mbps. "Base" still refers to the signaling type: baseband. The "T," however, doesn't refer to a distance limitation but to the type of cable used: twisted pair. For the record, the maximum distance allowed between a node and a hub is actually 100 meters. Once you have come to grips with 10BaseT, it is not a quantum leap to understand the key selling point of 100BaseT. Many modern Ethernet NICs automatically switch between 10 Mbps and 100 Mbps operation to match the hubs they're plugged into, and some modern hubs even support a mix of devices running at either speed.

Exam Tip

The distance limitation for 10BaseT is 100 meters.

Before we leave this section, you should know that there are two types of 100-megabit UTP Ethernet: 100BaseTX and 100BaseT4. 100BaseTX is by far the more popular version and runs over two pairs in a CAT 5 cable. 100BaseT4 is an earlier implementation that can run over CAT 3 cable, achieving the 100 Mbps speed by using all four pairs of wires. 100BaseT4 installations have become very rare as the installed base of CAT 5 cabling has grown.

Exam Tip

Although 100BaseT installations have become more common as costs have dropped, the Network+ exam continues to emphasize 10 Mbps standards such as 10BaseT and 10Base2.

Gigabit Ethernet

Modern developments have cranked Ethernet up to the heady speed of 1000 Mbps while retaining compatibility with the CSMA/CD standard. Various others have now been ratified by the 802.3z Gigabit Ethernet Standardization project, as follows:

- **IEEE802.3ab. 1000BaseT** Gigabit Ethernet over four pairs of CAT 5 UTP
- **IEEE802.3z. 1000BaseX** Gigabit Ethernet over fiber (including 1000BaseSX and 1000BaseLX)

10/100/1000BaseT Summary

Here are the key features that distinguish 10/100/1000BaseT cabling:

- Speed of 10, 100, or 1000 Mbps (megabits per second) according to standard
- Baseband signal type
- Distance of 100 meters from node to hub
- Two nodes per segment (node + hub port)

10 Gigabit Ethernet (10GbE)

For the highest-bandwidth applications, such as interconnecting servers and connecting high-speed switches in corporate datacenters, the new 10 Gigabit Ethernet standard, also known as *10GbE,* provides the fastest Ethernet-based networking technology available today. The IEEE recognized two 10GbE standards: 802.3ae for 10GbE over fiber optic cabling and 802.3ak for 10GbE over copper cabling.

In addition to speed, most 10GbE variations are designed to interoperate with SONET, making it an ideal choice for connecting local networks to preexisting long-distance fiber optic links that already use SONET. Refer to Table 3.1, and see Chapter 7 for more information on SONET.

TABLE 3.1 10GbE (10 Gigabit Ethernet) Standards

Standard	Maximum Distance	Cabling	SONET Compatible?
10GBase-SR	300 m	Multimode fiber	No
10GBase-SW	300 m	Multimode fiber	Yes
10GBase-LR	10 km	Single-mode fiber	No
10GBase-LW	10 km	Single-mode fiber	Yes
10GBase-ER	40 km	Single-mode fiber	No
10GBase-EW	40 km	Single-mode fiber	Yes
10GBase-LX4 over single mode	300 m	Single-mode fiber	No
10GBase-LX4 over multimode	10 km	Multimode	No
10GBase-CX4	15 m	Infiniband copper cabling	No
10GBase-T (Note that the 10GBase-T standard has not been finalized as of this writing.)	100 m	Category 5e/6/7 UTP	No

Exam Tip

The Network+ objectives specifically call out 10GBase-SR, 10GBase-LR, and 10GBase-ER. Focus on those 10GbE standards when preparing for the exam.

Objective 3.03 Ring Topologies

In a true ring topology, every computer system is connected together in a complete loop, but the loop itself is vulnerable to a single point of failure, so two loops are often implemented in a fashion known as *counter-rotating rings* (see Figure 3.19). The goal is to ensure that if the primary ring suffers a cable failure, the two nodes on either side of the problem can detect the fault and reroute the data signals to the secondary ring (see Figure 3.20). The data flow on the secondary ring proceeds logically in the opposite direction of the primary ring, hence the counter-rotation.

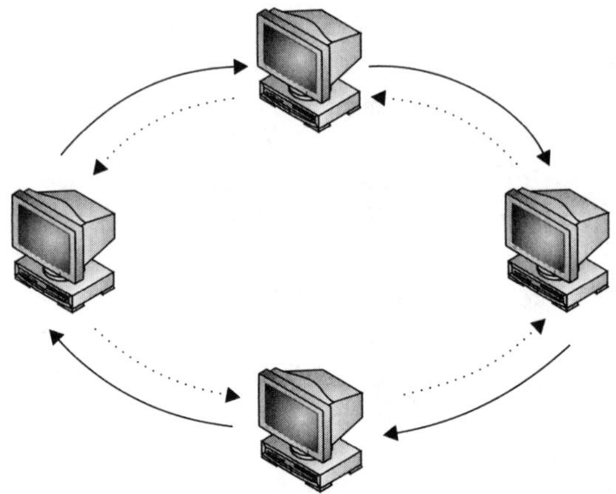

FIGURE 3.19 A ring topology network with counter-rotating rings

FDDI

The fullest implementation of a true ring topology is a fiber standard known as *Fiber Distributed Data Interface (FDDI)*. FDDI is not commonly used in LANs because of the expense to install and maintain. A variant of the full FDDI standard is sometimes used to link systems together in server rooms, but in that scenario the counter-rotating rings are actually built into the hubs, and the computer systems connect to the hub via fiber patch cables.

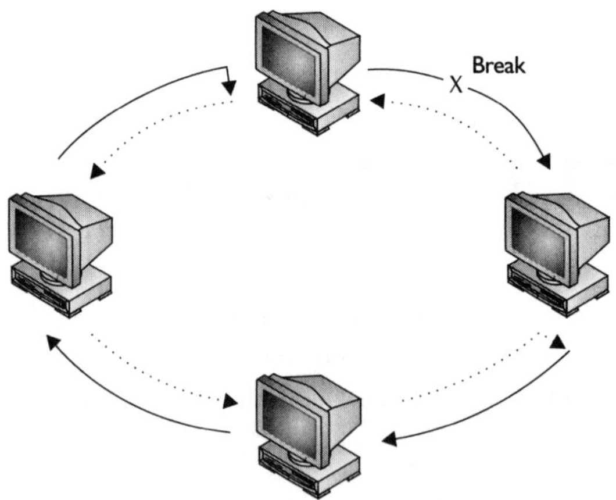

FIGURE 3.20 If the primary ring breaks, data is looped through the secondary ring.

FDDI's more common role lies in providing WAN links between remote sites. FDDI provides several vital features for use in these WAN links: high speed (100 Mbps) and long distances (2 km using multimode fiber, and longer distances using single-mode fiber), and redundancy (through the use of dual, counter-rotating rings). FDDI uses *token passing* to control access to the media. Token passing, although more complex to implement, yields more efficient performance than random access methods such as Ethernet's CSMA/CD. Because of the dual counter-rotating rings, if one ring fails, the network can continue to function using a single ring until repairs can be completed.

Here are the key features of FDDI:

- Speed 100 Mbps (megabits per second)
- Fiber optic cabling
- Useful for long distances (2 km with single-mode fiber, longer distances with multimode fiber)
- Redundancy through the use of two counter-rotating rings

Token Ring

If your wired network doesn't use Ethernet, it probably uses Token Ring. Although Token Ring provides a perfectly viable alternative to Ethernet—and, indeed, can offer greater speed and performance under load—its market share remains far smaller, mainly because the technology costs more to implement.

Token Ring was originally a proprietary IBM technology, but the IEEE 802.5 committee now defines and maintains the standard. Just as minor differences exist between the original Xerox Ethernet standard and IEEE 802.3, small differences exist between the original IBM standard for Token Ring and the IEEE 802.5 standard. These differences have little impact on the average network tech, and for all intents and purposes the terms "Token Ring" and "IEEE 802.5" refer to the same thing.

Exam Tip

Token Ring is defined by the IEEE 802.5 standard.

Although the IEEE 802.5 standard does support a true ring topology for a Token Ring network, where devices can be linked together in a ring, most practical implementations hide the physical ring by creating a logical ring inside a hub, technically referred to as a *multistation access unit (MAU);* see Figure 3.21.

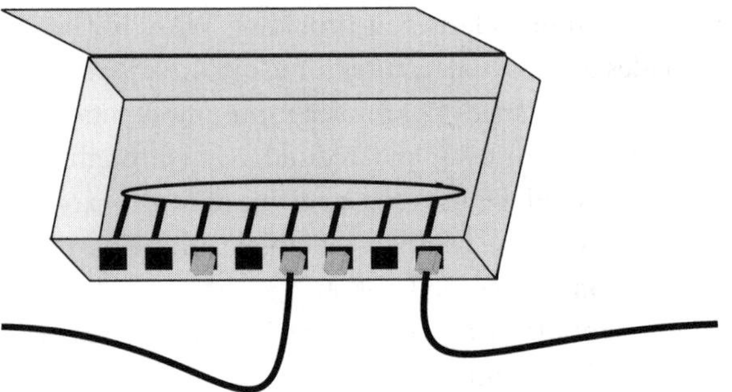

FIGURE 3.21 The logical ring is inside the MAU.

Local Lingo

multistation access unit (MAU or MSAU) A Token Ring hub.

Individual nodes connect to the hub using either unshielded twisted pair (UTP) or shielded twisted pair (STP) cabling (see Figure 3.22). This arrangement is known as a *star-wired ring.* Note that MAUs have special connectors—known as ring in (RI) and ring out (RO)—to link multiple MAUs together. Up to 33 MAUs can combine to form a single logical ring. Building a network with more than 33 MAUs requires the use of bridges or routers; these devices are covered in Chapter 4.

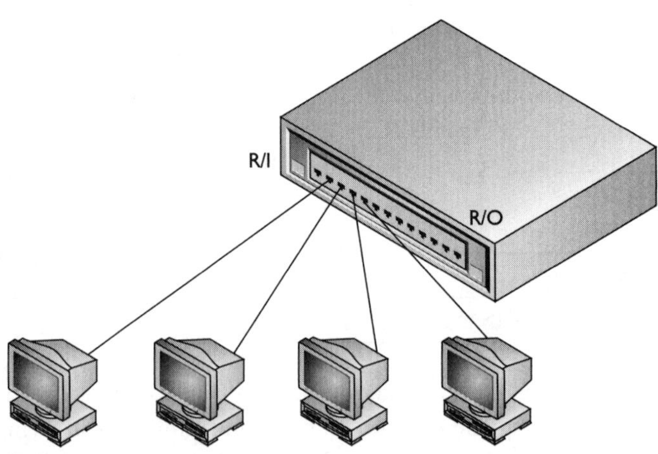

FIGURE 3.22 Token Ring nodes connect to the MAU.

Exam Tip

Token Ring networks can use a true ring topology, but most installations use MAUs in a configuration known as a *star-wired ring*.

Token Passing

Unlike Ethernet nodes, which broadcast their packets across a shared cable, Token Ring (and FDDI) nodes communicate directly with only two other machines: their upstream and downstream neighbors (see Figure 3.23). Access to the network is controlled by a technique known as *token passing* rather than the CSMA/CD system used by Ethernet. Token Ring nodes transmit data only when they receive a special packet called the *token* (see Figure 3.24). No collisions should ever occur using this token-passing method. By preventing all collisions, token passing operates more efficiently than CSMA/CD, allowing Token Ring nodes full use of the network's bandwidth.

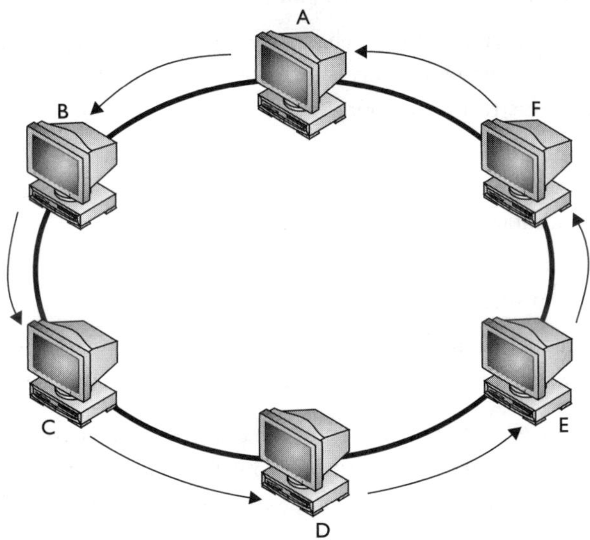

FIGURE 3.23 Node F is the upstream neighbor of node A; node B is the downstream neighbor of A.

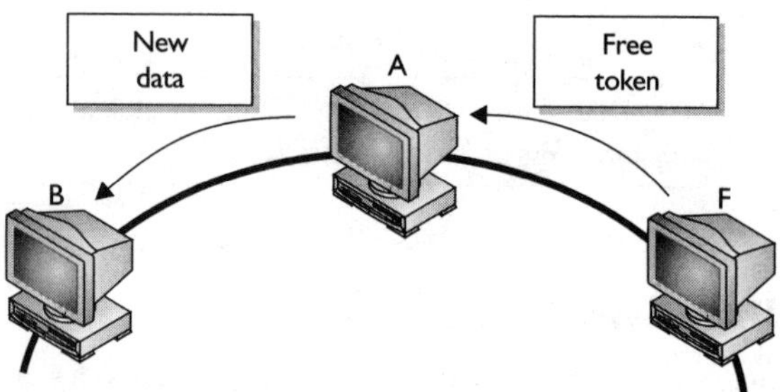

FIGURE 3.24 After receiving the free token, node A can send data around the network via its downstream neighbor, node B.

In a nutshell, token passing works like this:

1. A node receives a data packet containing the free token—it becomes that node's turn to use the network.
2. The node generates a packet addressed to its intended recipient and sends it to its downstream neighbor.
3. The downstream neighbor checks the destination MAC address to determine whether to process the data it contains or send the packet to its downstream neighbor.
4. Eventually, the data packet arrives at the intended recipient. The recipient reads the data, modifies the packet to indicate that it has been received, and sends it to its downstream neighbor.
5. The data packet makes its way back to the original sender, which registers a successful transmission.
6. The original sending machine generates a new token packet and sends it on its way to the next node to be given permission to use the network.

A Token Ring NIC requires more processing power than the equivalent Ethernet NIC. This increased processing power contributes to both the standard's robustness and the relatively high cost of the components. Because the Token Ring standard eliminates the randomness of network access associated with Ethernet and CSMA/CD, each node knows exactly when it should transmit, thus avoiding the inherent chaos and inefficiency of Ethernet's CSMA/CD technique.

Exam Tip

Token Ring networks are called *deterministic networks.* Ethernet networks, with their random-access behavior, are called *probabilistic networks.*

Token Ring Speed

The original Token Ring network ran at 4 Mbps, but this was later increased to 16 Mbps. Modern MAUs allow 4 Mbps and 16 Mbps devices to be mixed, but if there is a mix of 4 Mbps and 16 Mbps devices, the network will run at 4 Mbps.

Token Ring over STP

Originally, Token Ring networks used a heavily shielded version of twisted pair cabling referred to as *shielded twisted pair* (see Figure 3.25) and a special connector known as an *IBM Type 1* connector (see Figure 3.26). When using STP, a single Token Ring MAU can support up to 260 computers, and the STP cable connecting the computer to the hub may not be longer than 100 meters. STP cabling is an ideal choice for environments with high levels of electrical interference, but corporate networks operating under more typical conditions will use the less expensive UTP cabling. Token Ring MAUs using UTP can support up to 72 nodes, and each node must be within 45 meters of the MAU.

Exam Tip

If you mix 4 Mbps and 16 Mbps devices on some older MAUs, you will crash the network.

Token Ring vs. Ethernet

The two mainstream network standards and topologies are often compared, and many polite-but-heated discussions have taken place over the merits of 4/16 Mbps Token Ring versus 10/100 Ethernet. Advocates of Token Ring argue that its token passing system uses available bandwidth more efficiently than Ethernet's random CSMA/CD process, and that it is more *scaleable,* meaning that it handles growth better. Ethernet advocates argue that their system is cheaper to

FIGURE 3.25 Shielded twisted pair (STP) cabling

FIGURE 3.26 An IBM Type 1 connector

install, and the faster basic speeds overcome the problems associated with CSMA/CD. In reality, Token Ring's expense is its major drawback, and although it will continue to exist in niche markets and in organizations with a large installed base of Token Ring equipment, Ethernet will retain its dominance in the marketplace for the foreseeable future.

Other Topologies

Having covered bus, star, and ring topologies, we've now considered the three main ways of stringing together network devices, but that's not the whole story. Numerous other ways and means of linking systems have been tried over the years and are also evolving as technology improves. Although these topologies are not covered in as much detail as "the big three," don't skip over the next section, because you might learn something to your advantage (for the exam)!

Objective 3.04 Wireless Networking

The IEEE 802.11 working group is responsible for wireless networking standards and currently has three major wireless standards available collectively referred to as *Wi-Fi:* 802.11b, 802.11a, and 802.11g. These wireless networks use radio waves instead of cabling. A simple wireless network consists of one or more cells that can support one or more nodes communicating with a base station known as an *access point.* The access point links the nodes to each other and to the wired network (if present). In technical parlance, the 802.11 standard defines two pieces of equipment: a wireless station (say, a PC or notebook computer fitted with a wireless NIC) and an access point (AP), which connects the wireless devices to the wired network.

Networks based on 802.11b, the first widely implemented wireless standard, operate in the 2.4 GHz frequency range and provide 11 Mbps of shared bandwidth. Public wireless networks, known as *hotspots,* exist in many cities and provide a flexible and inexpensive method for connecting mobile computers to the Internet. Although 802.11b can sometimes coexist with other devices operating using the 2.4 GHz frequency range, be careful about mixing 802.11b wireless installations with 2.4 GHz cordless phones.

Although generally described as operating at 11 Mbps, 802.11b devices will "step down" to a slower speed of 5 Mbps, 2 Mbps, or 1 Mbps when interference or a weak signal makes higher speeds unreliable. In many cases, users will not notice the slow down in speed because even 5 Mbps is faster than the Internet connection they are probably trying to use. Under optimal conditions, an 802.11a network should reach out to around 150 feet in all directions from the access point. Of course, "optimal conditions" don't include inconveniences such as plumbing, electrical wiring, and brick walls.

802.11a, another wireless alternative, provides 54 Mbps of bandwidth and operates in the 5 GHz band. Although less susceptible to interference than 802.11b (mainly because fewer devices currently operate at 5 GHz), 802.11a requires more access points to cover the same area as an 802.11b network, and it's not backwardly compatible with 802.11b devices. 802.11a networks are mostly found in corporate environments that require higher bandwidth, but 802.11a networks are becoming more rare since the introduction of 802.11g.

802.11g provides the same 54 Mbps bandwidth as 802.11a, but uses the same 2.4 GHz band as 802.11b networks. 802.11g networks are backwardly compatible with 802.11b devices, providing an easy upgrade path for anyone wanting more speed but wanting to take advantage of their existing 802.11b investments.

All three of these wireless standards, referred to collectively as *802.11a/b/g,* support operation in two modes: infrastructure mode and ad-hoc mode.

Infrastructure Mode

In infrastructure mode, wireless devices connect to a wired network through an access point (see Figure 3.27). The wireless part of the network can have more than one AP, in which case a number of cells will exist, creating a larger area of coverage. With the right hardware, all this coverage will appear to wireless devices as a single wireless section of network, with devices able to roam between cells without losing their network connections. The reception coverage of the APs must overlap to allow for a handover period as the user of the mobile device moves between cells. Note that some inexpensive wireless routers, intended for home and small office use, do not support this kind of roaming.

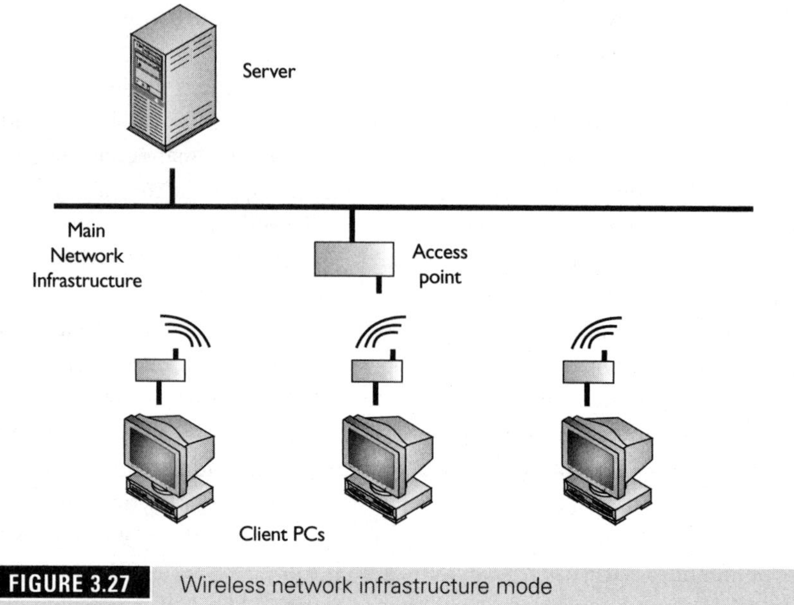

FIGURE 3.27 Wireless network infrastructure mode

Ad-hoc Mode

Ad-hoc mode (also called *peer-to-peer mode*) allows wireless NICs to connect to each other directly, without using an AP (see Figure 3.28). The idea behind this mode is, for example, to allow a group of notebook computers to be set up in a conference room or other location without the need to install an access point or other network device.

CSMA/CA

No, that heading is not a typo! Wireless networks that conform to the IEEE 802.11b spec use a modified version of CSMA/CD to get their data onto the network. This is known as *Carrier Sense Multiple Access/Collision Avoidance (CSMA/CA)*, or the *Distributed Coordination Function (DCF)*. CSMA/CA uses a similar method to 802.3's CSMA/CD technique, but adds an additional feature. When a node has determined that the media (in this case, the radio spectrum) is available, it will first send out a packet just to let other nodes know that it is about to send out data. If this first packet is received and the receiving node sends back an acknowledgment packet, the sending node will transmit its actual data payload. In essence, the sending station momentarily reserves the available bandwidth. These extra packets, which transmit no information beyond the message "Hey! I'm about to send some data so stay out of my way," add additional overhead that

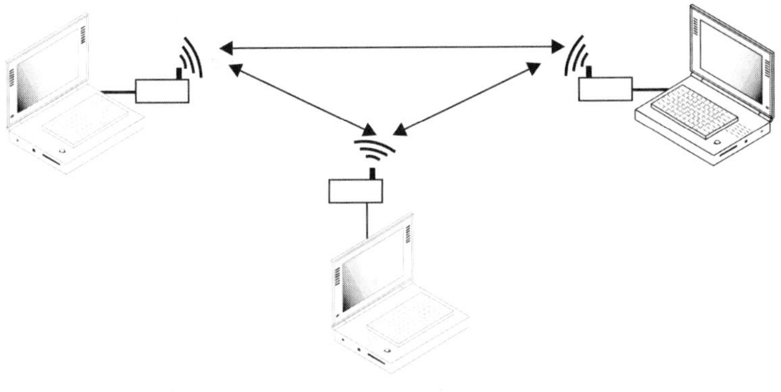

FIGURE 3.28 Wireless network ad-hoc mode

wired networks using CSMA/CD don't have. The benefit, however, is that CSMA/CD minimizes the number of collisions and helps to detect problems with radio interference.

Security

Wireless security remains a developing field. In general, assume that wireless network traffic can be intercepted by a motivated third party. Although a variety of wireless security advances are available or will become available in the near future, IEEE 802.11b originally included two basic security mechanisms: *Direct Sequence Spread Spectrum (DSSS)* breaks the available signal bandwidth into 14 overlapping 22 MHz channels and spreads the transmitted signal among the channels, which makes it difficult for an unsynchronized third party to keep track of the signal. However, the second security mechanism is a packet encryption scheme called *Wired Equivalent Privacy (WEP)*. Unfortunately, tools for intercepting wireless traffic and defeating WEP encryption quickly appeared. Wireless networks should not be used for sensitive information unless you take additional steps to secure your data. For example, using a VPN over a wireless connection would be relatively safe because the data that could be intercepted would be encrypted by the VPN.

The IEEE has begun work on an improved wireless security standard, called 802.11i, that will address many of the security weaknesses of current wireless implementations. In preparation for the move to 802.11i, the IEEE has begun to release pieces of the upcoming standard, including WPA (Wi-FI Protected Access) and AES (Advanced Encryption Standard). A full discussion of 802.11i, WPA, and AES is beyond the scope of the Network+ exam.

Distributed Star Topology—ARCNet

The distributed star topology was championed by an older networking standard called ARCNet (Attached Resource Computer Network). Although ARCNet predates the IEEE standards, it resembles IEEE 802.4, which defines a token-passing, bus-based network. In fact, ARCNet could be run over a bus-based or star-based topology at a blazing 2.5 Mbps (a later version called ARCNet Plus ran at 20 Mbps) and was very popular from its launch in 1977 to late 1980s, mainly because it supported a maximum distance of 2,000 feet (610 meters) from node to hub and because it was very easy to extend an existing installation. ARCNet supported coax and (later) UTP and fiber media, but it was really killed off by the mass adoption of Ethernet and UTP wiring systems (which also allow relatively easy expansion) and, of course, by faster networking standards.

Objective 3.06

Mesh Topology

The mesh topology connects each node with multiple links, providing multiple paths between any two nodes. The mesh topology is rarely if ever seen in local area networks because of cost: It requires so many separate links. A partial mesh, however, is used to connect networks together (see Figure 3.29). In essence, any series of interlinked networks where there is more than one possible data path between network locations can be considered to be using a mesh topology.

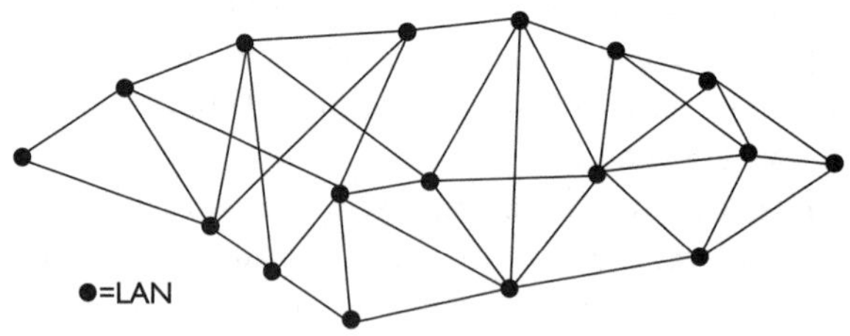

FIGURE 3.29 Mesh topology

Exam Tip

The best example of a mesh topology is the Internet.

Because mesh topologies support multiple paths between networks, the level of fault tolerance improves as the number of paths increases.

✔**Objective 3.01: The Bus Topology and Ethernet** Ethernet is a very common networking standard and was first developed for use with a bus topology, where all computing devices are interconnected via a single run of coaxial cable, known as a *segment.* Although bus-based networks are relatively simple to install, the main drawback to these types of networks is that they have a single point of failure—one break will stop the entire segment from working. The ends of the bus must also be terminated properly for correct operation. Ethernet networks use a system called Carrier Sense, Multiple Access/Collision Detection (CSMA/CD) to determine which computer should use the shared cable at a given moment. The IEEE 802.3 standard defines how Ethernet operates.

✔**Objective 3.02: The Star Bus Topology** This topology overcomes some of the limitations of the bus topology by placing a logical bus within a hub and allowing multiple hubs to be interconnected to form a larger network. The hubs isolate cable problems to individual ports and devices so that only the device attached to a faulty cable is stopped from using the network. Classic examples of this topology include the 10BaseT and 100BaseT standards.

✔**Objective 3.03: Ring Topologies** True ring topologies, such as a full implementation of a fiber standard known as FDDI, are expensive to install because they require a large amount of interconnection between all devices on the network, but a modified version, known as a *star-wired ring,* is used for Token Ring networks. The star-wired ring topology also uses hub-type units to connect devices to the network; the correct term for these hubs is Multistation Access Units (MAUs or MSAUs). Token Ring offers predictable (deterministic) network performance by using a system known as *token passing* to determine which computer can use the network at a given moment. The IEEE 802.5 standard defines how Token Ring operates.

✔**Objective 3.04: Wireless Networking** Wireless networking is defined by the various IEEE 802.11 standards. 802.11b, the most widely implemented version, uses the 2.4 GHz band to provide up to 11 Mbps of bandwidth. When using infrastructure mode, one or more access points (APs) provides access to the network for wireless devices. Direct NIC-to-NIC communication (ad-hoc mode) is also possible. Wireless networking solves the problem of providing network connectivity where physical cabling is not possible or not wanted, but the actual distances that can be achieved vary according to local conditions. IEEE 802.11b networks use a system called *Carrier Sense, Multiple Access/Collision Avoidance (CSMA/CA)* to determine which computer can use the network at a given moment.

✔**Objective 3.05: Distributed Star Topology—ARCNet** ARCNet is an older networking standard that is not common nowadays. ARCNet used a token-passing system over coaxial cable and ran at 2.5 Mbps. Now superseded by other systems, ARCNet's popularity was partly due to the long distances it supported. ARCNet approximates the IEEE 802.4 networking standard.

✔**Objective 3.06: Mesh Topology** The mesh topology is commonly used to interconnect networks, not just devices on individual networks. By providing multiple pathways between networks, the mesh topology provides fault tolerance in the event of problems on one or more pathways and is the topology used by the Internet.

REVIEW QUESTIONS

1. Which of the following network types uses a bus topology?
   - **A.** IEEE 802.5
   - **B.** IEEE 802.3
   - **C.** IEEE 802.11
   - **D.** FDDI
2. What name is given to the access method used by Ethernet networks to determine which device can have access to the media?
   - **A.** Token passing
   - **B.** Collision Domain Management (CDM)
   - **C.** CSMA/CA
   - **D.** CSMA/CD

3. You have been asked to extend an existing 10BaseT network to add ten machines to the existing 25 on the network. The required objective is to ensure that the new machines connect successfully to the network. One optional objective is for all the new machines to operate at a faster speed across the network to a new server (which is also one of the new machines). Your proposed solution is to install all new machines on a 10/100 hub daisy-chained to the existing hub. What will this achieve?

    A. This meets the required and optional objectives.

    B. This meets the required objective but not the optional objective.

    C. This meets the optional objective only.

    D. This meets neither the required nor the optional objective.

4. Removing a terminator from a 10BaseT network...

    A. will cause the entire network to fail.

    B. enables the network to expand.

    C. is not possible because 10BaseT networks don't use terminators.

    D. will improve network performance.

5. Which of the following network types can use a ring topology? (Select two answers.)

    A. IEEE 802.5

    B. IEEE 802.3

    C. IEEE 802.4

    D. FDDI

6. Which of the following connector types is similar to a MIDI/joystick connector?

    A. AUI

    B. BNC

    C. FDDI

    D. Coax

7. What network topology is most fault tolerant?

    A. Bus

    B. Ring

    C. Star

    D. Mesh

8. Which of the following is true of Token Ring networks?

    A. Collisions between packets slow down the network.

    B. Data packets are broadcast to all nodes using tokens.

- **C.** Data packets are transmitted in counter-rotating directions.
- **D.** Collisions do not happen.

9. Which of the following represents a wireless network standard?

- **A.** 10BaseT
- **B.** 10BaseW
- **C.** IEEE 802.5
- **D.** IEEE 802.11

10. Which of the following is *not* a feature of a network based on the 10BaseT standard?

- **A.** Uses screened cable.
- **B.** Maximum segment distance is 1,000 meters.
- **C.** Multiple token packets are supported.
- **D.** All of the above.

REVIEW ANSWERS

1. **B** Of the possible answers, only IEEE 802.3 represents a bus standard.

2. **D** Ethernet uses CSMA/CD. Token passing is used on FDDI and Token Ring networks, CDM is fictional, and CSMA/CA is used on wireless and AppleTalk networks only.

3. **A** Installing a 10/100 hub will provide the expansion needed and also allow all the new machines to operate at 100 Mbps.

4. **C** Sure enough, it's a "trick" question—10BaseT networks don't use terminators.

5. **A** **D** Both Token Ring (802.5) and FDDI networks can be configured as true rings. IEEE 802.3 is a bus topology standard, and 802.11 is a wireless networking standard.

6. **A** AUI ports are dangerously similar to the MIDI/joystick connector.

7. **D** The mesh topology is the only one to allow multiple pathways between networks.

8. **D** There should be no collisions on a fully working Token Ring network.

9. **D** IEEE 802.11 is a wireless network standard.

10. **D** All of the above.

Network Hardware

ITINERARY

- **Objective 4.01** Network Interface Cards
- **Objective 4.02** Repeaters and Hubs
- **Objective 4.03** Bridges and Routers
- **Objective 4.04** Gateways

NEWBIE	SOME EXPERIENCE	EXPERT
4 hours	2 hours	1 hour

So far, this book has covered the basics of networking and the components that make up the network infrastructure (all that media and connectors stuff—you were paying attention, weren't you?). I've also mentioned some hardware up to this point. Now it's time to go into greater detail on those items and some of the other gear that links the parts of your network together, or extends your network to another site.

As you read through this chapter, you'll notice yet again that I often reference the topics I cover to the OSI seven-layer model. The Network+ exam is quite keen on this, so make sure you store this information away for future use.

Exam Tip

Although all seven layers of the OSI model are covered on the Network+ exam, the first three layers—Physical, Data Link, and Network—are stressed for identifying devices.

Objective 4.01 Network Interface Cards

Network interface cards, or NICs, provide a computer with the ability to send and receive data across a network. They provide an interface between the equipment's data bus and the network medium, whether that network medium is copper (coax or UTP), wireless, fiber, or what have you. Many modern computer systems include a built-in NIC. Even when the NIC is integrated into the system motherboard, we still refer to it as a NIC. Many items, such as printers and other systems that might need to be shared directly via a network connection (for example, a stack of CD-ROM drives), may also come with a built-in NIC or the ability for a NIC to be installed.

Exam Tip

Network interface cards are Data Link layer (layer 2) devices with reference to the OSI seven-layer model.

Choosing a NIC

If you're familiar with PC technology, you might already understand terms such as "ISA" and "PCI expansion bus." These items are really the domain of the CompTIA A+ exam, so they won't figure into our plans for Network+ domination. It's worth remembering, though, that in the real world if you turn up onsite with a PCI Ethernet NIC and the customer's PC only has a spare ISA slot, you'll be making another roundtrip real soon to get a part that fits! Don't forget that there are also alternatives to the classic plug-me-in-the-PC network card; for example, notebook PCs have expansion connectors that conform to the various "credit card module" expansion standards (PC Card, CardBus, and PCMCIA) and external, plug-in USB (Universal Serial Bus) NICs are also available.

After this, what do you need to know? Well, how many mainstream network technologies do you know? That's right: Ethernet and Token Ring. So, your NIC also has to be right for the network type being used. No one has yet produced a dual- or multitechnology card that will configure itself to whatever standard is being used. Also, don't forget that there are other networking standards, too. Maybe your customer has an old ARCNet network; no good fitting an Ethernet card then!

All done? Hmm... not quite! How many *speeds* of each networking standard do you know? Great, you're way ahead of me here! Ethernet comes in three main flavors: 10 Mbps, 100 Mbps, and 1000 Mbps. Token Ring comes in two: 4 Mbps and 16 Mbps.

Some modern NICs will operate at various speeds—for example, 1000/100/10 Mbps or 10/100 Mbps Ethernet NICs or 4/16 Mbps Token Ring NICs. These components autosense how they should set themselves up, but be prepared for situations where the autosense gets it wrong, in which case you'll need to use the software supplied with the NIC. You can also use the Device Manager or Network settings under Windows, if the card is fully Plug-and-Play compatible, to set the speed you want. Finally, don't forget that there are two standards for 100Mb Ethernet networking—100BaseTX and 100BaseT4—and your NIC must support the right standard, or it'll be very quiet on that PC.

Don't forget about the media! Yes, it's a good idea if the NIC can interface with the network media—or put simply, if it can "plug in." Your head should already be full of terms such as "BNC," "RJ45," "AUI," and so on, so don't forget that the NIC you're installing must have a socket or connector that matches the ones being used by the network media.

Sometimes this requirement is straightforward. For example, if you're working with a coax-based Ethernet network, you know you'll need either a BNC (Thinnet) or AUI (Thicknet) connector. If the network media is UTP, though, you're dealing with RJ45. Token Ring networks may also be UTP based (RJ45 connectors), but the older style that used STP media requires a nine-pin female DB connector (a so-called DB-9F connector).

Many network cards have a combination of connector types to suit all possible media options. These so-called "combo" cards will often autodetect the interface being used, but some older ones need to be set via software, or you may need to adjust a jumper setting on the card itself (see Figure 4.1).

FIGURE 4.1 An Ethernet combo NIC

To summarize, when choosing a NIC, you must ensure that it meets specific criteria to work properly with your equipment and network. These criteria are as follows:

- The NIC must have the right interface for your PC (or whatever it is you're going to network): bus type or expansion port type (USB, PC Card, CardBus, PCMCIA, and so forth).
- The NIC must support the right networking technology (Ethernet, Token Ring, and so forth).
- The NIC must operate at the right speed (10 Mbps or 100 Mbps for Ethernet and 4 Mbps or 16 Mbps for Token Ring, for example).
- The NIC must be compatible with the media connector (BNC, RJ45, AUI, fiber, and so forth).

If all this sounds pretty obvious, then great—you're bound to get some points on the exam. So what's the catch? Well, look out for questions that mix and match all these issues to give plausible, possible answers that don't actually represent a valid combination. For example, there's no such thing as a BNC Ethernet NIC that supports 100 Mbps over coax.

Additional NIC Functionality

We're nearly done with NICs, but we still need to cover a few other features before we can move on.

Link LEDs

Most NICs have one or more diagnostic LEDs to give a quick visual indicator of the state of the network link. Typically, there will be a LINK LED, which confirms that the NIC senses that it is physically connected to usable media, and an ACT (for *activity*) LED, which blinks every time the NIC detects some data being sent or received (see Figure 4.2). Sometimes one LED serves both purposes. A quick look at these LEDs *before* diving into more complex troubleshooting procedures can sometimes pay dividends. How many times have you reconfigured Windows networking only to discover that the problem is due to a loose or disconnected cable?

Full-Duplex

NICs using coax-based Ethernet can only operate at *half-duplex,* meaning that they can either send or receive data at any one time. (You can talk or listen, but you can't do both at the same time.) Ethernet over fiber or UTP (10, 100, and Gigabit), however, can support *full-duplex* operation, meaning a NIC can be transmitting and receiving at the same time. If your NIC and hub both support full-duplex operation, you might want to enable this feature to give the PC-to-network connection a performance boost (see Figure 4.3). If you enable full-duplex operation at the NIC and it's *not* supported by the hub, things may go a bit quiet. Most hubs that support full-duplex operation autodetect that it has been enabled at the NIC, and don't need to be manually configured.

Exam Tip

Full-duplex Ethernet works on UTP and fiber only, not coax.

FIGURE 4.2 A 10Base2/10BaseT Ethernet NIC with LINK and ACT LEDs

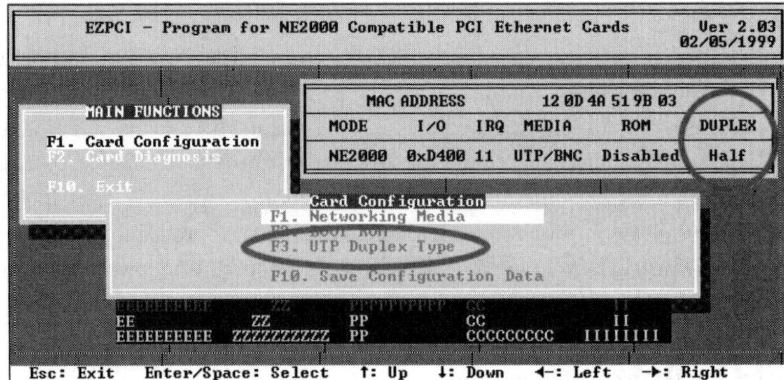

FIGURE 4.3 Configuring a network card to full-duplex using its setup program

MAC Address

Every network card has a built-in, unique ID known as its *Media Access Control (MAC)* address. This address will be used to identify the source and destination of every packet sent on the network. The MAC address is fundamental to the operation of all mainstream networking technologies, as it is the one address that can uniquely identify a specific card—and thus a specific computer (or other device)—on the network. As you'll see in Chapter 6, other addressing schemes are put in place when you're setting up a routed network, but these addressing schemes are *not* the ones used to pump data around the local network; that's the job of the MAC address. In general, it is not essential to worry about the MAC address of your NIC during installation and setup, because the software parts of your setup that *do* need to know it can easily find the MAC address out by asking the NIC. It is, however, worth knowing that the MAC address exists because some configuration and diagnostic tools will display it and that it can also be used for network security. (In fact, some programs will use the MAC address as a de facto machine identifier.) Network operating systems such as Microsoft Windows 2000, Linux, and Novell NetWare allow you to restrict the locations from which a user can log in by specifying the MAC addresses of the relevant workstations.

Travel Advisory

If you change the NIC inside a PC, you also change the PC's MAC address. Don't restrict a critical network account, such as Administrator, to one machine! If the NIC fails and has to be replaced, this account may not be able to log in and administer the network anymore.

In their raw form, MAC addresses are 48-bit binary numbers, such as the following:

000000001110000010011000000000010000100100001110

To make these numbers easier to read and document, they are usually written in hexadecimal (base 16) format. This means that the preceding address can also be written as

00 E0 98 01 09 0E

Being 48 bits long allows for a possible 2^{48} (281,474,976,710,656) MAC addresses—that should keep us going for a while!

Because the pool of possible MAC addresses is so large, the IEEE has been tasked with ensuring that no two network interface cards ever share the same MAC address. To achieve this, NIC manufacturers are assigned one or more *start* addresses—the top 24 bits of the MAC address, which the IEEE calls the *Organizationally Unique Identifier (OUI)*. The manufacturers then use the remaining 24 bits to give each card they produce a truly unique address. For example, the MAC address of the NIC inside the computer used to write this paragraph is 00 D0 59 0E 0B C8, the top 24 bits being 00 D0 59 (each hexadecimal pair of digits represents 8 bits).

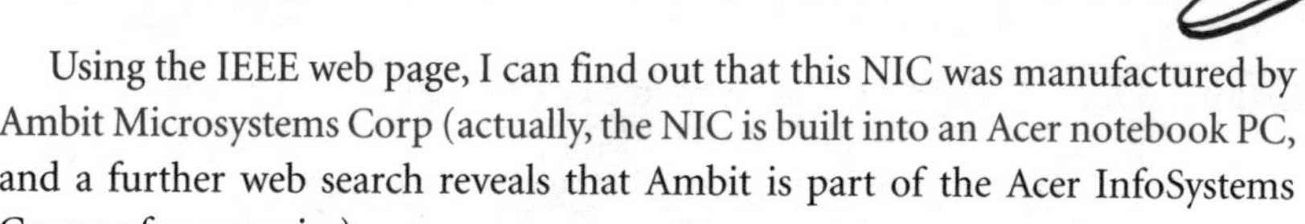

Travel Assistance

You can look up OUIs on the IEEE website at http://standards.ieee.org/regauth/oui/index.shtml.

Using the IEEE web page, I can find out that this NIC was manufactured by Ambit Microsystems Corp (actually, the NIC is built into an Acer notebook PC, and a further web search reveals that Ambit is part of the Acer InfoSystems Group of companies).

How can you find out the MAC address of your network card? Well, if you're running Windows 2000/XP, you can use the command-line utility IPCONFIG to display this information (see Figure 4.4). The same command works under Windows NT. In either case, to see the MAC address, use the command IPCONFIG/ALL. On Windows 9*x*, you can also run the WINIPCFG program, as shown in Figure 4.5. Note that these commands may only be available if the computer has the TCP/IP networking protocol installed (more about this later). The setup program supplied with many NICs will also probably show the MAC address of the card, and many manufacturers also place a MAC address label on the NIC, as shown in Figure 4.6.

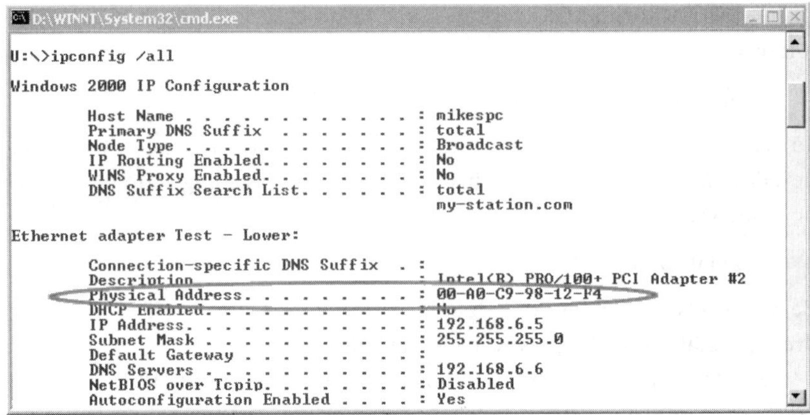

FIGURE 4.4 IPCONFIG showing the MAC address of the NIC

FIGURE 4.5 WINIPCFG also showing the MAC address

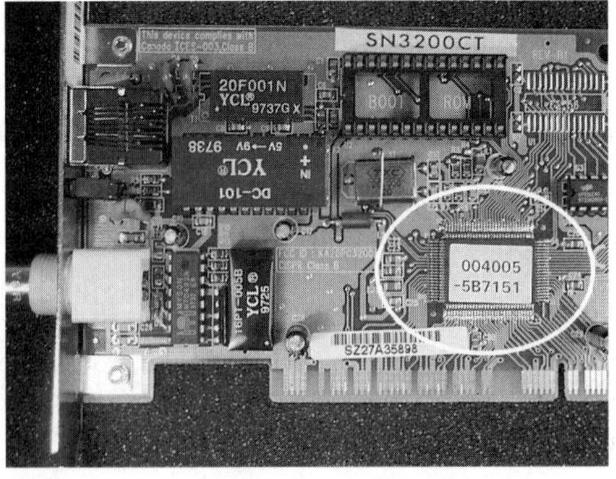

FIGURE 4.6 Label on a NIC showing its MAC address

Exam Tip

MAC stands for *Media Access Control*. A MAC address is a unique identifier for each machine (NIC) on a network.

Objective 4.02 Repeaters and Hubs

There comes a time in every network tech's life when he or she actually wants to connect a few computer systems together and (horrors!) build a network. Let's imagine such a tech, and let's name him Tom. Armed with a few basic facts, Tom knows that he can link together up to 30 nodes on a single run of up to 185 meters of Thin Ethernet (10Base2), or he can (theoretically) link together 1,024 computers using hubs and UTP (10BaseT). But what happens when Tom needs to add that 31st computer to the coax or stretch the network beyond 185 meters. And what if he's never actually seen a *1,024*-port hub?! Clearly, our tech needs some more insight.

Repeaters

If you want to stretch your Ethernet network beyond the basic distance limitations, you will need a *repeater*.

Local Lingo

repeater Any device that takes all the signals it receives on one Ethernet port and passes out a copy of them on all its other ports (and does pretty much nothing else).

Although the electrical signals handled by a repeater represent data bits that ultimately form packets of data, the repeater doesn't know this. A repeater simply takes the incoming electrical signals, corrects any voltage drops, and then retransmits the cleaned signals. In this respect, the repeater does *not* function as an *amplifier*, although this term is often used incorrectly to describe a repeater. Amplifiers boost signals, flaws and all, like a copy machine making a copy of a bad original.

A repeater increases the maximum possible distance between machines by linking together two or more segments. Each segment retains its own distance limitation. If a repeater connects two 10Base2 segments, for example, the maximum distance that can separate two machines on different segments is 370 meters (2×185 meters, see Figure 4.7). Two 10Base5 segments connected by a repeater can cover 1,000 meters (2×500 meters).

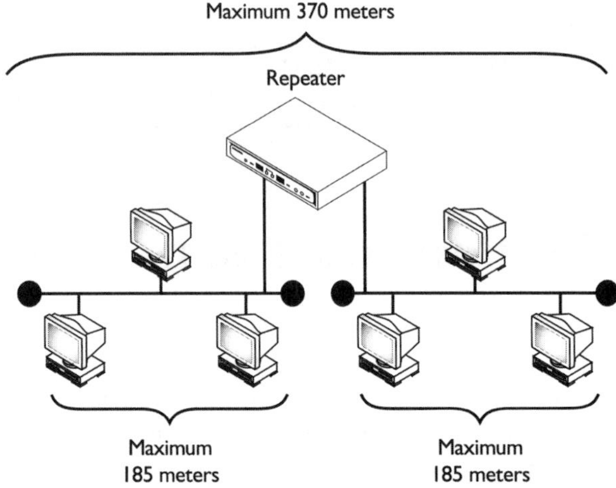

FIGURE 4.7 Two 10Base2 segments joined by a repeater

Repeaters also increase the number of machines that can connect to the network. If a repeater connects two 10Base2 segments, the network can have 60 computers attached to it (2 segments × 30 nodes per segment, see Figure 4.8).

Repeaters also add a degree of *fault tolerance* to a network: If one of the segments breaks, only that segment will fail. Computers on the remaining segment will continue to function, unaffected when communicating within their own

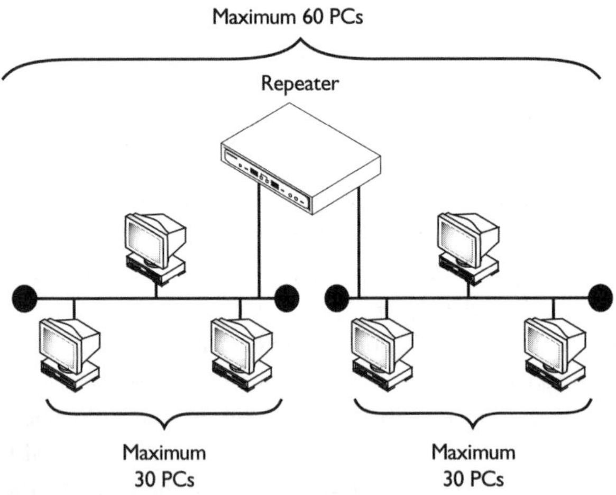

FIGURE 4.8 As well as increasing overall network distance, a repeater allows you to add more machines.

segment. The segment with the cable break fails because of reflections, but the segment on the far side of the repeater remains properly terminated and functions normally.

Local Lingo

fault tolerance The ability of a system to continue functioning even after some part of the system has failed.

Repeaters can also give network designers the flexibility to combine different cabling types on the same network. Both 10Base5 and 10Base2 networks use exactly the same packet structure, so a repeater can connect a 10Base5 and a 10Base2 segment without difficulty; many repeaters come with both AUI and BNC connectors for that purpose (see Figure 4.9).

Exam Tip

Many repeaters have only two ports, but they can have more (so-called *multiport repeaters*).

Repeater Summary

- They extend the distance that a network can cover.
- They increase the number of machines that can connect to the network.
- They provide a measure of fault tolerance, limiting the impact of breaks in the cable to the segment on which the break occurs.
- They can link different types of (Ethernet) cabling segments together.

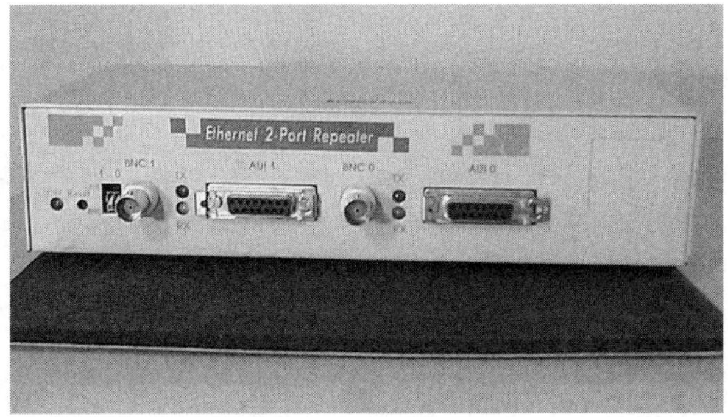

FIGURE 4.9 An Ethernet repeater with AUI and BNC ports

Repeaters do not help reduce or manage traffic on networks that experience too much traffic, but they remain important tools for network technicians and architects.

Hubs

Do UTP-based Ethernet networks use repeaters? You bet, but they're called *hubs* (see Figure 4.10). In other respects, there's not a great deal of difference between a multiport repeater and a hub. For example, they both operate at the Physical layer, and you can deduce from this that both repeaters and hubs don't do much except pass electrical signals from one port to another. When it comes to 10BaseT networking, though, hubs are essential parts of the topology, and they are not there just to extend the size of the network beyond some basic limits.

A multiport hub allows a specific number of devices to connect to the network (one per port) and often, but not always, includes a separate port to allow hubs to be linked together to grow the network. Some hubs also include connectors for different media types—BNC, AUI, and fiber—but they cannot interface between networks that are based on different technologies (for example, Ethernet to Token Ring). This would require capabilities beyond the scope of a simple Physical layer device.

Exam Tip

Repeaters and hubs are layer 1 (Physical layer) devices because they only work with electrical signals and don't understand more complex structures, such as data packets and network addresses.

FIGURE 4.10 UTP (10BaseT) hub, patch cable, and NIC. Note that this hub also has a BNC connector.

Repeater and Hub Diagnostic Indicators

Both device types often include a number of status LEDs. A repeater may have an LED for each port (network segment) to indicate whether the attached segment is terminated properly. If the repeater detects a faulty segment, in addition to turning on the LED it might (if it's part of the repeater's spec) isolate, or *partition,* the faulty segment in order to stop its signal reflections from affecting the rest of the network. Remember that repeaters pass everything—even reflections.

Here's a wonderful term: *jabber protection.* If a faulty Ethernet NIC starts to send out an endless stream of unintelligible data, it is said to be "jabbering." Jabbering is sort of similar to deliberately generated reflections, and will stop every other device from using the network. Many hubs and repeaters support jabber protection and will turn off the affected port until the problem is corrected. In the case of a repeater, this could possibly isolate all the machines on the affected coax segment from the rest of the network, but on a hub this will usually only affect the one machine on the one port.

The last indicator that's often seen on a repeater or hub is the *collision LED.* This will generally light up every time the number of collisions on a segment exceeds a specific threshold. Don't forget that collisions are fundamental to Ethernet's mode of operation (remember CSMA/CD?), so it is not necessarily a problem if the collision LED comes on. It's best to read the instructions that came with the repeater or hub to see what this LED is trying to tell you. In other respects, you'll probably get the feeling that excess collisions are a likely problem, because most of the network users will be on the phone every five minutes complaining that the network's very slow!

Hub Summary

- Hubs are found in UTP-based Ethernet environments and are similar in general function to multiport repeaters.
- Unlike a repeater, a hub can have only one device per port—either a NIC or another hub.
- Most hubs can detect problems on their ports (such as jabbering) and will isolate problem ports from the rest of the network.

You've Gone Too Far: The 5-4-3 Rule

Although it might seem feasible to create very large networks just by using many repeaters or hubs, in practice, technical limitations prevent the ability to sprawl without careful planning. The main problem is that repeaters pass all signals to all their ports. This means that the network, however large, appears as a single entity as far as all data traffic is concerned; in technical terms, the network has a single *collision domain.*

For Ethernet networks to function properly, each node must detect when its own transmissions collide with those of any other node (remember CSMA/CD, specifically the *CD* bit, *collision detection*). Ethernet nodes cease checking for collisions once they send the last byte of each data packet. If the network is large enough that the last byte leaves the sending node before the first byte reaches every other node on the network, undetected collisions can occur. If the sending node fails to detect a collision, it won't know that it has to resend the packet, so the packet is lost.

Exam Tip

The most common reason for a machine to fail to detect a collision is that the network is too large.

The 5-4-3 rule avoids the need for complex math to work out whether a real-life Ethernet network is physically too large. The rule states that in a collision domain, no two nodes may be separated by more than

- Five segments
- Four repeaters
- Three populated segments

A *populated segment* is an Ethernet segment with at least one machine directly connected to it, either a segment of coax or a UTP connection to a hub. Each hub also counts as a repeater. Figure 4.11 shows an example of a network with the maximum numbers of elements.

To see whether a network complies with the 5-4-3 rule, trace the worst-case path between two machines—that is, the path between the two machines that will yield the highest number of segments, repeaters/hubs, and populated segments. Figure 4.11 shows a network with five segments, four repeaters, and three populated segments. The path between machines A and C represents the worst-case path because the packets must pass through all the segments and repeaters on the network. The paths between A and B or B and C are irrelevant for calculating compliance with the 5-4-3 rule, because a longer path exists between two other machines. The path between machine A and machine C uses all five segments, all four repeaters, and all three populated segments. It is possible for a network with more than five total segments to comply with the 5-4-3 rule, as long as the worst-case path includes no more than five segments. Figure 4.12 illustrates such a network.

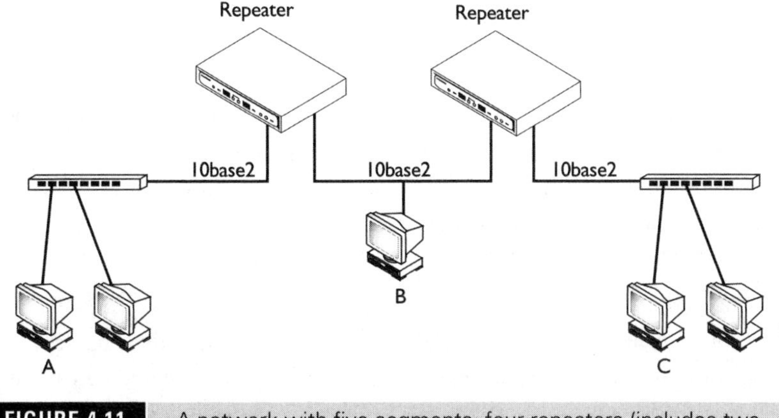

FIGURE 4.11 A network with five segments, four repeaters (includes two hubs), and three populated segments (A, B, and C).

Linking Hubs Together: Daisy Chaining

Extending a hub-based network—within the scope of the 5-4-3 rule, of course!—can be achieved by plugging a patch cable between a pair of ports on the hubs, but this won't work if you just plug the cable into any old port. Hub ports expect to be connected to NICs—not to other hubs—so this can lead to a

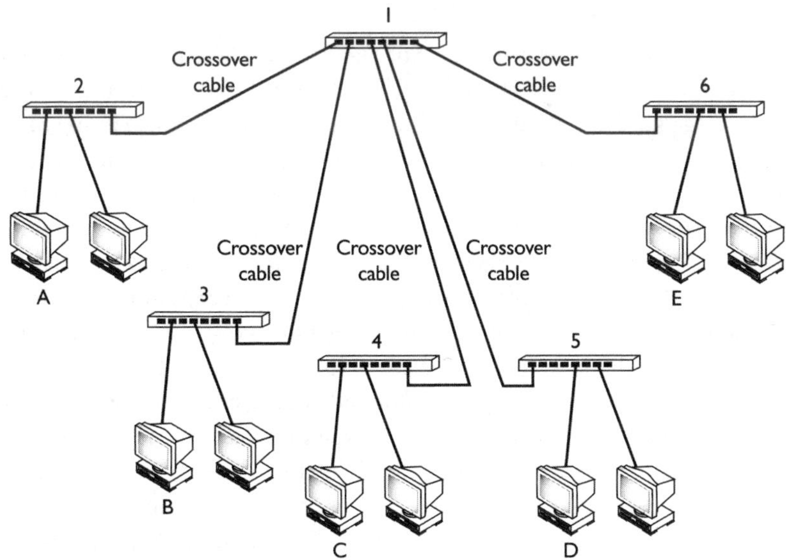

FIGURE 4.12 A network with six segments that still complies with the 5-4-3 rule

failed connection between the two devices. This problem is easily fixed, however, by using a patch cable that has been made up to cross over the misconnecting signals to correct the problem. It's even easier if the hub has a special *crossover* port that does this for you; sometimes one of the ports even has a switch that enables it to act as a standard NIC connection or as a crossover port without the need for a crossover patch cable. Look for a port marked "MDI-X" or a switch marked "MDI/MDI-X."

Stackable Hubs

Stackable hubs are hubs with a special proprietary connection that enables them to combine and function as a single device (in effect, they are not seen as daisy chained). For the purposes of the 5-4-3 rule, all the hubs in a stack are a single segment, repeater, and populated segment. There will still be a limit to the number of hubs that can be stacked, but this is usually (not always) more than the four allowed in a daisy chain. For example, the classic IBM 8237 Ethernet hub allows a stack of ten, creating a 170-port unit.

Switching Hubs: Hubs with Attitude

The curious (sorry, *probabilistic*) nature of Ethernet, with its CSMA/CD technology, means that, depending on the specific demands placed on the network's bandwidth, the number of machines that can peacefully coexist in a single Ethernet collision domain while still giving acceptable performance can vary from over 100 to as few as two.

Over the last few years, a new type of hub has become very fashionable: the so-called *switching hub,* or *switch.* Switching hubs have more intelligence than your average kind of hub, and they *do* analyze the sending and receiving MAC addresses of traffic passing through each port in order to decide where it actually needs to go. By passing data traffic only between a specific pair of ports, a switch isolates this traffic into its own collision domain, significantly improving overall performance. Network-wise, switches are often used to link sections of a building together and then feed everything into the server group. A classic installation is every floor in a building connected to its own 10 Mbps port on a switched hub, with the servers connected into the switch via its 100 Mbps port.

Switches have to analyze the data traffic and make decisions about what to do with it very rapidly. This makes them more expensive than basic hubs, but prices have dropped to the point that it almost doesn't make sense to buy plain-old hubs anymore. As the cost of switches has dropped, it has become cost-effective for some organizations to eliminate plain-vanilla hubs altogether and move to an entirely switched network. Switches can process the data packets in two ways:

- *Store-and-forward* switches *store* an entire data packet in memory while they analyze it, check its addressing, and check it for errors. Once a switch is happy with the data packet, it *forwards* the data packet to the appropriate port. If, however, the data packet doesn't look right—for example, if it seems to have been corrupted somehow—it will be discarded.
- *Cut-through* switches start to forward data packets as soon as the destination address (MAC address) of the packet has been read from the incoming packet. The remainder of the packet follows without any analysis. This approach improves performance at the expense of not stopping bad packets, which can lead to problems under some circumstances.

Some switches only support one or the other mode of operation, whereas others can be configured according to the network manager's wishes. Some modern switches can even be configured to perform cut-through switching on a per-port basis until a set error threshold is reached, whereupon they automatically change to store-and-forward mode. When the error rate falls below the threshold, the port automatically changes back to cut-through mode.

Exam Tip

Switches operate at layer 2 of the OSI model, also known as the Data Link layer, because they understand and can analyze data packets and MAC addresses.

Objective 4.03 Bridges and Routers

Two other major classes of devices exist to help manage bandwidth: bridges and routers. At the simplest level, both of these devices can also manage (filter) traffic between sections of a network in order to make the best use of available bandwidth, but they do that filtering based on different types of addresses.

Bridges

Bridges are essentially the same thing as switches: They filter and forward traffic between two or more segments of a network based on the MAC addresses contained in the data packets. To *filter* traffic means to stop it from crossing from one network segment to the next; to *forward* traffic means to pass traffic originating on one side of the bridge to the other. Figure 4.13 shows two Ethernet collision domains connected by a bridge. The bridge is represented as a simple box because the physical appearance of a bridge can vary a great deal. The bridge can be a standalone device that looks similar to an Ethernet repeater or hub, or it might be a PC with two NICs running special bridging software. The bridge might even be built into a multifunction device that provides other functions in addition to acting as a bridge.

How Bridges Function

Ethernet bridges behave just like repeaters when first switched on: They forward all data packets on the basis that they haven't got a clue whether they should or not. After a short while, however, a bridge starts to build up a list of the active MAC addresses on either side of its electronics. With a complete table listing each machine's MAC address and the side of the bridge on which it sits, the bridge can look at every incoming packet and decide whether to forward or filter it.

Exam Tip

Bridges operate at layer 2 of the OSI model, also known as the Data Link layer.

Bridges provide a performance benefit by forwarding or filtering data as required. Bridges also do exactly what a repeater can do—that is, extend the network over another segment (another 185 meters and/or another 30 nodes). Obviously, though, if that's all you want to do, a bridge is an expensive way of doing it!

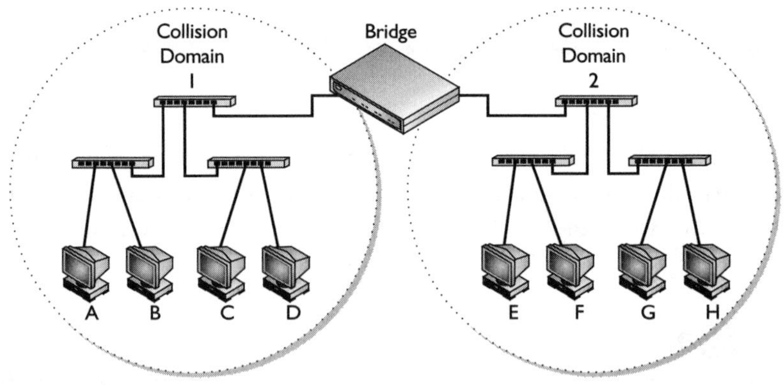

FIGURE 4.13 Two Ethernet collision domains connected by a bridge

One key difference between a bridge and a repeater is the fact that you can have five segments, four repeaters, and three populated segments of machines *on either side of the bridge.* This is because forwarded packets are seen to originate from the bridge—not the original sender—and the bridge will retransmit a forwarded data packet if it detects a collision.

Adding a bridge to a network does not require any major reconfiguration; simply split the network into two segments and rejoin them using the bridge. The individual network segments still behave and operate as one single network. The invisible nature of bridges makes them the easiest way to break an Ethernet network into multiple collision domains.

Exam Tip

Bridges also exist for other technologies, such as Token Ring, but they cannot connect an Ethernet network to a Token Ring network because of differences in the structure of the packets—something bridges cannot change.

Transparent Bridging

The type of bridging described here is *transparent bridging.* Some documentation, especially documentation that deals with networking theory, may refer to *translational bridges,* which *can* translate between different packet formats. Translational bridges rarely, if ever, appear in Ethernet or Token Ring networks. If you see the term "bridge," assume it refers to the transparent bridge discussed here unless specifically told otherwise.

Unicasts and Broadcasts

Most network traffic is *unicast* traffic—sent from one machine to another—but some network traffic is *broadcast* traffic, which is directed to all machines on the network. Because bridges recognize that broadcast traffic is not destined for a specific machine, they play it safe and forward all broadcast traffic. This behavior increases traffic on both sides of the bridge, but allows all functions that rely on broadcasts to work correctly. For example, MAC addresses are ultimately used to send data packets from one machine to another, but sometimes your system doesn't know the MAC address to which it wants to send the packets. In order to determine the MAC address, your system will broadcast a message asking the destination PC to respond with its MAC address based on some other identifying information, such as a computer name or IP address (we'll talk about IP addresses in more detail later).

Broadcast traffic is used for many purposes, one of which is to identify the relationship between a MAC address and the addressing scheme used by a specific network protocol. For example, if your computer wants to send a data packet to a computer known as SERVER1, it first broadcasts a request for SERVER1 to return its actual MAC address. Every machine on the network must examine that broadcast and determine whether its name and MAC address are the ones being sought. Most machines will ignore the broadcast, but the machine named SERVER1 will respond to your computer with a unicast packet confirming its MAC address.

Loops and Spanning Trees

If you like the sound of bridges so far, here's where I reveal their dark secret: They don't like loops! Figure 4.14 shows a network with multiple bridges that create a bridging loop. When machine A transmits a packet, bridges 2 and 3 will both forward the packet to bridge 1, making it appear to bridge 1 that machine A lies on both sides of bridge 1. This confuses many bridges and networked PCs, causing all sorts of weird error messages. In reality, *some* bridges don't actually mind loops (I confess I may have overplayed the dark secret bit) because they support an IEEE protocol called *802.1d*—also known as the *Spanning Tree Algorithm (STA)*—that detects loops and blocks traffic that would otherwise circle indefinitely. STA also allows blocked sections of a loop to unblock in the event that the other way around stops working, thus providing a rudimentary form of fault tolerance.

Exam Tip

The Network+ exam does not cover the Spanning Tree Algorithm; the term is mentioned here only for completeness.

Bridge Summary

- Bridges filter or forward traffic based on the MAC addresses contained in each data packet.
- Bridges always forward broadcast packets.
- Bridges operate at the Data Link layer, layer 2 of the OSI model.
- A bridge can only connect two network segments if they use the same type of data packets (for example, Ethernet to Ethernet, Token Ring to Token Ring).
- Some bridges cannot be used to provide multiple routes between machines.

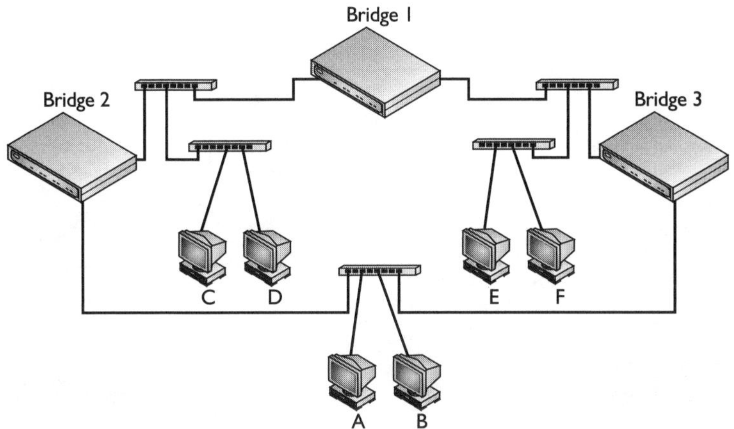

FIGURE 4.14 Bridges connected in a loop—only permitted if the bridges support the Spanning Tree Algorithm (IEEE 802.1d)

Routers

Routers provide a more flexible and robust alternative to bridges under many circumstances. They filter and forward traffic, as bridges do, but instead of relying on the layer 2 MAC addresses, routers use an additional level of layer 3 addresses. Because of the more sophisticated addressing schemes used by routers, they support multiple routes between networks. The networks connected by the routers can be different types of networks (for example, Ethernet and Token Ring). Routers provide a lot more flexibility for linking networks to each other than what bridges can provide.

Router technology holds together the Internet, providing multiple pathways between the hundreds of networks that make up the entire system (see Figure 4.15). Most routers, however, see much more humble service doing the same kind of thing as bridges, linking networks or sites together to form a wide area network (WAN). One very important difference is that the two sides of a router are considered to be separate *networks.* If you step back through this chapter, you'll note I was very careful to refer to the two *segments* on either side of a bridge or repeater—not two *networks.* What's the difference? Well, it affects how the networks are set up. Within a network, manufacturer-provided MAC addresses provide all the addressing information needed. When connecting multiple networks, the network architect must assign appropriate addresses to the machines on each network. You'll learn more about this in Chapters 5 and 6.

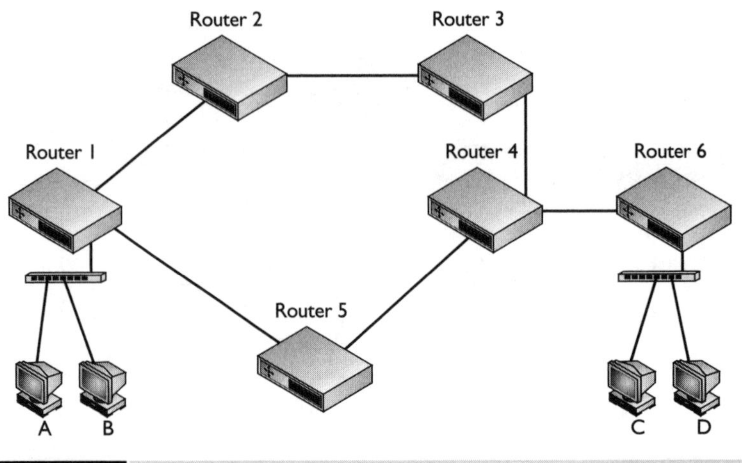

FIGURE 4.15 A network with multiple routers

Exam Tip

Because routers can change the structure of data packets (for example, convert them from Ethernet ones to Token Ring ones, or vice versa), and because routers can make decisions about the path a data packet takes between networks, they are said to operate at layer 3 of the OSI model, also known as the Network layer.

How Routers Function

Unlike bridges, routers discard all broadcast traffic by default. This is because routed networks tend to consist of two or more local area networks (LANs) connected to form a wide area network (WAN), and often the interconnections between the LANs have a limited bandwidth, perhaps down to 56 Kbps. If all the broadcast traffic from each LAN were forwarded over those slower WAN links, the internetwork links would quickly bog down. In addition, in very large WANs (such as the Internet), most broadcast traffic is irrelevant to most machines outside the local LAN and therefore does not need to be seen by them. Imagine how many machines there are on the Internet at any instant, and then imagine how much slower everything would be if every machine saw every other machine's broadcast packets (see Figure 4.16)!

Because routers discard broadcast packets, they cannot learn where all the machines on the network are by listening to their traffic the way that bridges do. Instead, they rely on an additional level of addressing called *network addressing* (remember we said that routers operate at the Network layer of the

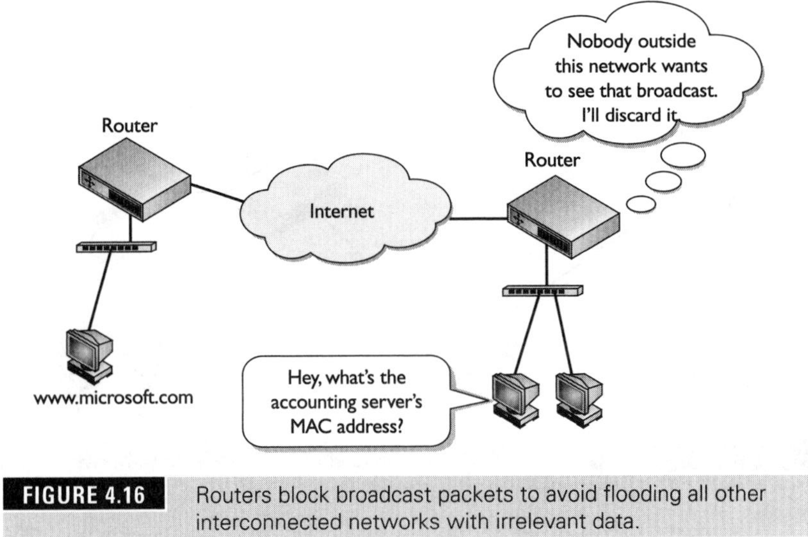

FIGURE 4.16 Routers block broadcast packets to avoid flooding all other interconnected networks with irrelevant data.

OSI model—well, here's one tie-in). A network address tells the router two pieces of information: the specific machine to which a packet should be delivered, and the network on which that machine lies. The IP addresses used on the Internet are examples of network addresses (see Chapter 5 for a discussion of IP addressing).

Given the destination network address, a properly configured router can determine the best route to the destination machine. In Figure 4.17, router 1 needs to deliver a packet from machine A to machine D. Assuming that all the links between the routers operate at the same speed, the most efficient route for the packet should be router 1 to 5 to 4 to 6. That route requires four hops. A *hop* is the process of passing through a router en route to the final destination. Alternative routes exist, but the router ignores them because they require more hops. In the event of a break in the link between routers 1 and 5, router 1 should automatically calculate the next-best route (if one exists) and redirect traffic to the alternative route: router 1 to 2 to 3 to 4 to 6 (see Figure 4.18).

Routed networks require significantly more planning and configuration than bridged networks. In a bridged network, the bridge does all the work, building up a table of MAC addresses found on each of its network interfaces. In a routed network, each node must know the network address of its local router. Although this can often be assigned automatically, it might actually be necessary for a network tech to key in this information on every machine on the network (and if there's a configuration change…!). The routers also need to know about

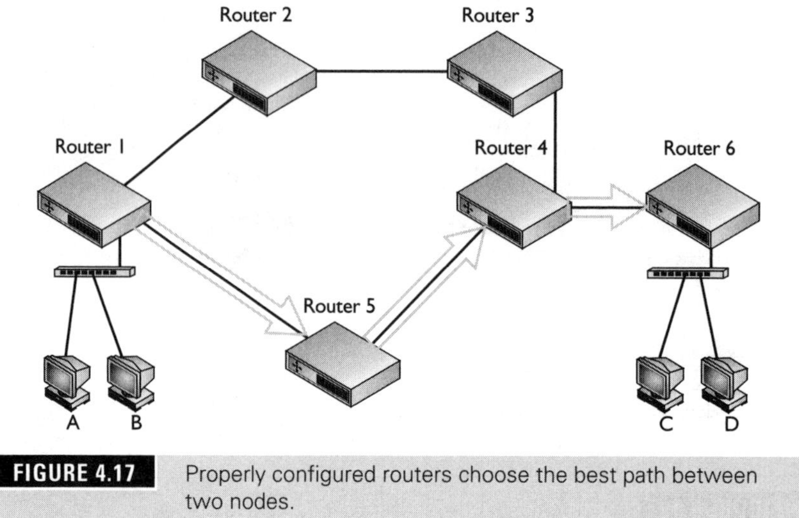

FIGURE 4.17 Properly configured routers choose the best path between two nodes.

all the possible networks to which they might route data packets, and this may also involve a degree of manual setup.

Although this might sound too complex to be worthwhile, the benefits of a routed network include fault tolerance and a high degree of control over how data gets around a WAN. For example, routers can be configured to favor faster routes over slower ones, or vice versa if the fast routes are getting bogged down. They can

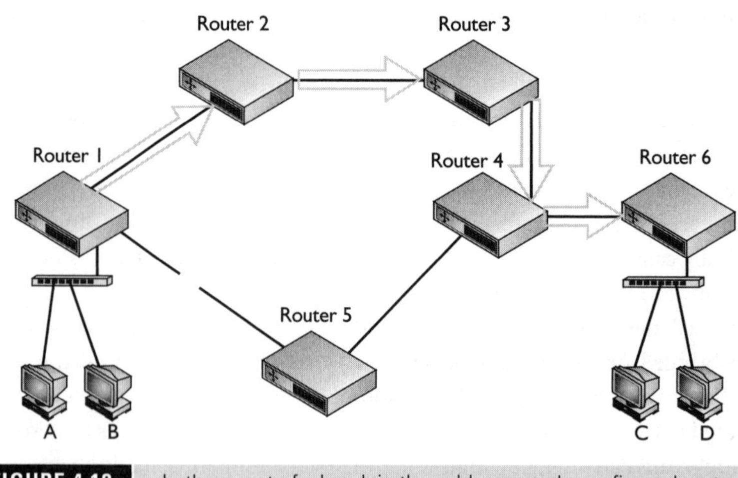

FIGURE 4.18 In the event of a break in the cable, properly configured routers automatically switch to an alternate route if one is available.

also make routing decisions based on how many intermediate networks exist between the source and destination ones (that is, the number of *hops*) and how much it costs to use a particular route.

Dynamic Routing Protocols

As the number of routers and networks grows, manually configuring each router with information about every other network becomes impractical. Fortunately, most routers can communicate with each other and dynamically determine the routes necessary to reach every network. Routers configured to use RIP (Router Information Protocol) or OSPF (Open Shortest Path First), for example, communicate with each other to build their routing tables without human intervention.

Exam Tip

Dynamic routing protocols such as RIP and OSPF provide automatic configuration of routes, simplifying network administration. Detailed discussions of RIP and OSPF are beyond the scope of the Network+ exam.

Routers and Wide Area Network Links

On a LAN, a router may not look much more exciting than a module with two network ports—in fact, the simplest form of router is two NICs in a server, with the server itself managing the routing. This would work on a small-to-medium network, but would place too much of a burden on a big, corporate server, and so the two-card trick—creating a so-called *multihomed server*—is not always the best approach. On a WAN, a router may be as simple as a modem connected to a server and an analog telephone line; this is workable but obviously very slow (maybe 56 Kbps). Other services, such as a *leased line,* may be more practical if speed is important—there's more about wide area networking and connectivity in Chapters 7 and 8.

Router Summary

- Routers filter and forward traffic based on network addresses (such as IP addresses), not based on MAC addresses.
- A router can choose among multiple paths between two nodes.
- Routers operate at layer 3 of the OSI model, known as the Network layer.
- A router can link two networks in-house or via communications circuits between sites to create a wide area network.

Objective 4.04 Gateways

You might have noticed that I've been slowly working my way up through the OSI layers—from hubs and repeaters at the Physical layer (layer 1), through bridges (layer 2), to routers (layer 3). So guess what's next? Yes! Gateways at layer… well, hang on a moment.

I've stopped for breath because in the networking world, the term "gateway" has two meanings. Yes, it can mean a device or system that operates at the higher OSI layers, but if our conversation is totally focused on the world of networking using the TCP/IP suite of protocols, then the term "gateway" is often used interchangeably with the term "router." So, in TCP/IP terms, a router is a gateway. Confused? Well, don't worry too much—just pay attention to the context. If you're talking about TCP/IP settings, the gateway will be a router. If not, then the gateway will be a device or system that allows two dissimilar networking or application environments to exchange information.

Exam Tip

Routers in TCP/IP-based networks are often referred to as *gateways*.

The principle of operation is that a gateway not only passes information between different systems, but can also change (*edit* or *translate*, if you like) the information to make it acceptable to the other system. You've probably used this type of gateway without even knowing it. For example, a mail gateway on your site might allow your PC-based e-mail system to transfer messages to and from a mail application based on an IBM mainframe, where the character set and text format is different; the gateway translates the PC text into IBM format, and vice versa, without you having to lift a finger. As another example, you might be running Microsoft's Gateway Services for NetWare on one of your NT servers. This allows users on the network to access file and print resources on a server running Novell NetWare via the NT server (the NetWare resources appear as if they were based on the NT server); the gateway software translates the Microsoft client requests into ones that the NetWare server can understand, and vice versa.

OK, so back to the OSI model—where does this definition of a gateway sit? Well, stand by for heated debates between groups of network techs. Some say that gateways operate at every level of the OSI model, whereas others say that they operate at layers 4–7 (Transport, Session, Presentation, and Application), because this is where data actually gets generated, processed, and generally managed.

In terms of identifying where devices fit into the OSI model, expect the Network+ exam to focus on the Physical, Data Link, and Network layers. Don't stress too much about identifying exactly where things fit at layers 4 through 7—very knowledgeable people often disagree about how some real-world products fit into that model. Don't expect too many probing questions based on the top end of the OSI model.

Exam Tip

Gateways act as translators between different operating system and application environments, and are said to operate at the higher OSI layers (4–7).

VLANs and 802.1Q

Virtual LANs, known as *VLANs,* provide an additional method of managing network traffic. Most of our energy in this chapter has been devoted to describing ways to segregate network traffic by dividing our network into discrete broadcast and collision domains using routers and switches. When two PCs are separated by a router, for example, they will not see each other's broadcasts. However, if those PCs communicate with each other frequently, the routing process adds additional processing overhead on the router and increases the latency between the PCs. In some cases, we may wish to avoid the performance impact of routing for communication between two machines on physically separate networks. VLANs allow us to forward traffic between machines on different segments using layer 2 information, reducing the amount of processing that must be done on each packet. The IEEE 802.1Q standard provides a Data Link layer method for creating VLANs by adding an additional VLAN tag to each Ethernet packet.

Exam Tip

Only nodes with the same VLAN tag can communicate with each other without going through a router. Even if two nodes are on the same physical network segment, they will ignore each other's data packets if their VLAN tags do not match.

The sending node, or the switch to which it connects, adds an additional 802.1Q tag to each Ethernet packet. 802.1Q-compliant layer 2 switches will then send those packets on to all other member nodes of that VLAN, either directly or by forwarding the packets to other switches that belong to the same VLAN. This sounds a lot like routing, except that in the case of VLANs the processing occurs at the Data Link layer. For network nodes that communicate frequently, such as two database servers that frequently replicate data, moving the traffic between network segments using layer 2 information (the 802.1Q tag in the Ethernet frame) instead of layer 3 information (the IP address) reduces latency by reducing the amount of data that must be read from each data packet. The VLAN switch can simply ignore any layer 3 information in the packet. Although the amount of extra processing involved in reading a few more bytes of data for each packet may seem trivial, remember that a router must read and interpret that data for every individual data packet—eliminating the need to make a routing decision on each packet can significantly improve performance in some cases.

VLAN Configuration

Although VLAN tags can be added by the sending node itself, more commonly the VLAN tag will be added by the switch on a per-port basis. The network administrator assigns each port to a VLAN and all traffic coming into that port will be tagged with the appropriate 802.1Q VLAN tag. The tagged Ethernet frames will then be sent on to all other ports that have been assigned to the same VLAN, even if those ports are part of a different switch. When a node needs to be moved to a different VLAN, no physical changes to the network are required—the administrator can simply reconfigure the port on the switch to use a different VLAN tag.

Troubleshooting VLANs

VLANs create some new troubleshooting issues. Two nodes on different VLANs cannot communicate directly with each other, even when connected to the same physical LAN. The only way they will communicate is if you use a router to route the data between the two VLANs. When two devices on the same physical LAN cannot communicate, you should confirm that the VLAN for each port on the switch has been set correctly. Also, older equipment that is not compatible with the 802.1Q standard will treat any Ethernet frame with a tag as an invalid frame and will discard it. Confirm that the sending node, the receiving node, and any switches in between them support 802.1Q tagging.

Exam Tip

802.1Q VLANs function at layer 2 in the OSI model, the Data Link layer.

802.1Q VLAN Summary

- Operates at layer 2 (the Data Link layer) in the OSI model.
- A VLAN tag is added to each Ethernet frame to specify the VLAN to which it should be delivered.
- Older hardware that is not 802.1Q compatible will discard tagged frames as invalid.
- VLANs can improve performance by eliminating the need for routing between nodes on the same VLAN, even if they connect to physically separate networks.
- VLANs ease administration by eliminating the need to make physical changes to the network when machines are moved from one logical network to another. To move a system to another VLAN, you simply associate the port the system is connected to with a different VLAN that has been configured on the switch.

✔**Objective 4.01: Network Interface Cards** A network interface card gets you on the network, but it must be the right fit for your computer system, or whatever you're plugging it into. You must also make sure that it has the right connectors for the network media and that it supports the right network standard and speeds—for example, 10/100 Mbps Ethernet or 4/16 Mbps Token Ring. Many NICs include diagnostic LEDs that help with basic fault-finding, so don't forget to check them. One very important task performed by a NIC is to give your computer system a unique address in the network; this is known as the *Media Access Control (MAC)* address. This address is unique on every NIC produced, but the top 24 bits of the MAC address can be used to identify the NIC (or NIC component) manufacturer.

✔**Objective 4:02: Repeaters and Hubs** Repeaters provide a simple way to extend a bus-based network over the basic 185 meter (Thinnet) or 500 meter (Thicknet), 30/100-device (Thin/Thick) segment maximums. Hubs behave like multiport repeaters to connect machines to a star-bus network. Both devices have no specific understanding of the data they are passing between ports and therefore do not provide any form of traffic management. Repeaters and hubs also have diagnostic LEDs and may be able to isolate faulty segments or devices if they detect problems such as a broken cable or jabbering NIC. There is a limit to the number of repeaters or hubs that you can link together (the 5-4-3 rule), but this can be overcome by using stackable hubs. A more sophisticated hub—known as a *switching hub*—can intelligently pass traffic between selected ports to reduce data collisions and thus improve throughput.

✔ **Objective 4.03: Bridges and Routers** Bridges can link sections of a network together, just like a repeater, but they also build up an internal MAC address table identifying the computer systems on either side of their interfaces so they can determine whether a data packet does actually need to pass across the bridge; this helps with traffic management and thus improves overall network performance. Bridges pass broadcast network traffic to ensure that computer systems on the network can identify the MAC addresses of other machines with which they want to communicate. Routers can do all the things that bridges can do, but they also support multiple paths between networks and can link together dissimilar network types, such as Ethernet and Token Ring. Routers are often used for wide area networking, providing interconnectivity between networked sites. Routers do not pass broadcast traffic; instead, they manage the identification of machine locations themselves, using network addresses that contain both a machine's address and the network on which it is located.

✔ **Objective 4.04: Gateways** In TCP/IP terms, "gateway" is another word for a router. In general networking language, however, a gateway is a device or program that can pass information between different operating environments or applications, changing (translating) the data being processed if necessary. A classic example of this type of gateway is an application that can take formatted messages from one e-mail environment and pass them on to another—for example, between a PC-based mail system and a mainframe computer.

REVIEW QUESTIONS

1. A user complains that his PC has just stopped letting him log in to the network, although he can log in successfully from another system. You have checked the PC's network setup and it seems fine, and the NIC also passes its diagnostics. What should you do next?
   - **A.** Replace the NIC.
   - **B.** Replace the BNC T-piece.
   - **C.** Check the MAC address of the NIC.
   - **D.** Check the LINK LED on the NIC.
2. Your corporate 10BaseT network is running slowly and you have been tasked with improving overall performance. Which of the following options provides the most practical, lowest-cost solution?
   - **A.** Install a router.
   - **B.** Install a switch.

C. Upgrade to 100BaseT hubs and NICs.

D. Install a fiber backbone.

3. Which of the following will improve performance on a 10Base2 network?

A. Installing a switch

B. Setting the NICs to full-duplex

C. Reconfiguring to use AUI ports

D. None of the above

4. Which address type is built into every NIC made?

A. A unique MAC address

B. A common Ethernet network address

C. A TCP/IP address

D. None of the above

5. What is the maximum possible end-to-end network distance on a 10Base2 network?

A. 185m

B. 200m

C. 500m

D. 925m

6. At which layer of the OSI seven-layer model does a bridge operate?

A. 2

B. 3

C. 4

D. 5

7. At which layer(s) of the OSI seven-layer model does a mail gateway operate? (Select all that apply.)

A. 3

B. 4

C. 1

D. 2

8. Which is the most cost-effective and simple way to link two hubs?

A. A fiber duplex cable

B. A switch

C. A crossover patch cable

D. A full duplex cable

9. Which of the following statements is true?
   - A. Bridges pass broadcast traffic.
   - B. Bridges block unicast traffic.
   - C. Routers pass broadcast traffic.
   - D. Routers block network packets.
10. Which of the following correctly represents the 5-4-3 rule?
   - A. Five hubs, four segments, three populated segments
   - B. Five segments, four repeaters, three populated segments
   - C. Five populated segments, four repeaters, three crossover cables
   - D. Five hubs, four populated segments, three routers

REVIEW ANSWERS

1. **D** Check the LINK LED. The card diagnostics may not tell you whether there's a good connection to the network.
2. **B** Installing a switch is the best solution. A router won't improve network speed overall, and fiber would be very expensive.
3. **D** Switches are for hub-based networks, and 10Base2 is coax. Similarly, full-duplex mode is only supported by hub-based networks. AUI ports aren't used on 10Base2 networks (they're used on 10Base5), and they wouldn't offer any performance increase anyway.
4. **A** Every NIC has a unique MAC address.
5. **D** The maximum end-to-end distance, according to the 5-4-3 rule, would be five segments of 185 meters each, for a total of 925 meters.
6. **A** Bridges operate at the Data Link layer (layer 2).
7. **B** Gateways operate at layers 4–7, but only answer B (layer 4) is in this range.
8. **C** Linking two hubs requires a crossover patch cable.
9. **A** Bridges pass broadcast traffic; all other statements are false.
10. **B** The 5-4-3 rule states that the maximum end-to-end distance on a bus-based network can be five coax segments connected together by four repeaters, with only three populated segments.

Protocols and Protocol Suites

ITINERARY

- **Objective 5.01** Overview of Protocols and Protocol Suites
- **Objective 5.02** Role and Function of NetBEUI
- **Objective 5.03** Role and Function of IPX/SPX
- **Objective 5.04** Connection-Oriented vs. Connectionless Protocols
- **Objective 5.05** Core Network Operating System Protocols

NEWBIE	SOME EXPERIENCE	EXPERT
2 hours	1 hour	30 minutes

Standards, standards everywhere! There's an old joke that a giraffe is actually a horse designed by committee—and that animal we call networking has also had its share of committees and standards over the years. Actually, the standards committees have done a darn good job, although you might not think so when you're knee deep in service packs and your main server's a quaking mass of unbootable metal. The standards and protocols that define the main networking protocols function pretty well, in part due to the modular nature of the key networking protocols (remember the OSI seven-layer model from Chapter 1?). Each protocol handles a specific set of tasks, and as network standards have matured, the standards committees have been able to add improvements without rewriting the entire "network stack."

Overview of Protocols and Protocol Suites

The moment that you press a key on your keyboard or click your mouse button, you use protocols and standards. Take a key press as an example. First, the keyboard controller chip in your PC senses that you have pressed a key and works out which one. Next, the keyboard controller turns this information into a *scan code,* a piece of data that represents the key you pressed, and stores it in a small block of memory called a *buffer.* The PC's operating system then checks the keyboard buffer for data, sees that something is in there, and reads it. Finally, the data is passed back to the application currently waiting for input, where the keyboard data is analyzed and acted upon—maybe adding a character to a document or completing a password-entry sequence. All the way through this process, things must happen just so, or the process won't work properly; in other words, there are *protocols* involved. To handle input from the keyboard, for instance, several protocols and standards are in place to eliminate potential problems:

- If every manufacturer used a different set of scan codes for its keyboards, the operating system would have to cater to every possibility. Just imagine: Windows 2000 for Compaq keyboards, Windows 2000 for Dell keyboards, Windows 2000 for that budget keyboard you bought at the local store for not much more than the cost of a fast-food burger (please, please, please let it be supported)—it would be a nightmare! With minor exceptions, all modern keyboards use the same scan codes to represent the keys.

- What would happen if the operating system read the keyboard buffer data just as the keyboard controller was updating it? Would the data be valid? How do we know when it's valid?
- How does the operating system pass data to a specific application? Wouldn't it be sensible if the handover sequence was standardized so that it was the same in every case? Of course it would be, and in fact it is.

Phew! And that's just for a keyboard!

Protocol Categories

We can break down networking protocols into several broad categories:

- Protocols that state how and when data can be placed on the network media and what that media can be.
- Protocols that identify the format of data structures, such as packets.
- Protocols that help identify individual computers and systems and how to get data between them.
- Protocols that handle errors in transmission and manage the flow of data across a network.
- Protocols that help establish initial communication between systems that want to exchange information.
- Protocols that give meaning to specific data sequences.
- Protocols that allow general applications to work with the networking environment.

Hey, have you spotted something? No? How many categories are in this list? Seven. Hmm.... Now where has that number come up before?

Yes, you've got it! We've broadly mapped our protocol categories to the OSI seven-layer model, and that's no coincidence because that's where you'll find all the protocols you need to know for the Network+ exam.

Protocol Suites

To create a network, you cannot simply randomly pick one protocol from each layer and expect to create a working system. In reality, protocols work together in families, known as *protocol suites* or *protocol stacks*. Even though there may be several protocols listed as operating at a layer of the OSI model, your network will not necessarily support and use all of them (see Figure 5.1). The three most popular protocol families you're likely to encounter in the real world and on the

Network+ exam are NetBEUI, IPX/SPX, and TCP/IP. To see the point here, consider this: Within the TCP/IP protocol suite, IP is the protocol responsible for device addressing. The IPX/SPX network standard (the IPX protocol) uses another way of managing addresses, but there's no such thing as the TCP/IPX protocol suite. It's theoretically possible, but don't even *think* about it, because your network would be the only one in the world using it. Try asking Microsoft to write a Windows 2000 protocol driver for *that!*

The protocol suite you need to know most intimately for the Network+ exam is TCP/IP, but TCP/IP is *such* an important part of the exam (and in real-life networking, too) that it has its own chapter (Chapter 6, right after this one). As you'll see, there's much more in the suite than just TCP and IP; the same is true for IPX/SPX and NetBEUI. In an ideal world, you'd have only one networking protocol suite to learn about—TCP/IP may well get there one day—but for now, you also need to know the ins and outs of IPX/SPX and NetBEUI as well.

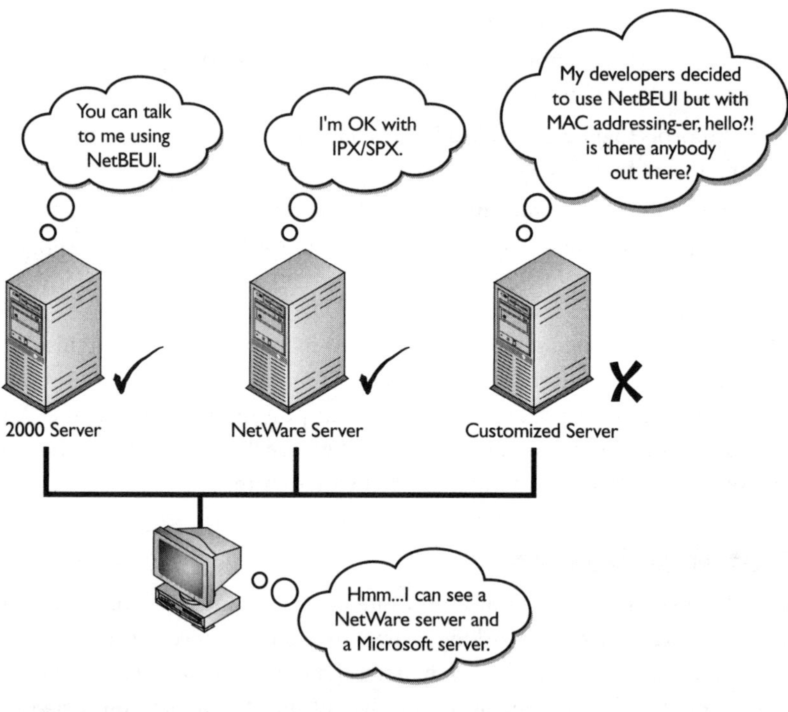

FIGURE 5.1 You can't arbitrarily mix protocols.

Role and Function of NetBEUI

NetBEUI provides a fast, simple set of network protocols, mainly for use with smaller LANs. This protocol suite is most closely associated with IBM and Microsoft networking environments such as the ancient IBM LAN Manager, OS/2, and Windows 9*x*. All of Microsoft's general desktop environments (Windows NT, 9*x*, 2000, Me, XP) can use NetBEUI for small peer-to-peer networks (see Figures 5.2 and 5.3); some third-party products, such as Artisoft's LANtastic, also support it. The NetBEUI protocol suite consists of two main protocols: NetBIOS and NetBEUI (see Figure 5.4). When you install NetBEUI for a Microsoft product, you are actually installing both protocols.

NetBIOS

NetBIOS handles the Session layer functions for NetBEUI networks, managing the connections between machines. NetBEUI creates connections for data transmission and closes the connections after the completion of a transmission.

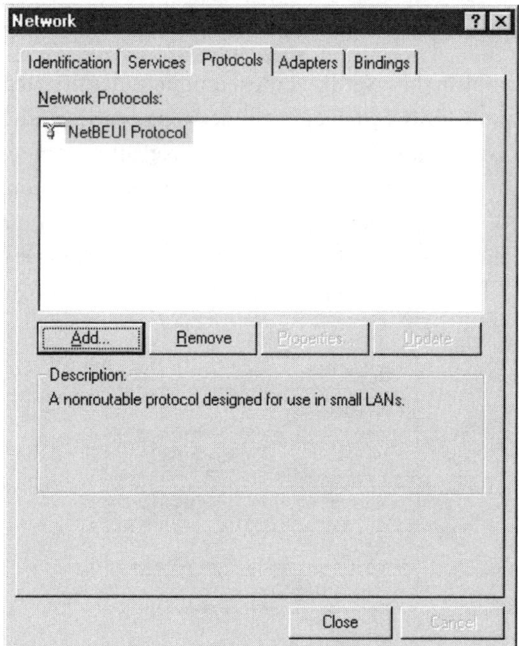

FIGURE 5.2 NetBEUI in a Windows NT environment

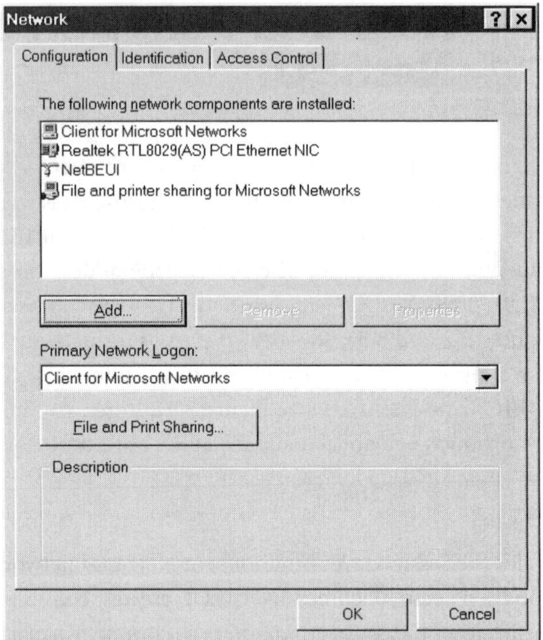

FIGURE 5.3 A peer-to-peer computer running Windows 9*x* using NetBEUI

In order to accomplish this, NetBEUI must uniquely identify each machine with a NetBIOS name. NetBIOS manages connections based on the names of the computers involved. Figure 5.5 shows a typical NetBIOS name.

NetBIOS can handle the Session layer for other protocol suites in a Microsoft-based network, although Microsoft has begun to move away from NetBIOS as a default with Windows 2000 and Windows XP (see the discussions of IPX/SPX and TCP/IP later in this chapter and in Chapter 6, respectively).

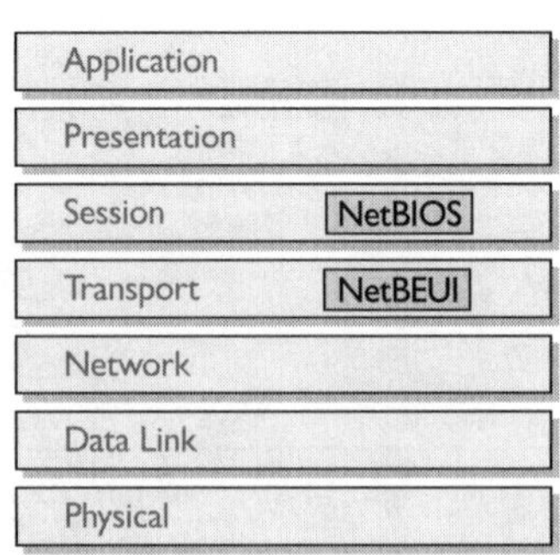

FIGURE 5.4 NetBIOS and NetBEUI in the OSI model

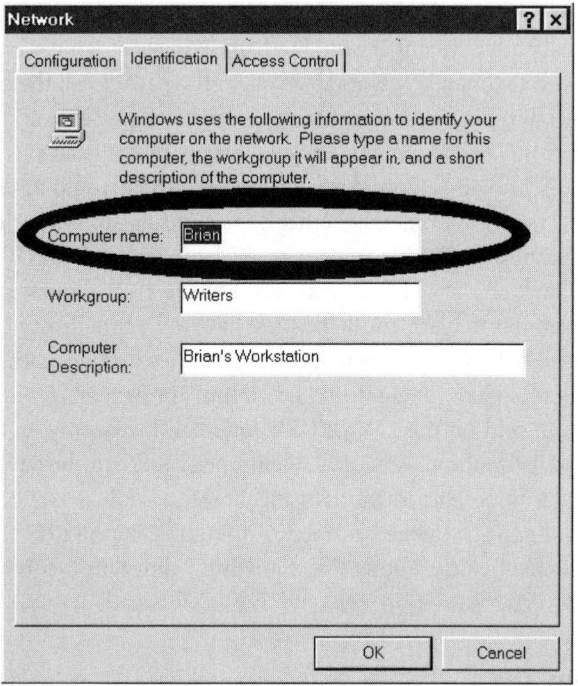

FIGURE 5.5 You can configure the NetBIOS computer name in Windows 98 by using the Network control applet on the Control Panel.

NetBIOS Names

NetBIOS names can be up to 15 characters long and must be unique so that machines can be uniquely identified. If duplicate names existed on a network, it would be like several houses in your neighborhood having the same telephone number: Messages (data) wouldn't get through to the right location. If duplicate addresses are set up on your network, the affected machines will detect this and display an error message.

Exam Tip

NetBEUI (through the NetBIOS protocol) identifies individual computers by their computer names.

NetBIOS does not scale well for larger networks. NetBIOS uses a *flat name space* model, meaning that every machine has a single name to identify it, but no way to identify a location. Each machine has a *node* address (a layer 2 address), but no *network* address (a layer 3 address). If this type of flat model were applied to the national phone system, it would be like having telephone numbers but no area codes. You *could* make a workable system (boy, would all the phone numbers be long!), but because you couldn't automatically assume a location for a specific telephone, every time you dialed a number—for example, your friend Jo on 23664322214045—every exchange in the country would have to see your dialing request so it could check whether it's responsible for the phone you want to ring. If you now apply this analogy to a (theoretical) NetBEUI-based wide area network (WAN), you'd have a situation where *every* request by one computer to communicate with another would have to be broadcast to *every* other interconnected network, in effect swamping the network and bringing everything to a grinding halt. There would be no time for data on *this* network!

OK, are you sold on this? NetBEUI is for small LANs only. In fact, routers block NetBEUI for the reasons just mentioned. You can, however, still split a large LAN into smaller sections using bridges, because these *do* forward NetBEUI data packets. Repeaters are also still usable because they forward everything—remember, they don't know anything about protocols and packets, just electrical signals.

Exam Tip

NetBEUI is a nonroutable protocol.

On your small LAN, though, once NetBIOS establishes a connection, it passes the packet down to the NetBEUI protocol, which operates at the Transport layer.

The NetBEUI Protocol

NetBEUI (as an individual protocol, not the name of the suite—you'll have to get used to this double-meaning stuff because it happens a lot!) does what all good Transport layer protocols do: It breaks larger chunks of data into smaller pieces on the sending machine (fragmentation) and reassembles them on the receiving end (defragmentation). This is shown in Figure 5.6.

Because NetBEUI is a nonroutable protocol, there's no need for the Network layer (where routing activities take place) to do anything, so there's no Network layer protocol in the NetBEUI protocol suite. If a router receives a NetBEUI packet, it simply discards it (see Figure 5.7). Everything gets passed directly to the Data Link layer, where it's all packaged up ready to whiz around the network to the destination machine.

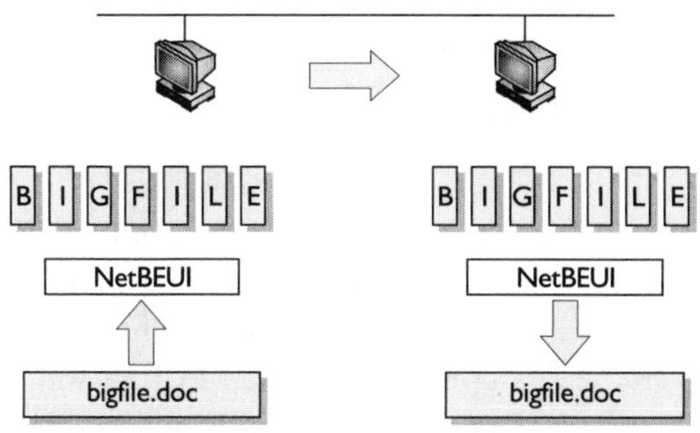

FIGURE 5.6 NetBEUI breaks a file into smaller pieces for transmission and reassembles the pieces on the receiving end.

NetBEUI Summary

If you need a simple LAN, NetBEUI might be the protocol for you. Here's a summary of its key features:

- Fast, Transport layer protocol suitable for small networks (LANs)
- Nonroutable and therefore not suitable for WANs
- Uses the NetBIOS protocol at the Session layer to identify and manage computer names and connections
- Traditionally associated with IBM and Microsoft networking environments

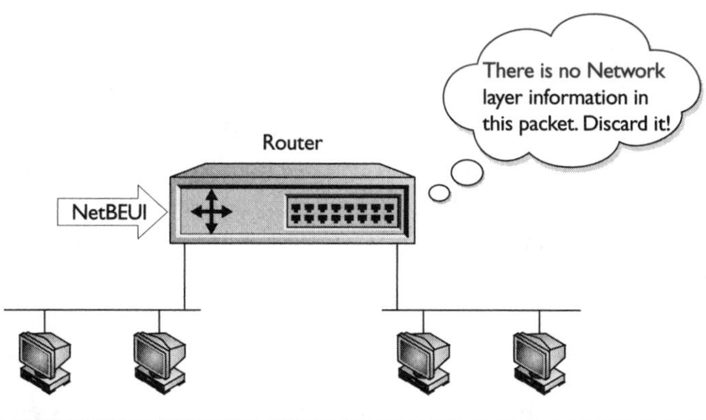

FIGURE 5.7 Routers discard NetBEUI packets

Role and Function of IPX/SPX

The IPX/SPX protocol suite is firmly associated with the NetWare series of network operating systems from Novell. Based on an older Xerox protocol called XNS, IPX/SPX provides a more scaleable solution for networks than NetBEUI (NetWare servers don't support NetBEUI anyway). From the late 1980s to the mid-1990s, NetWare was *the* network operating system to use, with a claimed market share in the 70-to-80-percent range. NetWare remains strong today, but Windows and the Linux operating system have seriously eroded Novell's market position. Nevertheless, a large base of client/server networks still use NetWare as their main server software platform. Even Microsoft supports IPX/SPX through its own version of the protocol, called NWLink, allowing Windows-based clients to access NetWare resources as well as Microsoft-based servers (you could also use true IPX/SPX by installing a Novell-supplied client kit). Modern versions of NetWare also fully support the TCP/IP protocol.

The IPX/SPX Protocol Suite

IPX/SPX represents a much more sophisticated protocol suite compared to NetBEUI, and it includes protocols that operate at layers 3 through 7 of the OSI model. The layer 3 functions include routing, which makes IPX/SPX suitable for WAN use.

Figure 5.8 shows some of these protocols in relation to the OSI model. At the Network layers, the Internetwork Packet eXchange (IPX) protocol handles the routing of data packets between networks. At the Transport layer, Sequenced Packet eXchange (SPX) handles the process of breaking data into smaller chunks on the sending machine and reassembling the data on the receiving machine. The Service Advertising Protocol (SAP) handles the Session layer by regularly broadcasting the availability of servers, print servers, and other services across the network, and the NetWare Core Protocol (NCP) handles a variety of Presentation and Application layer issues.

Exam Tip

IPX operates at the Network layer; SPX operates at the Transport layer.

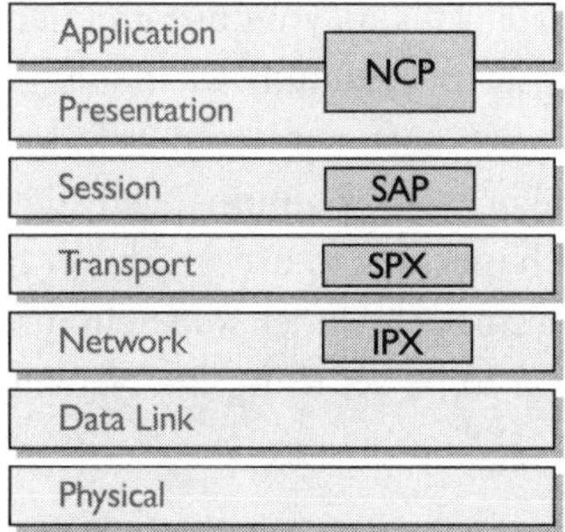

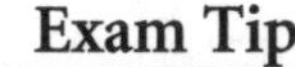
FIGURE 5.8 IPX/SPX includes protocols operating at OSI layers 3 through 7.

IPX/SPX Addressing

IPX/SPX uses the MAC address built into the network interface card (NIC) to uniquely identify a computer on the network; therefore, unlike NetBEUI, which requires someone to assign each computer a name, IPX/SPX node addressing requires no manual setup. Because IPX/SPX is routable, however, every client needs a network address, which is entered as part of a server's configuration. The important point to remember here is that every server on the same network must be configured with the *same* network address. Think of our earlier phone analogy: Your telephone and that of your neighbor will have the *same* area code (unless your two houses straddle phone districts, but let's assume they don't).

Exam Tip

IPX/SPX uses MAC addresses to identify computers.

NetWare Packet Formats

NetWare has evolved over time, and one of these evolutionary stages brought NetWare's packet (frame) format into alignment with the rest of the industry. Early versions of the NetWare operating system use a slightly nonstandard packet format that Novell, somewhat confusingly, called Ethernet_802.3. Later versions of NetWare fell in line with the rest of the world and used, by default, a packet format that Novell called Ethernet_802.2. To cap it all, NetWare also supports two other Ethernet frame types called Ethernet_II (used with TCP/IP) and Ethernet_SNAP. The upshot of this is that every machine on a NetWare-based network must use a common frame format (usually now Ethernet_802.2) to be able to communicate. This may require the network techs to check the configuration of existing servers carefully when adding a new server to ensure that the required frame type(s) are supported. Windows 9*x* and Windows NT/2000 systems simplify the process by automatically detecting IPX traffic by default and configuring each machine to use whichever frame type is detected on the network first (see Figure 5.9). Under some circumstances, however, a specific frame type may need to be set using the Network Control Panel applet, shown in Figure 5.10.

Wide Area Networking with IPX/SPX

Although IPX/SPX is a routable protocol, it does not scale well for large WANs. The main problems center around the way that servers and other network services broadcast their availability and the way that routers and servers exchange routing information. Although these problems can be overcome, most network architects prefer TCP/IP for large WANs.

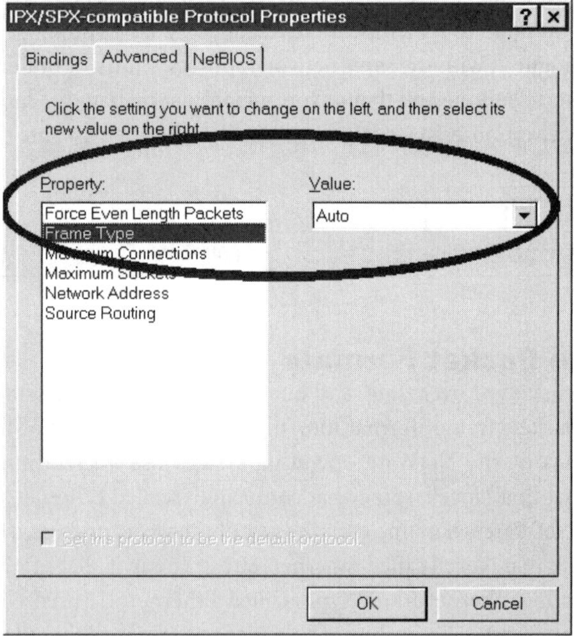

FIGURE 5.9 Microsoft's NWLink default setup autodetects IPX/SPX frame types.

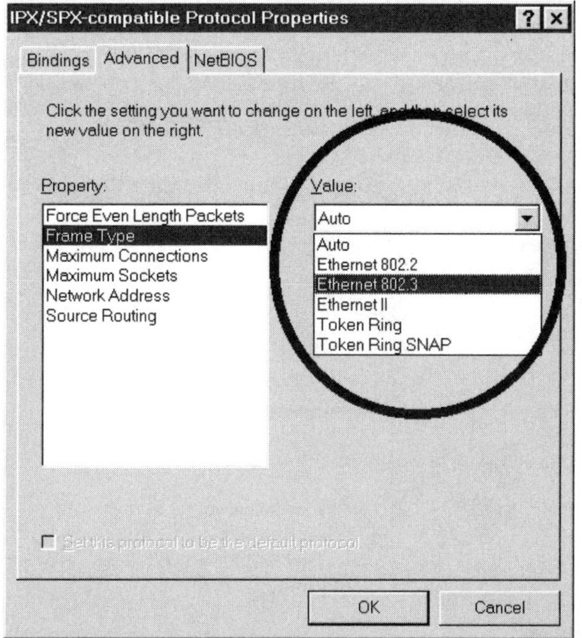

FIGURE 5.10 Microsoft's NWLink setup can also have the frame type set manually.

SAP Traffic

On a NetWare network or WAN, servers and other network services broadcast their availability using the SAP protocol every 60 seconds. Although this configuration works well on small- and medium-sized networks, as a network grows to include hundreds of servers and thousands of clients, the SAP traffic increases to a point where it begins to use a significant part of the available network bandwidth, thus slowing down the network.

RIP Traffic

Novell's Routing Information Protocol (RIP) is used by NetWare servers to broadcast information about available routes on WANs, and this can lead to further congestion. Like SAP, RIP broadcasts everything, every 60 seconds, even if the information hasn't changed since the last broadcast. More recent versions of NetWare address this traffic congestion by using a different protocol, called NetWare Link Services Protocol (NLSP), that broadcasts only *changes* to routing information as they occur (see Figure 5.11).

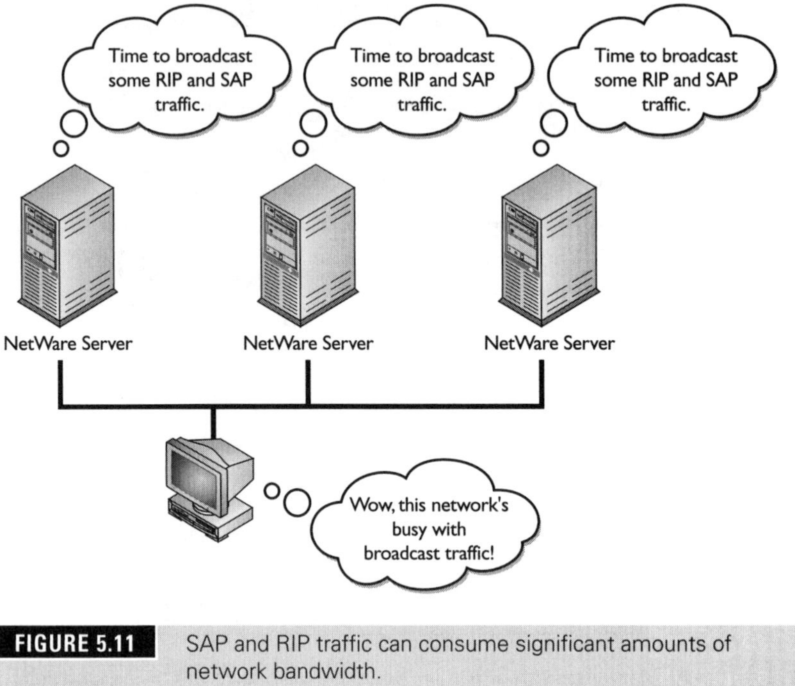

FIGURE 5.11 SAP and RIP traffic can consume significant amounts of network bandwidth.

IPX/SPX Summary

Here's the bottom line on NetWare:

- Routable protocol
- Supported by Microsoft using the Microsoft NWLink equivalent protocol
- Uses MAC addressing to identify nodes on the network
- Supports different packet (frame) types
- Uses SAP broadcasts to advertise network services, often slowing down very large networks
- Uses RIP to broadcast routing information, although later NetWare server products can also use NLSP
- Modern NetWare servers can support TCP/IP in addition to, or instead of, IPX/SPX

Connection-Oriented vs. Connectionless Protocols

In networking terms, a connection-oriented protocol is a protocol that verifies the delivery and receipt of *each and every* packet sent. Connection-oriented protocols also check whether the destination device is actually present before sending it any data—they establish a connection between the sending and receiving devices prior to data transmission.

On the other hand, *connectionless* protocols assume that some other mechanism or protocol (usually at a higher level in the OSI model) will detect when things have gone wrong and request retransmission. The difference in the two approaches can be summed up (a bit crudely, but it will do) this way:

- Connection-oriented (reliable) protocols are pessimistic and paranoid, and they check everything before and after data transmission.
- Connectionless (unreliable) protocols assume that everything's working fine and expect something elsewhere to notice any problems.

Because of the smaller data transmission management overhead, connectionless protocols tend to be faster than connection-oriented ones and therefore are preferable in some circumstances, especially where the underlying network can be considered stable, such as on a LAN. Connectionless protocols are also used where there's no guarantee that the data recipient is actually present on the network; for example, all broadcast traffic must, by definition, be connectionless, because you don't know exactly who's going to receive it.

Exam Tip

SPX is a connection-oriented (reliable) protocol. IPX is connectionless (unreliable). NetBEUI can provide both connection-oriented and connectionless packet delivery services. Later chapters contain further examples you should remember.

Core Network Operating System Protocols

The protocols covered so far in this chapter have to do with getting data around a network, but when a packet is received by a machine, it has to know what to do with the packet. Is it part of a file, a login request, or an instruction for the server to do something? This short section outlines three protocols that are responsible for deciding what to do with the contents of a packet. Because these protocols ultimately interface with the network operating system in question—in fact, they are generally part of the network operating system—they are said to operate at the Application, Presentation, and Session layers of the OSI model (layers 7 down through 5).

Microsoft Networking: Server Message Blocks

All the functionality of a Microsoft server is defined by a set of protocols (procedures) known collectively as Server Message Blocks (SMBs). If a client wants to log onto an NT server, for example, the client sends a data packet formatted with the appropriate SMB data to attempt a login; this reaches the server and travels up through the OSI layers until the data itself hits the core operating system, where it is decoded and understood.

Novell Networking: NetWare Core Protocol

The NetWare Core Protocol defines the functionality of a NetWare server in a way similar to what SMB does for a Microsoft-type server: An NCP request (packet) from a client machine is interpreted by the NetWare NOS and causes a specific action to take place.

UNIX/Linux and SAMBA

UNIX and Linux have traditionally provided a high-performance, centralized data-processing environment that people can access using a screen and keyboard terminal. This remains true today. UNIX continues to have a strong presence in corporate environments, and the Linux operating system provides a low-cost method for introducing UNIX-like functionality at all levels of an organization, not just in the datacenter. In particular, UNIX and Linux solutions run a significant portion of the Internet. In 1992, Andrew Tridgell published the code for an installable UNIX environment that would make the UNIX system look and behave like a Microsoft server, in effect implementing the SMB protocol on the UNIX system. The result was an open-source product called SAMBA. Once SAMBA is installed and configured, Microsoft clients see shared disk space and printers on a UNIX system in exactly the same way they would if they were accessing a true Microsoft server (see Figure 5.12). Before SAMBA, you could share files between UNIX systems and other platforms using various file transfer programs and disk tools, but SAMBA makes things much simpler. SAMBA also provides client tools for UNIX and Linux workstations to access Windows servers, making SAMBA a key tool for integrating UNIX and Linux systems into a Windows environment (or vice versa).

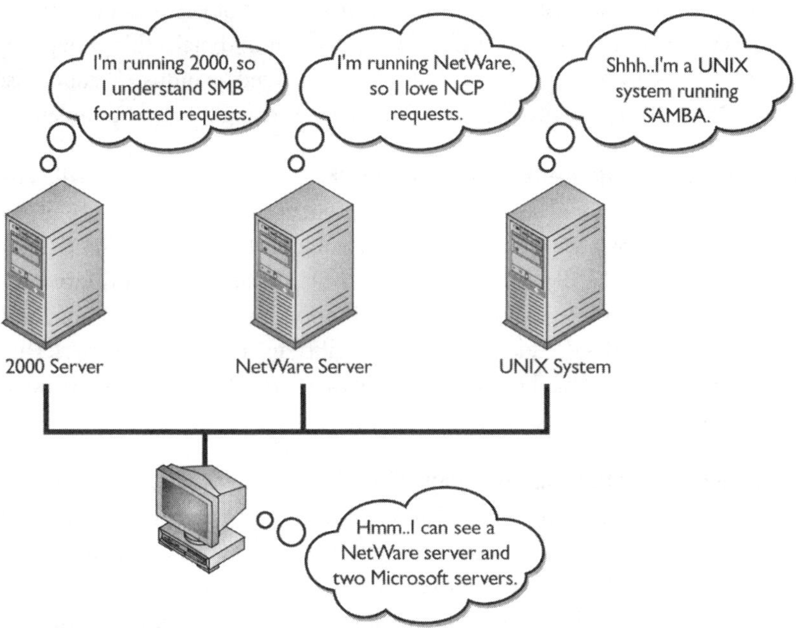

FIGURE 5.12 SAMBA makes a UNIX server look like a Microsoft server to its clients.

Exam Tip

The Common Internet File System (CIFS) is a backward-compatible development of SMB, published as a public-domain standard. CIFS is defined by Microsoft as "a standard remote file system access protocol for use over the Internet," and many publications and technicians now treat SMB and CIFS as the same thing.

✔**Objective 5.01: Overview of Protocols and Protocol Suites** Protocols define how everything works, at various levels, on a network, from the format that a packet of data must have to how machines are uniquely addressed. There is no single protocol that covers every aspect of networking; instead, families, or suites, of protocols work hand in hand to make things happen. Over the years, three protocol suites have emerged as industry standards: NetBEUI, IPX/SPX, and TCP/IP, with the latter being the most popular.

✔**Objective 5.02: Role and Function of NetBEUI** NetBEUI is a small, fast networking protocol suite suitable for small networks. Because it's a nonroutable protocol, NetBEUI is not suitable for wide area networks. Within the NetBEUI protocol suite, NetBEUI itself is the Transport layer protocol responsible for packet fragmentation and defragmentation, and NetBIOS provides the addressing functionality, using computer names. Historically, NetBEUI has been associated with Microsoft and IBM networking products.

✔**Objective 5.03: Role and Function of IPX/SPX** IPX/SPX was developed by Novell for its NetWare range of network operating systems. This protocol uses MAC addresses to identify computers on a network. Also, because a unique MAC address is built into every NIC, there's no need to set addresses manually. Although IPX/SPX is a routable protocol, it does not scale well for big WANs because its SAP (Service Advertising Protocol) and RIP (Routing Information Protocol) traffic can consume significant network bandwidth. Later versions of NetWare can use the NetWare Link Services Protocol (NLSP) to reduce the amount of RIP traffic on the network. Partly because of NetWare's popularity, Microsoft implemented its own, compatible version of IPX/SPX, called NWLink.

✔**Objective 5.04: Connection-Oriented vs. Connectionless Protocols** Connection-oriented protocols, such as SPX, check every data packet for successful transmission and also establish a network connection to the recipient before actually sending any data. By contrast, connectionless protocols just send data packets without any before or after checking. This makes them faster, but not suitable for applications that need to be sure of complete data transmission integrity at all times. In general, however, most client-to-server network traffic uses a connectionless protocol. NetBEUI is capable of both connection-oriented and connectionless operation.

✔**Objective 5.05: Core Network Operating System Protocols** Up to this point, our discussions have focused on protocols for getting data across a network to its destination. This section refers to the protocols or standards that lie at the heart of a network operating system and define how specific data patterns can be sent to a server to make certain things happen. In the Microsoft world, the functionality of a server is defined by a set of protocols known collectively as Server Message Blocks (SMBs). In the NetWare world, server functionality is defined in a similar way by the NetWare Core Protocol. Finally, we discussed SAMBA, an application that allows UNIX-based systems to understand SMBs and to look and behave on a network like a Microsoft server.

REVIEW QUESTIONS

1. You have been asked to network three computers in a small office. The main objective is to share a printer and some disk space. A secondary objective is to allow for future wide area networking. Your chosen solution uses the NetBEUI protocol. This solution:
   - **A.** Meets both objectives
   - **B.** Meets the main objective only
   - **C.** Meets the secondary objective only
   - **D.** Doesn't meet either objective
2. At which layer of the OSI model does the NetBEUI protocol operate? (Select one answer.)
   - **A.** Application
   - **B.** Session

C. Transport

D. Network

3. Your office has three NetWare servers installed and one NT server. Which of the following protocols would *not* allow you to communicate with all the servers? (Select one answer.)

A. TCP/IP

B. NetBEUI

C. NWLink

D. They would all be suitable

4. Which of the following statements about the IPX/SPX protocol is true?

A. IPX/SPX supports computer name addressing.

B. IPX/SPX is not a routable protocol.

C. SPX handles machine addressing.

D. IPX/SPX uses MAC addressing.

5. You have just added a client computer to a NetWare server–based network, and the machine cannot access any of the servers. You have checked the cabling, NIC, and driver setup. What should you check next? (Select one answer.)

A. The computer name

B. The power supply

C. The frame type

D. The server's NCP address

6. Which of the following is a connectionless-only protocol? (Select one answer.)

A. SPX

B. IPX

C. NetBEUI

D. They are all connectionless

7. You have been asked to add a NetWare server to your existing network of Microsoft systems. Which of the following protocols could you add to your client PCs to allow access to the NetWare server? (Select two answers.)

A. NCP

B. IPX/SPX

C. NetBEUI

D. NWLink

8. Which of the following devices will forward NetBEUI data packets? (Select all that apply.)
   - **A.** Repeaters
   - **B.** Routers
   - **C.** Hubs
   - **D.** Bridges
9. You have been asked to install a Linux-based system on your Microsoft network. The primary objective is to allow data to be transferred to the Linux system from the Microsoft servers. A secondary objective is to allow all users easy access to the Linux printers. You decide to install NWLink on the NT servers. This solution meets:
   - **A.** Neither of the objectives
   - **B.** The primary objective only
   - **C.** The secondary objective only
   - **D.** Both objectives
10. Which of the following is a Session layer protocol? (Select one answer.)
    - **A.** NetBIOS
    - **B.** NetBEUI
    - **C.** NCP
    - **D.** SMB

REVIEW ANSWERS

1. **B** NetBEUI will certainly meet the main objective and let you share resources, but it won't meet the secondary objective. This is because NetBEUI is a nonroutable protocol and therefore is not suitable for wide area networking.
2. **C** NetBEUI is a Transport layer protocol.
3. **B** NetWare does not support the NetBEUI protocol.
4. **D** NetWare uses MAC addressing to identify computers on the network.
5. **C** Always make sure that clients on a NetWare network are using the right frame type—the same frame type used by the servers. Autodetect works under most circumstances, but you may need to set the frame type manually.
6. **B** IPX is the only completely connectionless protocol on the list.

7. **B D** You could use IPX/SPX (B) using a NetWare client kit, or you could use NWLink (D) using Microsoft's client.
8. **A C D** NetBEUI is nonroutable, so that eliminates routers (B), but all the other devices listed will forward NetBEUI data packets.
9. **A** NWLink is generally used to connect to NetWare servers and is not a protocol associated with Linux. Installing TCP/IP on a Windows machine and SAMBA on the Linux boxes would be the most straightforward way to share both files and printers between Windows and Linux systems.
10. **A** NetBIOS is a Session layer protocol originally used by the NetBEUI protocol suite. Versions of Microsoft Windows prior to Windows 2000 also used NetBIOS as a Session layer protocol for TCP/IP.

TCP/IP

ITINERARY

- **Objective 6.01** The TCP/IP Protocol Suite
- **Objective 6.02** IP Addressing
- **Objective 6.03** Subnet Masks and Subnetting
- **Objective 6.04** IP Version 6
- **Objective 6.05** Routing
- **Objective 6.06** Transport Layer Protocols
- **Objective 6.07** Session Layer Protocols
- **Objective 6.08** Name Resolution
- **Objective 6.09** TCP/IP Utilities

NEWBIE	SOME EXPERIENCE	EXPERT
6 hours	3 hours	2 hours

Take the fact that we've given TCP/IP its own chapter as an indication that it's an important topic for the Network+ certification exam! All major operating systems, including UNIX, Linux, Windows 95/98/Me, Windows NT/2000/XP, and Novell NetWare, support TCP/IP. In fact, UNIX has used TCP/IP since the protocol was first announced in the early 1970s.

The U.S. Defense Advanced Research Projects Agency (DARPA) first proposed TCP/IP as a standard for connecting various existing networks so that they could exchange information in 1973. One aim was to develop a common standard to replace the growing number of proprietary and incompatible ones that were emerging. The work undertaken as part of the DARPA project eventually led to the development of the TCP/IP protocol suite, and the Internet as we know it today. To read more about the history of TCP/IP, visit the Internet Society's web page at: http://www.isoc.org/internet/history/.

One of TCP/IP's great virtues lies in its use for *heterogeneous* computing environments—environments that include more than one type of system. If you want your Macs to talk to your mainframe, and your NetWare server to talk to your Windows 2003 Server, or your laptop to talk to your wireless router, TCP/IP provides a common language that each of these environments understand. Each of the protocols within the TCP/IP protocol suite defines a set of rules for passing data between hosts, so the packet structure of an IP packet coming from a PC should look no different from an IP packet originating on a Macintosh.

Local Lingo

host In TCP/IP, a *host* is any machine that can send or receive data on the network (clients, servers, printers, routers, and so forth). Every host needs at least one IP address.

So what have we got then? An "ancient" protocol from the 1970s that is, at this very moment, responsible for carrying the data passing through the world's high-tech Internet infrastructure? Sounds about right! The DARPA folks designed the TCP/IP for adaptability, and they succeeded brilliantly.

The TCP/IP Protocol Suite

The first thing to know about TCP/IP is that it is not a single protocol; it is a *suite* of protocols. The term "suite" indicates that a number of protocols are included. TCP/IP is made up of a number of protocols that work together to make this protocol the most popular protocol in networking today. Each protocol in the TCP/IP protocol suite performs a specific role. This section identifies some of the popular protocols in the TCP/IP protocol suite and what their role is.

Application Protocols

The first type of protocol to discuss is the application-level protocols within the TCP/IP protocol suite. Application-level protocols are responsible for initiating some sort of request (on the client) or answering that request (on the server). For example, when you surf the Internet, you are using an application (your web browser) that is sending a request to a web server for a specific page. This communication happens across TCP/IP using an application protocol known as *HTTP (Hypertext Transfer Protocol)*. In this example, the client is sending an HTTP request (requesting a web page), which gets sent across the network to the HTTP server, and the server answers this request by sending the web page back to the web browser.

To summarize, application protocols are used by applications to send out requests to other systems on the network (or Internet). Here are some examples of popular application-level protocols:

- **SMTP** This protocol is used to send mail across a TCP/IP network.
- **POP3** One of the protocols used to read e-mail over a TCP/IP network.
- **IMAP4** An alternative protocol used for reading e-mail over a TCP/IP network. IMAP4 supports additional features not available using POP3, such as server-based folders for storing e-mail.
- **FTP** A protocol used to transfer files over a TCP/IP network.
- **HTTP** The protocol used to deliver web pages from a web server to a web browser.
- **DNS** The protocol used to convert an FQDN (fully qualified domain name) to an IP address (we will discuss this protocol more, later in the chapter).

Transport Protocols

When an application sends out a request, the request needs to be specified as either a connection-oriented request or a connectionless request. A *connection-oriented* request means that before data can be sent between two hosts, they must first introduce themselves (create a connection to the remote system) and agree upon the rules for their conversation. This is very similar to the way you have conversations with individuals you meet at a party. You don't just walk up to someone and start talking. You first introduce yourself: "Hi, my name is Glen Clarke...." After the formal introduction, the communication starts. A connection between two systems is known as a *session.* Connection-oriented protocols are also responsible for monitoring the session and ensuring that the data sent throughout the session is received at the other end. If data is not received at the remote host, it will then be re-sent. Transport protocols decide on how data is transported, either with a session or without a session being established.

Connectionless communication is a type of communication where a host does not establish a session with the remote system (the system it is talking to) before sending the data, and when data is sent to the remote host it is not monitored to ensure that it has reached its destination. Connectionless communication is like throwing a piece of data out on the wire and if it reaches its destination, great, and if it doesn't, that is okay, too.

TCP (Transmission Control Protocol) is the connection-oriented protocol in the TCP/IP protocol suite. When an application-level protocol passes the request to TCP, TCP will establish a session with the remote host and monitor the session for its duration. TCP ensures that the data reaches the destination. HTTP, SMTP, and FTP are a few of the application protocols that use TCP as the transport for communication.

UDP (User Datagram Protocol) is the connectionless protocol in the TCP/IP protocol suite. If an application-level protocol creates a request that does not need to establish or monitor a session, it will use the UDP protocol. DNS queries are a type of application request that use UDP instead of TCP as the transport, meaning that there is no session involved in the conversation.

Exam Tip

Be sure to know the difference between TCP and UDP when preparing for the Network+ exam.

Internet Protocols

Before we discuss the next set of protocols within the TCP/IP protocol suite, let's review what we have so far. When you sit at a machine and surf the Internet, the request that is made uses the HTTP application-level protocol. Before this request can leave your system, it must decide whether it will be a TCP (connection oriented) or a UDP (connectionless) request. HTTP as a protocol always uses TCP, which means TCP will ensure that the data reaches the destination and that a session is created with the remote web server before your system can send the request. Now the next step. How does your system identify itself on the network (or Internet), and how does it route (or send) the data to the remote system? This is not the role of TCP but rather the role of IP (Internet Protocol).

IP (Internet Protocol)

The IP (Internet Protocol) found in the TCP/IP protocol is responsible for the addressing and routing of data to the remote system—*addressing* meaning that IP is responsible for some sort of addressing scheme used to identify each system on the network (or Internet) and for determining how we use that address to route the data to the destination. The addressing scheme that IP uses is known as an *IP address.* The IP address is a unique number assigned to your system that looks something like 192.168.1.10. An entire section is devoted to IP addressing later in this chapter, so I will leave the rest of our discussion on IP for that section.

ARP (Address Resolution Protocol)

When a host sends data to a remote system, it must send the data to the MAC address of the remote system. The problem is, at this point your system only knows the IP address of the machine it wants to talk to. At the low level, you actually send the data to the MAC address that is burned into the network card of the destination computer. How does your system figure out what the MAC address is of the destination system? That is the purpose of the Address Resolution Protocol (ARP). ARP converts the IP address of the destination computer to the MAC address. It does this through broadcast. If computer A sends to computer B (which resides on the same local area network), computer A will yell out to everyone on the network (a broadcast), "Whoever has this IP address, I need your MAC address!" Then, the machine with that IP address will send its MAC address to whichever computer sent the broadcast out (computer A).

Exam Tip

Address Resolution Protocol (ARP) is responsible for converting an IP address (layer 3 address) to a MAC address (layer 2 address).

ICMP (Internet Control Message Protocol)

Another protocol that is important to mention in the TCP/IP protocol suite is the Internet Control Message Protocol (ICMP). ICMP is the reporting protocol of the protocol suite. If you have ever used the PING utility to verify that a remote system is up and running, you have seen replies come back to you (if that machine was up and running). ICMP is the protocol used by PING to report the replies to you. Or, if you have ever received the "destination host not found" error message when performing a PING, this message is also generated by ICMP.

To enable operating system developers to create programs and driver code to support all these protocols, the standards for the protocols were (and still are) published for all to see and comment on—and that's where our "designed by committee" statement comes in. Anyone who has a vested interest in the standards associated with TCP/IP can contribute to their development. Unlike most things designed by committee, TCP/IP actually works pretty well.

RFCs

The TCP/IP protocols are really a set of rules for communication. So where are these rules written down? The designers of TCP/IP standards record the details of each standard in a document called a *Request for Comment (RFC)*. For every TCP/IP protocol or application, there will be an associated RFC defining exactly how things are supposed to work. The Internet Architecture Board (IAB), a committee of the Internet Engineering Task Force (IETF), manages the RFC process. By looking up the appropriate RFCs, you can find out how a protocol works so that you can develop a version of it for your system. As you might expect, there have been many developments in networking technology since the 1970s, and the RFC process anticipates that these changes will occur. When a standard is updated, the original RFC is never revised. Instead, a new RFC *obsoletes* (that is, *replaces*) the older RFC as the definitive document defining the standard.

Always consult the most recent RFC on any particular topic. The File Transfer Protocol (FTP), for example, was originally proposed in 1971 (RFC 265) and has been updated numerous times as new capabilities have been added to the standard. RFC 959, the most recent definition of the RFC standard, was written in 1985 and *obsoletes* (*replaces*) all older definitions of the FTP standard, including RFC 265 (1971) and RFC 765 (1980). To find the most current RFC on a particular topic, visit the IETF's RFC repository at: http://www.ietf.org/rfc.html.

Some RFCs aren't actually about protocols but contain useful information and tutorials (and poems—see RFC 1121) about TCP/IP and the Internet. RFC 1118 is a great example. Titled "The Hitchhiker's Guide to the Internet," this document contains a very useful introduction to the Internet, its concepts, and terminology (even though it was written in 1989, the basics still hold true). Download a copy today—it will provide valuable background information that may help with your Network+ studies.

Travel Assistance

RFC 1118, "The Hitchhiker's Guide to the Internet," can be found at various locations, including http://www.ietf.org/rfc/rfc1118.txt.

In addition to the RFCs, there are two other categories of documents:

- **Standards documents (STDs)** These documents represent individual Internet (TCP/IP) standards and are released periodically in order to condense the relevant information from numerous related RFCs into a single document.
- **For Your Information (FYI) documents** These documents contain general information about Internet- and TCP/IP-related issues.

Exam Tip

You will not be expected to remember and quote RFC numbers on the exam—they are included here for your reference and optional further study.

Objective 6.02 IP Addressing

When installing TCP/IP on a system (or device), you are responsible for the configuration of the protocol. You will be responsible for configuring at least three settings in order to participate on the Internet or a WAN type environment:

- **IP address** A unique value that represents your system on a TCP/IP network.
- **Subnet mask** A value used to help you distinguish what network the host is a part of.
- **Default gateway** The IP address of the router for your network. The router is responsible for sending data off your network if needed.

Figure 6.1 displays the TCP/IP configuration dialog box on a system. In this figure you can see that the system has been configured with the IP address 192.168.75.38. Let's take a look at breaking this address down.

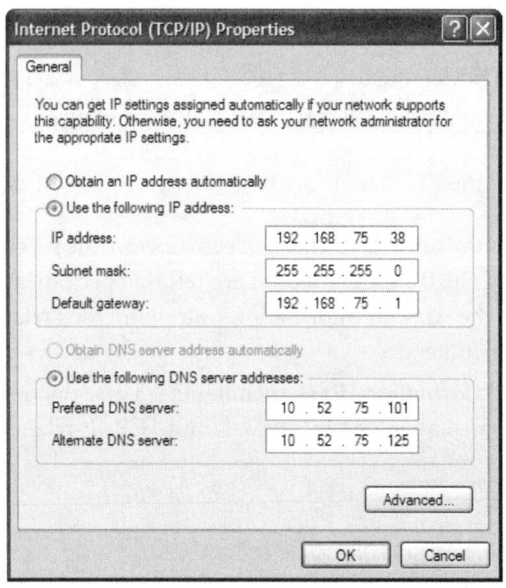

FIGURE 6.1 The basic TCP/IP settings in Windows XP

What Is an IP Address?

An IP address consists of four numbers separated by periods (such as 192.168.75.38). Each of these numbers has a binary representation (hidden from us in the background) of 8 bits. Because there are four numbers of 8 bits each (4×8=32), an IP address is a 32-bit value. Each of the 8 bits that is separated by a period is known as an *octet*. There are four octets in an IP address. 192 is an octet, 168 is an octet, 75 is an octet, and finally 38 is an octet.

Exam Tip

An IP address is a 32-bit number that is known as a layer 3 address. IP addresses are displayed in dotted decimal notation (for example, 192.168.4.56).

An IP address is divided into two parts; a network ID and a host ID. The network ID portion of the IP address will be the same for all hosts on the same network. For example, looking at Figure 6.1, the network ID for that IP address is 192.168.75 (the first three octets), which means that every system on this network will begin with 192.168.75. In this example, the last octet is the host ID portion, which is responsible for uniquely identifying the host within the network. In this example, every host on the network will begin the IP address with

192.168.75 because that is the network ID assigned. The first host on this network will get assigned 192.168.75.1 as an address, the second host will be given the IP address 192.168.75.2, and so on.

What Is a Subnet Mask?

How do you know what the network ID portion of your IP address is? This is the role of the subnet mask. If the subnet mask has "255" in an octet, the corresponding octet in the IP address is part of the subnet mask. Let's take a look at the configuration found in Figure 6.1 again in the following table:

	Octet 1	Octet 2	Octet 3	Octet 4
IP Address	192	168	75	38
Subnet Mask	255	255	255	0

The shaded cells in this table help you identify the fact that when you view your TCP/IP settings, the subnet mask determines what portion of the IP address is used by the network ID. Why is it so important for the configuration to identify what the network ID is? When you communicate with another system, your IP address is compared against the IP address of the destination to determine if the destination computer exists on the same network as you. For example, let's say that your system is configured as shown in the preceding table, and let's assume you are trying to communicate with a web server that has the IP address 192.163.45.10. Is this system on the same network as you? The answer is no, because the network IDs are different. The philosophy here is if these systems were on the same network, they would have the same network ID. Now look at the following table:

	Octet 1	Octet 2	Octet 3	Octet 4
IP Address	192	168	75	38
Subnet Mask	255	255	255	0
Destination IP	192	163	45	10

Your system uses this network ID to determine whether the destination computer exists on the network because, if the destination system does exist on the same network, your system can send the data directly to it. If your computer is on a different network (as determined by the subnet mask), your computer will need to forward the data to the router, which will then send the data off the network. You don't want to bother the router unless you have to, so only data destined for a different network is passed to the router. Your computer knows who the router is because of the default gateway entry in your TCP/IP settings. The default gateway specifies who the router is on the network.

Let's summarize what we know about your TCP/IP configuration. Your system has an IP address that is made up of a network ID and a host ID. The network ID identifies the network, whereas the host ID identifies that system on the network. The combination of the two ensures uniqueness in the world. The network ID is determined by the subnet mask and is used to decide whether the computer you wish to send data to is on the same network. Your system needs to know this so it can decide whether it needs to send the data to a router (for remote communication).

Understanding Binary

Let's focus on just the IP address for a bit (no pun intended). I mentioned that an IP address is a 32-bit value, which contains 8 bits in each octet. When troubleshooting TCP/IP, we work with the decimal representation of the IP address, whereas the computer (more specifically, the IP protocol) uses the binary representation. Let's look at how to convert a decimal value to binary, and a binary value to decimal; we will use the first octet of the IP address used earlier in the discussion as the example (192). The 8 bits that make up an octet each have a numeric value associated with them. The following table displays the numeric values associated with each of the 8 bits in an octet:

Bit	**1**	**2**	**3**	**4**	**5**	**6**	**7**	**8**
Value	128	64	32	16	8	4	2	1

When converting from decimal to binary, you will need to find out what bits need to be enabled (set to a "1" or "on" state) to come up with the decimal value desired. For example, our first octet has a decimal value of 192. We can accomplish 192 by enabling (setting to 1) the first bit and the second bit (128+64). This will give us the value of 192. All other bits are disabled, or set to an "off" state (set to 0). In our example, because we did not use bits 3 to 8 to reach a decimal value of 192, those bits are set to 0. Therefore, the binary representation of 192 is 11000000.

Let's look at one more example—the number 37. What is the 8-bit pattern for 37? To reach a value of 37, we will need to enable the third bit (which has a value of 32), the sixth bit (a value of 4), and the eighth bit (a value of 1):

32+4+1=37

Therefore, the 8-bit pattern to get the decimal value of 37 is 00100101. This is shown in the following table:

Bit	1	2	3	4	5	6	7	8
Value	128	64	32	16	8	4	2	1
State	0	0	1	0	0	1	0	1

You would take the exact opposite approach if you needed to convert binary to decimal. Suppose you have the binary value 10111001. To convert this to its decimal equivalent, you would add the values associated with each of the bits together (in this example, 128+32+16+8+1=185).

If you add the values of all 8 bits in an octet, you will get the number 255; therefore, 255 is the maximum number you will ever see in an octet. This also means that there are 256 possible numbers in an octet ranging from 0 to 255.

Exam Tip

We use the term "layer 3 addresses" when referring to IP addresses to distinguish them from MAC addresses, which we refer to as "layer 2 addresses." Keep in mind that IP addresses do not replace MAC addresses—they serve different functions and operate at different OSI layers. You need the MAC addresses to handle the addressing of hosts for physical delivery, and you need IP addresses to support the routing of the data to the destination network.

IP Address Classes

You know that the subnet mask determines which octets map out to the network ID and which octets map out to the host ID portion. But how do you know what the subnet mask is? The subnet mask is based off what address class the address is. The IANA (Internet Assigned Numbers Authority) broke up all the possible IP addresses into smaller blocks known as *licenses.* These licenses were then granted to various organizations so that they could connect to the Internet and be certain that their addresses were unique.

Recognizing that large organizations (such as major universities, the U.S. government, and large Internet service providers) would need large numbers of addresses while smaller organizations (such as local schools and small companies) would need far fewer addresses, the IANA wisely did not pass out the addresses in equal chunks. Instead, they divided the available addresses into three classes:

- **Class A** These networks use the first 8 bits of the IP address (the first octet) to specify the network ID and use the remaining 24 bits to identify individual hosts. If the first octet is the network ID, that makes the subnet mask 255.0.0.0 for class A networks. A class A network can have up to 2^{24} different host IDs, which means the network can have up to 16,777,214 hosts (two host addresses are reserved for the network ID and the broadcast address—more on that later).
- **Class B** These networks use the first 16 bits of the IP address (the first two octets) to specify the network ID and use the remaining 16 bits to identify individual hosts. If the first two octets are used for the network ID, that makes the subnet mask 255.255.0.0 for class B addresses. A class B network can have up to 2^{16} different host IDs, so the network can have up to 65,534 hosts (two host addresses are reserved for the network ID and the broadcast address).
- **Class C** These networks use the first 24 bits of the IP address (first three octets) to specify the network ID and use the remaining 8 bits to identify individual hosts. If the first three octets are used for the network ID, that makes the subnet mask 255.255.255.0 for class C addresses. A class C network can have up to 2^{8} different host IDs, so the network can have up to 254 hosts (two host addresses are reserved for the network ID and the broadcast address).

Exam Tip

Class A addresses have a default subnet mask of 255.0.0.0, class B addresses have a default subnet mask of 255.255.0.0, and class C addresses have a default subnet mask of 255.255.255.0.

We now know that a class B address has a subnet mask of 255.255.0.0, but how do we know that the address we are looking at is a class B over a class A or C? If you look at the first octet of any IP address, you can identify what address class it is. If the first octet has a number between 1 and 126, the address is class A. If the first octet has a number between 128 and 191, it is a class B address. If the first octet has a number between 192 and 223, you are working with a class C address. Table 6.1 summarizes the IP address classes.

Let's look at an example. If you are troubleshooting a system that has an IP address of 192.168.7.124, using Table 6.1 you can determine that this address is a

TABLE 6.1 IP Class Table

If the first octet is between…	…then the address class is…	…which has a default subnet mask of…	…which means that the network ID portion of the address is…	…leaving the host ID as…	…so this split (network ID/host ID) looks like this…
1 and 126	A	255.0.0.0	the first octet	the last three octets	N.H.H.H
128 and 191	B	255.255.0.0	the first two octets	the last two octets	N.N.H.H
192 and 223	C	255.255.255.0	the first three octets	the last octet	N.N.N.H

class C address. Also, you know that a class C address has a default subnet mask of 255.255.255.0. A subnet mask of 255.255.255.0 means that the first three octets in the IP address are the network ID, while the last octet is the host ID. This means that every computer on that network must begin with 192.168.7.x. Otherwise, they will not be able to communicate with one another.

Class D and E Addresses

If the first octet is between 224 and 247, the address is a class D (multicast) address—used for sending data to a "group" of systems, such as you might want to do for a videoconference. Addresses with the first octet set between 248 and 255 are class E (experimental) addresses.

Exam Tip

The Network+ exam doesn't cover class D and E addresses. However, multicast technology will be worth watching as companies begin to send more rich media content across their internal networks.

The Loopback Address

If you look at the preceding table a little more closely, you'll see that the number 127 does not appear in any of the ranges for the first octet. TCP/IP sets aside address 127.0.0.1 for internal testing (actually, the entire 127.0.0.0 subnet is reserved for internal testing, but in practice the 127.0.0.1 address is the only one that really gets used). Referred to as the *loopback address,* messages sent to 127.0.0.1 never leave the sending machine; instead, they are redirected back through the internal software layers to communicate with network software running on the "localhost," a fancy name for "this machine." The loopback address comes in handy for confirming whether the TCP/IP software stack has initialized properly on your system.

Travel Advisory

When you're assigning an IP address to a system, 127 can appear in the host ID portion of the IP address, but not in the first octet of the network ID.

When troubleshooting why you cannot communicate with a remote host, if you want to verify that your system has initialized the TCP/IP software stack, you could "ping localhost" or "ping 127.0.0.1" at a command prompt. If you get a reply from either of these commands, you can be sure that TCP/IP is working on your system. If you don't get a reply, you may consider reinstalling TCP/IP.

Exam Tip

The loopback address, 127.0.0.1, is also known as *localhost.*

How Many Hosts Can Exist in an Address Class?

Each address class has support for a specific number of hosts on that network; you can determine this by looking at the IP address. Our example, 192.168.7.124 is a class C address (we know this because of the 192 in the first octet). A class C address has 255.255.255.0 as the subnet mask, which means that the first three octets are the network ID, and the last octet is the host ID. The numbers that can appear in this last octet are 0 (which is 00000000 in binary) to 255 (which is 11111111 in binary). Having host IDs that range from 0 to 255 will allow for 256 possible addresses, which means that with a class C network you can have 256 hosts in total. However, we are not allowed to use the first number in that range (which is 0), and the last number in that range (which is 255) because they are reserved as a way to refer to "the network" (192.168.7.0) and the broadcast address (192.168.7.255). Therefore, the number of hosts that can exist on a class C address is 254 (256 minus the two illegal addresses). Refer to the rules in the next section for more about the network address and the broadcast address.

While class C addresses may have 254 hosts (256 minus the two illegal addresses of 0 and 255), a class B address has a subnet mask of 255.255.0.0, so you have the last two octets that are used by the host ID. Because you can have 256 values in each octet, you can calculate the number of hosts as 256×256, which equals 65,536 hosts on the network (don't forget to take the two illegal addresses away). You can calculate this a different way as well. We have 16 bits that appear in the host ID portion of the IP address, and because each bit can have two possible values (1 or 0) you can calculate the total number of hosts that may exist on the network by using this formula:

$$\text{Number of hosts} = 2^{(\text{number of host bits})}$$

Our example would give us the formula 2^{16}, which equals 65,536. Table 6.2 summarizes how many hosts may exist on each class network.

TABLE 6.2 IP Network and Host Address Ranges

Address Class	Number of Bits in Network ID	Number of Bits in Host ID	Maximum Number of Hosts on That Class of Network
A	8	24	$2^{24}-2=6,777,214$
B	16	16	$2^{16}-2=65,534$
C	24	8	$2^{8}-2=254$

IP Address, Facts, Rules, and Regulations

There are some additional rules to remember when assigning IP addresses to systems on the network. Here are some fundamental rules that cannot be broken:

- *IP addresses cannot be duplicated.* You are not allowed to assign two systems the same IP address; doing so will result in an IP address conflict message and a system that is unable to communicate on the network.
- *127 cannot appear in the first octet.* You are not allowed to use 127 as the first octet of the IP address. It is reserved as the loopback address (also known as *localhost*).
- *All host bits cannot be set to zero.* The host ID portion of an IP address is not allowed to have all the host bits set to zero. This is reserved as a way to refer to the network ID. For example, the 192.168.7.x network is a class C address and has a subnet mask of 255.255.255.0. This means that the first three octets make up the network ID whereas the last octet is the host ID. The host ID bits cannot be set to 0000000. This is reserved as a way to refer to the network. To reference the 192.168.7.x network properly, use 192.168.7.0 (the zero comes from adding the value of the 8 bits in the host ID, which is 0).
- *All host bits cannot be set to one.* The host ID portion of the IP address is not allowed to have all the bits in the host ID set to an enabled state (all 1s) because this address is reserved for broadcast. A broadcast is a way to send data to everyone on the network. In our 192.168.7.x example, all host bits set to 1 would make the decimal value of 255. Therefore, 192.168.7.255 is illegal to assign to a host because it is the broadcast address for that network.

IP Address Summary

- IP addresses are 32-bit values.
- IP addresses are commonly referred to in dotted decimal notation (for example, 192.168.7.34), which uses a decimal number between 0 and 255 in each of the four octets. Each octet is an 8 bit value.
- The IP address consists of two parts: a network ID and a host ID.
- You can determine an IP address class by examining the first octet. If the octet ranges from 1 to 126, it is a class A address; if the first octet ranges from 128 to 191, you are looking at a class B address; and if the first octet ranges from 192 to 223, you have a class C address.
- The network itself is represented by an IP address. The IP address that represents "the network" will have all host bits (host bits being all the bits in the host ID portion of the IP address) set to zero. This address is illegal to assign to an actual host.
- The network also has a broadcast address. The broadcast address is how a system sends data to all other hosts on the network. Having all bits within the host ID portion set to 1 represents the broadcast address. This address is illegal to assign to an actual host.
- To verify that TCP/IP has initialized on your system and is functioning correctly, you may "ping" the loopback address. The loopback address is known as 127.0.0.1, or by the name "localhost."

ANDing: Are You on My Network?

You know that the network ID is used to determine whether the destination host exists on the same network as the sending computer. If the network IDs are the same for the source and destination systems, the two are on the same network, but if the network IDs are different, the two systems exist on different networks. If the systems exist on different networks, the data must be passed to the default gateway, which is the router for the network.

When communicating from one system to another, the IP protocol on the sending computer determines whether the destination system exists on the same network through a process called *ANDing*. ANDing is done at the bit level. The first thing that needs to be done when ANDing is that the sending system has to AND its IP address with its own subnet mask to create an answer. Then the *sending* system uses the destination IP address and ANDs it with the same subnet mask to generate an answer. If the two answers are equal, the two systems exist on the same network. Let's look at an example.

Let's assume your system has an IP address of 181.107.3.15, and my system has an IP address of 216.83.11.24. Do these systems exist on the same network? You can figure it out quickly by looking at the first address, and based off the first octet you know it is a class B address (class B addresses use the first two octets as the network ID). This would mean that my system would need to use the same first two octets if we were on the same network. In this example, the first two octets (the network ID) are different, so the two systems exist on different networks. Let's see if ANDing will lead us to the same conclusion.

First, convert the sending computer's (your system) IP address and subnet mask to binary values and place them one above the other like you were to do some addition. Then add the two together. If there is a 1 in one placeholder of the IP address and a 1 in the corresponding position of the subnet mask, when you add those two bits together you get a 1. But if any other combination is ANDed together, the answer is 0. Our example is shown here:

```
Sender IP address in binary: 10110101.01101011.00000011.00001111
(181.107.3.15)
      Subnet mask in binary: 11111111.11111111.00000000.00000000
(255.255.0.0)
                     result: 10110101.01101011.00000000.00000000
```

Now that you have the result of the sending system ANDed against the sender's subnet mask, you do the same thing with the destination address to generate a result:

```
     Destination IP address: 11011000.01010011.00001011.00011000
(216.83.11.24)
      Subnet mask in binary: 11111111.11111111.00000000.00000000
(255.255.0.0)
                     result: 11011000.01010011.00000000.00000000
```

When comparing the results from the two ANDing operations, you can see that the two results are different, which means that the two systems are on different networks. Your system would send the data to the default gateway because it knows that my system is on a different network.

IP Addresses: Classless Notation

Now that you have the rules for IP address classes, it's time to start breaking them. IP addresses that divide themselves into network and host IDs based on the address class (which is based off the value of the first octet) are called *classful addresses.* Modern networking hardware can be configured to ignore the class addresses and use an arbitrary number of bits for the host and network IDs. Instead of relying on the class of the address, we can use *classless* IP addresses and simply indicate how we want to divide up the address. Table 6.3 shows one way

TABLE 6.3 Classless (CIDR) Address Notation

Sample Address	Class	Classless Notation
14.12.23.244	A	14.12.23.244/8
132.12.23.233	B	132.12.23.233/16
214.123.2.93	C	214.123.2.93/24

that we can indicate the number of bits used for the network ID. We just add a slash (/) to the end of the IP address and specify the number of bits assigned to the network portion of the IP address. For example, you know that the IP address 131.107.5.10 uses the first two octets as the network ID when you see the subnet mask of 255.255.0.0. You may also indicate this by using the CIDR (Classless Inter Domain Routing) notation 131.107.5.10/16, which means that the first 16 bits are the network ID. This way of specifying an IP address and its network ID portion is called *classless* or *CIDR* notation, and is shown in Table 6.3.

Classless notation makes it easier to see straightaway the number of IP address bits actually assigned to the network ID. Whereas the old "classful" rules required network architects to use either 8, 16, or 24 bits for the network address, CIDR allows them to divide up their network address space more flexibly. See the discussion on subnetting later in this chapter for more detail.

Private Networks

Although you can use pretty much any address range you want if you're not connecting to the Internet, RFC 1918 defines a range of class A, B, and C addresses that have been declared "nonroutable" on the Internet. "Nonroutable" means that if you *do* use them *and* you have connectivity to the Internet, your Internet routers (or *gateways* in proper TCP/IP lingo) won't pass your in-house traffic on elsewhere. Using these special addresses, you run *absolutely* no danger of your IP addressing scheme clashing with anyone else's (see Figure 6.2). These so-called "private IP addresses" are shown in Table 6.4.

TABLE 6.4 Private IP Address Ranges

Address Class	Private Address Range
A	10.0.0.0 to 10.255.255.255
B	172.16.0.0 to 172.31.255.255
C	192.168.0.0 to 192.168.255.255

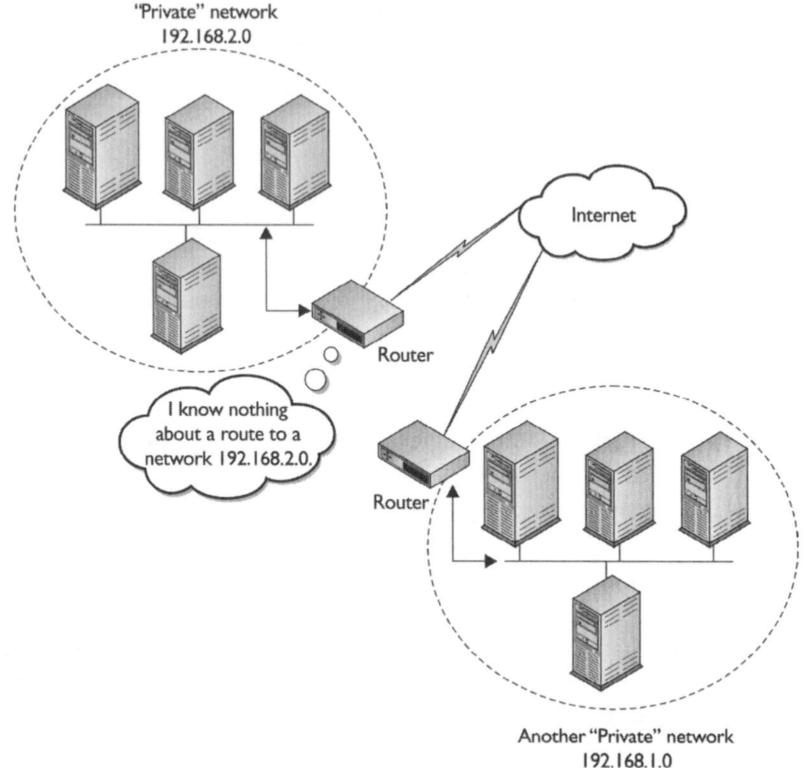

FIGURE 6.2 Private IP addresses are not routable.

Travel Assistance

Be aware that it is possible to use private addresses inside your network and still use the Internet. Most networks use technologies such as network address translation (NAT) to translate the private address to a public address on the way out through the router to reach the Internet.

Objective 6.03 Subnet Masks and Subnetting

Before we get into the basics of subnetting, let's review what you know of a subnet mask. You learned that the class of an IP address determines what

TABLE 6.5 Default Subnet Masks

IP Class	Default Subnet Mask
A	255.0.0.0
B	255.255.0.0
C	255.255.255.0

the *default* subnet mask of a system is. The subnet mask defines how many bits of the IP address refer to the network ID portion of the IP address. Table 6.5 reviews the various main IP classes and their corresponding default subnet masks.

If an octet has "255" (11111111 in binary) in the subnet mask, the corresponding octet in the IP address is part of the network ID. If an octet equals zero in the subnet mask, the corresponding octet in the IP address refers to part of the host ID. On a bit-by-bit basis, if a specific bit in the subnet mask is a 1, the corresponding bit in the IP address given is part of the *network* address. If a specific bit in the subnet mask is a 0, the corresponding bit in the IP address given is part of the *host* address.

Let's look at a few examples of these default subnet masks at work. For the class B address 187.12.54.123, the default subnet mask is 255.255.0.0. Address 187.12.54.123 translates to "host 54.123 on network 187.12.0.0." Table 6.6 shows other examples of translating IP addresses into their equivalent network and host IDs using the subnet mask.

Notice that we keep talking about the "default" subnet mask. Just because it's the default doesn't mean that we have to use it. We can change the subnet mask to split the IP range, which is currently one network ID, into multiple network IDs by using a feature called *subnetting*.

Subnetting Basics

Subnetting allows you to take a single IP-based network address and divide (subnet) it into smaller sections. You accomplish subnetting by borrowing bits

TABLE 6.6 Translating IP Addresses into Network and Host IDs Using the Subnet Mask

IP Address	Default Subnet Mask	Network ID	Host ID
210.35.156.198	255.255.255.0	210.35.156.0	198
125.25.210.12	255.0.0.0	125.0.0.0	25.210.12
180.220.215.19	255.255.0.0	180.220.0.0	215.19
155.35.123.99	255.255.0.0.	155.35.0.0	123.99
142.98.189.222	255.255.0.0	142.98.0.0	189.122
85.123.225.19	255.0.0.0	85.0.0.0	123.225.19

from the host ID portion of the IP address and use them as network ID bits (or in this case, subnet bits). This allows you to have more networks, but less hosts per network (because you took some of the host bits away). Subnetting is ideal for situations where you need to split a network address space into multiple subnets, or networks. You may want to split your one network into multiple physical networks so that you can optimize network performance and cut down on broadcasts by placing a router between the two network segments. But, if you only have one IP range, you will need to manipulate the addressing so that you have two address ranges instead of one—one range for each side of the network. Figure 6.3 shows a subnetted network.

The first step when subnetting is to decide how many subnets (sections) you want to break your network address into (we will use the network address 131.107.0.0 in our example), because this determines how many binary bits of the host ID you will need to borrow. To determine how many bits you will need to take, we have a little cheat method. Picture that you want four networks. To

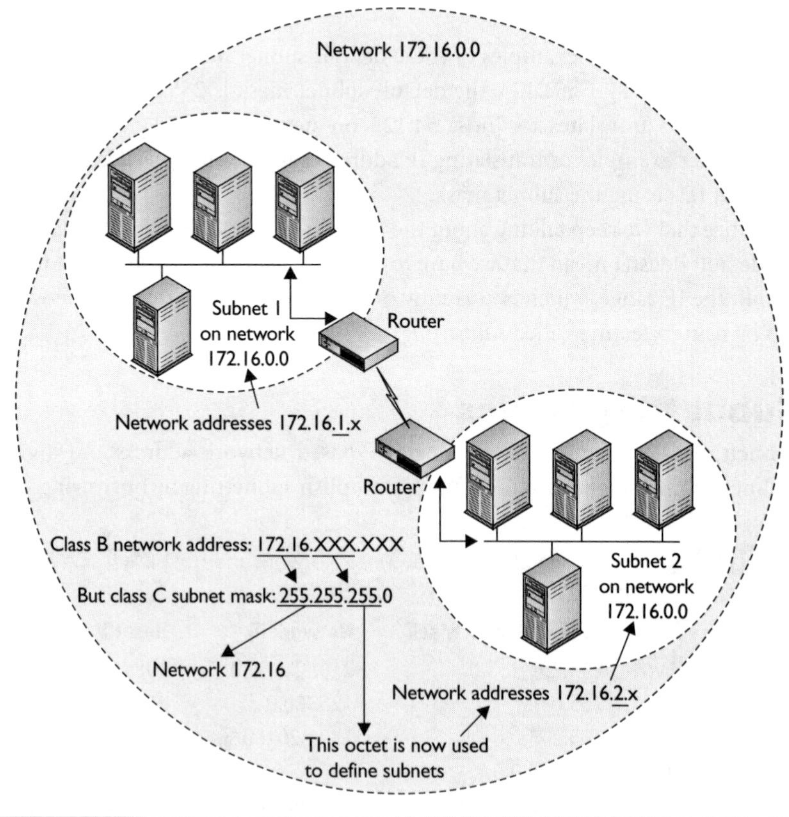

FIGURE 6.3 A subnetted network

determine how many bits you need to take, you simply look at the binary table of 8 bits and enable the bits that would make the number 4. This should be 00000100. Then, as shown in the following table, you count the number of bits (from right to left) used to get to your last enabled bits. In this example, we have 3 bits. Therefore, we need to take 3 bits from the host ID portion of the address range to create four networks.

Value	128	64	32	16	8	4	2	1
Enabled						**1**	**0**	**0**

The next step is to look at your network address and determine what the subnet mask is. Because 131.107.0.0 is a class B address, you know that you have a subnet mask of 255.255.0.0. The next step is to place this in binary and take the 3 bits from the host ID and enable them (set them to 1; see the following bolded bits) to make them subnetted bits:

```
Original Subnet mask in binary:
 11111111.11111111.00000000.00000000 (255.255.0.0)
Using 3 bits for subnetting:
 11111111.11111111.11100000.00000000 (255.255.224.0)
On our class B network, every host must now use the subnet mask
255.255.224.0
```

Looking at this example, you can see that once you steal 3 bits from the host ID portion and use them for the subnet bits, it changes what the default subnet mask is in decimal format. The new subnet mask for each of the four networks will be 255.255.224.0.

The next thing you need to do is determine what the network ID, broadcast ID, first valid IP address, and last valid IP address are for each of the four subnets. You can figure this out by focusing on the 3 bits you have stole. Using the original network ID (131.107.x.y), you figure out all the possible combinations of on and off states for the 3 bits in the third octet. Once you have the different combinations figured out, you convert the last two octets to decimal values using your newly acquired binary math skills! You should come up with the following:

```
Subnet 1:    131.107.00000000.00000000 (131.107.0.0) -
               ILLEGAL TO USE
Subnet 2:    131.107.00100000.00000000 (131.107.32.0)
Subnet 3:    131.107.01000000.00000000 (131.107.64.0)
Subnet 4:    131.107.01100000.00000000 (131.107.96.0)
Subnet 5:    131.107.10000000.00000000 (131.107.128.0)
Subnet 6:    131.107.10100000.00000000 (131.107.160.0)
Subnet 7:    131.107.11000000.00000000 (131.107.192.0)
Subnet 8:    131.107.11100000.00000000 (131.107.224.0) -
               ILLEGAL TO USE
```

The first thing to note is that you are not allowed to use the network ranges where all subnet bits are set to 0 and where all subnet bits are set to 1. So, of the eight possible combinations, only six are usable networks. Let's break down what we have in the six subnets. The 3 bolded bits are the subnet bits, and the remaining 13 bits to the right are the host bits. The next step is to determine the network ID, first valid address, last valid address, and broadcast address by manipulating the host bits.

To determine the network ID, you will convert the binary addresses to decimal while the host bits are all disabled (a value of 0). This means that the first valid network ID (which is the second subnet) is 131.107.32.0. The first valid address on that network can be determined by enabling the least significant bit in the host ID (the bit farthest right; the most significant bit is the bit farthest left). When you enable the least significant bit, you have a binary value (for the last two octets) of

```
131.107.00100000.00000001 = 131.107.32.1
```

This would make the address 131.107.32.1 the first valid address on the 131.107.32.0 network. Next, you need to calculate the last valid address on that network; you do this by enabling all host bits except for the last one, like this:

```
131.107.00111111.11111110 = 131.107.63.254
```

So that's the last valid address of the 131.107.32.0 network. The final address to calculate for the 131.107.32.0 subnetwork is the broadcast address. The broadcast address can be determined by enabling all host bits, as shown here:

```
131.107.00111111.11111111 = 131.107.63.255
```

You have now completed subnetting the 131.107.0.0 network and have calculated all the required information for the first subnet. Let's review what the final outcome for the first subnet is. The network ID is 131.107.32.0, and the new subnet mask for this network is 255.255.224.0. The first valid address is 131.107.32.1, and the last valid address is 131.107.63.254. The broadcast address for this subnet is 131.107.63.255. You just need to calculate the same four pieces of information for each of the remaining subnets. Here is what you should come up with (don't forget that the subnet mask is the same for all subnets—255.255.224.0):

Subnet	Network ID	First Valid Address	Last Valid Address	Broadcast
Subnet 2	131.107.32.0	131.107.32.1	131.107.63.254	131.107.63.255
Subnet 3	131.107.64.0	131.107.64.1	131.107.95.254	131.107.95.255

Subnet	Network ID	First Valid Address	Last Valid Address	Broadcast
Subnet 4	131.107.96.0	131.107.96.1	131.107.127.254	131.107.127.255
Subnet 5	131.107.128.0	131.107.128.1	131.107.159.254	131.107.159.255
Subnet 6	131.107.160.0	131.107.160.1	131.107.223.254	131.107.223.255

Travel Assistance

For a useful guide to subnetting, visit http://support.microsoft.com/support/kb/articles/q164/0/15.asp.

Objective 6.04 IP Version 6

The word is out (actually, it has been for some time)—the Internet's running out of spare 32-bit IP addresses. What to do? Simple, use bigger addresses. Make everything backward compatible with the existing address scheme? No problem; here's IP version 6….

Sounds easy, but it has taken many years to perfect a replacement for the 32-bit IP addressing scheme—known, by the way, as IP version 4, or IPv4. ("What happened to version 5?" I hear you ask. Well, it never really existed, so don't worry about it!)

Exam Tip

The 32-bit IP addressing scheme is known as IP version 4 (IPv4). The new 128-bit scheme is known as IP version 6 (IPv6) or "IP, Next Generation" (IPng).

With a 128-bit address range, IPv6 supports a mind-blowing 340,282,366,920,938,463,463,374,607,431,768,211,456 addresses, which equates to (so we're reliably informed) approximately 665,570,793,348,866,943,898,599 addresses per square meter of the surface of the planet Earth.

IPv6 is in use today on parts of the Internet, but it's not having much impact on the desktop (yet). The new addressing scheme was designed to slide in place of IPv4 relatively seamlessly, and parts of the Internet infrastructure are being upgraded all the time without us noticing. IPv6 will address three major issues that plague IPv4: a shortage of addresses, the increasing complexity of routing information, and problems caused by network address translation (NAT). For more information on network address translation, see Chapter 9.

Don't worry too much about IPv6 for the Network+ exam. You don't need to memorize the long numbers mentioned earlier—they're just there out of interest and to give you some sense of what "128-bit addressing" means. For the exam, you only need to know that IPv6 exists and that it uses a 128-bit address space. You may also be asked to identify the IPv6 loopback address, 0:0:0:0:0:0:0:1, so that you can determine whether IPv6 is properly installed.

Travel Assistance

Further information on IPv6 can be found at http://playground.sun.com/pub/ipng/html/ipng-main.html and http://www.microsoft.com/ipv6/.

Objective 6.05 Routing

If the data packets you're sending need to be forwarded to another network, your host machine must send these packets to a router. The router is responsible for routing (sending) the data to a different network. The router must know how to find every other network within the *internetwork,* which is the larger "network" made up of all the subnetted networks within your infrastructure.

Travel Advisory

The IP address for a host's default gateway must lie on the same network as the host (see Figure 6.4).

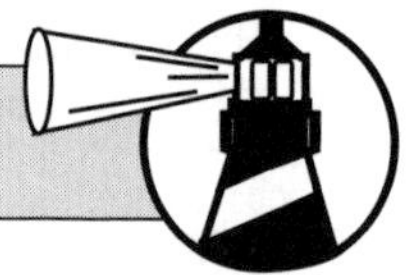

In order to route the packets to a remote network, the router uses a routing table that's built into the router's memory. The routing table lists all the destination networks and how the router can reach each of those destination networks. A router knows about any networks it is connected to, but it's typically programmed by the router administrator for any additional networks. You may use a dynamic routing protocol to have the routing tables built automatically by each router sharing the routes it knows about with the other routers.

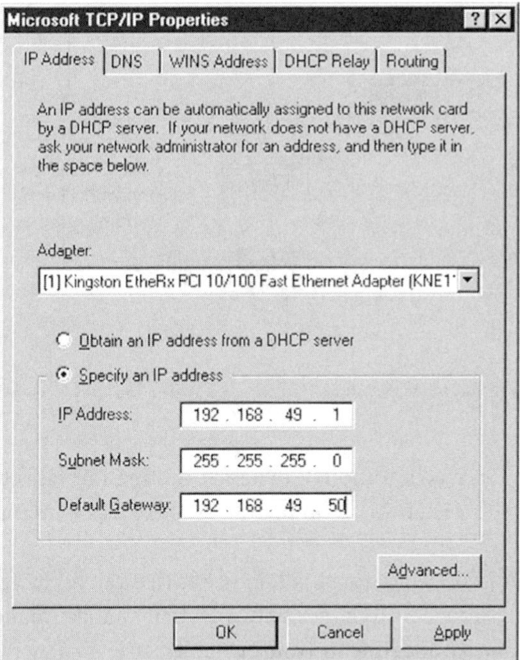

FIGURE 6.4 If you want to communicate with remote networks, you must specify the address of your default gateway.

Exam Tip

In a TCP/IP network, a host's nearest router is called its *default gateway*.

For proper routing to take place, all the routers must learn the location of the other networks within their internetwork.

Static and Dynamic Routing

Static routing requires a network tech to sit at each router and manually enter a route to each of the networks within the internetwork. The commands used vary from router to router, depending on the brand, but all supply the same essential information. With *dynamic routing* (see Figure 6.5), the routers automatically exchange information with the other routers, building their own list of routes to the various networks. The routers build this list, called a *routing table*, by sending out messages to other routers on the network, informing them of the

FIGURE 6.5 Dynamic routing takes place automatically between routers.

networks they can reach. Although dynamic routing increases traffic between the routers, it relieves network administrators of the task of manually configuring the routers.

Static routing works best for small networks that rarely change, whereas dynamic routing works best in larger networks that change frequently or lack a centralized authority to define the routing tables. In a small network with relatively few routers to configure, the network tech can easily take the time to set any necessary routes manually. In addition to eliminating dynamic routing traffic between the routers, static routing gives the network tech control over the routes used. In a larger network with dozens or even hundreds of routers, updating manual configurations becomes so time-consuming that some type of dynamic routing protocol becomes essential. Network architects can choose from a variety of dynamic routing protocols, with names such as Router Information Protocol (RIP), Open Shortest Path First (OSPF), Exterior Gateway Protocol (EGP), and Border Gateway Protocol (BGP). Each dynamic routing protocol has advantages and disadvantages in terms of ease of use and efficiency. As a general rule, the larger the network managed by a routing protocol, the more complex its configuration becomes.

Exam Tip

Routers configured with *static* routing require manual configuration of the routing table; routers configured with *dynamic* routing protocols such as RIP or OSPF communicate with each other and automatically calculate routes on their own.

Transport Layer Protocols

Remember that TCP is the Transmission Control Protocol (TCP), a *connection-oriented* protocol, establishing a connection between two hosts before transmitting data and verifying the receipt of the data before closing the connection (see Figure 6.6). TCP has a Transport layer colleague called UDP—the User Datagram Protocol (UDP).

UDP is a connectionless protocol and is used by applications that don't feel the need for all that connection-oriented mumbo jumbo. We do not concern ourselves with choosing a Transport layer protocol for a particular application—the programmers who designed the applications choose the appropriate protocol. Applications that send short bursts of data typically use UDP because of its low overhead (see Figure 6.7). Applications that send larger pieces of data typically use TCP because the cost of establishing the connection becomes less significant as the amount of data sent over that connection grows.

Exam Tip

TCP is connection oriented; UDP is connectionless.

Objective 6.07 Session Layer Protocols

Protocols at the Session layer manage the actual connections between communicating systems. TCP/IP networks currently support two major Session

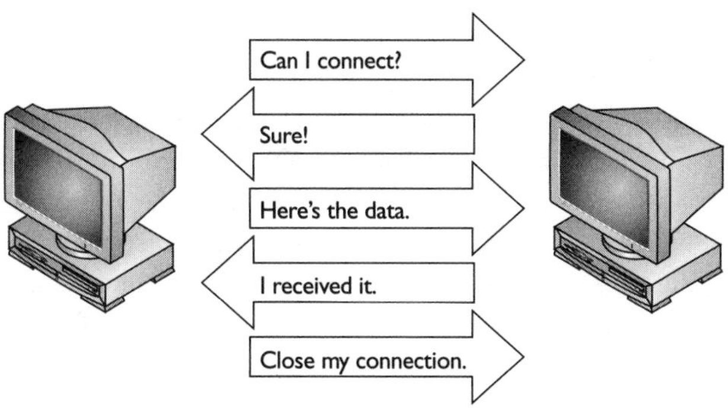

FIGURE 6.6 TCP is a connection-oriented protocol and checks every stage of the data transmission process.

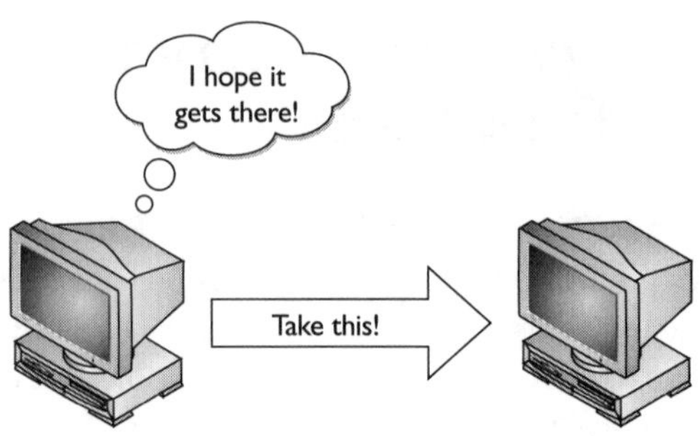

FIGURE 6.7 UDP is a connectionless protocol and sends data without any pre- or post-transmission setup and checking.

layer protocols: NetBIOS and Sockets. Microsoft operating systems using TCP/IP employ NetBIOS names to track connections, whereas typical Internet applications such as web browsers and FTP clients use Sockets, the traditional TCP/IP Session layer protocol. The way that these two protocols work is radically different, and they require specific configuration to work properly.

NetBIOS and Sockets

As you know, NetBIOS manages connections between machines using NetBIOS names—essentially the "computer name." The Sockets standard manages connections based on an IP address and a port number.

Local Lingo

socket A *socket* is a combination of a port number, protocol (either TCP or UDP), and an IP address. A socket defines the endpoints of communication, uniquely identifying a TCP/IP application that runs on a system.

The IP address identifies the machine at the other end of the connection, and the port number identifies the application on that system you wish to communicate with—for example, web servers use the Hypertext Transfer Protocol (TCP port 80) to accept traffic from a web client. The server sends the requested page to the client, using the socket to keep track of the connection.

Table 6.7 lists the most common Application layer protocols in the TCP/IP suite and their corresponding port numbers.

TABLE 6.7 The Most Common Application Layer Protocols

Application Layer Protocol	Ports	UDP or TCP	Description
FTP	20 and 21	TCP	File Transfer Protocol (FTP) transfers files between clients and servers. FTP uses two ports: 21 for control messages and 20 for the actual data. Note that FTP usernames and passwords are sent in clear text, posing a potentially serious security risk.
SSH	22	TCP	Secure Shell, a secure replacement for Telnet, encrypts both login information and any additional data sent over the connection.
SCP	22	TCP	Secure Copy uses the encryption provided by SSH to securely transfer files between hosts. Use SCP instead of FTP when available.
Telnet	23	TCP	Telnet allows a user to log in remotely and execute commands on a remote host. Typically, Telnet is often used to log into UNIX/Linux hosts and managed network devices such as routers and switches. Telnet sends usernames and passwords in clear text, posing a potentially serious security risk. When available, use SSH instead of Telnet.
SMTP	25	TCP	Simple Mail Transfer Protocol (SMTP) sends e-mail messages between mail servers. Mail clients also use SMTP to send outgoing e-mail to a mail server.
DNS	53	TCP and UDP	Domain Name Service (DNS) provides domain name resolution. TCP 53 is used for DNS zone transfers, whereas UDP 53 is used for DNS queries.
TFTP	69	UDP	Trivial File Transfer Protocol (TFTP) transfers files between servers and clients without requiring any user login. It's most commonly used for downloading operating systems and configuration files to systems with no local hard disk (for example, diskless workstations and routers).

TABLE 6.7 The Most Common Application Layer Protocols *(continued)*

Application Layer Protocol	Ports	UDP or TCP	Description
HTTP	80	TCP	Web servers use the Hypertext Transfer Protocol to accept connections from web browsers such as Internet Explorer and Netscape Navigator.
POP3	110	TCP	E-mail clients (such as Outlook Express) use Post Office Protocol, Version 3 (POP3) to retrieve e-mail from mail servers.
NNTP	119	UDP	Network News Transfer Protocol transfers Usenet newsgroup messages between servers and between clients and servers.
NTP	123	UDP	Network Time Protocol is used to synchronize the time on TCP/IP hosts.
NetBIOS	137, 138, 139	TCP	Used to support functions such as Microsoft File and Print Sharing over TCP/IP networks.
IMAP	143	TCP	E-mail clients use Internet Message Access Protocol to access e-mail messages while leaving the messages themselves stored on the server.
SNMP	161	UDP	Simple Network Management Protocol enables network management applications to remotely monitor network devices.
LDAP	389	TCP	Clients use the Lightweight Directory Access Protocol (LDAP) to search and update information in directories over a TCP/IP network. Directory services such as Microsoft's Active Directory and Novell eDirectory can be accessed using LDAP.
HTTPS	443	TCP	HTTP over SSL (Secure Sockets Layer) provides an encrypted connection between a web server and a web client. Most web browsers display a closed padlock to indicate a secure connection.
Raw SMB	445	TCP	When NetBIOS support is disabled, Microsoft File and Print Sharing uses port 445.
IGMP	463	UDP	Clients use Internet Group Multicast Protocol (IGMP) to register as members of a multicast group.
LPR	515	TCP	The Line Printer protocol is used to communicate between the LPR client and the LPD (Line Printer Daemon) server. Typically used for printing using UNIX/Linux systems.

Exam Tip

It is important to memorize the popular ports and protocols for the common Internet applications mentioned in Table 6.7. For example, HTTP uses TCP port 80, whereas FTP uses TCP port 21.

Objective 6.08 Name Resolution

If we had to remember the IP address of every computer we wanted to access, we'd probably go nuts! It's much easier to use proper (computer) names such as DATA1 or web addresses such as http://www.gleneclarke.com. Imagine trying to remember the phone numbers of hundreds of people without an address book, and you get a good idea of the kind of problem we need to address.

TCP/IP networks require some means of "name resolution" so that people can use names instead of numbers and the computers can determine the IP addresses to which these names refer. In a local area network, name resolution is easy; our host can simply broadcast on the network to get the name of a particular system. When routing becomes involved, however, broadcasting is no longer a viable option—remember, routers do not forward broadcasts.

Just like we have directory assistance for phone numbers, a TCP/IP network may provide "directory assistance" for IP addresses. TCP/IP networks treat name resolution differently depending on whether an application uses a NetBIOS name (computer name) or a fully qualified domain name (FQDN) to make a connection to a service. DNS (Domain Name System) provides name resolution for fully qualified domain names (www.gleneclarke.com) and WINS (Windows Internet Name Service) provides name resolution for NetBIOS names used by applications that connect to computer names.

Exam Tip

Text files reside on the hard drives of client computers that can be used for name resolution. The HOSTS file is used to resolve FQDNs to IP addresses, whereas the LMHOSTS file is used to resolve NetBIOS names to IP addresses.

Sockets, Applications, and DNS

TCP/IP Sockets-based applications, such as web browsers and e-mail client programs, do not require that computers have names in order to function; instead, they require IP addresses. When we type in an address such as **www.gleneclarke.com** or **ftp.microsoft.com**, our system uses DNS to look up the associated IP address. In very simple terms, DNS is an application running on a computer system providing an address lookup service. We may have a DNS server on our local network, or we may use the DNS services available through our Internet service provider, the Internet itself, or all three.

A local DNS service (running on, perhaps, a Linux or Windows 2003 server) maintains a database of known addresses and their DNS style names, either entered manually or through an association with another DNS server (such as the one provided by our ISP). DNS management uses a hierarchical structure to divide up responsibility among different organizations on the Internet, with the DNS namespace broken into domains.

A *DNS domain* is a specific branch of the DNS namespace, as shown in Figure 6.8. The DNS namespace starts at the root, which is controlled by InterNIC (Internet Network Information Center). InterNIC does not have to know the name of every computer in the world. Instead, it delegates authority for particular subdomains to other organizations. InterNIC contracts with Network Solutions (www.networksolutions.com), for example, to maintain the .com subdomain.

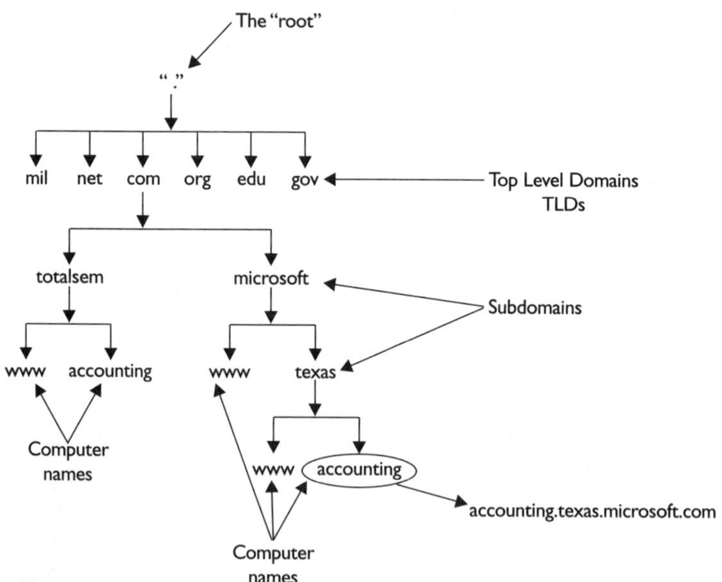

FIGURE 6.8 The DNS namespace

There are a variety of top-level domains similar to .com in the Internet world. Table 6.8 shows the common top-level domains used in the United States. This first level of domains, including the .com, .org, and .net domains, are often referred to as *TLDs* (for *top-level domains*).

DNS Name Resolution

When you enter an address such as www.microsoft.com into your web browser, the chain of events used to identify the actual address of the web server is as follows:

1. The host contacts its local DNS server (if present) and requests the IP address, as shown in Figure 6.9.
2. If the local DNS server does not know the address for www.microsoft.com, it will refer to a DNS root server. The root servers, maintained by InterNIC, know all the addresses of the top-level domain DNS servers. The root servers do *not* know the address of www.microsoft.com, but they do know the address of the DNS server in charge of all .com addresses.
3. Your local DNS server refers your request to the DNS server responsible for .com addresses. The .com DNS server identifies the IP address of the microsoft.com DNS server.
4. Your DNS server asks the microsoft.com DNS server for the IP address of www.microsoft.com and then passes this information back to your browser. Figure 6.10 shows the process of resolving a fully qualified domain name into an IP address.

TABLE 6.8 Common Top-Level Domains

Top-Level Domain	Refers To
.com	Originally intended for companies involved in commercial activities, but anyone can register a .com address.
.net	Companies involved in providing network access, such as Internet service providers (ISPs), but anyone can register a .net address.
.org	Organizations not involved in commerce, especially nonprofit organizations, but anyone can register a .org address.
.mil	United States military organizations.
.edu	United States educational institutions, especially higher education.
.gov	United States federal government organizations.

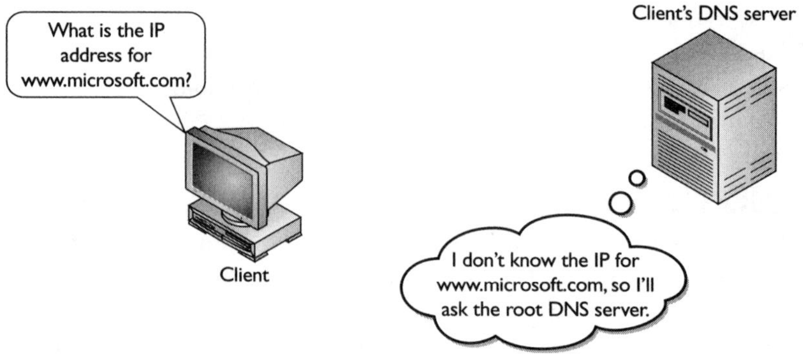

FIGURE 6.9 A host contacts its DNS server

Although this procedure might sound a bit complex, it works very well and provides a great deal of flexibility. Prior to the existence of DNS, every computer that wanted to use domain names had to have a local file—called a HOSTS file—that contained a table of IP addresses and their associated names. This file

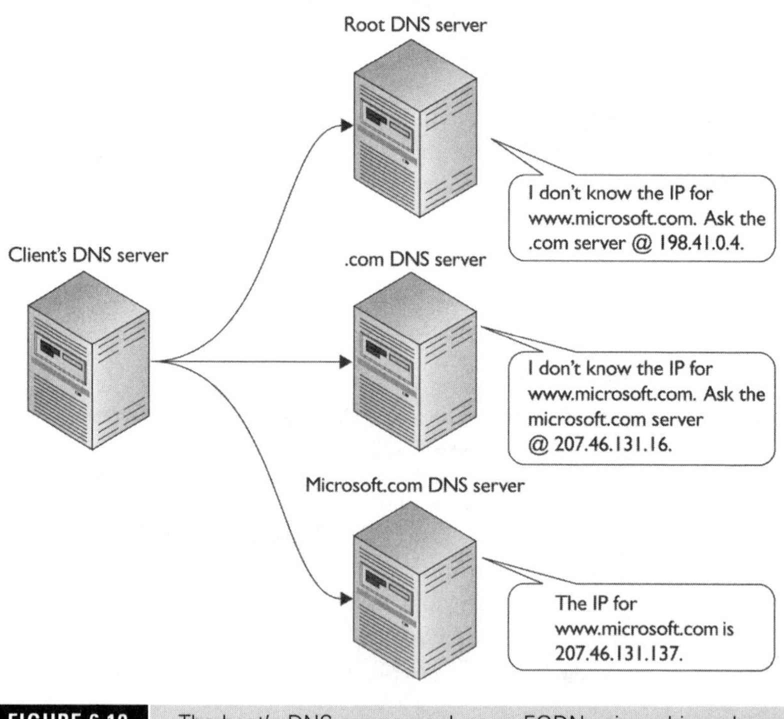

FIGURE 6.10 The host's DNS server resolves an FQDN using a hierarchy of DNS servers.

was stored on every system's hard disk. Because the HOSTS file changed on a daily basis, network techs had to keep downloading updates from the Internet! You can still use a HOSTS file today if you just have a small number of computers on a local network, but DNS is the way to go for bigger networks. A simple HOSTS file would look something like this:

```
109.54.94.197      dan.glensworld.com
138.125.163.17     glen.glensworld.com
127.0.0.1          localhost
```

Notice that the name "localhost" appears in the HOSTS file as an alias for the loopback address 127.0.0.1.

NetBIOS Applications and WINS

NetBIOS applications include basically every program that has the word "Microsoft" in front of its name except Microsoft Internet Explorer. Because NetBIOS-based applications can run over protocol suites other than TCP/IP, NetBIOS applications themselves must remain aloof from details like IP addresses that only exist in a single protocol suite; instead, these programs use NetBIOS names (a.k.a. computer names) instead of sockets when connecting to talk to other computers. NetBIOS applications connect to a NetBIOS name, or computer name, which is then converted to an IP address by a Windows Internet Name Service (WINS) server.

Exam Tip

WINS servers are very popular on larger pre-Windows 2000 (Windows NT) networks. Starting with Windows 2000 and continuing on to Windows XP and Windows 2003, Microsoft is focusing on DNS as the primary method of name resolution.

WINS Name Resolution

When a WINS client (that is, any machine using WINS) boots up, it sends a message to its specific WINS server (specified in the client's TCP/IP settings) registering its name and IP address in the WINS database. The WINS clients do not broadcast their registrations—they send them directly to the IP address of their WINS server. After registering with the WINS server, the WINS clients have a means of determining the IP address that corresponds with a particular NetBIOS name. When a client on the network wants to connect to a particular computer name, it simply contacts the WINS server and asks the WINS server for the IP address of the computer instead of depending on broadcasts over the network to resolve the name.

WINS performs another vital task on a NetBIOS-based network—ensuring name uniqueness. If a second computer tries to register a duplicate NetBIOS name, the WINS server will send a message to the second computer, telling it to get off the network. The user of the machine that has its name refused sees the error message shown in Figure 6.11.

Travel Advisory

The LMHOSTS file can resolve NetBIOS names to IP addresses, but it cannot guarantee unique NetBIOS names across a routed network.

In the absence of a WINS server, a file called LMHOSTS (located on the hard disk of each system) offers another means of resolving names to IP addresses. This is very similar to the way that a HOSTS file functions for DNS host name resolution. Whereas a WINS server acts much like directory assistance, the LMHOSTS file acts like a little black book of phone numbers. The WINS server provides a centralized database to which every machine can refer, whereas the LMHOSTS file exists on each machine's individual hard drive for that machine's exclusive use. A simple LMHOSTS file would look something like this:

```
102.54.94.97     rhino       #PRE #DOM:networking  #net group's DC
 102.54.94.102    "appname  \0x14"              #special app server
 102.54.94.123    popular        #PRE           #source server
 102.54.94.117    localsrv       #PRE           #needed for the include
```

Travel Advisory

Windows NT/2000/XP/2003–based operating systems store the HOSTS and LMHOSTS file in c:\%windir%\system32\drivers\etc. Also note that the existing LMHOSTS file has a .sam extension (for "sample"). You will need to remove this extension before the file performs its function.

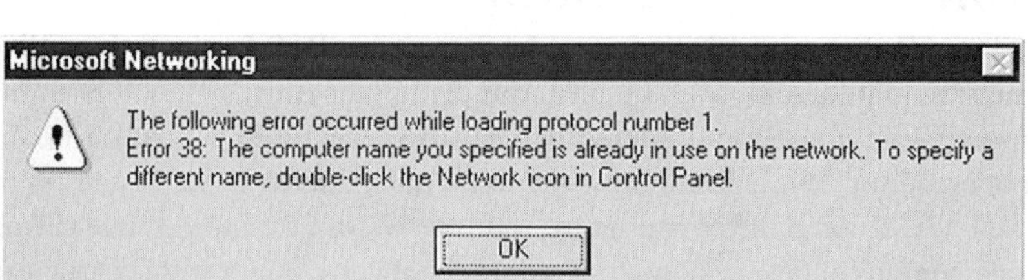

FIGURE 6.11 When a client tries to register a duplicate NetBIOS name, it receives an error message.

The use of WINS servers is the preferred and recommended method for handling NetBIOS name resolution over an LMHOSTS file. Although LMHOSTS files can be used, they are difficult to maintain as the network grows. In addition, administrators must manually edit the LMHOSTS file of each machine to ensure that every system is aware of a name change. Typically, LMHOSTS files are used when a WINS server cannot easily be added to the network because of cost or other factors, and sometimes for remote users dialing into a network where WINS is not available to remote users for security reasons.

DNS vs. WINS

DNS and WINS serve a similar function on TCP/IP-based networks, providing centralized databases of names and addresses for network hosts to consult, but there are some key differences between them. The DNS namespace is hierarchical, whereas the NetBIOS namespace used by WINS is flat. In the past, administrators had to maintain DNS databases manually, whereas WINS builds its databases as clients register. Windows 2000/2003 DNS supports having clients self-register the records with DNS, making a more attractive solution for all network name resolution. The key difference, however, lies in the type of name they resolve and the types of applications that use each service. TCP/IP Sockets-based applications (web browsers, e-mail clients, and so forth) use DNS, whereas Microsoft-based NetBIOS applications (Network Neighborhood, map network drive) use WINS. Table 6.9 summarizes the distinctions between DNS and WINS.

Exam Tip

You may know of some real-world examples that contradict the clear distinctions made in Table 6.9 between WINS and DNS. In particular, the Dynamic DNS functions provided in Windows 2000 offer a very "WINS-like" automatic registration capability for DNS client machines. However, the current exam does not cover Dynamic DNS. Any question about DNS that appears on the exam will assume that all addresses must be manually configured by a network administrator.

TABLE 6.9 DNS vs. WINS

Area of Difference	DNS	WINS
Used by:	Sockets applications	NetBIOS applications
Database built:	Manually (typically)	Dynamically
Text file alternative:	HOSTS	LMHOSTS
Namespace:	Hierarchical	Flat

DHCP

With so many settings (IP address, subnet mask, default gateway, DNS servers, WINS servers) to specify, the typical TCP/IP network administrator can spend days properly configuring each host manually. Fortunately, TCP/IP provides a protocol that takes much of the drudgery out of TCP/IP configuration: Dynamic Host Configuration Protocol (DHCP).

DHCP servers distribute IP addresses and additional IP settings to machines on the network, freeing the network tech from the wear and tear on the tennis shoes inflicted by manual configuration. Machines that can handle this automatic configuration are called, appropriately, *DHCP clients.* Most network client software can be set up to accept DHCP (see Figure 6.12).

When a DHCP client boots up, it sends out a broadcast message requesting its configuration. If a DHCP server receives that message, it returns the appropriate values to the DHCP client, as shown in Figure 6.13. The DHCP server keeps track of the addresses it assigns to ensure that it does not assign the same address to two machines.

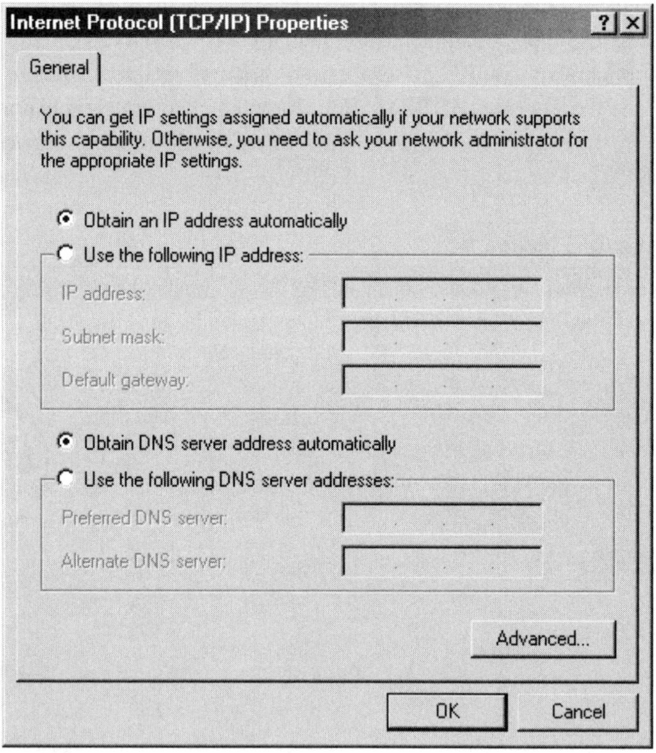

FIGURE 6.12 Configuring a DHCP client

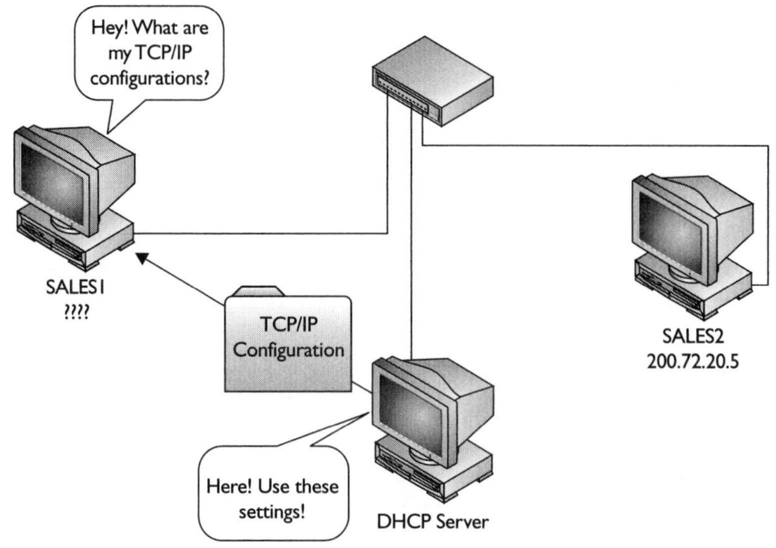

FIGURE 6.13 A DHCP server supplies TCP/IP configuration to clients.

When using DHCP, network techs may need to check the configuration of specific machines to ensure that the DHCP server has assigned the appropriate configuration. Every operating system that supports TCP/IP will include a utility that displays the current TCP/IP configuration. In Windows 9*x*, for example, you can run the WINIPCFG program from a command line to display the screen shown in Figure 6.14.

On a Windows NT/2000/XP/2003 system, the command IPCONFIG /ALL displays similar information:

```
C:\> ipconfig /all
Windows 2000 IP Configuration
     Host Name . . . . . . . . . . . . : nk-mobile
     Primary DNS Suffix  . . . . . . . :
     Node Type . . . . . . . . . . . . : Peer-Peer
     IP Routing Enabled. . . . . . . . : No
     WINS Proxy Enabled. . . . . . . . : No
Ethernet adapter Local Area Connection:
     Connection-specific DNS Suffix  . :
     Description . . . . . . . . . . . : Intel 8255x-based PCI
                                         Ethernet Adapter
                                         (10/100)
     Physical Address. . . . . . . . . : 00-D0-59-0E-0B-C8
     DHCP Enabled. . . . . . . . . . . : Yes
     Autoconfiguration Enabled . . . . : Yes
     IP Address. . . . . . . . . . . . : 192.168.2.77
     Subnet Mask . . . . . . . . . . . : 255.255.255.0
     Default Gateway . . . . . . . . . : 192.168.2.1
```

```
DHCP Server . . . . . . . . . . . : 192.168.2.1
DNS Servers . . . . . . . . . . . : 192.168.2.1
                                    192.168.2.1
Primary WINS Server . . . . . . . : 192.168.1.10
Lease Obtained. . . . . . . . . . : Sunday, October 07,
                                    2004 16:54:00
Lease Expires . . . . . . . . . . : Wednesday, October 10,
                                    2004 16:54:00
```

In UNIX, the command used to display this information can vary, but it's usually ifconfig. Regardless of the operating system, a utility exists that can display the current configuration.

Exam Tip

The ipconfig command is used to view the TCP/IP setting on a Windows NT/2000/XP/2003 machine, whereas ifconfig is used on a UNIX or Linux.

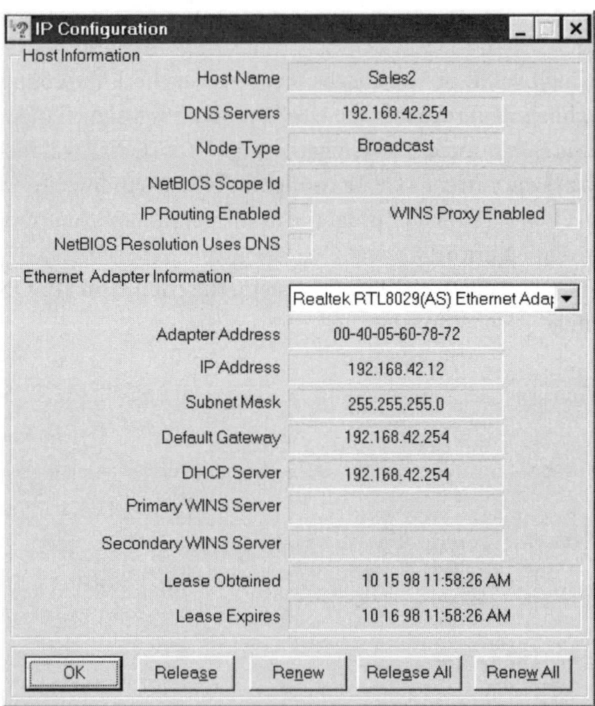

FIGURE 6.14 The Windows 9*x* WINIPCFG utility

TCP/IP Utilities

TCP/IP—in all OS flavors—comes with a powerful set of troubleshooting utilities with which all network techs should familiarize themselves.

PING

The PING utility tests connections between two hosts. To test the connection between two hosts, sit at one of the systems and type in **PING** followed by the name or IP address of the other host. PING uses a special protocol called the *Internet Control Message Protocol (ICMP)* to determine whether the other machine can receive the test packet and reply. A host that can be reached will respond back, and the PING command will report success. PING can also be used to test for the availability of Internet-based services using fully qualified domain names, but note that some sites block PING to dissuade their sites from being used for testing—and some corporate Internet security systems will also block PINGs to external sites. The output of the PING command will look like this:

```
C:\>ping 192.168.2.1
Pinging 192.168.2.1 with 32 bytes of data:
Reply from 192.168.2.1: bytes=32 time<10ms TTL=255
Reply from 192.168.2.1: bytes=32 time<10ms TTL=255
Reply from 192.168.2.1: bytes=32 time<10ms TTL=255
Reply from 192.168.2.1: bytes=32 time<10ms TTL=255
Ping statistics for 192.168.2.1:
    Packets: Sent = 4, Received = 4, Lost = 0 (0% loss),
Approximate round trip times in milli-seconds:
    Minimum = 0ms, Maximum =  0ms, Average =  0ms

C:\PING www.google.com
Pinging www.google.com [216.239.33.100] with 32 bytes of data:
Reply from 216.239.33.100: bytes=32 time=270ms TTL=49
Reply from 216.239.33.100: bytes=32 time=271ms TTL=49
Reply from 216.239.33.100: bytes=32 time=270ms TTL=49
Reply from 216.239.33.100: bytes=32 time=271ms TTL=49
Ping statistics for 216.239.33.100:
    Packets: Sent = 4, Received = 4, Lost = 0 (0% loss),
Approximate round trip times in milli-seconds:
    Minimum = 270ms, Maximum =  271ms, Average =  270ms

C:\ping www.madethisup.com
Unknown host www.madethisup.com.
```

You should read the messages PING reports back when it cannot reach another machine—they can contain important clues about the source of the problem. If PING cannot turn a name into an IP address, for example, it will report back "Unknown host" or some similar message, indicating that PING was unable to determine the proper IP address for the name used. (The exact message returned by the PING command varies depending on the operating system.) If PING resolves an IP address (either because the tech specified one or because PING resolved it using DNS) but cannot reach the specified address, PING will display a different message, such as "Destination host unreachable." Keep the following points in mind when you receive such a message:

- **Unknown host** This message means "I don't know the IP address!" You probably specified an invalid/unused DNS name.
- **Destination host unreachable** This message means "I can't get to that IP address." In this case, you should check for possible routing problems—for example, have you specified a default gateway?

If a (seemingly) valid host is specified but that host doesn't appear to be responding, you will see a sequence similar to the following:

```
C:\> ping 192.168.2.223
Pinging 192.168.2.223 with 32 bytes of data:
Request timed out.
Request timed out.
Request timed out.
Request timed out.
Ping statistics for 192.168.2.223:
    Packets: Sent = 4, Received = 0, Lost = 4 (100% loss),
Approximate round trip times in milli-seconds:
    Minimum = 0ms, Maximum =  0ms, Average =  0ms
```

TRACERT

TRACERT (or TRACEROUTE on some operating systems) traces the route between two hosts. TRACERT will send a response back with each router it hits. This will allow you to determine if communication is slow because a link has gone down between you and the destination. If you know there are normally three routers between you and the destination, and the TRACERT returns back six responses, you know that your packets are taking an indirect pathway (due to a link being down). TRACERT lists each router between the host and the destination. The following listing shows a trace to the Total Seminars' web server from a machine in the UK (the –d switch tells TRACERT to display IP addresses without the corresponding domain names):

```
C:\> tracert -d www.totalsem.com
Tracing route to www.totalsem.com [64.226.214.168]
over a maximum of 30 hops:
  1    <10 ms   <10 ms   <10 ms  192.168.2.1
  2     80 ms    70 ms    80 ms  194.159.254.93
  3     80 ms    90 ms    90 ms  194.159.254.100
```

```
  4     90 ms     91 ms     90 ms  194.159.252.54
  5     90 ms    100 ms     90 ms  194.159.36.234
  6     90 ms     90 ms     90 ms  213.206.130.81
  7     81 ms     90 ms     90 ms  213.206.128.41
  8    130 ms    131 ms    120 ms  213.206.129.38
  9    130 ms    120 ms    121 ms  80.77.64.33
 10    200 ms    200 ms    201 ms  144.232.19.29
 11    210 ms    210 ms    211 ms  144.232.19.98
 12    210 ms    200 ms    211 ms  144.232.7.253
 13    220 ms    211 ms    220 ms  144.232.9.198
 14    220 ms    221 ms    220 ms  144.232.12.18
 15    220 ms    221 ms    220 ms  160.81.204.10
 16    220 ms    221 ms    220 ms  64.224.0.99
 17    230 ms    221 ms    240 ms  totalsem.com [64.226.214.168]
Trace complete.
```

ARP

The ARP utility helps diagnose problems associated with the Address Resolution Protocol (ARP). TCP/IP hosts use the Address Resolution Protocol to determine the physical (MAC) address that corresponds with a specific logical (IP) address. The ARP utility, when used with the –a option, displays any IP addresses that have been resolved to MAC addresses recently. Here's an example:

```
C:\>arp -a
Interface: 192.168.43.5 on Interface 0x1000002
  Internet Address      Physical Address      Type
  192.168.43.2          00-40-05-60-7f-64     dynamic
  192.168.43.3          00-40-05-5b-71-51     dynamic
  192.168.43.4          00-a0-c9-98-97-7f     dynamic
```

NETSTAT

NETSTAT enables the network tech to examine network statistics about a system. These statistics include information such as the ports listening on the system and any connections that have been established. The following is some output from the netstat command:

```
C:\>netstat
Active Connections
  Proto  Local Address      Foreign Address          State
  TCP    brian:1030         BRIAN:1274               ESTABLISHED
  TCP    brian:2666         totalsem.com:pop3        TIME_WAIT
  TCP    brian:2670         totalsem.com:pop3        TIME_WAIT
  TCP    brian:2672         www.cnn.com:80           TIME_WAIT
  TCP    brian:2674         www.nytimes.com:80       ESTABLISHED
  TCP    brian:2460         MARSPDC:nbsession        ESTABLISHED
  TCP    brian:1273         NOTES01:2986             TIME_WAIT
  TCP    brian:1274         BRIAN:1030               ESTABLISHED
```

NETSTAT can provide a wide range of information depending on the command line switches used. Type **NETSTAT /?** at a command prompt to list the optional command line switches:

```
NETSTAT [-a] [-e] [-n] [-o] [-s] [-p proto] [-r] [interval]
  -a          Displays all connections and listening ports.
  -e          Displays Ethernet statistics. This may be
              combined with the -s option.
  -n          Displays addresses and port numbers in numerical form.
  -o          Displays the owning process ID associated with
              each connection.
  -p proto    Shows connections for the protocol specified by
              proto; proto may be any of: TCP, UDP, TCPv6, or
              UDPv6.  If used with the -s option to display
              per-protocol statistics, proto may be any of:
              IP, IPv6, ICMP, ICMPv6, TCP, TCPv6, UDP, or UDPv6.
  -r          Displays the routing table.
  -s          Displays per-protocol statistics.  By default,
              statistics are shown for IP, IPv6, ICMP, ICMPv6,
              TCP, TCPv6, UDP, and UDPv6; the -p option may be
              used to specify a subset of the default.
  interval    Redisplays selected statistics, pausing interval
              seconds between each display.  Press CTRL+C to stop
              redisplaying statistics.  If omitted, netstat will
              print the current configuration information once.
```

NBTSTAT

NBTSTAT (NetBIOS over TCP/IP statistics) enables a network tech to check information about the NetBIOS names. This includes viewing the names that have been registered by the local system (nbtstat –n), viewing the names registered by a remote system (nbtstat –A), and viewing the NetBIOS name cache, which shows the NetBIOS names and corresponding IP addresses that have been resolved by a particular host. Here's some sample output:

```
C:\ >NBTSTAT -c
Node IpAddress: [192.168.43.5] Scope Id: []
                 NetBIOS Remote Cache Name Table
  Name                   Type          Host Address     Life [sec]
-------------------------------------------------------------------
WRITERS          <1B>  UNIQUE        192.168.43.13    420
DAN              <20>  UNIQUE        192.168.43.3     420
VENUSPDC         <00>  UNIQUE        192.168.43.13    120
GLEN             <20>  UNIQUE        192.168.43.2     420
NOTES01          <20>  UNIQUE        192.168.43.4     420
```

When properly used, NBTSTAT helps network techs diagnose and troubleshoot NetBIOS problems, especially those related to NetBIOS name resolution. NBTSTAT enables the network tech to determine whether the WINS server has supplied inaccurate addresses to the WINS client.

Like NETSTAT, NBTSTAT can provide a wealth of information using different switches. Here are some of the popular switches:

```
NBTSTAT [ [-a RemoteName] [-A IP address] [-c] [-n]
        [-r] [-R] [-RR] [-s] [-S] [interval] ]

  -a  Lists the remote machine's name table given its name
  -A  Lists the remote machine's name table given its IP address
  -c  Lists NBT's cache of remote [machine] names and their IP
      addresses
  -n  Lists local NetBIOS names.
  -R  Purges and reloads the remote cache name table
```

Exam Tip

Note that NBTSTAT allows you to purge and reload the NetBIOS name cache with the command **NBTSTAT –R**. Remember that, unlike most Windows command-line utilities, NBTSTAT is case sensitive when it comes to its switches. Therefore, **NBTSTAT –R** and **NBTSTAT –r** are *not* the same command.

NSLOOKUP

NSLOOKUP provides a command-line utility for diagnosing DNS problems. In its most basic usage, NSLOOKUP returns the IP address, as shown here:

```
C:\ >nslookup example.com
Server:  dns.example.com
Address:  192.168.31.211
Non-authoritative answer:
Name:    server1.example.com
Address:  192.68.67.12
```

NSLOOKUP also offers an interactive mode, which allows you to specify a wide range of options as you diagnose and troubleshoot DNS issues. To see the full range of options, type **?** at the NSLOOKUP prompt:

```
> ?
Commands: (identifiers are shown in uppercase, [] means optional)
NAME            - print info about the host/domain NAME using
                  default server
NAME1 NAME2     - as above, but use NAME2 as server
help or ?       - print info on common commands
set OPTION      - set an option
    all                 - print options, current server and host
    [no]debug           - print debugging information
    [no]d2              - print exhaustive debugging information
    [no]defname         - append domain name to each query
    [no]recurse         - ask for recursive answer to query
    [no]search          - use domain search list
```

```
    [no]vc                 - always use a virtual circuit
    domain=NAME            - set default domain name to NAME
    srchlist=N1[/N2/.../N6] - set domain to N1 and search list
                               to N1,N2, etc.
    root=NAME              - set root server to NAME
    retry=X                - set number of retries to X
    timeout=X              - set initial time-out interval to X
                             seconds
    type=X                 - set query type (ex. A,ANY,CNAME,MX,NS,
                             PTR,SOA,SRV)
    querytype=X            - same as type
    class=X                - set query class (ex. IN (Internet), ANY)
    [no]msxfr              - use MS fast zone transfer
    ixfrver=X              - current version to use in IXFR transfer
                             request
server NAME        - set default server to NAME, using current
                     default server
lserver NAME       - set default server to NAME, using initial
                     server
finger [USER]      - finger the optional NAME at the current
                     default host
root               - set current default server to the root
ls [opt] DOMAIN [> FILE] - list addresses in DOMAIN (optional:
                        output to FILE)
    -a             - list canonical names and aliases
    -d             - list all records
    -t TYPE        - list records of the given type (e.g. A,CNAME,
                     MX,NS,PTR etc.)
view FILE          - sort an 'ls' output file and view it with pg
exit               - exit the program

>
```

In addition to NSLOOKUP, UNIX/Linux systems offer another DNS diagnostic utility, DIG.

Using command-line utilities such as PING, TRACERT, ARP, NETSTAT, NBTSTAT, and NSLOOKUP, an experienced network tech can diagnose most TCP/IP problems quickly and begin working on solutions. If two hosts can ping each other by address but not by name, for example, the wise network tech knows to leave the routers alone and concentrate on name resolution (DNS, WINS) issues instead.

To function effectively as a network tech, you need to learn TCP/IP. Supported by most operating systems, the TCP/IP suite provides excellent tools for integrating multiple operating systems within the same network. Its importance will continue to grow as the Internet continues to increase its importance in both business and everyday life.

✔ **Objective 6.01: The TCP/IP Protocol Suite** TCP/IP has been around since the 1970s, but it is a dynamic suite of protocols and is still being enhanced today through the use of RFC documents. Underpinning the Internet's functionality has allowed TCP/IP to become universally adopted as a networking standard for most computer platforms.

✔ **Objective 6.02: IP Addressing** The original IP addressing scheme (IPv4) uses a 32-bit address to identify a host address and its network address based on a series of addressing schemes known as *IP classes.* The associated subnet mask identifies where the boundary between the network and host address lies and also allows us to change this boundary if we wish. Various IP addresses have been defined as nonroutable and therefore can be used to create "private networks," thus reducing potential WAN configuration issues.

✔ **Objective 6.03: Subnet Masks and Subnetting** Altering the default subnet mask allows us to subdivide a network into smaller sections, called *subnets.* Subnetting can help with general network management and also traffic management.

✔ **Objective 6.04: IP Version 6** IPv6 uses a 128-bit addressing scheme to provide a (in effect) limitless supply of IP addresses and is needed because the 32-bit address range of IPv4 is running out of spare addresses. Parts of the Internet are already using IPv6, but it is not generally in use at the desktop yet.

✔ **Objective 6.05: Routing** You must configure your host PC to know the address of its default router ("default gateway" in TCP/IP-speak); otherwise, it will not be able to communicate with hosts on other networks. Routers also need configuring to know the other networks to which they are able to forward data packets; this can be done manually (static routing) by a network tech, or automatically by the routers "talking" to each other using one of several route discovery protocols (dynamic routing).

✔ **Objective 6.06: Transport Layer Protocols** The TCP/IP protocol suite supports two main Transport layer protocols: TCP (Transmission Control Protocol) provides reliable, connection-oriented packet delivery, whereas UDP

(User Datagram Protocol) is a faster, connectionless (unreliable) protocol more often used with applications that send short bursts of data.

✔ **Objective 6.07: Session Layer Protocols** Session layer protocols manage the connections between devices communicating across a network. Microsoft operating systems using TCP/IP employ NetBIOS names to track connections, whereas traditional Internet functions such as web browsing use Sockets, the traditional TCP/IP Session layer protocol. The Sockets standard uses a combination of IP address, protocol, and a port address to manage connections; each major TCP/IP-based protocol has its own port address that identifies its functionality—for example, HTTP (the protocol used by browsers to communicate with web servers) uses port 80.

✔ **Objective 6.08: Name Resolution** Although it's easier for humans to refer to computer systems using computer (NetBIOS) names or fully qualified domain names (such as www.totalsem.com), communication between two systems can only take place if the target machine's IP address is known. In the Microsoft networking world, WINS (Windows Internet Name Service) is used to resolve IP addresses from NetBIOS computer names, but pure TCP/IP environments (such as the Internet) use a database system called DNS (Domain Name System) to resolve IP addresses from fully qualified domain names, such as www.totalsem.com. DNS uses a hierarchical structure, with separate servers (or groups of servers) managing the resolution of various parts of a domain name.

✔ **Objective 6.09: TCP/IP Utilities** There are a number of basic TCP/IP- and NetBIOS-related utility programs that every tech should know about: PING tests connections between hosts (and can also be used to test the local installation of TCP/IP using the command PING 127.0.0.1 or PING localhost). PING uses a special protocol called the Internet Control Message Protocol (ICMP). TRACERT (TRACEROUTE) traces the route between two hosts and can be used to identify routing problems. The ARP (Address Resolution Protocol) utility can be used to display the contents of the local ARP cache, which holds a table of IP addresses against their host's known MAC addresses. NETSTAT displays a list of current Sockets-based connections active on the local host. NBTSTAT displays the current NetBIOS name cache, which shows the NetBIOS names and corresponding IP addresses that have been resolved by a particular host.

REVIEW QUESTIONS

1. Which of the following correctly defines a TCP/IP host? (Select one answer.)
   - **A.** Any server on a TCP/IP network
   - **B.** Any device on a TCP/IP network that can send or receive data packets
   - **C.** A device on a TCP/IP network that forwards data packets to other networks
   - **D.** A device on a TCP/IP network that resolves names to IP addresses
2. Which of the following is a valid class B host address? (Select one answer.)
   - **A.** 147.28.0.0
   - **B.** 192.168.14.50
   - **C.** 12.12.12.12
   - **D.** 128.14.255.0
3. Which of the following commands would produce the following output? (Select one answer.)

```
Active Connections
 Proto Local Address  Foreign Address State
 TCP   brian:1030     BRIAN:1274      ESTABLISHED
 TCP   brian:2666     totalsem.com:pop3          TIME_WAIT
 TCP   brian:2670     totalsem.com:pop3          TIME_WAIT
 TCP   brian:2672     www.cnn.com:80  TIME_WAIT
 TCP   brian:2674     www.nytimes.com:80         ESTABLISHED
 TCP   brian:2460     MARSPDC:nbsession          ESTABLISHED
 TCP   brian:1273     NOTES01:2986    TIME_WAIT
 TCP   brian:1274     BRIAN:1030      ESTABLISHED
```

   - **A.** NBTSTAT
   - **B.** ARP
   - **C.** NETSTAT
   - **D.** TRACERT
4. What is the minimum number of data bits required for subnet addressing to allow a total of five subnets to be created? (Select one answer.)
   - **A.** 1
   - **B.** 2
   - **C.** 3
   - **D.** 4

5. Sue is checking a customer's machine onsite. The machine can access devices on the local network, but nothing else on the WAN. What is the most likely cause of this? (Select one answer.)
   - **A.** The computer has an invalid NetBIOS name.
   - **B.** There is no WINS server running.
   - **C.** The machine does not have a default gateway address set.
   - **D.** The ARP cache is corrupt.
6. What port number does Telnet use? (Select one answer.)
   - **A.** 443
   - **B.** 23
   - **C.** 80
   - **D.** 43
7. Which of the following protocols provide TCP/IP name resolution? (Select two answers.)
   - **A.** WINS
   - **B.** SNMP
   - **C.** Telnet
   - **D.** DNS
8. Jo issues the command PING 127.0.0.1 and receives the reply "Request timed out." What should Jo check first? (Select one answer.)
   - **A.** That the correct default gateway has been specified
   - **B.** The NIC LEDs
   - **C.** That DNS is running on the network
   - **D.** That TCP/IP has been installed correctly
9. Which of the following will resolve NetBIOS names to IP addresses? (Select two answers.)
   - **A.** A HOSTS file
   - **B.** A WINS server
   - **C.** A router
   - **D.** An LMHOSTS file
10. Which protocol provides automatic host IP address assignment? (Select one answer.)
   - **A.** DHCP
   - **B.** DNS
   - **C.** NetBIOS
   - **D.** BOOTR

REVIEW ANSWERS

1. **B** Any device on a TCP/IP network that can send or receive data packets is called a host.
2. **D** Only D is a valid class B address. Although choice A is a class B address, it is an invalid host address of all zeroes (x.x.0.0).
3. **C** The listing shows the output from the NETSTAT command.
4. **C** Three bits allow a total of six subnets to be created, giving scope for the five we want to create. Two bits (choice B) would only allow two subnets.
5. **C** Because we cannot see past the local network, it sounds like Sue has a default gateway (router) issue.
6. **B** Telnet uses port 23.
7. **A** **D** WINS and DNS provide name resolution. SNMP is for network management, and Telnet provides terminal emulation functionality.
8. **D** Pinging 127.0.0.1 runs a local loopback test, and if this doesn't work, something's wrong with the installation of TCP/IP on that machine.
9. **B** **D** A WINS server or an LMHOSTS file can be used for NetBIOS name resolution.
10. **A** DHCP—the Dynamic Host Configuration Protocol—provides automatic host IP address assignment.

Wide Area Networking

ITINERARY

- **Objective 7.01** Basic Equipment Requirements
- **Objective 7.02** PSTN—The Analog Telephone System
- **Objective 7.03** ISDN—The Digital Telephone System
- **Objective 7.04** Fixed-Line (Always-on) Services

NEWBIE	SOME EXPERIENCE	EXPERT
3 hours	1 hour	30 minutes

In this chapter, we'll take a look at ways to connect multiple LANs into a larger wide area network (WAN). Keep in mind that the Internet is not the only WAN out there—many organizations maintain their own private WANs. The technology and equipment used, however, will be much the same whether we're talking about a private corporate WAN or the Internet. We'll still need routers, telecommunications links, and network techs to make it all work.

Basic Equipment Requirements

You should be familiar with the term "router" by now, and you should also know that routers can be used to link sites (networks) together to provide either a direct, point-to-point link or a mesh-type topology with multiple pathways between your network and the destination network or networks. Well, routers and routing *are* part of the solution, but how do these routers link to other sites?

The basic requirement for wide area connectivity is some device that can interface between the network and the communications circuit in use, as shown in Figure 7.1. When you create a WAN link, some kind of routing device must be used to prevent local traffic from swamping the relatively slow WAN link. Remember that a 2–3 Mbps WAN link is considered pretty high end, but your local network most likely runs at 10, 100, or even 1000 Mbps. The first rule: Keep local traffic on the LAN!

Figure 7.1 shows a generic WAN connection; the physical interface between the WAN unit and the network is likely to be simply a connector that matches the existing network topology—for example, a BNC or RJ45 connector on an Ethernet device or perhaps a pair of fiber connectors. The interface to the communications circuit will depend on what that communications circuit is—it might be just an RJ11/telecom phone connector, or it could be a specialized interface that conforms to a specific data communications standard.

So let's have a look at the technologies you're going to use to link your networks together.

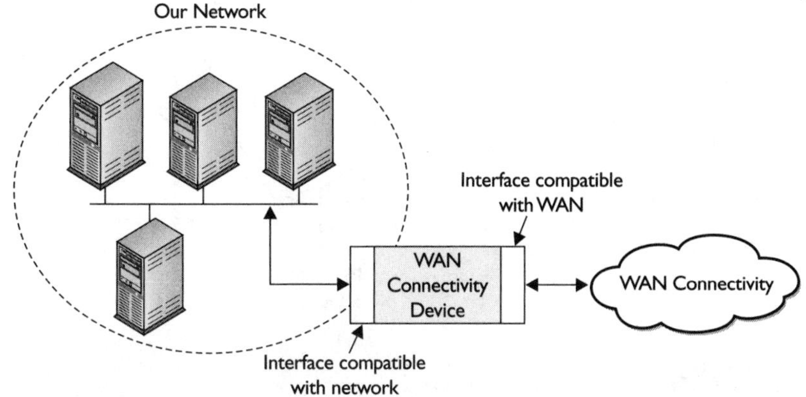

FIGURE 7.1 The generic requirements for a wide area connection

PSTN—The Analog Telephone System

The use of dial-up services (phone circuits) for data communications is a well-established practice. The two services generally available fall into two easy-to-remember categories: analog and digital.

The public switched telephone network (PSTN—sometimes also known as the plain-old telephone system, or POTS) is capable of carrying data, but because the system was originally designed for (analog) voice traffic only, the maximum bandwidth for data is quite limited, even though the systems in most countries now use digital technology for almost everything except the wire between the exchange and your phone socket (sometimes called the *local loop*). Figure 7.2 shows a typical modem setup.

To connect a computer system to the PSTN requires a *modem*—a device that can convert a computer's digital signals into a PSTN-compatible analog signal (perform *mo*dulation) and do the reverse for incoming signals (perform *dem*odulation). Modems come in all shapes and sizes—external boxes connected via a serial port, internal PCI or ISA cards, PC cards for laptops, or even integrated into

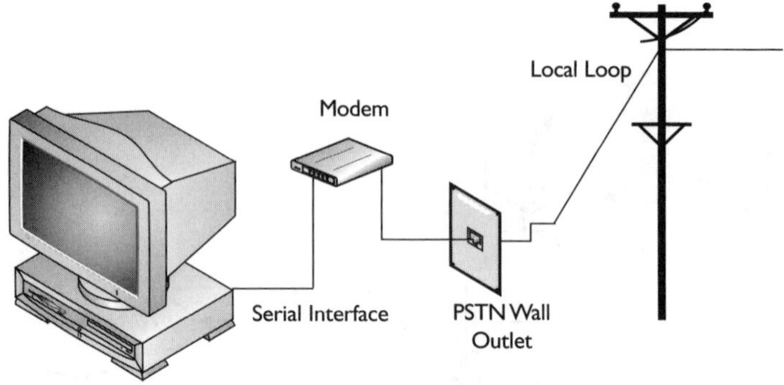

FIGURE 7.2 Typical modem setup

the motherboard. Figure 7.3 shows an internal and an external modem. The hardware alone doesn't make the network connection, of course, but every modern operating system has built-in modem support. Figure 7.4 shows the network configuration for a Windows 98 system.

The main limitation of a configuration that uses a modem and serial port for a network connection is the speed. The two current fastest standards for modems are V.90 and V.92, and if your modem is capable of supporting these standards, then under the *best* conditions you will get an *asymmetric* connection (different speeds in either direction), *receiving* at 56 Kbps and *transmitting* at 33.6 (V.90) or 48 (V.92) Kbps. It's also worth remembering that for a V.9*x* link to work properly, the device at the other end of the link (usually your ISP, but this

FIGURE 7.3 Internal and external modems

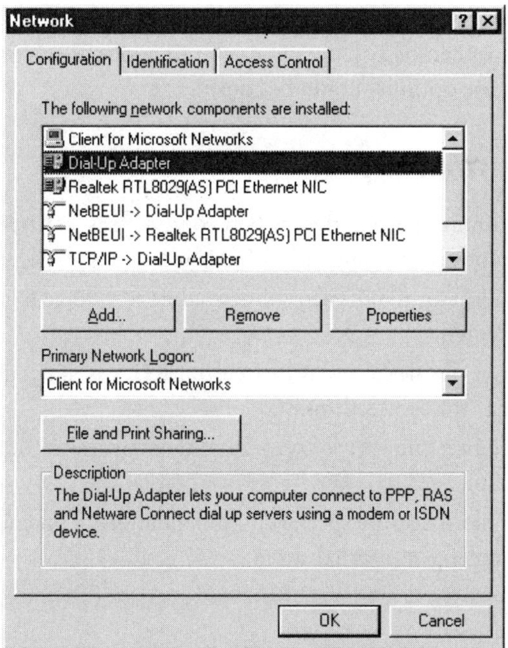

FIGURE 7.4 Windows 98 network configuration showing modem support (Dial-Up Adapter)

would need to be in your computer room if you are setting up your own remote access solution) can't just be another V.9*x* modem. Instead, special equipment is needed. If you use a pair of V.9*x* modems to link systems, they will slow down to around 33.6 Kbps for both transmitting and receiving.

Modem Performance

As a rough guide, you divide the modem speed (in kilobits per second) by ten to get the approximate throughput in bytes per second. Therefore, a 56K link will average around 5.6 Kbps (actually a bit more when you take data compression into consideration)—not the kind of bandwidth that you'd want to use as a wide area link for a business network with even just a few people on it.

Of course, telecommuters will often use modems for remote access to the corporate network. The limited bandwidth for a single user is not as big an issue. Setting up a system to accept modem dial-in links provides a cheap and flexible remote access solution.

Under some circumstances, in some countries, local telephone calls are free, and this makes using a modem for local dial-up users very attractive (if the users can live with the 56K bandwidth), but for a permanent connection between distant sites, the cost can be frightening due to long distance charges, and other more cost-effective options should be considered.

PSTN Summary

- The maximum speed under the best conditions is 56 Kbps (for receiving data)—probably not suitable for WAN links.
- PSTN is ideal for remote access by a mobile workforce if high bandwidth is not required.
- The cost of (local) calls may be free, but PSTN is not generally suitable for permanent connections.
- PSTN requires support software to route network traffic through the modem link.
- V.9*x* standards require special equipment at the main end of the link to provide the top supported speed.

ISDN—The Digital Telephone System

The integrated services digital network (ISDN) has been around for some time and provides more bandwidth than the PSTN service. Being digital in nature and not subject to as many bandwidth-crushing influences (such as noise on the line and electrical interference) as the analog phone system, ISDN generally offers stable 64 Kbps performance for received *and* transmitted data. Many ISDN circuits run over preexisting copper phone lines, and the quality of these lines from your office to the central office (CO) is a limiting factor in determining whether ISDN will actually work from your premises. In general, you must be within 18,000 feet (about 3.4 miles, or 5.5 km) of the nearest CO for ISDN to work.

Local Lingo

central office (CO) The local premises used as a customer connection point by a telecom or data services company—for example, a local telephone exchange.

We've carefully avoided the word "modem" in this section. Although the basic ISDN communications kit *looks* like a modem, it doesn't perform any *mo*dulation or *dem*odulation (see the previous section). ISDN is *already* in a digital (not analog) format, and it makes connections through a terminal adapter (TA).

Exam Tip

Many techs refer to "ISDN modems," but the correct term is "terminal adapter" (TA). In reality, a TA does sort of the same job as a modem—it connects you to the communications system. Therefore, in general-speak, we'd let you get away with "ISDN modem," but not for the Network+ exam, please!

ISDN Bridges and Routers

Because it's more data friendly than PSTN, ISDN has more data-oriented devices available; in addition to a basic internal or external TA, you can purchase routers with built-in ISDN interfaces (see Figure 7.5). Some of these routers include a built-in hub so that connecting your LAN requires nothing more than plugging in a patch cable. Many workgroup ISDN routers also have a built-in DHCP server to assign IP addresses automatically.

Basic Rate Interface (BRI)

ISDN services vary from country to country, but the standard service is called Basic Rate Interface (BRI) and is provided to the user as two 64K data channels, known as the *bearer* (or *B*) channels, plus a low-speed (16 Kbps) channel that's used for call setup, control, and other signaling, called the *delta* (or *D*) channel. For this reason, Basic Rate Interface is sometimes described as 2B+D.

An ISDN TA might support data communications using only one B channel (see Figure 7.6), providing a 64K connection (the other channel could be used at

FIGURE 7.5 ISDN TA/router

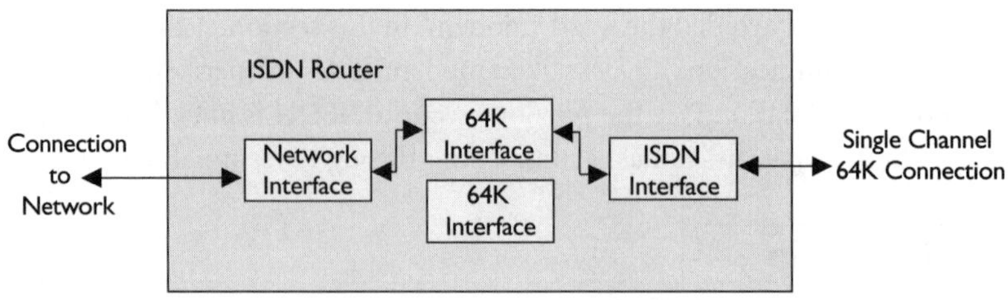

FIGURE 7.6 ISDN router using one channel

the same time for an ISDN phone), but some TAs can aggregate the two B channels to provide a 128K link—provided the kit at the other end (your other office or your Internet service provider) also supports channel aggregation, or *bonding* (see Figure 7.7). However, remember that each B channel counts as one phone call for charging purposes; therefore, if your ISDN package doesn't offer unlimited connection time, you will be billed for *two* calls every time you use your 128K link.

Local Lingo

channel aggregation Channel aggregation, also known as *bonding,* combines multiple channels into a single link.

The ISDN Network Terminator

In the United States, the user must provide the local interface to the ISDN service; this is called a *network terminator,* or *NT-1,* and is built into most ISDN communications equipment. In Europe (for ISDN2e, the European 2B+D service) NT-1 is provided by the telecom company as a wall-mounted box with two RJ45 data outlets, allowing two pieces of equipment to be connected.

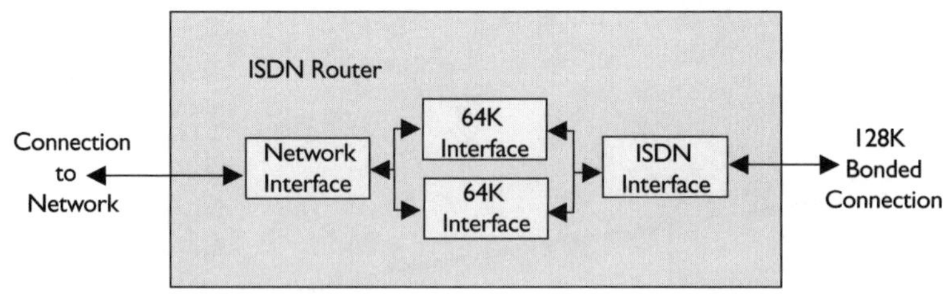

FIGURE 7.7 ISDN channel bonding

Primary Rate Interface (PRI)

Primary Rate Interface provides multiple B channels—the most common configuration in the United States is 23 × 64K B channels + 1 × 64K D channel (23B+D), providing a bandwidth of 1.544 Mbps (megabits per second). European PRI—known as ISDN30e—can be configured with any number of channels between 8 and 30, with 30B+D providing a bandwidth of 2 Mbps.

Using ISDN

ISDN-related data technology has been around for some time and is considered stable and mature, making it a popular choice for business use, even when other options are available (see the next sections of this chapter). For general networking, Primary Rate Interface is widely used for interoffice connections (WAN links) and for "fat pipes" between businesses and the Internet service provider (see Figure 7.8). ISDN has also traditionally been used as a fallback service that kicks in if the (faster) permanent WAN connection between two sites fails, and *ISDN fallback* is built into many WAN bridges.

Circuit Switching

ISDN is a dial-up (circuit switching) service—you need to dial the number of the host system to which you want to connect (every time), perform the data transfer, and then close the connection. Although this sounds like a bit of a pain, ISDN dial-up service connects very quickly—users will not typically notice a delay. ISDN also allows you to dial into different systems according to your need

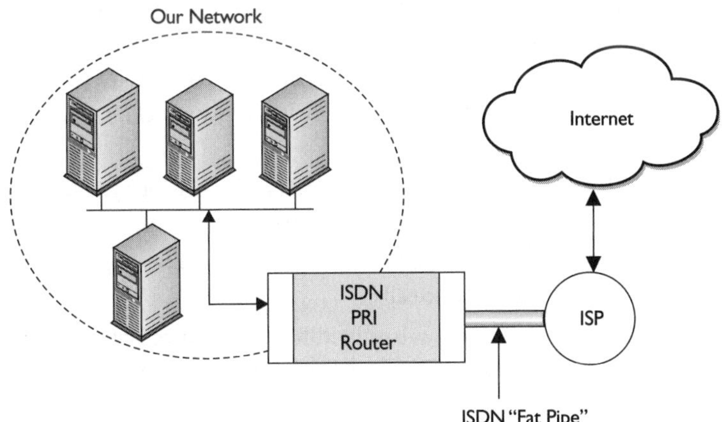

FIGURE 7.8 A Primary Rate Interface fat pipe

(unlike a fixed WAN link between two sites), making it ideal for connecting computer systems to commercial services, such as printers and graphics design studios, where you can establish a direct PC-to-PC link and upload large files such as artwork and layouts.

Local Lingo

circuit switching The principle of establishing a connection (circuit) through a communications service, sending and receiving data, and then closing the call.

Costs can be high if calls are charged by the second/minute/unit, but many service providers now offer flat-rate packages. More recently (especially in Europe), the delay in rolling out more IT-friendly and low-cost services, such as ADSL, has led to widespread use of ISDN for home systems, too.

ISDN Spoofing

If you are *not* on a flat-rate fee scheme, do make sure that your ISDN setup is configured correctly. Many network protocols send out regular broadcasts, and your ISDN kit may keep establishing a link with another site to pass on these broadcasts. Guess what? You still have to pay the phone bill! Many ISDN routers support *spoofing*, where they pretend to establish a link (to keep the broadcasting kit happy), but they don't actually do so (see Figure 7.9).

ISDN Summary

- ISDN is a stable technology providing digital data and telephony services.
- Basic Rate ISDN (BRI) provides a 64K or 128K data circuit with two bearer (B) channels for data and one delta (D) channel for signaling and control.
- Primary Rate ISDN (PRI) provides a 23B+D, 1.544 Mbps (up to 30B+D, 2 Mbps in Europe) circuit for faster connectivity.
- ISDN is a dial-up service, and calls may be charged per second/minute/unit just like regular phone calls.
- ISDN is widely used for low-bandwidth WAN connectivity, as a fallback for faster links, and as a dial-up service between businesses.

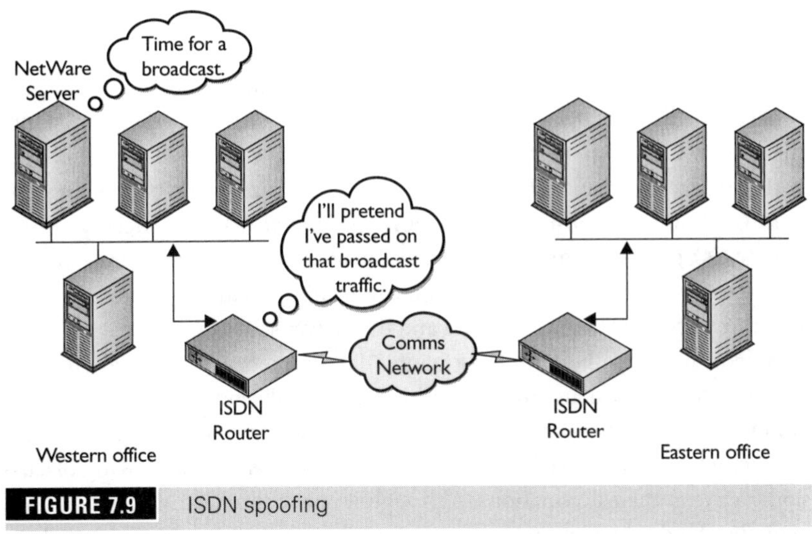

FIGURE 7.9 ISDN spoofing

Objective 7.04 Fixed-Line (Always-on) Services

When dial-up service cannot meet your needs for bandwidth or a constant connection, a leased line will be your next option. Unlike a PSTN or ISDN line, you cannot dial phone numbers from a leased line—it is a hard-wired, always-on link between two locations. You can choose from among several competing technologies, depending on your specific needs.

Packet-Switching Circuits

A packet-switching network breaks data up into smaller pieces called *packets* and routes them individually to their destination. By "routes them individually," we mean that there is no dedicated path between the sending and receiving site—the path for each packet is determined on-the-fly as the packet arrives on the network. When you use a packet-switching circuit, you rent space on a WAN owned by someone else (usually a telecom company) that's then used to carry your data between sites. Because the WAN won't usually run all the way to your premises, the telecom company will provide lines between local access points (the central office or local exchange) and your premises. The distance between the two COs sometimes defines what is known as the *charging distance,* which is used to calculate your rental bill. Some packet-switching options charge by the amount of data transmitted across the network instead.

Although with a packet-switching circuit, from your perspective you appear to have a dedicated, always-on WAN link between sites, your data is actually mixed with that from all the other customers using the packet-switched network. This may seem like a bit of a mess and also a security risk, but your equipment is set up to establish a *permanent virtual circuit (PVC)* between your site and the CO, giving the appearance that your site is the only one on the network (see Figure 7.10). Your data travels on the same physical media as the other customers, but you never see their data and they never see yours.

As you might gather from the name, data packets are switched (routed) round the network in an arbitrary fashion, ultimately ending up at the correct destination. The route that individual packets take varies according to numerous factors, but all the packets eventually (we hope—see the following discussion) arrive at their destinations. Although we are concentrating on data links here, the standard telephone system is actually a packet-switching network, as most voice traffic is carried today as digital data.

Packet-switching networks don't have to be fast. Some packet-switching networks use fairly old technology and run at speeds of only 9.6 Kbps, but this

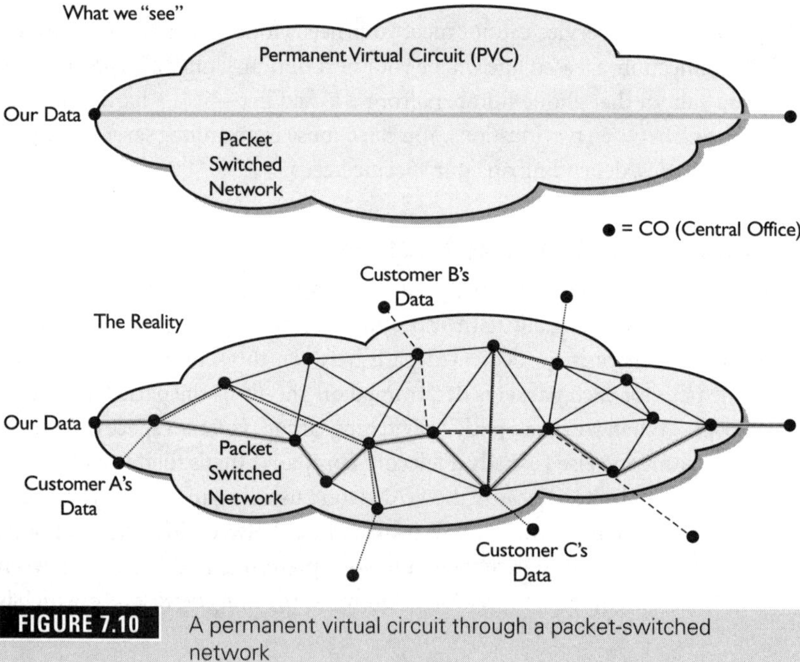

FIGURE 7.10 A permanent virtual circuit through a packet-switched network

speed is adequate for simple tasks such as linking ATM machines to a central location. Obviously, a WAN link running at 9.6 Kbps is going to be a bit slow, but other packet-switching circuits offer greater speed, as you'll see later.

X.25

One of the oldest commercial packet-switching networks (from the 1970s) goes by the name X.25. This is a connection-oriented (reliable data delivery) analog system that can carry data, interfacing with your networking equipment through a device known as a *Packet Assembler/Disassembler (PAD)*. X.25 is generally used for terminals and other low-end devices, and a PAD typically has a standard serial (RS232) interface, not a LAN connection, although X.25 solutions are available for link speeds up to 2 Mbps. The X.25 spec operates at layers 1 through 3 of the OSI model (Physical, Data Link, and Network).

Frame Relay

Frame relay is a simplified (still connection-oriented), digital version of X.25. It provides no built-in error control (it works at the OSI Physical and Data Link layers only). Therefore, external, higher-level (OSI layer) protocols are used to ensure data integrity. Because the transmission protocols are stripped down to the basics (packets may make it to their destination, or they may not), frame relay is faster than X.25 and can be used successfully for WAN (data) and voice applications; speeds up to around 50 Mbps are available.

One other main difference between X.25 and frame relay is that with X.25, your data packets are sent individually across the switched network to their destination. With frame relay, data packets are mixed together (multiplexed) for transmission, which maximizes the use of available bandwidth, further contributing to frame relay's high performance (see Figure 7.11). Many of the general high-speed circuits used for WAN interconnectivity today are based on frame relay technology.

Exam Tip

Frame relay networks use multiplexed data to maximize bandwidth. Packet-switching networks send every data packet individually.

Quality of Service

Unlike X.25, frame relay provides a Quality of Service (QoS) facility, meaning that the bandwidth a connection gets depends on what that connection is doing.

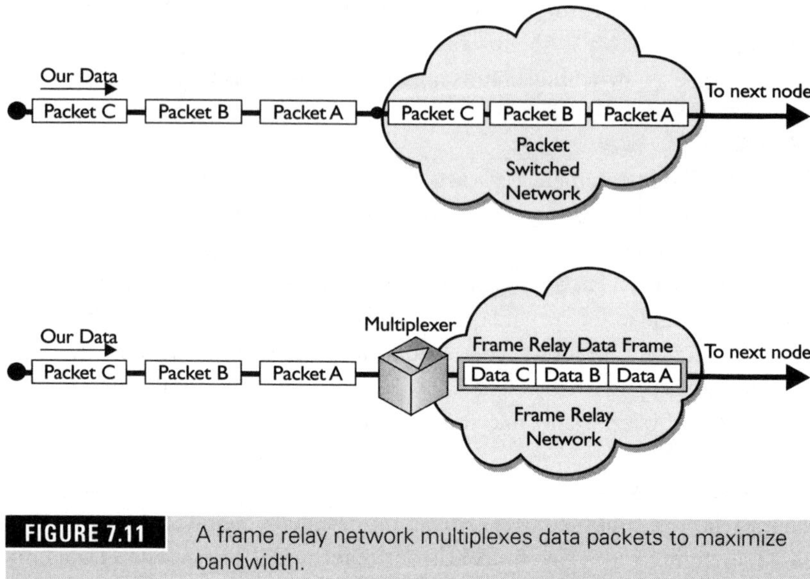

FIGURE 7.11 A frame relay network multiplexes data packets to maximize bandwidth.

If it's sending general data, this data may be carried at normal speed, but a videoconferencing link can be given greater bandwidth to ensure the best possible link (sound and video) quality.

At the low-speed end, frame relay networks can be accessed via ISDN, and this allows for *switched virtual circuits,* where you choose a specific destination for the task at hand. If you use ISDN for connecting to an Internet service provider, you may find that when you dial into the ISP, your telecom provider routes your data to the ISP using a frame relay network.

ATM

Most modern, digital, switched networks use Asynchronous Transfer Mode (ATM). ATM was developed from the technology first implemented on digital voice circuits. In fact, it is also possible (but expensive!) to implement a "to-the-desktop" ATM LAN using ATM NICs and hubs, with standard speeds of 25, 50, 155, and 622 Mbps, the latter using fiber media. The performance of ATM WAN links varies according to the carrying media, but speeds into the gigabits per second are available.

ATM also supports Quality of Service to provide optimized bandwidth on demand, but its main claim to fame is its use of very small, fixed-size data packets—called *ATM cells*—only 53 bytes in total (48 bytes of data) per packet (see Figure 7.12). When it was originally implemented for carrying voice traffic, the loss of the odd cell in transit wasn't a problem because 48 bytes of digitized speech is barely a click and won't be noticed by the listener. When it comes to data, however, losing the odd 48 bytes of a database would be a tad worrisome, and this was one of the main challenges for ATM data network designers. Thankfully, they got it right, and the whole thing works, delivering all the packets safely, with control protocols in place to ensure reliability.

Local Lingo

cell switching The switching technology used on ATM networks with very small data packets (cells).

ATM networks can easily connect to other networks using a router, and this remains a very popular choice for high-performance WAN connectivity.

The small packet size implemented in ATM can cause problems under some circumstances, where larger data packets (such as those used by protocols such as IPX/SPX and TCP/IP) are fragmented for transmission, but modern ATM bridges and routers have mostly overcome these problems, using various techniques to accommodate the fragmentation.

Switching Circuits Summary

Here are the basic points to remember about switching circuits:

- Switching circuits typically provide an always-on connection between sites and are very popular for WAN links.
- Some services provide only a point-to-point *permanent virtual circuit* between two sites, but others also support a *switched virtual circuit,* which allows you to choose the destination, as required.

Modern switched networks, based on frame relay and ATM technology, are capable of providing high-speed WAN connectivity.

Header: 5 bytes	Payload: 48 bytes

FIGURE 7.12 ATM cell—that's it!

General Fixed-Line Services

Sometimes we don't worry about the nature of the network providing our WAN connectivity—we just want to pay for (lease) a fixed bandwidth between sites and have it installed; whether our data goes via copper, fiber, ATM, or frame relay, we don't care, as long as everything works.

Many telecom companies and WAN solution providers offer a generic connection to their service, and one of the most popular options is a 1.544 Mbps circuit (24 × 64K channels) known as a T-1 (or DS-1) carrier. T-1 provides a service akin to Primary Rate Interface and often uses the same interface equipment. Many of the services behind the scenes are, in fact, based on frame relay technology, although ATM is becoming increasingly popular. Table 7.1 lists the two most popular T-carriers (see if you can work out which is the most expensive to lease).

In Europe, a different carrier system is available, offering other levels of performance (see Table 7.2). The principle is the same, though: multiple 64K channels are provided according to your needs and budget.

To connect to your T- or E-circuit, you use a pair of devices known as a *Channel Service Unit (CSU)* and a *Data Service Unit (DSU)*. Often, but not always, these items are built into one module, providing a CSU/DSU, which, for all intents and purposes, can look just like a humble modem. Keeping things simple, the CSU provides the interface to the network, whereas the DSU provides an interface to the T-*x* or E-*x* carrier circuit. The actual interface to your T-*x*/E-*x* connection will depend on how the service is provided—it may be a copper or fiber connection.

Travel Advisory

Some information sources state that the designator T-*x* is for copper-based circuits, and the designator DS-*x* is for fiber. Technically, the term "T-*x*" refers to the copper transmission medium, whereas "DS-*x*" refers to the service rather than the medium, but these terms frequently are used interchangeably.

TABLE 7.1 T-1 and T-3 Lines for the U.S. and Canada

Carrier	Bandwidth	Channels
T-1 (DS-1)	1.544 Mbps	24
T-3 (DS-3)	44.736 Mbps	672

TABLE 7.2 E-1 and E-3 Lines for Europe

Carrier	Bandwidth	Channels
E-1	2.048 Mbps	32
E-3	34.368 Mbps	512

SONET and SDH

The Synchronous Optical Network (SONET) is an American National Standards Institute (ANSI) standard for data transmission over optical fiber, and it's very popular for telecommunications and WAN connectivity and with Internet service providers. SONET is also used extensively for metropolitan area networks (MANs) because of its ability to carry a mix of services, including data, voice, and video. SONET is widely used in the United States, Canada, and Japan, and it provides a range of services (speeds), known as *Optical Carrier (OC) levels* (see Table 7.3).

The European equivalent of SONET is the Synchronous Digital Hierarchy (SDH). There are some minor speed differences between SONET and SDH at the lower end, but the European SDH speed standard STM-1 closely maps to OC-3, which also closely maps to the 155 Mbps ATM standard, making OC-3 a very popular connectivity option because it fits so many requirements.

Exam Tip

You don't have to remember all the OC-*x* speeds, but it is worth noting that OC-3 is a popular option.

TABLE 7.3 OC-*x* Carrier Speeds

OC-1	51.84 Mbps
OC-3	155.52 Mbps
OC-12	622.08 Mbps
OC-24	1.244 Gbps
OC-48	2.488 Gbps
OC-192	10 Gbps
OC-256	13.271 Gbps
OC-768	40 Gbps

SONET backbones form part of many of the connectivity options we have discussed here, so your PSTN voice traffic, ISDN, ATM, T-1, or switched circuit data may well make its way toward its ultimate destination via a SONET/SDH pathway (see Figure 7.13). Some top-end service providers can also provide you with a direct, point-to-point SONET connection (so-called *private* SONET) between offices, using their main SONET network to create a permanent virtual circuit.

Other WAN Services

This chapter has covered the mainstream wide area networking connectivity options. Other wide area services are also available if you have the need, the business case, and the cash—services such as satellite links and national wireless networks. Although the focus of the Network+ exam is on wide area networking, to link LANs together, remember that in the real world there are often wide area requirements that don't need 10+ Mbps WAN performance; we've already mentioned cash machines, and we can add to that list other services such as the updating of stock levels overnight in retail stores, the transmission of financial information, and the transmission of data from traffic-monitoring stations. If you don't need to send megabytes of data instantaneously, some of the slower—and therefore cheaper—wide area networking options may be perfectly suitable.

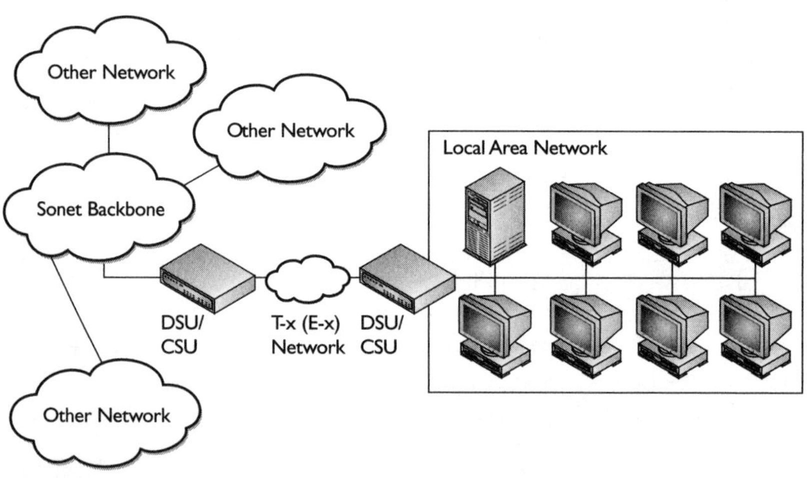

FIGURE 7.13 SONET backbones often carry other data services between destinations.

✔ **Objective 7.01: Basic Equipment Requirements** At the most fundamental level, your wide area networking kit must provide two interfaces: one to your network and one to the communications circuit you are using for the WAN link. The equipment may also do other things, such as compress and encrypt data, and will almost certainly provide routing or bridging functionality.

✔ **Objective 7.02: PSTN—The Analog Telephone System** PSTN, also known as *POTS (plain-old telephone service)* is the least attractive option for a WAN connection due to its speed: 56 Kbps on a good day, and probably only 33.6 Kbps if you don't have the full V.90/92 setup. For dial-in remote users, it is a viable option if the speed is acceptable (more about this in the next chapter).

✔ **Objective 7.03: ISDN—The Digital Telephone System** Although Basic Rate Interface (BRI) starts by offering only a 64K link—which seems to be only marginally better than the PSTN—this 64K is pretty much guaranteed, and you can also aggregate the two 64 B channels actually provided to create a 128K link—provided that the terminal adapter or bridge/router equipment at the other end of your WAN link supports this option, too. Flat-rate charging options for ISDN also make it look attractive, but if you're not on such a scheme, remember that you'll generally be charged by the second/minute/unit for each channel in use and that incorrect network setups can make a lot of regular calls just to exchange routing and other information, so check your kit's ability to block these regular calls using a procedure called *spoofing*. Primary Rate Interface (PRI) offers up to 23 (30 in Europe) B channels and therefore can offer a bandwidth of up to 1.544 Mbps (2 Mbps in Europe). PRI ISDN is widely used for interoffice links and connectivity to ISPs where there's need for a "big" connection (well, bigger than BRI anyway!).

✔ **Objective 7.04: Fixed-Line (Always-on) Services** Leased line options are best suited to site-to-site links, and they generally provide a packet-switched, permanent virtual circuit between sites through the communications company. The old, analog X.25 system is not designed for today's high-speed demands, but it is still suitable for slow-speed links and is mainly used for applications that don't transfer a lot of information. Frame relay switched networks, on the other hand, can provide decent bandwidth and are often used for WAN connectivity. ATM technology also provides a high-speed, switched option using small, 53-byte data packets called *cells*. Among the most popular switched solutions are those defined by the designations T-1 and T-3 (E-1 and E-3 in Europe); these provide connectivity at 1.544 and 44.736 Mbps, respectively (2 and 34.368 Mbps in Europe). The SONET (SDH in Europe) standards provide very high bandwidth and are generally used by telecom carriers and network service providers to form their main backbones. SONET speeds are referred to as *Optical Carrier (OC)* levels, with OC-3 (155 Mbps) being a very popular choice.

REVIEW QUESTIONS

1. Which of the following provides the fastest service? (Select one answer.)
   - **A.** BRI ISDN
   - **B.** PRI ISDN
   - **C.** PSTN
   - **D.** V.92
2. John wants to connect his laptop computer to an ISDN port. Which of the following will probably be suitable? (Select one answer.)
   - **A.** V.90 modem
   - **B.** V.92 modem
   - **C.** NIC
   - **D.** A terminal adapter
3. You have been asked to provide a wide area network between two offices. The primary objective is to provide data connectivity, and a secondary objective is to allow your videoconferencing system to receive optimum bandwidth. Your proposed solution is a 128K BRI using channel bonding and ISDN routers. What goals does this solution meet? (Select one answer.)
   - **A.** Both the primary and the secondary objectives
   - **B.** The primary objective only
   - **C.** Neither of the above
4. Which of the following apply to an ATM WAN? (Select all that apply.)
   - **A.** The ATM WAN uses wireless technology.
   - **B.** ATM offers a QoS facility.
   - **C.** The WAN supports kilobyte-sized, variable-length packets.
   - **D.** ATM uses small, fixed-length data packets called cells.

5. Which of the following services provides the greatest throughput? (Select one answer.)

   A. T-1

   B. V.90

   C. OC-3

   D. E-3

6. Which of the following is not an optical WAN standard? (Select one answer.)

   A. X.25

   B. STM-1

   C. SONET

   D. SDH

7. What type of interface is required to connect to a T-1 circuit? (Select one answer.)

   A. X.25

   B. PAD

   C. 2B+D

   D. CSU/DSU

8. Harry has just been asked why the company's telecom bill for the WAN link is so high, and he has noticed that the bill includes a significant number of short-duration dial-up calls. What is the most likely cause? (Select one answer.)

   A. The ATM interface is faulty.

   B. The V.90 modem has been set to dial a not-in-service number.

   C. ISDN spoofing is not configured correctly.

   D. Harry has set the wrong ATM frame format.

9. What is the maximum distance allowed to the CO for a BRI link? (Select one answer.)

   A. 100 meters

   B. 2,048 meters

   C. 1,800 feet

   D. 18,000 feet

10. Which of the following is a packet-switching network? (Select one answer.)
    - **A.** ISDN
    - **B.** ATM
    - **C.** X.25
    - **D.** V.90

REVIEW ANSWERS

1. **B** Primary Rate Interface provides the fastest service: BRI = 128 Kbps max, PRI = 1.544 Mbps max, PSTN = 56 Kbps, V.92 = 56 Kbps.
2. **D** John needs an ISDN terminal adapter. ISDN lines are already digital, so no modem is required.
3. **B** The ISDN connection will provide connectivity but no Quality of Service and therefore will not give any form of priority to the videoconferencing data.
4. **B** **D** ATM provides QoS and also uses small packets called cells.
5. **C** OC-3 = 155.52 Mbps, T-1 = 1.544 Mbps, V.90 = 56 Kbps, E-3 = 34.268 Mbps.
6. **A** X.25 is provided over a copper wire circuit and therefore is not an optical standard.
7. **D** A CSU/DSU combination is required for a T-*x* connection. The CSU connects to your local network, whereas the DSU handles communication on the T-*x* connection.
8. **C** Because the WAN link is clearly working, all the answers that relate to configuration problems (A, B, and D) are unlikely to be true. In any case, this is a dial-up problem; Harry's not looking at an ATM issue because he's not even using ATM (A and D), and if he were dialing a not-in-service number with a V.90 modem (B), he would not be charged. Unless Harry set up spoofing, the ISDN line will connect every time one of the systems on the network sends out a broadcast, even if the broadcast is entirely for local purposes.
9. **D** ISDN works only if you are within 18,000 feet of the nearest CO.
10. **C** X.25 is a packet-switching network.

Remote Access

ITINERARY

- **Objective 8.01** Defining Remote Connectivity
- **Objective 8.02** Dial-In Remote Access
- **Objective 8.03** Dial-In Software Requirements
- **Objective 8.04** Fixed-Point Remote Access

NEWBIE	SOME EXPERIENCE	EXPERT
3 hours	2 hours	1 hour

Mobile computing, once the province of the occasional road warrior, has become the norm for many organizations. It's not unusual to walk into an urban coffee shop and see dozens of "information workers" toiling away over their favorite overpriced coffee drink. Telecommuting, once a bold experiment, has become commonplace. To support all these mobile workers, network techs must provide remote access. Chapter 7 covered the WAN technology used to link networks together, but now we have to connect remote users to the network resources they need.

Defining Remote Connectivity

The *L* in LAN stands for "local," and in a classic LAN all the systems (clients and servers) are said to be local to each other. Each system connects to the network using some type of *dedicated* connection, usually a cable. A remote system, in contrast, accesses your LAN via a connection that your organization does not own or control—for example, a telephone line or the Internet. The remote system will likely spend at least some of the time disconnected from the network.

Until recently, most remote users accessed the network using a dial-up connection, and dial-up connections remain common. Dial-up remote access requires both a client and server (see Figure 8.1). The remote access server has a dedicated connection to a LAN and some type of modem. The server runs special software that works with the modem to listen for rings, authenticate the user, and provide network access. The remote access client also uses a modem, and software to communicate with the server.

Remote or Local?

If you have a remote access server and a remote access client, which is local and which is remote? Two different definitions exist. Many people define the terms "remote" and "local" in a relative way—from their own viewpoint. Thus, their local system is the one with them, and the remote system is the one elsewhere (back at the office, perhaps). For remote access terminology, however, the office-based server is always the local system and the users *out there somewhere* are always remote. This second definition is the preferred way to define a local and remote system, but you should be prepared for Network+ to throw questions at you from either perspective (see Figure 8.2).

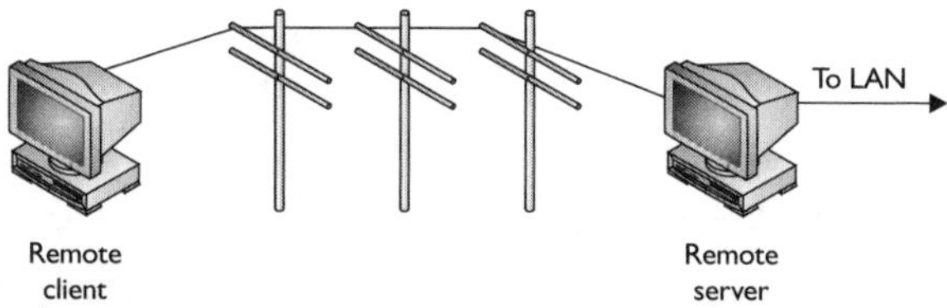

FIGURE 8.1 Remote client and server

Objective 8.02 Dial-In Remote Access

Most remote users connect using a dial-up service. Dial-up service includes both regular phone lines and ISDN lines. Regular phone lines, known as either public switched telephone network (PSTN) lines or plain-old telephone service (POTS) lines, support maximum access speeds between 56 Kbps and 64 Kbps. ISDN lines support speeds of up to 64 Kbps per channel. (You will sometimes see ISDN speeds of 128 Kbps advertised—to achieve 128 Kbps you have to combine two ISDN channels.) Although faster alternatives exist, PSTN and ISDN lines reach far more users because they piggyback on the existing telephone infrastructure.

Client Hardware Requirements

In order to use a dial-in remote access server, your PC, notebook, or whatever will need a compatible terminal adapter (TA) for using an ISDN line or a modem for using a POTS line. The speed standards for ISDN are fixed, but modems come in a variety of shapes and sizes—internal, external, USB, serial, and so forth—and support different standards. Fortunately, all the important modem standards (protocols) have been well defined over the years and are now managed by the

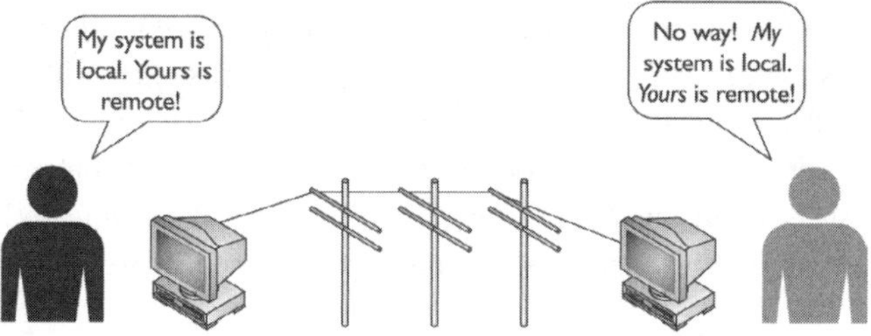

FIGURE 8.2 Relative local and remote systems

International Telecommunications Union-Telecommunication (ITU-T) to ensure that a Brand X modem can always talk to Brand Y.

V Standards and Bits per Second

We already discussed the ITU V.90 and V.92 (56 Kbps) protocols in Chapter 7, but there are three other protocols, unrelated to speed, that all decent modems will support:

- **V.42** Used for error checking
- **V.42bis** Used for data compression
- **MNP5** Defines error-correction and data-compression protocols

A modern modem will support these protocols to maximize throughput and to cope with data-transmission errors. With most modems that support these protocols, there's nothing you have to do to turn the support on—you just enjoy the benefits.

Modem speed is measured in *bits per second (bps)*. You will see the term "baud" used to refer to speed, but baud actually refers to the "electronic state change" of the signal and not to the amount of data being transmitted. The POTS lines in the United States top out at around 2400 baud, so any speed beyond 2,400 bps cannot be referred to as a "baud" rate. Modems today manage to send more than one bit with each state change, allowing for the higher speeds we see with today's modems. The Network+ exam doesn't worry about the ins and outs of the baud/bps issue—just remember that modem speed is measured in bits per second (bps) and not baud.

Exam Tip

The speed of a modern modem is measured in bits per second (bps), not baud.

In order for two modems to run at their fastest, they must modulate signals in the same fashion. The two modems must also query, or negotiate with, each other in order to determine the fastest speed of each modem. The International Telecommunications Union has put forth its ITU-T (V.) standards to define a series of common speeds, and a pair of modems will negotiate to determine the best standard they both support. The most common speed standards are as follows:

- V.22 1,200 bps
- V.22bis 2,400 bps

- **V.32** 9,600 bps
- **V.32bis** 14,400 bps
- **V.34** 28,000/33,600 bps
- **V.90/V.92** 57,600 bps

Serial Port Speeds

Many people get a little confused on the concept of port speed and modem speed. All versions of Windows give you the opportunity to set the port speed, which is the speed of the data between the *serial port* of your PC and the *modem*—not between the modems. As a rule, always set this speed to 115,200 bps, regardless of the capabilities of your modem. This setting will allow for the most efficient transfer of data. Setting a slower speed is likely to result in slower modem performance.

The Serial Port Interface

The electronic device that manifests itself as a serial port is known as a *Universal Asynchronous Receiver/Transmitter (UART;* see Figure 8.3). The original IBM PC (and many clone machines) used a design based on an Intel UART chip known as the 8250. The 8250 UART performs poorly at speeds over 9,600 bps, and newer PCs use a newer chip design based on an Intel chip called the 16550. If you happen to stumble across an old PC and you set its modem serial port to 115,200 bps, your modem will perform poorly if at all. Faced with this problem, all you can do is install a new serial port card (with a 16550-based design) or use an internal modem, which will include its own serial port circuitry. If you think you have encountered this problem, the modem icon in the Windows Control Panel includes a diagnostics option that tells you your UART type.

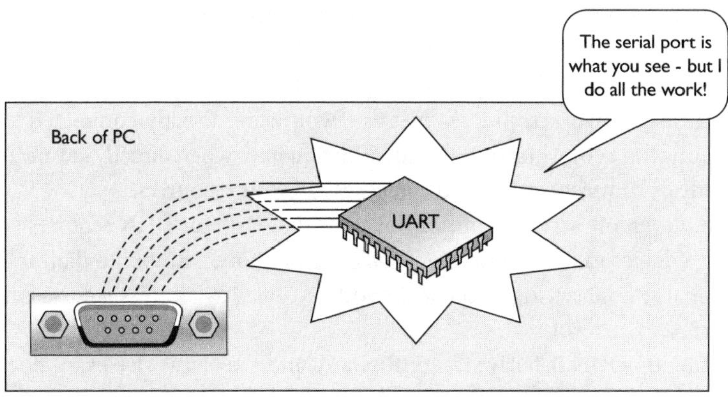

FIGURE 8.3 PC serial ports are controlled by a UART chip.

Windows Modems or Soft Modems

Many low-cost PCs use a new breed of modem called a *soft modem* or *Winmodem* (Windows modem). These units do *not* have a UART, and instead rely on the PC's processor to perform the data-processing tasks normally associated with this chip. Although many people will never notice that they are using a Winmodem, be aware that on slower PCs these modems can tie up processing power and slow things down during heavy data transfers. With today's fast PCs, you may never notice this performance hit. If you only occasionally use your modem, using a soft modem may not be a significant disadvantage. On a fast PC, the main disadvantage of using a soft modem is that many soft modem manufacturers only supply drivers for Windows, leaving users of alternative operating systems such as Linux and BSD with a modem that they cannot use. If performance or support for non-Windows operating systems is a factor, avoid using soft modems.

Dial-In Software Requirements

OK, so you have the hardware for dial-in. Now, what's going to make it work? You need some software!

Client Side: Microsoft Dial-Up Networking

Microsoft's Dial-Up Networking (DUN), configured through Network and Dial-Up Connections on Windows 2000 or through Network Connections on Windows XP, allows you to configure your modem to dial into a remote access server. DUN supports a wide range of authentication protocols, including PAP, CHAP, MS-CHAP, MS-CHAP2 v2, EAP, and Kerberos. These authentication protocols are detailed in Table 8.1. Once you dial up and log on to the network, you can use network resources just as if you were directly connected to the LAN. You won't enjoy the same bandwidth you have when directly connected to a 100 Mbps connection, but you can access all your resources.

Like all remote access clients of this type, the setup for DUN requires you to specify a device to use (modem or ISDN TA), a phone number to dial, and any additional special settings, such as IP address, gateway address, and so on (see Figure 8.4).

Setting up DUN is fairly straightforward, and the Network+ exam does not dive into the intimate details. The sole exception would be your choice of the protocol used to provide you with a network connection through a telephone line. This is covered later.

TABLE 8.1 Remote Access Authentication Methods

Authentication Protocol	Description
PAP (Password Authentication Protocol)	Sends passwords in clear text, so it's less secure than other options but widely supported.
CHAP (Challenge Handshake Authentication Protocol)	Passwords are encrypted in transit using MD5 encryption scheme, but stored in plain text on the server. The most commonly used authentication protocol for dial-up connections.
MS-CHAP	Proprietary Microsoft version of CHAP.
MS-CHAP v2	Updated version of MS-CHAP that allows for two-way authentication.
EAP (Extensible Authentication Protocol)	Enables the use of newer authentication methods such as smart cards and certificates.
Kerberos	Strong cryptography solution that enables clients and servers to authenticate each other. Useful both for remote access and within LANs.

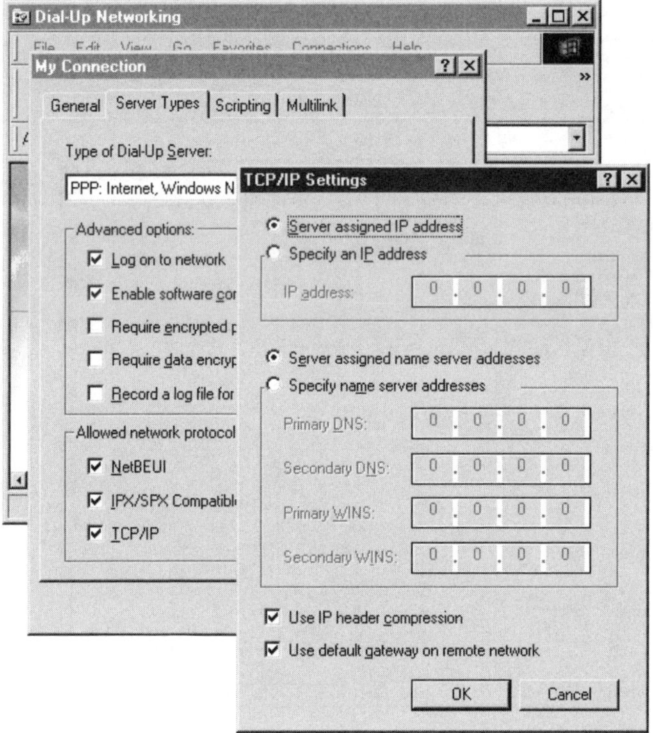

FIGURE 8.4 Configuring DUN

Server Side: Microsoft Remote Access Service (RAS)

If you are using Microsoft Dial-Up Networking to connect yourself to your organization's network, you may well then be using Microsoft's Remote Access Service (RAS) on your Windows NT/2000 server to manage your dial-in services. You do not need to know the ins and outs of RAS for the Network+ exam, but you should be generally aware that you need to configure the server to accept calls, provide the necessary passwords (many RAS servers have a separate logon password just to allow the user to access the remote access server), and set the dial-up user's rights/permissions on the server. (Many remote servers have a separate set of permissions for dial-up users). Figure 8.5 shows Remote Access Service being configured.

Remote Access Protocols

All the Data Link layer networking protocols you encountered in previous chapters are designed for use with networks using LAN media such as coax or UTP

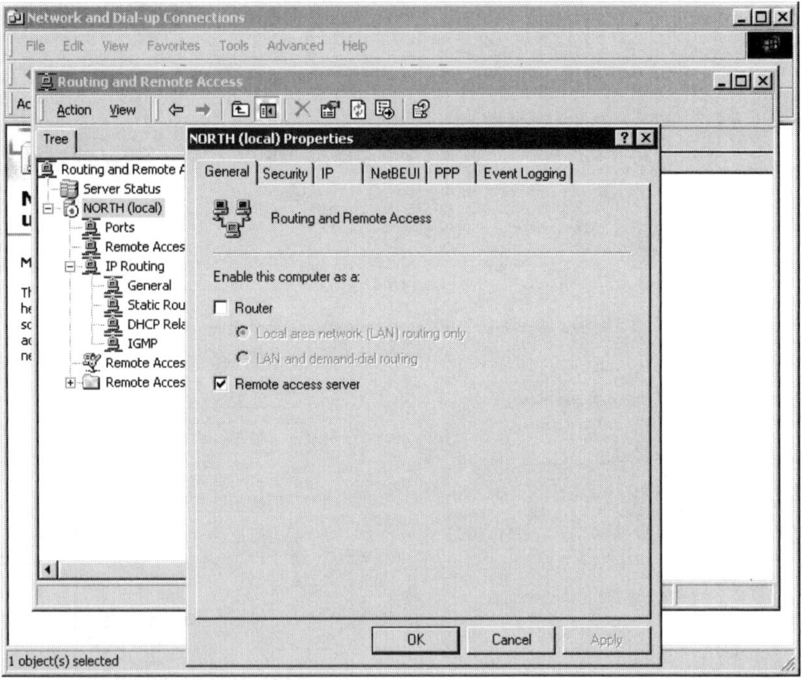

FIGURE 8.5 Configuring RAS

wiring. Telephone lines and serial port network connections also require a Data Link layer protocol.

SLIP

SLIP (Serial Line Internet Protocol), the first widely used Data Link protocol for serial interfaces, has many limitations. First, SLIP only supports IP; you can't use it for NetBEUI or IPX networks. Second, any system that uses SLIP requires a static IP address. Static IP addresses weren't too big an issue in the early days of direct system-to-system connections, but today's shortage of IP addresses makes SLIP unacceptable. Most remote access programs continue to support SLIP as a backward-compatibility option, but SLIP is not a good choice for today's requirements. Let's be clear: Don't use SLIP unless you need to connect to an older, legacy system that doesn't support PPP.

Exam Tip

SLIP only works with IP and requires a static IP address.

PPP

PPP, the Point-to-Point Protocol, addresses all of SLIP's shortcomings and has replaced SLIP in most cases. PPP supports IPX and NetBEUI in addition to IP and supports dynamic IP address allocation. All modern remote access software comes with PPP support. Use PPP, not SLIP, for your dial-up connections, as shown in Figure 8.6.

Exam Tip

PPP can work with TCP/IP, NetBEUI, and IPX.

Remote Control Software

Using Dial-Up Networking and RAS extends your organization's network to your remote PC. A network connection that runs at (let's hope!) around 56 Kbps is not going to be much fun if you have to retrieve and work on a large spreadsheet. Let's say you have 1MB (1,024KB) of data to download; assuming your modem connection makes 56K, that's around 6KB of data transfer per second. That spreadsheet's going to take about 170 seconds—or nearly 3 minutes—to get to you!

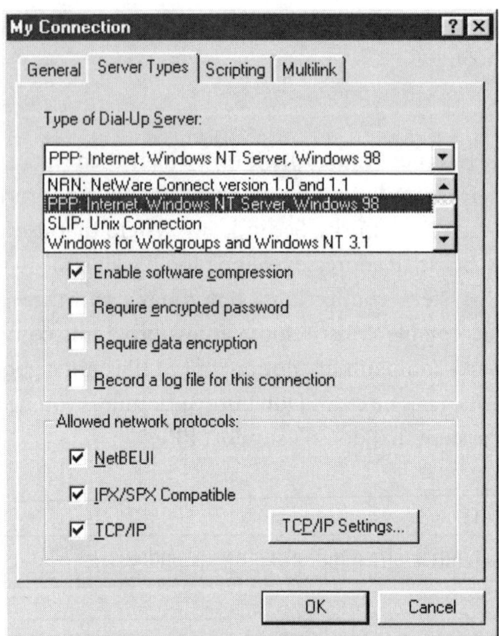

FIGURE 8.6 Use PPP for your remote access requirements—everyone else is!

An alternative to a DUN-type link is to dial into a computer on your in-house network and take it over, operating it remotely. This way, all that comes down the wire is the screen information, and all that goes up the wire is the data for your keyboard and mouse operations. This way of working forms the basis of a number of remote access options where the applications involved are data-heavy.

Various remote access products of this type are available. Common ones include Symantec's pcAnywhere, Altiris's Carbon Copy, and VNC (Virtual Network Computing).

Heavy-duty Remote Access: Remote Desktop

Sometimes, there is nothing like sitting in front of your own computer—or at least that used to be true. Today, you have many options for taking remote control of you PC from another computer, enabling yourself to enjoy the benefits of your own PC without actually having to be sitting in front of it. By "remote control," I mean that the screen on the computer in front of you will look just like the desktop on the remote computer. Also, your keyboard and mouse input will be transferred over the network to the remote PC.

Windows XP includes its own Remote Desktop software, and third-party utilities such as VNC (Virtual Network Computing) exist to allow you to take remote control of other systems. These utilities work well for occasional use, but some network architects will choose to take advantage of a more powerful alternative—the server-based remote desktop.

Rather than making each user responsible for maintaining their own desktop, we can use a high-performance solution based on a Windows NT/2000/2003 server that runs a virtual PC, called a *session,* for every remote user on top of its core operating system (see Figure 8.7). In effect, this solution shares the hardware of the server among the remote users who have sessions, which is a bit like the remote control software described earlier but without the need for a separate physical PC for each remote user. The two main products in this field are Citrix MetaFrame, with what they term their *Independent Computing Architecture (ICA),* and Microsoft's Windows Terminal Server (WTS) with its *Remote Desktop Protocol (RDP).* Both of these solutions can be used with remote access (dial-up or via the Internet) or for local users on the LAN. Because all the users' processing is done by the central server (which has to be fairly powerful because of its workload), the desktop PCs do not need to be that powerful. In fact, some organizations are now installing low-end systems that are barely more than a NIC, keyboard, monitor, mouse, and printer port in a single unit—a so-called *thin client.* In the event that a desktop PC or a laptop begins to fail, you can hand the end user a replacement system and have them back up and running just as soon as they log into their remote desktop—no need for the user to wait for you to rebuild their system.

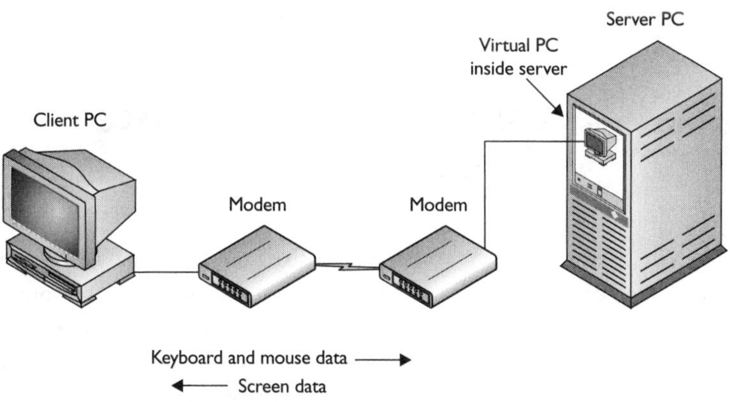

FIGURE 8.7 ICA and RDP create virtual PCs in the central server.

Access Through the Internet

So far, all the remote access options discussed have been dial-up services available from wherever there's a suitable connection point (probably PSTN) directly to your organization's network. Products such as DUN can also connect you to the Internet, so if your organization's server (or whatever you want to connect with) is also on the Internet, you can take this route. In fact, this would be a very flexible option because you could get to your systems from anywhere there's an Internet connection. Cost-wise, there may also be benefits; for example, imagine the following scenarios:

- John is on a business trip to London, England and needs to download a PowerPoint presentation from the corporate server in Atlanta, in the U.S. John hooks his notebook PC to the hotel room's telephone line and dials the remote access server in Atlanta, logs in, and begins to download the presentation—all 12MB of it!
- Isabel is on a business trip to Paris, France and needs to download a PowerPoint presentation from the corporate server in Phoenix, in the U.S. Isabel hooks her notebook PC to the hotel room's telephone line and dials the number of a local Internet service provider, fires up her remote access software, logs in to the corporate server, and begins to download the presentation—all 12MB of it!

Spot the main difference? OK, the names and locations are different, but who do you think will have the biggest phone bill—Isabel with her local call or John with his international call to Atlanta? If you're not sure, then you've never seen a hotel room phone bill—ouch!

Connecting through the Internet raises security issues that we will discuss in Chapter 10.

Fixed-Point Remote Access

If there's a need for remote access from a fixed location—say an employee's home—then dial-up access may not be fast enough. Depending on your location, you may have faster Internet access options. If the systems you need to access are available through the Internet, you can abandon your modem and enjoy the benefits of "broadband" Internet access. (Although this term has a specific meaning in traditional data communications, many people use the word "broadband" to indicate any form of high-speed Internet access.)

ADSL

Asymmetric Digital Subscriber Line (ADSL) provides a high-speed Internet connection using the existing telephone infrastructure. By deploying special equipment in their "central offices," the telephone company can provide download speeds up to 9 Mbps and upload speeds of up to 1 Mbps using your existing phone lines (see Figure 8.8). In this context, the "central office" (or CO) is not some office building but instead refers to locations at which the telephone company terminates customer lines and connects those lines into their larger telephone network. The big downside to ADSL is that you have to be relatively close to one of these central offices, and not all the central offices have been upgraded with the equipment necessary to support ADSL connections. Whether ADSL is available to you depends on where you live. Also, don't forget about the "asymmetric" part—with ADSL you don't get to upload at the same speed that you download.

ADSL has roughly the same distance restrictions as ISDN (18,000 ft, 3.5 km), so if you are too far from the local CO, you will not be able to use the service. ADSL has many variations in upload/download speed, according to the service provider and the country you're in; the more basic service gives a download speed of 512 to 2,048 Kbps maximum and an upload speed of 128 Kbps. Faster and more expensive services may provide a download of 9 Mbps maximum, and an upload of 384 Kbps.

ADSL is one type of a group of similar technologies known as xDSL. The fact that the upload and download speeds are different is the *asymmetric* part of ADSL; other xDSL technologies provide equal upload and download speeds.

ADSL shares a high-bandwidth local distribution point, provided by your local telecom or cable services company, between premises in your area. This sharing arrangement (known as *contention*) can lead to a slowdown in performance if the local area has a lot of ADSL users. Overall, though, performance is significantly greater than a dial-up or ISDN connection.

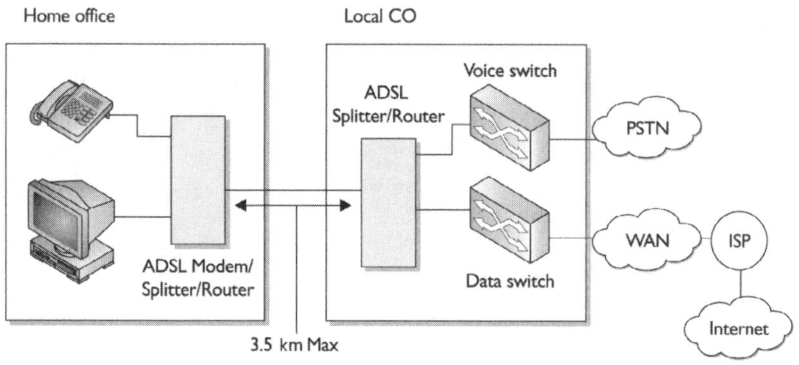

FIGURE 8.8 ADSL connectivity

ADSL providers should tell you what their contention ratio is. Typically, it's 50:1 for home users and 20:1 for business users—that's 50 or 20 connections (not necessarily all in use at the same time) sharing a local 512, 1,024, or 2,048 Kbps download connection. In reality, this *doesn't* mean that each user gets, say, 512/50 Kbps performance, because it's the overall load at the local exchange—where all the connections to the groups of 50 users or 20 users are linked together—that actually limits the available per-user bandwidth.

ADSL Hardware

The most common installation for ADSL consists of an *ADSL modem* that connects to the wall jack. This device is not a modem—it's more like an ISDN terminal adapter—but the term "modem" has stuck, and even the manufacturers of the devices now call them ADSL modems. The ADSL modem connects to a standard NIC, providing the ADSL service. If you want to use the ADSL line for your regular telephone service, you must add a *POTS splitter* to the line between the ADSL modem and the wall outlet (see Figure 8.9). Of course, there are also ADSL cards that connect to the PC, combined ADSL/hubs, USB adapters, and ADSL-capable routers. Which equipment you choose depends on your provider.

ADSL Summary

- ADSL is generally faster than PSTN or ISDN connections for Internet connectivity.
- Depending on how much you want to pay, ADSL typically offers an upload speed between 128 and 384 Kbps and a download speed of 512, 1,024, or 2,048 Kbps.

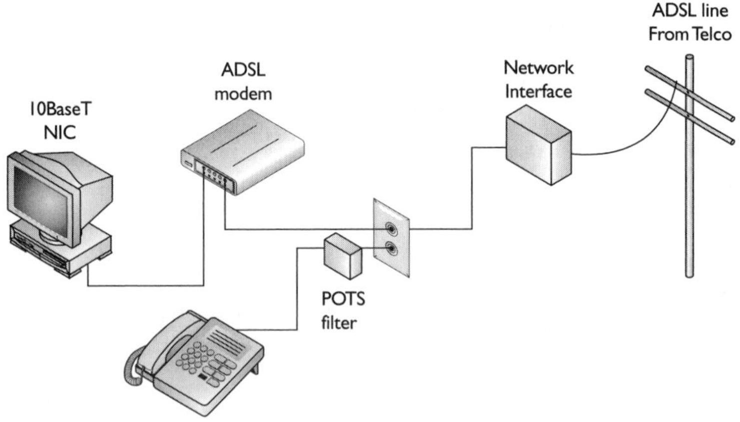

FIGURE 8.9 ADSL modem and telephone sharing one line

Cable Modems

The big competition to ADSL comes from the cable companies. Cable modems also provide an always-on Internet service, and can provide even greater bandwidth than ADSL—sometimes as high as 8 Mbps. However, just as ADSL users must deal with contention, cable modem users have to share that throughput with all their neighbors who also have cable modems. As more people in the neighborhood connect, the throughput will drop unless the cable company installs additional infrastructure to handle the increased load.

A cable modem installation consists of a cable modem connected to a cable outlet. In most cases, the cable modem gets its own outlet separate from the one that goes to the television. The cable is no different from the coax running into your TV or cable box—it's just split from the main line as though you were adding a second cable outlet for another television. Like ADSL, the cable modem connects to a PC via a standard NIC (see Figure 8.10).

Travel Advisory

Are cable modems faster than ADSL? It depends on the implementation. Either one will bog down if the service provider adds more subscribers than they can handle. Consult resources such as http://www.broadbandreports.com/ for reviews of specific broadband providers before choosing a service.

Cable Modem Summary

- Cable modems offer very high performance, but the bandwidth is shared, so the exact speed you attain will vary.
- Typical speeds are 1 to 3 Mbps (download) and 256 Kbps to 2.5 Mbps (upload).

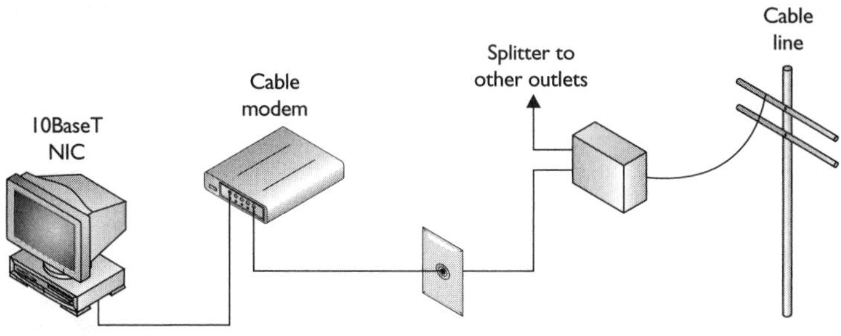

FIGURE 8.10 Cable modem connectivity

- It is only available if your location has a cable service *and* the service provider offers Internet access.

Satellite Modems

One exotic solution remains for your Internet connectivity: satellite! But forget massive dishes and powerful beams of energy radiating from your own personal satellite transponder towards the sky—it doesn't quite happen like that! Satellite communications use a regular modem for your uplink, usually via the PSTN or ISDN, but the data you request is beamed to you via satellite using an encoded MPEG2 (a video compression standard) data stream (see Figure 8.11).

The satellite modem system offers asymmetric performance—different upload and download speeds—and the actual speed in the downlink direction can be anywhere up to 52 Mbps (although 400 Kbps is more the norm) and the uplink speed will vary according to the service you use (PSTN, ISDN, and so forth). Satellite modems may be the only broadband option for remote locations.

Remote Access Security: Radius

Although you can configure each remote access server individually with the usernames, passwords, and other restrictions on remote users, in an environ-

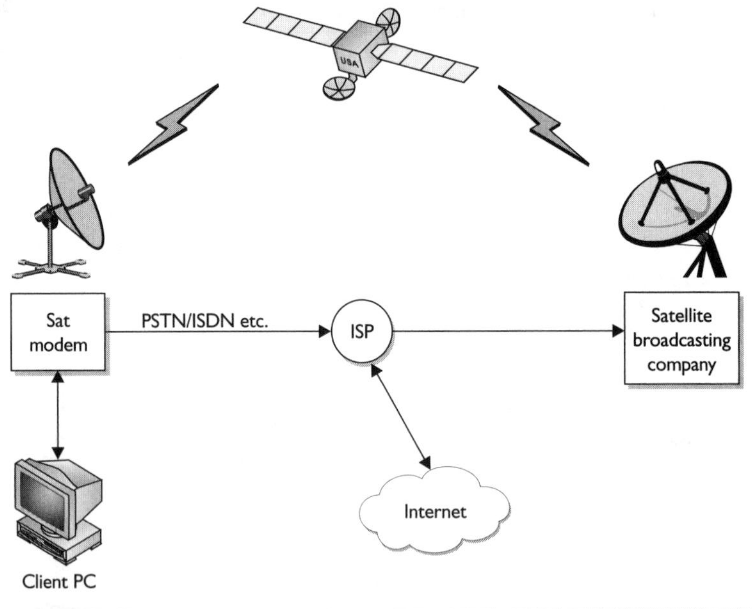

FIGURE 8.11 Satellite modem configuration

ment with many remote access servers the wise network tech will centralize this authentication information on a RADIUS (Remote Authentication Dial-In User Service) server. Each remote access server (now known as a *RADIUS client*) consults the RADIUS server when a remote user attempts to log in, and the RADIUS server authenticates the user and returns any additional configuration (such as restrictions on accessing certain resources) that the administrator has applied to remote users. Because the remote access server actually communicates directly with the remote access client, you can use any authentication mechanism (PPP, PAP, CHAP) supported by the remote access server. The RADIUS standard allows for extensions, so the exact options available will vary depending on which vendor's RADIUS server you deploy in your network.

Key features of RADIUS include the following:

- Centralized control of remote access user accounts
- Supports any authentication mechanism (PPP, PAP, CHAP, EAP) supported by the remote access servers

The secret to succeeding on the remote access questions on Network+ is to keep it simple. What do you need to make remote access work? You need a communications link, hardware, a Data Link protocol, and the correct software. Make sure you know the difference between PSTN and ISDN and the other options covered. Know that you want to use PPP instead of SLIP. Finally, know the types of remote access software available, and you'll do fine!

✔**Objective 8.01: Defining Remote Connectivity** Remote connectivity means being able to access resources on an organization's network from a remote site. In order to establish remote access using a dial-up (PSTN or ISDN) connection, you need client software on the remote machine and also a remote access server product running on a system in your office.

✔**Objective 8.02: Dial-In Remote Access** Dial-in remote access is very popular for two main reasons: First, it's a well-established way of remotely connecting to a network. Second, it's very flexible because it can be used anywhere, provided that you have access to a compatible phone socket. International modem standards—known by their "V." prefix—ensure that you can use your modem anywhere in the world. Just watch those call costs, even with a modern, fast V.90 modem capable of up to 56 Kbps. Take care to remember to use bps/Kbps rather than the term "baud" when referring to the speed of a modem. Baud is not technically correct, and is widely misused. One common problem with older PCs is that their serial port chip (a UART) is based on an older design and cannot cope with modern, fast modems; if your modem's struggling, make sure the serial port to which the modem is connected is using a 16550-type UART. If not, install a replacement serial interface or fit an internal modem. A cheap type of modem, called a Winmodem or soft modem, doesn't have a UART but can cause your PC to slow down during heavy data transfers because it requires the PC's main processor to perform some of the UART's functions.

✔ **Objective 8.03: Dial-In Software Requirements** Once you have the modem installed, you need dial-up software. The most common dial-in software is Microsoft Dial-Up Networking (DUN). DUN is simple to configure and allows you to establish a connection to a remote access server or an Internet service provider (ISP). On the server side, Microsoft's Remote Access Server (RAS) is also easy to set up and provides a degree of access control for remote users. One important point to watch is the choice of Data Link protocol for your serial port/phone line (PSTN or ISDN) link. SLIP is an older standard that supports TCP/IP only, using a fixed IP address, and has been largely replaced by PPP, which supports TCP/IP using a dynamically assigned IP address and/or IPX/SPX and/or NetBEUI. Dial-up networking extends a LAN to your location, but the speed of your link is limited to that of your modem, meaning it's v-e-r-y slow compared to a regular connection through a NIC. An alternative approach is to connect to a PC on the LAN and just send the screen, keyboard, and mouse information across the link. This type of remote access can be done on a PC-by-PC basis using a program such as pcAnywhere, Carbon Copy, or VNC. There is also similar software built into Windows XP called Remote Desktop, or you can use heavy-duty products such as Citrix MetaFrame and Microsoft Windows Terminal Server, which create virtual PC environments inside a central server on the network. All the access options discussed in this section can also be implemented via a dial-up connection to the Internet; although this opens up the possibility of local-call access to your systems from anywhere in the world, it also raises important security issues, which are tackled in Chapter 10.

✔ **Objective 8.04: Fixed-Point Remote Access** Dial-up services are flexible—they can be used from almost anywhere—but they're also slow. If you don't need the mobility of a dial-up solution (for example, you're providing remote access from a home worker's house), then faster Internet-based solutions are available. Asymmetric Digital Subscriber Line (ADSL) provides an always-on digital connection through a regular phone line (provided you're close enough to the local CO), and cable modems provide similar services through a local cable TV connection. If you don't have the luxury of such services in your location, it may be possible to install a satellite modem system. All these systems offer greater speeds than PSTN/ISDN dial-up connections, but ADSL and cable performance varies according to the number of other users sharing your local bandwidth.

REVIEW QUESTIONS

1. Which of the following is a data-compression protocol?

A. V.90

B. V.42bis

C. V.92

D. V.22

2. What is the name of Microsoft's remote access client?

A. Microsoft Client for Networks

B. Dial-Up Networking

C. ICA

D. RAS

3. Kyle is having problems getting good performance from his new V.90 modem on his trusty old PC. Everything seems to connect properly, and he has set his serial port speed to 115,200 bps, but file transfers often grind to a halt. What might be the cause of his problem?

A. Wrong brand of modem.

B. V.42 has been disabled.

C. Faulty NIC.

D. Old UART type.

4. Which of the following protocols are supported by Microsoft Dial-Up Networking? (Choose all that apply.)

A. TCP/IP

B. NetBEUI

C. IPX/SPX

D. XNS

5. Which of the following is not a Data Link protocol for telephone lines? (Select all that apply.)

A. SLIP

B. IP

C. PPP

D. ICA

6. Joe needs to provide a dial-up service for a home worker. Which of the following options are viable? (Select all that apply.)

   A. ISDN

   B. ADSL

   C. Cable modem

   D. PSTN

7. Alex works from a remote, converted farmhouse approximately 5 miles from the nearest town and telephone exchange. Alex needs some form of Internet access and would prefer a high-speed connection for downloading information. Which of the following would provide the best solution?

   A. Satellite modem

   B. ISDN

   C. ADSL

   D. Token Ring

8. Which of the following statements about ADSL are not correct? (Select two.)

   A. ADSL provides a dedicated connection running at approximately 2 Mbps.

   B. ADSL provides contention-based asymmetrical bandwidth.

   C. ADSL provides a high-speed, dial-up service.

   D. ADSL routers are available.

9. Which of the following V standards defines error checking?

   A. V.42

   B. V.42bis

   C. V.22bis

   D. MNP 8

10. Which of the following UARTs is required for high-speed modem use?

   A. 8250

   B. 82550

   C. 16550

   D. 80486

REVIEW ANSWERS

1. **B** V.42bis is a data-compression protocol. V.90 and V.92 are current standards for 56 Kbps modems. V.40 is not a common modem standard. V.22 is an older standard for modems running at 1,200 bps.
2. **B** Microsoft's remote access *client* is Dial-Up Networking.
3. **D** Kyle should check the UART type on his trusty *old* PC. If it's an 8250, that's the problem because the 8250 cannot support speeds above 9,600 bps.
4. **A** **B** **C** DUN supports the three main network protocols (TCP/IP, NetBEUI, and IPX/SPX). XNS is an old Xerox protocol from which IPX/SPX was developed, but it is not supported by DUN.
5. **B** **D** SLIP (A) and PPP (C) are Data Link protocols, whereas IP (B) and ICA (D) are not.
6. **A** **D** Joe needs a *dial-up* service; therefore, using ADSL (B) or a cable modem (C)—both always-on services—will not meet the requirement.
7. **A** Using a satellite modem (with a PSTN uplink) would provide the best option. ISDN and ADSL won't be available due to the distance from the nearest town, where the CO (exchange) is located.
8. **C** ADSL is *not* a dial-up service (C).
9. **A** V.42 is an error-checking standard.
10. **C** The 16550 UART is the modern, high-speed version.

Network Security

ITINERARY

- **Objective 9.01** Protecting Your Server
- **Objective 9.02** Reliability and Fault Tolerance
- **Objective 9.03** Logon and Access Security
- **Objective 9.04** WAN Security
- **Objective 9.05** Internet-Specific Security

NEWBIE	SOME EXPERIENCE	EXPERT
4 hours	2 hours	1 hour

Data security includes all the operating-specific tools we discussed in previous chapters (user IDs, passwords, access controls), but in real life (and on the Network+ exam) those are not the only security issues you will face. You must also protect your data from other dangers, including equipment failures, accidental erasure, and general network problems. Security includes both protecting your network and data from accidents and protecting it from unauthorized access.

Protecting Your Server

Your servers face potential attacks 24 hours a day—and we're not talking about hackers. Your servers can fall prey to power-related problems, environmental issues (heat, dirt, being kicked, and so on), user mistakes, the laws of physics, and plain, simple theft! All these are potential sources of data loss, so do all you can to prevent a catastrophe.

Protecting Against Power Problems

All the components in a PC run on electrical power. Without a clean, steady supply, they stop working. Electricity must travel through a number of stages between the power company and those components. A failure at any one of those stages will stop your PC from working. You can take several actions to safeguard your hardware to make sure this doesn't happen, starting with the power company.

In most developed countries, you can count on a good electrical supply *most* of the time; it's those other times that will get you. Electrical power sometimes stops (because of power outages) and sometimes goes bad (because of spikes, which are caused by nearby electrical storms or the operation of heavy motors, and sags, which are caused by supply equipment failures or other equipment being switched on nearby), as illustrated in Figure 9.1. Additionally, techs (and non-techs) can mess up perfectly good electricity on their own by overloading circuits with too much equipment. You can protect your servers from problems of power outages, electrical spikes, and overloaded circuits using several important technologies: dedicated circuits, surge suppressors, uninterruptible power supplies, and backup power.

Dedicated Circuits

A *dedicated circuit* is an electrical supply circuit that runs from a building's central power distribution point to specific power outlets—perhaps directly (and

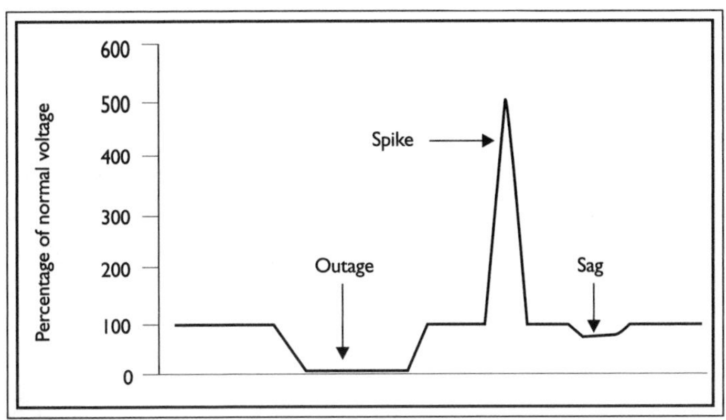

FIGURE 9.1 Power problems

only) to the computer room. Compare this to a general power circuit that supplies many outlets, feeding copiers, water coolers, PCs, printers, and the occasional vacuum cleaner or floor polisher. Using too many devices on one circuit causes the power to sag (dip), and these sags can cause computer systems to lock up or spontaneously reboot, depending on how lucky (or unlucky) you are at that moment. Dedicated circuits keep this from happening. They will (theoretically) prevent some uninformed person from plugging a vacuum cleaner into the circuit and bringing down the entire corporate computer system.

Surge Suppressors

An electrical surge—a sudden increase in the voltage on a circuit caused, for example, by a nearby lightning strike—can destroy an unprotected computer. In some cases, individual components will bear the brunt of the damage, but often the entire computer will be rendered inoperable. All modern PCs and other equipment have a degree of built-in protection, but additional, external suppressors add an extra layer of security for not much money. When buying a surge suppressor, remember that not all power surges come from the power outlet. Many current surge suppressors offer additional protection for other wires coming in and out of your computer, such as the network cable and the phone line.

Exam Tip

Suppressors are also called *passive filters* or just *filters*.

UPS

An uninterruptible power supply (UPS) should be standard equipment for your servers. A UPS contains a bank of batteries and a DC-to-AC converter circuit so that the batteries (DC) can provide AC power for the server in the event of a main power failure (many UPSs also provide protection from spikes and sags). UPSs often provide only a few minutes of power, but that will usually be enough to enable the server to shut down cleanly or for the backup power supply to kick in. More advanced UPSs will even shut down the server automatically in the event of a power failure, communicating with the system via a serial or USB cable (see Figure 9.2).

Exam Tip

All servers should be connected to a UPS.

Ironically, a power failure caused by a local high-voltage cable fault occurred while this book was being written, and office power was lost for nearly two hours—the first such major outage in the area since a bad storm in 1997. Fortunately, the office server was protected by a UPS, which shut down the system safely, and work on the book was being done using a local file on a laptop PC at the time, so we carried on by flashlight!

Backup Power

If your business cannot function without its computer systems, you need a backup power system, which will kick in when the electricity supply fails completely for a long period of time. This will usually be in the form of a gasoline or

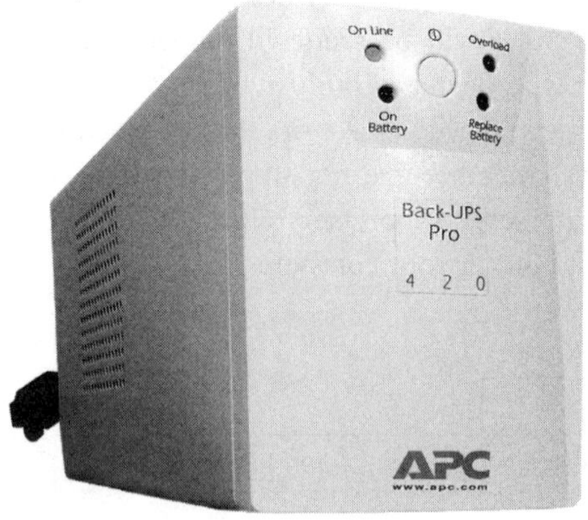

FIGURE 9.2 Typical UPS

diesel generator. A generator can supply power to your main systems, the networking equipment, and key computer systems, if not the whole building. It is *vital* that backup power systems be tested regularly to ensure they will fire up when needed.

Travel Advisory

Backup power should be just one part of your overall *business continuity plan,* your plan for keeping the business running when disaster strikes. Before disaster arrives in any one of its many forms (flood, fire, hurricane, Godzilla, etc.), you should create a plan. For example, could you set up your business in an alternative location if necessary?

Environmental Issues

All this wonderful protection is useless if someone walks off with your mission-critical server. It has happened! Here are some points to keep in mind:

- Keep the server room locked at all times, install a card lock or combination lock/doorknob, and make sure that only the right people have access.
- The closed environment of a computer room also allows you to reduce the thermal stress on the system. This will prolong the life of sensitive components, especially the power supply and hard disks.
- Use air conditioning to keep the humidity low, but not too low—around 40 percent is about right for most electronics.
- Keep the room a little on the cool side—about 68°F (20°C) is just about perfect, although most PCs can handle up to 80° or 85°F (26°C or 29°C) before overheating becomes a problem.
- Check with the system's manufacturer for recommendations.

Finally, be aware of the potential hazards from sources of electromagnetic interference (EMI). For example, documented reports have indicated that the signals radiated from cell (mobile) phones can interfere with sensitive electronic equipment, so many organizations ban cell phones from their main computer rooms.

Travel Advisory

Cell phones can crash computers—see http://catless.ncl.ac.uk/Risks/18.60.html#subj4.

Reliability and Fault Tolerance

Ever seen a bathtub? No, sorry, we're not questioning your bathing habits—maybe we should have said bathtub *curve*! What's that? Well, to find out, see Figure 9.3.

The bathtub curve is a classic figure, often used when discussing the reliability of any item—it shows how, for any manufactured object, there will be a number of early life failures due to component defects and manufacturing-related issues, then a period of low defects during the life of the unit, followed by a rise in failures as the item and its components come to the end of their life (wear out). Nothing is immune to the bathtub effect, which means that at some time or other you *will* experience a PC equipment or network failure—it's unavoidable!

A sudden loss of data—or the ability to get to their data—would cripple most organizations. Computers can be replaced and new employees hired, but the data is what makes most organizations function.

Providing Redundancy

One of the ways to reduce the impact of a failure is to install redundancy in a system—duplicate the bits that might fail. Many components inside a system can

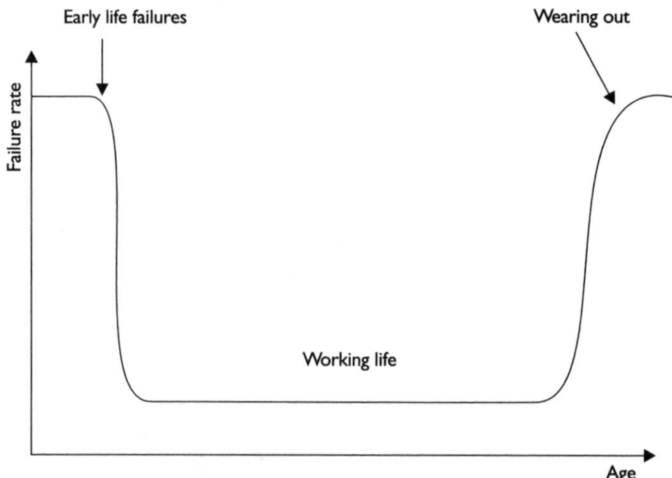

FIGURE 9.3 Bathtub curve

be made redundant. It is very common to find servers with redundant power supplies, where a power supply can be removed without even shutting down the PC. You can buy NICs that work together in the same PC, covering for each other if one dies; there are even NICs you can replace without rebooting the PC. There are also methods for making the entire server redundant—two or more servers can be mirrored, providing the ultimate in reliability, assuming the cost is bearable.

Protecting Disks

One of the most unreliable components inside a PC is the hard disk. Hard disks have moving parts, and anything with moving parts will wear down eventually. Assume that your hard drives will fail eventually and make plans for protecting your data. Fortunately, we have several methods available to protect our data in the event of a drive failure.

You could, for example, install a fancy hard drive controller that reads and writes data to two hard drives simultaneously. The data on each drive would always be identical, so if one drive were to fail you would still have a good copy of your data. One drive would be designated as the *primary* drive, and the other drive, called the *mirror* drive, would not be used unless the primary drive failed. This process of reading and writing data at the same time to two drives is called *drive mirroring* (see Figure 9.4).

If you really want to make data safe, you can use two separate controllers for each drive. With two drives, each on a separate controller, the system will continue to operate even if the primary drive's controller stops working. We call this drive mirroring technique *drive duplexing* (see Figure 9.5). Drive duplexing also offers faster performance than drive mirroring because a single controller does not have to write each piece of data twice.

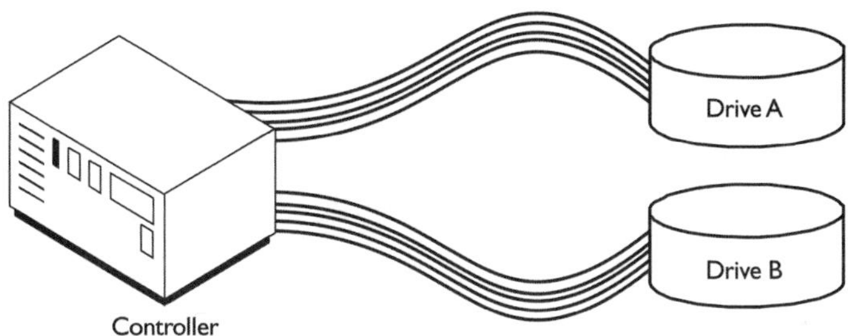

FIGURE 9.4 Mirrored drives

Exam Tip

The difference between mirroring and duplexing is that disk duplexing mirrors data to a second drive that is located on a second disk controller. This increases the level of fault tolerance.

The third, and most popular, way to create redundant data is a process called *disk striping with parity.*

Disk striping by itself is the process of spreading data among multiple (two or more) drives. Disk striping by itself provides no redundancy. If you save a small text file, for example, the file is split into multiple pieces; some of the pieces are stored on one drive, some on the other (see Figure 9.6).

The only advantage of disk striping by itself is speed. Disk striping improves performance because it reduces the amount of time the system waits for the mechanical part of the hard drive to find the correct part of the physical disk. But if any of the drives fails, *all* data is lost. Disk striping, by itself, is not something you should ever want to do—unless you simply don't care about your data. Nobody does *just* disk striping! However, we would really like to get that performance improvement, wouldn't we? We can, by implementing disk striping with parity.

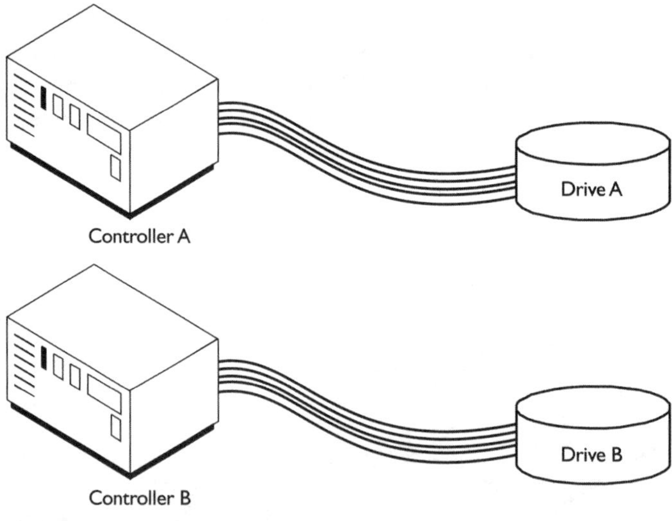

FIGURE 9.5 Duplexed drives

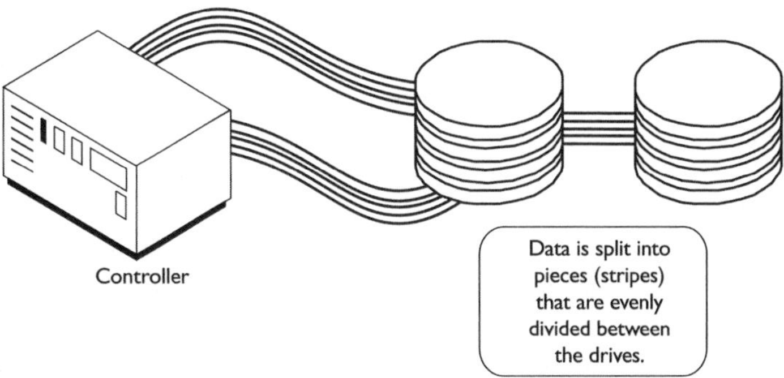

FIGURE 9.6 Disk striping

Exam Tip

Remember that disk striping (also known as RAID 0) does not protect data. To protect your data, you need to use either RAID 1 (disk mirroring or disk duplexing) or some version of RAID that supports disk striping with parity (RAID 3, 4, 5, and 6).

Disk striping *with parity* (also known as *RAID 5*) protects data by adding an additional drive, called a *parity drive.* The parity drive stores information that you can use to rebuild data should one of the data drives fail. Look at that same text file we used earlier. The data is still stored on the two data drives, but this time a simple, but very accurate, calculation is performed on data from equivalent locations on the data drives to create parity information on the parity drive. The calculation is similar to dividing two numbers and storing the result of the division, but the specifics are not what's important. Having parity data you can use to rebuild either drive, however, can become very important!

To do disk striping with parity, you must have at least *three* drives to stripe, and it is very common to use more than three. Unfortunately, the more drives you use, the greater the chance one might fail. Disk striping with parity can recover data only when just one drive fails. If two drives fail, you're stuck reaching for the backup tapes!

Exam Tip

Disk striping with parity (also known as RAID 5) requires a minimum of three disks and is a fault-tolerant solution.

Disk striping with parity combines the best of disk mirroring and plain disk striping. It protects data and is quite fast. The majority of network servers use a type of disk striping with parity to provide both data protection and maximum performance.

Using RAID

Disk mirroring and striping are both forms of RAID (Redundant Array of Inexpensive Disks or Redundant Array of Independent Disks—like some other computer acronyms, the meaning of the letters has changed over time, but the basic concept is the same). There are seven official levels of RAID, numbered 0 through 6:

- **RAID 0** Disk striping. (No data protection!)
- **RAID 1** Disk mirroring and disk duplexing.
- **RAID 2** Disk striping with multiple parity drives. (Unused; ignore it.)
- **RAID 3 and 4** Disk striping with parity. The differences between RAID 3 and 4 are trivial.
- **RAID 5** Disk striping with parity, but parity information is placed on all drives. This is the fastest way to provide data redundancy. RAID 5 is the most common RAID implementation.
- **RAID 6** RAID 5 with the added capability of asynchronous and cached data transmission. Think of it as a super RAID 5.

Exam Tip

RAID 5 requires three or more disks. Five disks are often used, but that's not why it's called RAID 5.

Disk Types

When configuring a server, you have two main types of hard disk technology available to you, defined by the type of interface used to connect the disks to their controller system. The Network+ exam doesn't expect you to know the technologies intimately, but you should be aware of some key terms and issues.

EIDE

Enhanced Integrated Drive Electronics (EIDE) disks are most commonly found in desktop PCs. The EIDE interface supports a maximum of four devices, which can be CD-ROMs, tape backup systems, and removable drives as well as hard disks. EIDE has always been intended for internal devices only, but you can get adapters to allow external units to be plugged in (if you really need to). The EIDE interface is quite fast, but it was not designed with multitasking environments, such as a NetWare server or UNIX system. Network techs will look at a server with EIDE disks and shake their heads in disapproval. There's nothing inherently wrong with using EIDE disks, but you will not get the best performance possible from your system. For that, you have to use SCSI.

Travel Advisory

Today, you can have more than four EIDE drives in a single system by adding additional EIDE controllers, such as those sold by Promise Technologies, to your system. For the purposes of the Network+ exam, however, assume that the maximum number of EIDE devices is four.

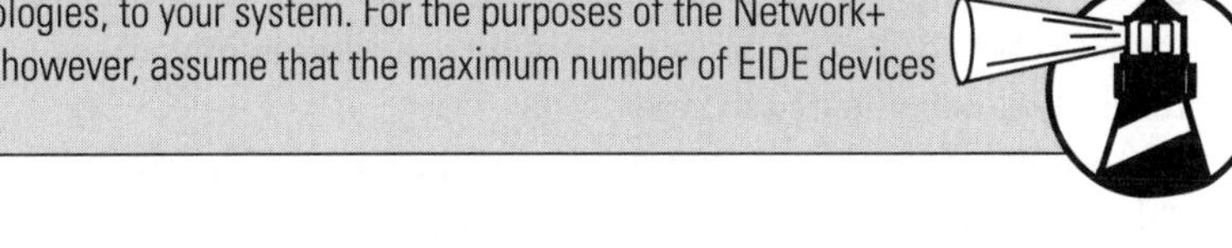

SCSI

Small Computer System Interface (SCSI) also supports a wide variety of devices, including hard disks, and performs much better than EIDE under heavy load conditions. Many SCSI controllers (the proper term is actually *host bus adapters,* or *HBAs*) support 7, 15, or 31 internal or external SCSI devices and therefore are ideal for RAID implementations. Better host adapters come with internal and external connectors, enabling both types of devices to exist on the same SCSI chain. Setting up a SCSI-based disk/tape/CD-ROM/whatever system is a relatively straightforward process, although there are a couple of specific requirements: Every device (disk, tape unit, and so on) connected to the HBA must be set to a unique ID using switches or jumpers on the unit, and just as with an Ethernet bus, the end devices must be terminated properly; otherwise, the system will not work. Fortunately, the Network+ exam isn't interested in your ability to configure SCSI, but you will be expected to know the connector types used (covered in Chapter 12).

In general, then, SCSI disks are best for servers, but they are more expensive than their EIDE equivalents. There's nothing wrong with using EIDE devices in a server that supports a small user base, but for anything bigger, SCSI is the way to go.

Travel Advisory

The gap between EIDE and SCSI in terms of performance has narrowed in recent years, and current EIDE implementations offer performance that is comparable to SCSI in many situations. SCSI continues, however, to hold the performance edge in the most data-intensive computing situations.

Making Tape Backups

Think about how much work you have done to create your nice, stable servers, workstations, and network. Imagine how many hours your users have spent creating data and storing it on those servers. Now imagine a virus (or user!) that deletes critical data or configuration files. As you can also imagine, this situation is not good for either your blood pressure or your job security.

Common sense dictates that you create backups of your data—and this will usually mean a *tape* backup; simply because tape offers high capacity, fast speed, and low cost (see Figure 9.7). If your needs are simple (and your amount of vital data small), you *might* consider alternatives, such as burning a CD/DVD or using a Zip-type drive, but the capacity of these devices is limited, and they can be relatively slow compared to tape.

A variety of tape backup types (all non-interchangeable, of course!) are available. You don't have to know the full technical specs, but they may be mentioned in the Network+ exam, so here's an overview of the most common types:

- **QIC (Quarter Inch Cartridge)** This is an old technology that has been surpassed by many of the others listed here. Tape capacities up to 15GB are available.
- **Travan** This is magnetic tape similar to QIC but it supports higher densities—it's very popular with home users and small businesses. Capacities up to 20GB are available. Travan drives can read and write (some) QIC tapes/formats.
- **DAT (4mm)** This very popular tape type is based on a data-grade version of the digital audio tape format known as the *digital data specification (DDS)*. It's now showing its age a bit, and new, sexier technologies are trying to steal the market. Capacities up to 40GB per tape are available.

FIGURE 9.7 An 8mm backup tape

- **8mm** This is another spin-off from a consumer product (8mm video tapes), but using a higher-quality tape system. Capacities up to 150GB per tape are available.
- **DLT (Digital Linear Tape)** This tape type is very popular due to its speed and tape capacities—it's quite a whizzy system, and a tape can pack up to 80GB.
- **AIT (Advanced Intelligent Tape)** AIT is a (relatively) new kid on the block. It is fairly fast, with high capacity—up to 100GB per tape. It's a bit pricey at the moment.
- **ADR (Advanced Data Recording)** ADR is a low-cost digital tape format that's popular with home users and small/medium-sized businesses. Capacities up to 60GB per tape are available.

Schedule Your Backups

You can't use a backup tape created several weeks ago to restore a file if the missing live file was updated yesterday. To make sure you always have current data available, you should create a backup schedule that ensures your data is backed up regularly and can be restored easily. The best way to start is to make sure you have a backup plan in place. The backup plan should include answers to the following questions:

- When will backup occur, and what will the tape rotation schedule be?
- What types of backups will be performed at each backup time?
- Where will the backups be stored?
- Who is responsible for managing the backups, and what should be done if that person is not available?

Perhaps the most important details are the types of backups and the backup schedule or strategy.

Types of Backups

The goal of backing up is to ensure that whenever a system fails, a recent backup will be available to restore the system. At first thought, you might simply back up the complete system at the end of each day, or whatever interval you feel is prudent to keep the backups fresh. This can work if the amount of data to be backed up is small enough to be copied to tape during an available off-hours timeslot, but if you are responsible for a massive repository of data, this may not be possible. And if you are running a 24/7 operation, there may be no after-hours time, so you might want to avoid arranging a mass backup of everything that would slow down the system noticeably for those currently using it.

Exam Tip

Avoid running backups during live system hours because they will slow down the network for all users.

Most backup software solutions have a series of options available other than the old complete (usually called *full* or *normal)* backup.

The Archive Bit

The key to understanding how backups are managed and performed is knowing about the existence and use of a file attribute called the *archive* attribute. All files have a series of attributes (or archive bits) that act as on/off or set/unset indicators for the status of the file. Here are the most common attributes (they vary somewhat depending on the file system):

- **Hidden** Don't show the file in normal directory listings.
- **System** The file is a critical file for the system.
- **Read-Only** The file can be read but not written to or erased.
- **Archive** The file is new or has been changed since the archive bit was last cleared.

Backup programs can use the archive bit to decide whether a file should be backed up; if the archive bit for a file is set (on), the file is a likely candidate for backup. If a file's archive bit is turned off, there's likely a backup of that file on some tape (because the backup process is configured to copy a file to tape and then clear the archive bit). Figure 9.8 shows two files: one with the archive bit on, and one with it off.

Using the archive bit allows a complete range of backups to be performed, as shown in Table 9.1.

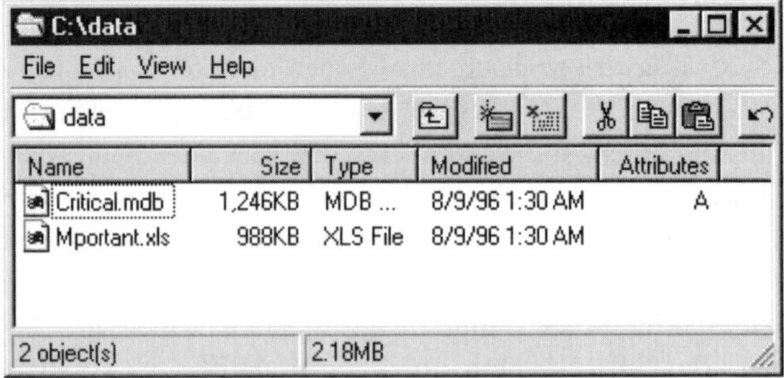

FIGURE 9.8 Archive bit

TABLE 9.1 Types of Backups

Backup Type	**Description**	**Archive Bit Status (*After* Backup Is Complete)**
Full/Normal	Backs up everything regardless of the archive bit setting.	Cleared
Copy	Makes copies of all data regardless of the archive bit setting.	Unchanged
Incremental	Backs up all files that have the archive bit set.	Cleared
Differential	Backs up all files that have the archive bit set.	Unchanged

Exam Tip

Remember the different types of backups, including which ones clear the archive bit and which ones do not.

Exam Tip

Be sure to memorize the differences between the different backup types when preparing for the Network+ exam.

The motivation for having both incremental and differential backups is not always clear—they seem to do pretty much the same job. Incremental seems the better option at first. If a file is backed up, you would want to turn off the archive bit, right? Well, maybe. But there is one scenario where that may not be too attractive a choice. Most backup procedures include a big weekly normal backup, with daily incremental or differential backups at the end of every business day. Figure 9.9 shows the difference between the two types.

Notice that a differential backup is a cumulative backup. Because the archive bits are not set, it keeps backing up all changes since the last normal backup. Clearly, the backups will get progressively larger through the week as more files are changed. The incremental backup, in contrast, backs up only the changes since the last backup. Each incremental backup will be small and also totally different from the previous backup. Now assume that the system is wiped out on Thursday. How will the system be restored? Well, with an incremental backup, you need first to restore the weekly backup, then the Tuesday backup, and then the Wednesday backup before the system is restored. If you use a differential backup, on the other hand, you need only the weekly backup and then the

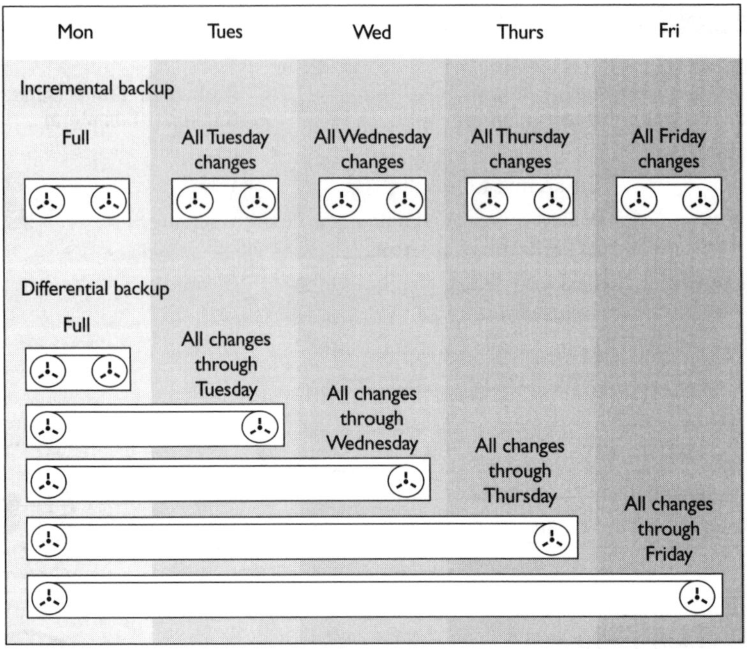

Mon
Tues
Wed
Thurs
Fri
Incremental backup
Full
All Tuesday changes
All Wednesday changes
All Thursday changes
All Friday changes
Differential backup
Full
All changes through Tuesday
All changes through Wednesday
All changes through Thursday
All changes through Friday

FIGURE 9.9 Incremental versus differential backups

Wednesday backup to restore the system. The greater the distance between normal backups, the more incremental backups you need to restore. With a differential backup, you will always need only two backups to restore the system (see Figure 9.10). Suddenly, the differential backup looks better than the incremental!

Incremental restore
Full
All Tuesday changes
All Wednesday changes
Differential restore
Full
All changes through Wednesday

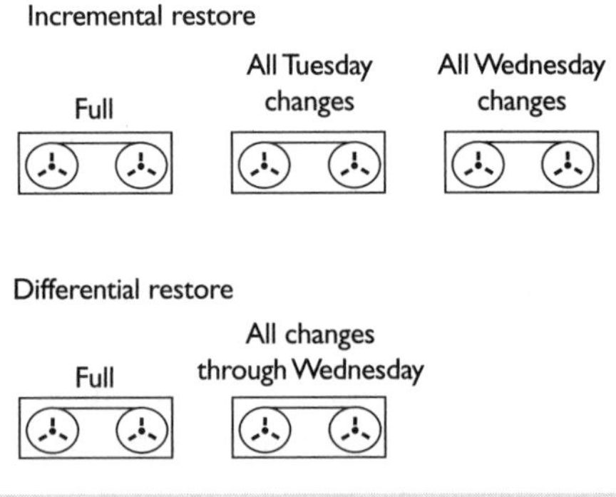

FIGURE 9.10 Recovering from Thursday's crash

Backup Strategies

Putting your data onto tape is one step in the right direction, but managing your backups is also a vital issue. How are you going to store them? Where are you going to store them? Is the backup system actually putting anything on tape? Backing up to tape is not a fit-and-forget exercise. Consider, and remember, the issues discussed here.

Verification

After you have backed up all your data, you should give some thought to data integrity on the backup tapes as well as to the safekeeping of those tapes. To verify data integrity, test the restore procedures on a regular basis. All this entails is performing a restore operation on some of the files from a tape to an alternate location and then comparing the data to make sure it is usable and correct. Many organizations have religiously backed up their systems on a daily basis only to discover sometime down the line (during a crisis) that there's nothing on the tapes.

Tape Reliability

Tapes do wear out. If you have used the same tapes for a long time, buy some new ones. Set a schedule for taking tapes out of production and either archiving them or destroying them and replacing them with new tapes. Also, you do not want to store all your backups on a single tape. You should rotate tapes so that you always have the tapes necessary to run a full restore back to your last full backup. Depending on the type of backup you have chosen to perform, this may entail having a full week's worth of tapes that you rotate—maybe more. Some organizations, for example, keep their Friday tapes for a month and their monthly tapes for a year, just in case. Figure 9.11 shows a comprehensive tape backup set.

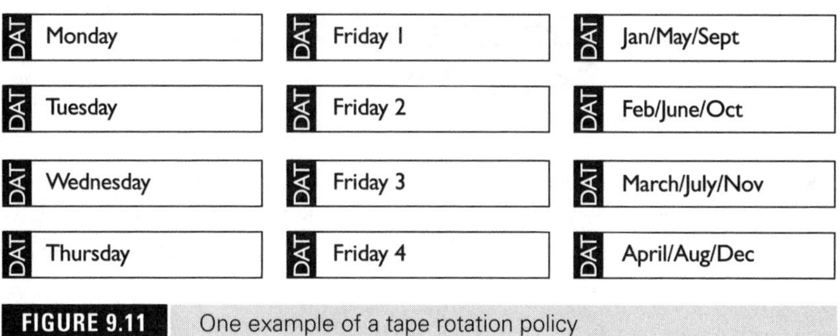

FIGURE 9.11 One example of a tape rotation policy

With the tape setup in Figure 9.11, differential backups are stored on the daily tapes, and full backups are stored on the Friday tapes, with the tapes rotated throughout the month, and a month-end backup on the last Friday of the month that's kept for three months before being reused.

Storage

If possible, you should always store backups offsite in a secure location so that they are not damaged by catastrophic events such as a fire or flood. The next-best solution is a fireproof safe, and this should ideally be located in another part of the building (*not* in the computer room), preferably somewhere secure on the ground floor. Why not in the basement? Basements fill with water if the building floods or is pumped full of water during a fire.

Disaster Recovery

Always plan for the worst. It's a depressing thought, but we all know, realistically, that bad things *do* happen. Every IT department should have a disaster recovery plan (also known as a *business continuity plan*) that includes the relocation of equipment to a suitable offsite location or the hiring of replacement equipment—some disaster recovery companies have mobile computer rooms in freight containers that they can bring by truck to your site. Your plan should also include procedures for the retrieval and restoration of backups; using backup power supplies; and setting up a network for users, telecom facilities, cell phones, links for remote workers, and so on. Decide how key techs will be contacted and what their responsibilities will be. Finally, *test* the plans—see how quickly everything can be brought back to functionality. Yes, it's tedious; yes, it takes time and money; and yes, your business may fail if you have an emergency and you haven't planned for it. Your organization must balance the cost of preparing for disaster with the potential cost of *not* preparing.

Logon and Access Security

Now that you have confidence that servers will stay up and running (or will shut down properly if a major electrical failure occurs) and you have planned for all foreseeable events, it's time to consider how unavailable you can make your servers to the "wrong" people.

Basic security issues common to all networks include the level of security, the proper use of passwords, and the centralization of control. Most decent computer systems won't let you get very far unless you can prove you are a recognized user—you need either a password for the resource you are trying to access, or you need a username and a password.

Implementing Share-Level Security

A network designer can choose from two levels of security: share level and user level. With share-level security, a network administrator assigns each shared *resource* a password (see Figure 9.12). These resources are generally either shared folders, where data or programs are stored, or shared printers. All users attempting to access the resource must supply the same password. Network administrators usually consider share-level control to be weak and difficult to manage. It's the kind of security used most often with simple peer-to-peer networks.

Figure 9.13 shows the share-level security options under Windows 9*x*; you can choose to have a password (or not), and it can be for read-only or full access to the resource—and that's it!

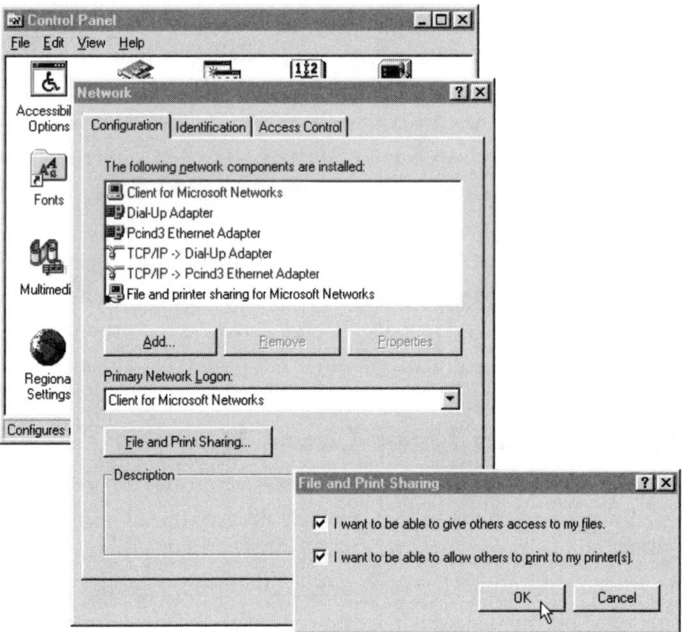

FIGURE 9.12 Turning on share-level security under Windows 9*x*

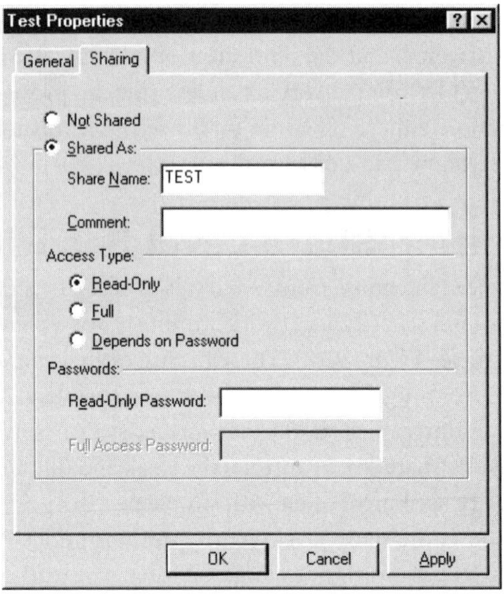

FIGURE 9.13 Share-level security options under Windows 9*x*

Because share-level passwords aren't personal, they tend to be treated as less important than they are (many a resource password has been spotted on a yellow sticky note fixed to the corner of someone's monitor!). Worse yet, the poor users may need to remember dozens of different passwords for all the resources they use. Although share-level control can provide some benefit for small, trusting companies with few computers and few users, they can be a pain to manage because there's no centralization—for example, a peer-to-peer network with 20 computers each sharing resources will have 20 locations at which share-level security needs to be set up and managed. Large networks require a more sophisticated scheme: user-level security.

Implementing User-Level Security

With user-level security, a network administrator creates an account for each user, usually on a central server that can itself manage the access to resources on other systems. Most administrators prefer to have a single place to go when adding, changing, or deleting a user account. A *user account* defines the rights and privileges of a specific person when that person accesses a computer system or network. When a user sits down at the computer, that user supplies an account name and password, which the computer checks against its security database. If the password specified matches the one listed for that user account in the database, the computer assumes from that point forward that the user is valid and grants the user all the rights and privileges that have been assigned to that user account. The user doesn't need to remember a share-level password for each resource he or she wants to access.

To avoid the excessive workload of assigning specific rights to each user individually, network administrators organize users with similar needs into *groups* (see Figure 9.14). It *would* be possible to manage each user individually, but supposing 30 users need access to both the SALESDOCS shared resource and the SALESPRINT printer, which would be easier?

- To create a group called SALES, add the 30 users to the group, and give SALES access permission to the two resources (by virtue of their membership in that group, the 30 users can now access both resources).

or

- Give 30 user accounts permission to access SALESDOCS and then repeat the same exercise for SALESPRINT.

Think what would happen if you now needed to give the users access to SALESDATA—you would either go through the 30 accounts again or just change the group permission once (see Figure 9.15).

Take your pick—either approach will work, but one's much less effort (and who doesn't prefer an easy life?). In large organizations with hundreds of employees with similar needs, the time and effort saved quickly becomes significant. In most instances, a user's rights are cumulative, meaning that a user

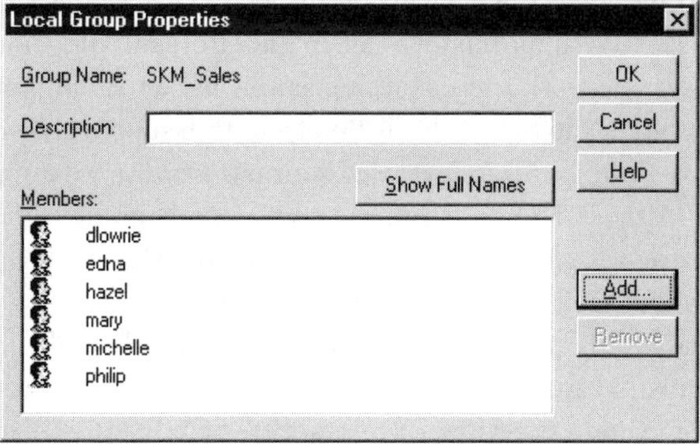

FIGURE 9.14 Group management on a Windows server

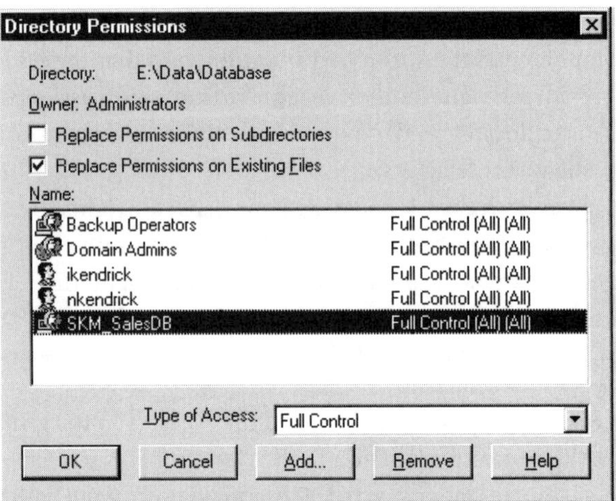

FIGURE 9.15 The SKM_Sales team can get to their favorite database.

receives the sum of the rights granted to his or her user account and the rights granted to any of the groups to which that user belongs.

Using Passwords

Of course, user-level security only works well when users keep their passwords secure. Passwords, for example, should never be written down where another user might find them, and users should never reveal their passwords to anyone, even the administrator of the network. In most cases, the administrator can reset a user's password without knowing the old password. Many end users, however, remain unaware of this and fall prey to one of the oldest hacker tricks in the book—the fake tech support phone call. In a large organization, most users will not know every network support technician. A hacker simply phones one of these hapless users and says, "This is Bob from tech support. We're upgrading the forward deflector grid, and we need your password so we can reset it when we're done." A shocking number of users will simply give out their password when asked over the phone. A large part of password security is educating network users about the proper care of their passwords.

A good password cannot be guessed easily. A password should never be based on any information about the user that can be easily obtained, such as elements of a user's name, address, relatives' name, or pet's name. Strangely enough, hackers also know about "qwerty," "letmein," and such. Ideally, a password should not be a real word at all. Hackers probing a network often run password-guessing utilities that simply try common dictionary words at random, but network administrators can reduce the effectiveness of such password-guessing programs by requiring all passwords to be longer than six or eight characters and by locking accounts after a specific number of failed login attempts. Hackers have a more difficult task when guessing longer passwords because there are many more possible combinations.

The most secure passwords contain a combination of letters (some in uppercase), numbers, and symbols. The following list contains examples of strong passwords:

- Jar56o$imum
- RhjP!!op11
- 100bobot&w

A good network administrator should assume that, over time, some users' passwords will become public knowledge. To limit the impact of these exposed passwords, a careful network administrator sets passwords to expire periodically, usually once every 30 days or less. Should a password become public knowledge, the gap in network security will automatically close when the user changes the password.

In summary, a strong password should

- Be longer than six or eight characters.
- Contain a combination of letters, numbers, and symbols.
- Not be based on easily guessed information.
- Be changed on a regular schedule.

Objective 9.04 WAN Security

If you're going to extend your network outside the boundary of your building, *expect* and *plan* for third-party attempts to break in. Maybe your organization isn't a likely target for industrial espionage, but that's not the only problem—remember that hacking is "fun," and some people do it simply for the challenge. Also remember that viruses, worms, and other such malicious programs may find their way to the borders of your system—*don't* let them in!

All remote users should be equipped with a secure account with access via a username and secure password, but this data needs to be passed across the WAN to be verified. If the data is in plain-text format, it's a fairly simple job for a hacker to snare it and have a look. Data packets can be easily read using diagnostics equipment (or suitably equipped PCs) running so-called *promiscuous drivers*, making picking up unencrypted passwords easy.

Local Lingo

promiscuous mode drivers NIC drivers that allow a host PC to read every data packet regardless of the actual destination MAC address.

Common Connection and Encryption Standards

A number of common standards and protocols are related to network connectivity, user authentication (logon), and data encryption. Setting up and using these standards and protocols is fairly straightforward: You simply enable the right features in your software or install the appropriate add-on. The following sections tell you all you need to know for the Network+ exam; they cover the common standards you will encounter and where they are used.

Travel Advisory

For a more detailed overview of encryption, see http://www.rsasecurity.com/rsalabs.

Layer 2 Tunneling Protocol (L2TP)

L2TP is used for connecting virtual private networks (VPNs) over public lines and networks, such as the Internet. L2TP itself doesn't provide encryption, but it combines the functionality of PPTP with a protocol called Layer 2 Forwarding (L2F), developed by Cisco Systems, and CHAP (see the next section), which provides encrypted user authentication. Many modern VPN connectivity packages support L2TP. For example, Figure 9.16 shows the VPN configuration options under Windows 2000.

PAP and CHAP

The Password Authentication Protocol (PAP) and Challenge Handshake Authentication Protocol (CHAP) are used by dial-up networking connections

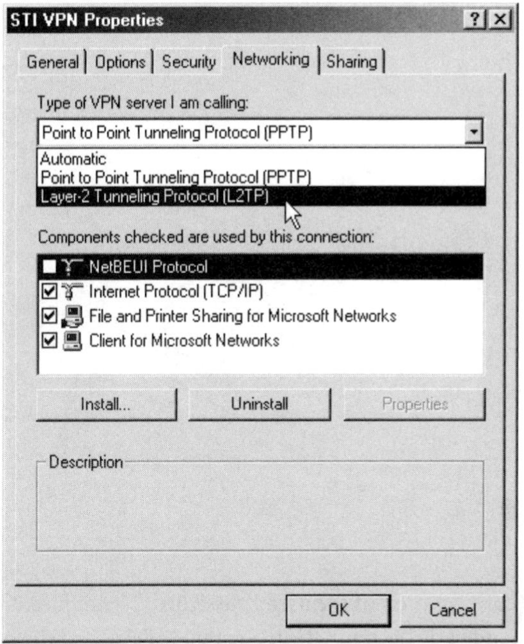

FIGURE 9.16 Configuring a VPN connection to use L2TP under Windows 2000

(and some VPN configurations) to verify login details. Essentially, they are the password and user verification protocols used with PPP/PPTP connections. All Windows dial-up connection utilities support both PAP and CHAP.

PAP PAP is a very simple protocol. After a PPP link has been established, a username/password pair is repeatedly sent (in plain text) until authentication is acknowledged or until the connection is terminated (see Figure 9.17). Although we're talking here about encryption and security, PAP doesn't do either, but it's included because it is still widely used.

Exam Tip

PAP sends user information as plain text and does not provide any encryption.

CHAP CHAP is more secure than PAP. After a remote connection is established, the server sends a *challenge message* to the system dialing in (the

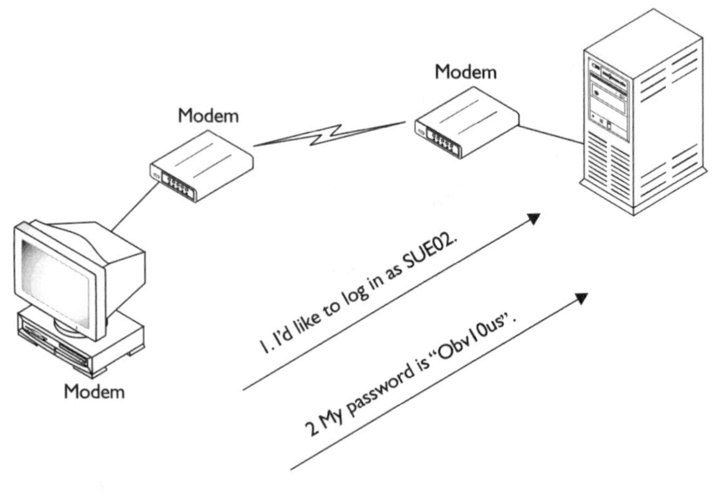

FIGURE 9.17 PAP checking a password

requestor) for confirmation of the user's password. The requestor generates a response using a one-way hash function—called MD5—and the server compares the response to its expected hash value (see Figure 9.18). If the values match, the connection is acknowledged; otherwise, it is terminated. In this way, a server can ask you if you know what your password is without your actually having to send it to the server for comparison. The server can generate a new challenge message at any time, which makes CHAP very secure because the authentication can be refreshed at any time. Instead of using MD5, CHAP can also encrypt its messages using the Data Encryption Standard (DES) algorithm—a very popular way of encrypting information using a long binary key, but it's not as secure as MD5.

Local Lingo

one-way hash function A computing function that takes a variable-length string as the input and produces a fixed-length binary value (hash) as the output. The process is irreversible—it is extremely difficult to find a string that produces a given hash value (hence, it's a one-way function). Message Digest 5 (MD5) is a common hash algorithm.

Although it would seem that PPP links should be configured for CHAP authentication, you can do so only if the remote end also supports CHAP.

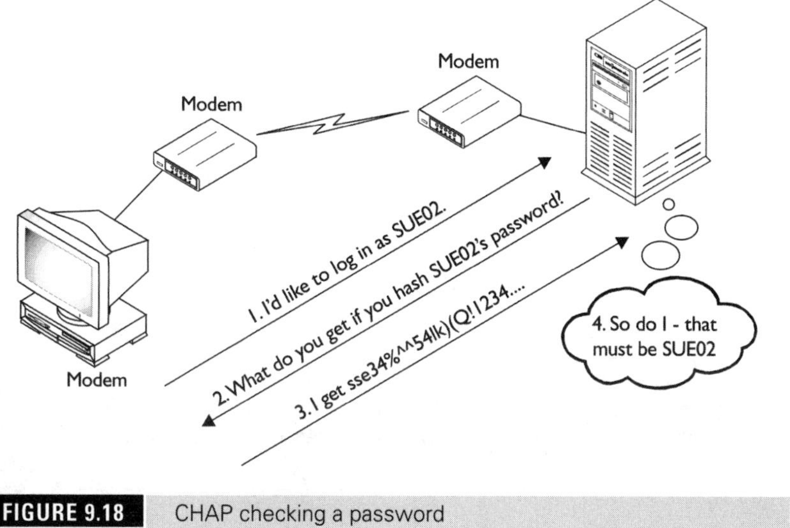

FIGURE 9.18 CHAP checking a password

IPsec

IP Security (IPsec) is a collection of open standards for ensuring secure private communications using a VPN over the Internet. Because IPsec works at the OSI Network layer, it can be used with many different (higher-level) protocols without modification. Once enabled, IPsec will authenticate and encrypt all data crossing an IP WAN. IPsec is built into Windows 2000/XP/2003 (see Figure 9.19) and is available for use with other platforms, such as UNIX and Linux.

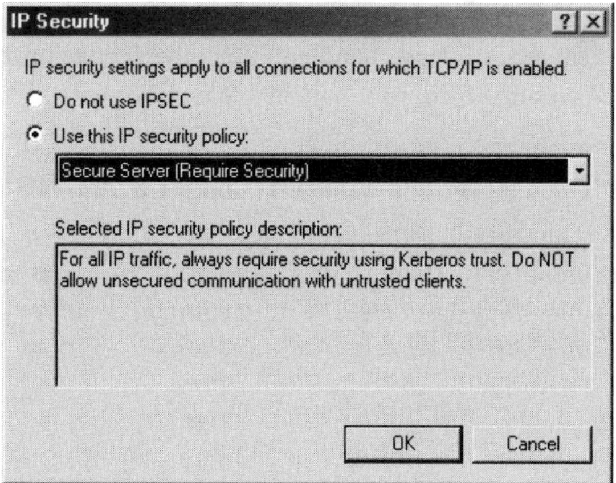

FIGURE 9.19 Turning on IPsec under Windows 2000

Kerberos

Kerberos is a network authentication protocol, providing authentication for client/server applications using secret-key cryptography. Kerberos was developed by the Massachusetts Institute of Technology. MIT publishes free versions of the protocol, and many commercial and open-source products also now support it. The Kerberos protocol allows a client to prove its identity to a server (and vice versa) across an insecure network connection. After a client and server have established an authenticated connection, they can also encrypt all their communications to guarantee privacy and data integrity.

Local Lingo

secret-key cryptography An encryption system that uses a common unlocking code (key) that is known only to the sender and recipient of the encoded message.

Microsoft has adopted the Kerberos standard as a feature of the login authentication and resource access system for Windows 2000 and 2003 servers, albeit with a few custom tweaks here and there that have upset open standards supporters.

Internet-Specific Security

We can't avoid it, I'm afraid—some people will insist on using the Internet! This opens the floodgates to potential evildoers intent on stealing the latest copy of your résumé from your personal folder—or worse.

Using Proxy Servers and Firewalls

Putting an intermediary between your main network and the Internet is one way of adding a control mechanism that allows you to monitor what's going on and attempt to block any nastiness. The most common forms of border control are proxy servers and firewalls.

Firewalls

Remember that each TCP/IP Application layer protocol had its own port number? Figure 9.20, for example, shows Microsoft's Outlook Express and its POP3 and SMTP settings.

A firewall lets you fine-tune the services (by port number) allowed in either direction into or out of your network (see Figure 9.21). Firewalls can also often block functionality by IP address; for example, you could allow incoming access from a range of known, fixed IP addresses (used by your remote workers), but from nowhere else. The reverse is also usually true; for example, you could allow web surfing (HTTP, using port 80) from only certain machines in your organization.

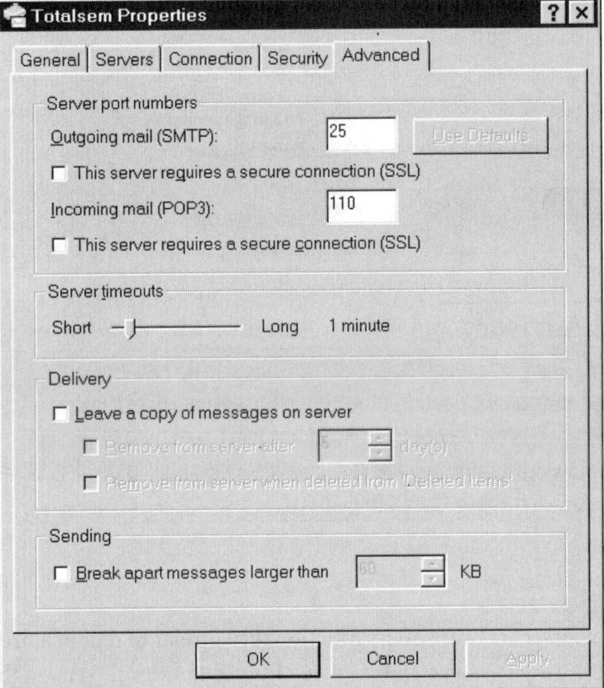

FIGURE 9.20 POP3 and SMTP settings

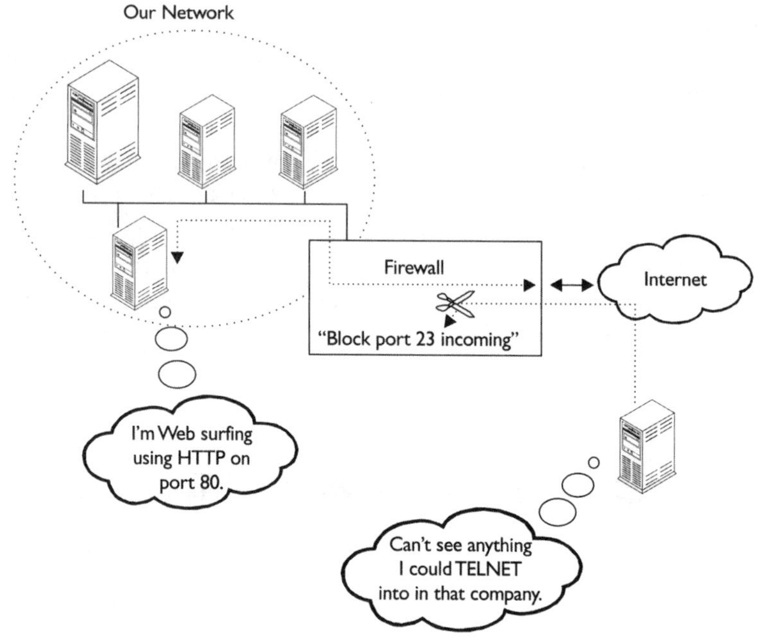

FIGURE 9.21 A firewall controls what services are allowed, both incoming and outgoing.

Travel Advisory

Remember that port numbers are arbitrary and can be changed. Just because you block port 21, the standard session control port number for FTP, doesn't mean that someone can't configure their FTP server to use a different port number. Port blocking is a good place to start, but it's not fool-proof.

Proxy Servers

Most proxy server software offers functionality similar to that of a firewall, but a *proxy server* also acts as a go-between, fetching data from servers on the Internet on behalf of clients on the local network. When you use a proxy server, the client application does not try to connect directly to the server; instead, it sends a request to the proxy server, asking it to get what it wants (see Figure 9.22). Proxy servers typically accept requests for web (HTTP), FTP, and e-mail (POP3 and SMTP) resources, but do not support requests for other TCP/IP application

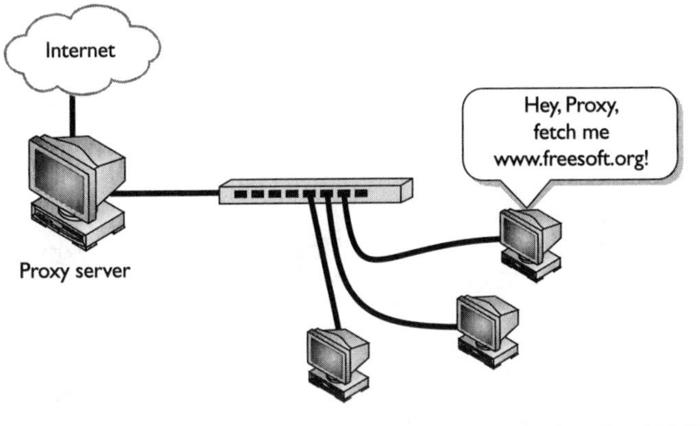

FIGURE 9.22 A client application asks the proxy server to fetch what it wants.

protocols unless the proxy server vendor specifically adds support. Proxy servers can enhance both the performance and security of a network.

Proxy servers improve the performance of a network by reducing the traffic that results when multiple users request the same data. For example, without a proxy server, if three users on Sherman's network all go to www.cnnsi.com to check the latest baseball scores, Sherman's network downloads the same information from the Internet three times, as shown in Figure 9.23.

When a proxy server is used, however, a copy of the page is kept the first time a user requests it (see Figure 9.24). When another host requests the same page, the proxy server gives the client that cached copy instead of contacting the web server again, thus reducing the amount of traffic going across the Internet and providing a faster response to the client (see Figure 9.25).

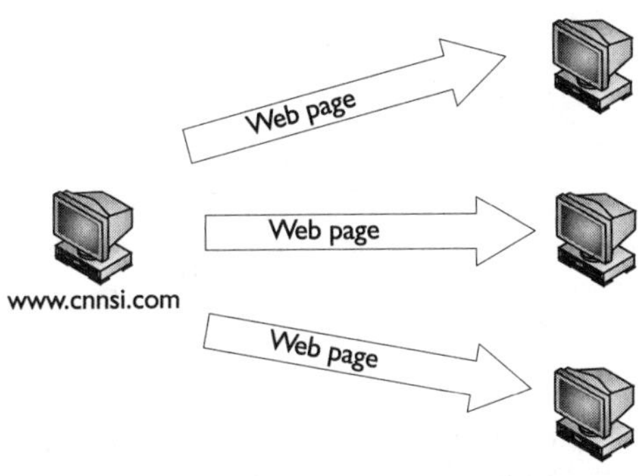

FIGURE 9.23 If three users request the same web page, it's fetched three times.

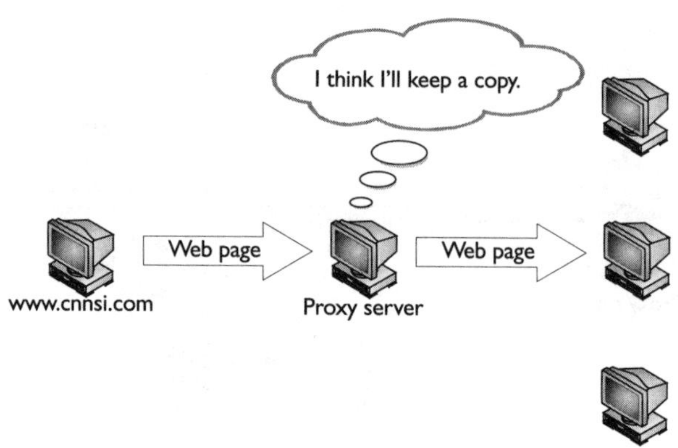

FIGURE 9.24 A proxy server retrieves and caches the web page so it's fetched only once.

Proxy servers enhance the security of a network by hiding individual hosts on the local network from hosts on the Internet at large. Figure 9.26 shows three computers, MO, LARRY, and CURLEY, protected behind a proxy server. As far as the evil hacker lurking somewhere in the dark recesses of the Internet with his computer NEO can tell, MO, LARRY, and CURLEY do not exist. The evil hacker can see only the proxy server. By limiting the number of machines that directly connect to the Internet, wise network techs ease their own workloads. Properly securing a single machine, the proxy server, consumes much less time and effort than properly securing hundreds of individual machines on a network.

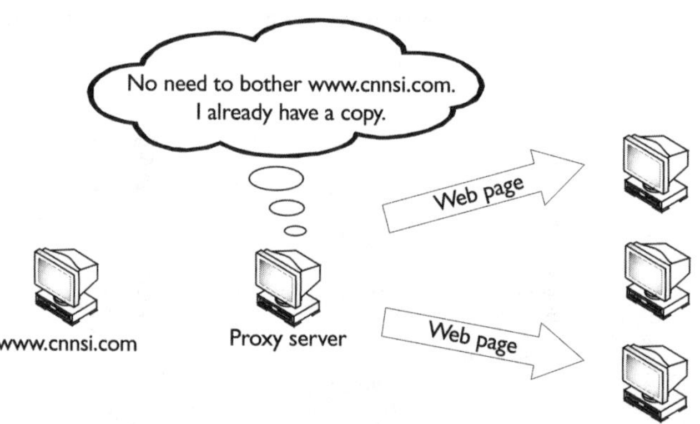

FIGURE 9.25 A proxy server delivers a page from the cache, if the page has already been accessed.

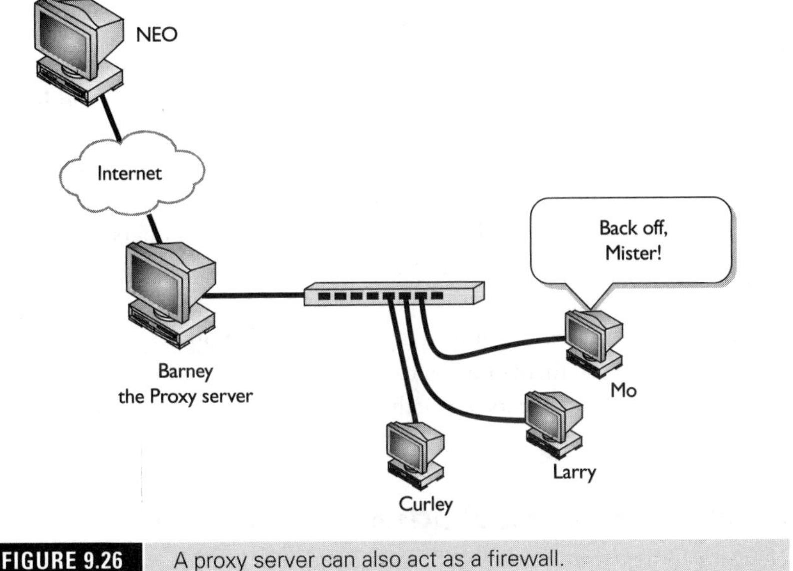

FIGURE 9.26 A proxy server can also act as a firewall.

If you have installed a proxy server, your web browsers will need to be told about it because they will no longer access the Internet directly (they will ask the proxy server for all that they want), as shown in Figure 9.27.

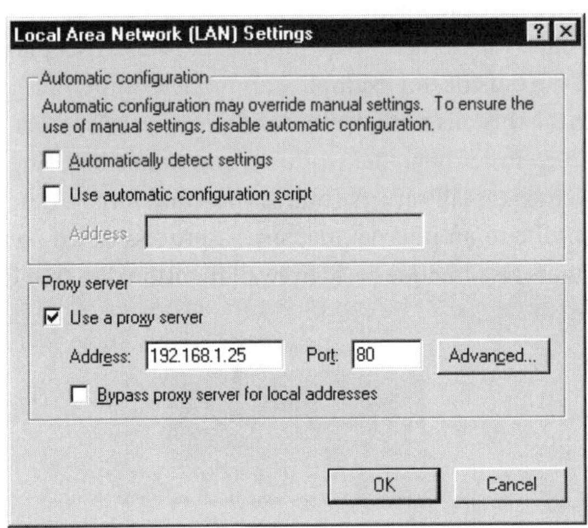

FIGURE 9.27 Microsoft Internet Explorer being told about a proxy server

Using HTTP and SSL

Ever wondered what that padlock thingy was at the bottom of your web browser (see Figure 9.28)? Well, when it's open (Netscape) or hidden (Microsoft IE), it's telling you that you are using plain-text HTTP to exchange information with a web server. When it's locked (Netscape) or present (Microsoft IE), however, you have switched, by magic, to Hypertext Transfer Protocol over SSL (HTTPS), a protocol that uses an encryption algorithm called RC4 that offers much better security, especially when you need it, such as when you're paying for an online transaction using a credit card. HTTPS (port 443) uses the Secure Sockets Layer (SSL) protocol for its encryption. Many websites will jump to and from HTTPS mode as required, so there's no need for you to worry about whether it's on or off, but some sites let you choose whether you want to access them using HTTPS (Figure 9.29).

Using Network Address Translation (NAT)

Network address translation (NAT) was intended to provide a temporary resolution to the problems caused by the shortage of spare IP addresses. Commonly implemented in IP routers, NAT allows multiple computers on a network to connect to the Internet through a single IP address (see Figure 9.30). The function of NAT is to ensure that incoming data packets are actually passed to the correct machines. NAT keeps track of outgoing requests and redirects responses to the correct internal machine.

Using NAT hides the details of your internal network from the outside world. Computers on the outside, for example, cannot determine your internal IP addresses. In general, this means that all communication using NAT must be initiated by machines inside your network, so you won't be using any of those machines as web or e-mail servers (unless you configure NAT to forward specific types of traffic to an internal machine, a process called *port forwarding*). Many NAT routers also include basic firewall functionality (see Figure 9.31).

FIGURE 9.28 Padlock (Netscape) unlocked

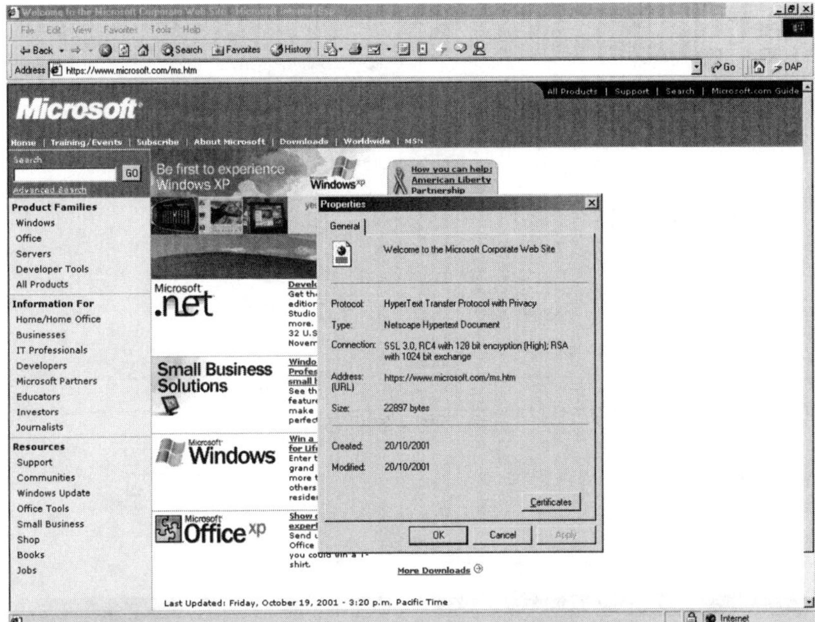

FIGURE 9.29 Microsoft's home page via HTTPS (Microsoft Internet Explorer). Notice the padlock.

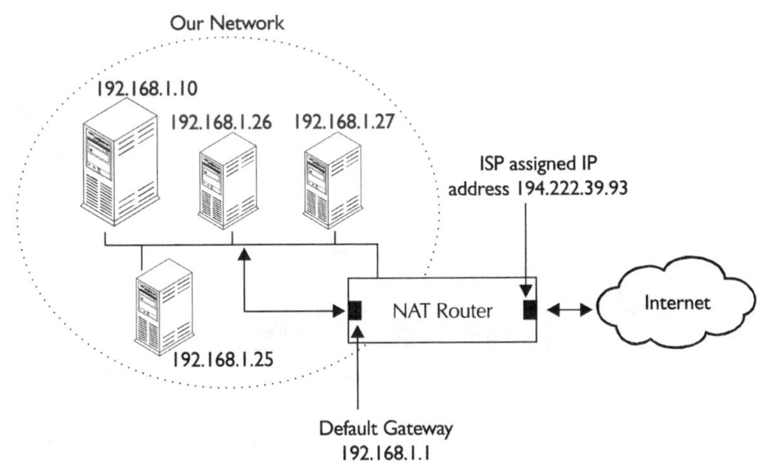

FIGURE 9.30 Using a NAT router to connect to the Internet

DrayTek Router Web Configurator
> Advanced Setup> IP Filter / Firewall Setup> Edit Filter Set> Edit Filter Rule <<Main Menu
Filter Set 1 Rule 1 <<Back | Clear |
Comments : Block NetBios ☑ Check to enable the Filter Rule
Pass or Block: Block Immediately | Branch to Other Filter Set: None
☐ Duplicate to LAN | ☐ Log
Direction IN | Protocol any

	IP Address	Subnet Mask	Operator	Start Port	End Port
Source	any	255.255.255.255 (/32)	=	137	139
Destination	any	255.255.255.255 (/32)	=		

☐ Keep State ☐ Source Route Fragments Don't Care
OK
Copyright (c) 2001, DrayTek Corp. All Rights Reserved.

FIGURE 9.31 Configuring a NAT router's firewall services via a web browser

Travel Advisory

Although most applications work just fine across a NAT connection, some applications won't. Conferencing applications that rely on the H.323 standard (such as Microsoft NetMeeting), for example, may not work properly when used across a NAT connection.

✔**Objective 9.01: Protecting Your Server** Remember that data protection goes well beyond username and password control. These issues are certainly important, but you must also consider what might happen to your server in the event of a system failure or power problem—or, indeed, if someone walks off with it! Physical protection, such as a locked computer room or a UPS, is just as important as the access controls you set up and manage.

✔ **Objective 9.02: Reliability and Fault Tolerance** Computer systems *will* break—it's unavoidable—but you can take steps to ensure that system failures do not bring down the entire network and that the systems can be fixed with minimal disruption. Redundant power supplies and NICs can be installed to keep the systems going in the event of a single failure, RAID systems can be used to reduce the chance of a disk failure, and you can plan for the inevitable by implementing a formal tape backup procedure.

✔ **Objective 9.03: Logon and Access Security** The simplest level of access control is reserved mainly for peer-to-peer networks and is called *share-level security.* This allows you to choose which folders and printers are available to your user base, and you can restrict access by setting up common passwords for these shares. The downside of this scheme is that the one resource password has to be known by everyone who is allowed access to the resource—there's no concept of validating a user's specific identity. A better setup is to have servers manage their resources on a per-user basis, controlling access to resources by verifying a user's logon name and password. Users can also be placed in groups, which further simplifies access management. The key to good user-level security is the proper management of user passwords, which, oddly enough, comes down to educating the system's users. Proper password management means not using obvious words or phrases, not writing passwords down, and changing passwords on a regular basis.

✔ **Objective 9.04: WAN Security** As soon as your network makes its way into the world at large, you must assume that someone will try to break into it. Several levels of protection can be added to your VPN to minimize the risk of intrusion: For example, data can be encrypted using standards such as IPsec, and user authentication can be checked using protocols such as CHAP and Kerberos.

✔ **Objective 9.05: Internet-Specific Security** The Internet is a real melting pot—it's a professional tool, a means of sending e-mail, a means of linking systems together, and a hunting ground for hackers. Protecting your systems from outside attack involves installing a firewall or proxy server of some type to filter IP traffic by address and/or port number. A proxy server can also help to speed up web browsing by locally caching frequently accessed pages. Sites that use network address translation (NAT) Internet connections have a high degree of inherent protection due to the way the system works.

REVIEW QUESTIONS

1. Which of the following will protect a network server from power outages? (Select all that apply.)
   - **A.** A dedicated power circuit
   - **B.** A UPS
   - **C.** A filter
   - **D.** A surge suppressor
2. John has allowed Tracy, Kyle, and Neil access to the SALES01 printer and has told them what password to use. What type of security system is being used? (Select one answer.)
   - **A.** Peer-to-peer
   - **B.** User-level
   - **C.** Kerberos
   - **D.** Share-level
3. Which RAID level provides disk mirroring only? (Select one answer.)
   - **A.** 0
   - **B.** 1
   - **C.** 3
   - **D.** 5
4. Your servers are configured with dual disk controllers, each hosting an independent disk. Data is automatically copied to both disks in its entirety. What fault-tolerant system are you using? (Select one answer.)
   - **A.** Disk duplexing
   - **B.** Disk mirroring
   - **C.** RAID 2
   - **D.** RAID 5
5. Which backup scheme uses a daily tape backup for all files that have changed since the last full backup? (Select one answer.)
   - **A.** Normal backup
   - **B.** Incremental backup
   - **C.** Differential backup
   - **D.** Copy
6. Which backup scheme uses a daily tape backup for all files that have changed since the last daily backup? (Select one answer.)

A. Normal backup
B. Incremental backup
C. Differential backup
D. Copy

7. Which of the following protocols or standards does *not* provide secure password authentication? (Select all that apply.)
   A. CHAP
   B. PAP
   C. L2TP
   D. Kerberos

8. You have been asked to improve Internet security on your network. As a secondary requirement, you have been asked to improve web browsing performance. You choose to install a firewall. Which of the following requirements does this fulfill? (Select one answer.)
   A. The main requirement only
   B. The secondary requirement only
   C. Both the main requirement and the secondary requirement
   D. Neither

9. Which of the following is *not* a feature of a proxy server? (Select one answer.)
   A. Web caching
   B. Port blocking
   C. Cache mirroring
   D. IP address filtering

10. Which protocol is used by HTTPS to encrypt data? (Select one answer.)
   A. Kerberos
   B. MD5
   C. CHAP
   D. RC4

REVIEW ANSWERS

1. **B** A UPS can supply power in the event of an outage, providing time for the system to shut down safely or for backup power to kick in.

2. **D** John is using share-level security. You can tell because he has to give a common password to all users of the shared network resource.
3. **B** Disk mirroring is also known as RAID level 1.
4. **A** Using multiple disks on independent controllers is known as *duplexing.*
5. **C** Differential backups store on tape everything that has changed since the last full backup.
6. **B** Incremental backups store on tape everything that has changed since the last daily backup.
7. **B** PAP does not provide secure password authentication. It passes plain-text passwords to the host system.
8. **A** A firewall will improve security but will not speed up web browsing because a firewall does not have a web cache.
9. **C** Cache mirroring is a made-up term. All the others refer to proxy server features.
10. **D** HTTPS uses the RC4 encryption algorithm.

The Complete Network

ITINERARY

- **Objective 10.01** Network Operating Systems
- **Objective 10.02** Network Clients
- **Objective 10.03** Maintaining the Network Infrastructure
- **Objective 10.04** Planned Maintenance
- **Objective 10.05** Viruses and Vulnerabilities

NEWBIE	SOME EXPERIENCE	EXPERT
4 hours	2 hours	1 hour

This chapter begins by discussing the features of the mainstream network operating systems and clients and then discusses the administrative side of networking, including one essential job that everyone hates—paperwork! Don't ignore this stuff—it's important information for the Network+ exam and may help you back at the office, too!

Objective 10.01 Network Operating Systems

Only a few years ago, you could choose one network operating system and concentrate on mastering it, but times have changed. In the "old days," you could content yourself with mastering one NOS (probably either NetWare, Windows, or some variety of UNIX) and be done with it. Today, however, you will rarely find a homogeneous network. Even if you run a "pure" Windows network, that network will connect to the Internet, which includes systems running just about every NOS ever created. Most large networks today will include a variety of network operating systems, and the wise network tech prepares for work in these heterogeneous environments.

Exam Tip

"Heterogeneous" and "homogeneous" are just fancy words we use to mean "a mix of different things (heterogeneous) and "all of one type" (homogeneous). A heterogeneous network is simply a network that includes a variety of operating systems and hardware.

All NOSs share the same fundamental goal: to enable *users,* the human beings that sit at the computers, to get work done. The routes to that goal vary, of course, depending on the nature of the work. Some networks simply enable users to share files and printers, whereas others supply users with access to sophisticated applications that execute on a server. Before choosing the right network operating system or systems for a network, you should evaluate the roles that need filling for the clients, file and print servers, and application servers (see Figure 10.1).

Roles

The majority of most networks consists of *clients,* the machines at which users sit and do work. Client systems run applications such as word processors, spreadsheets, and web browsers while providing access to resources on the network. Most networks today use a Microsoft operating system such as Windows 2000

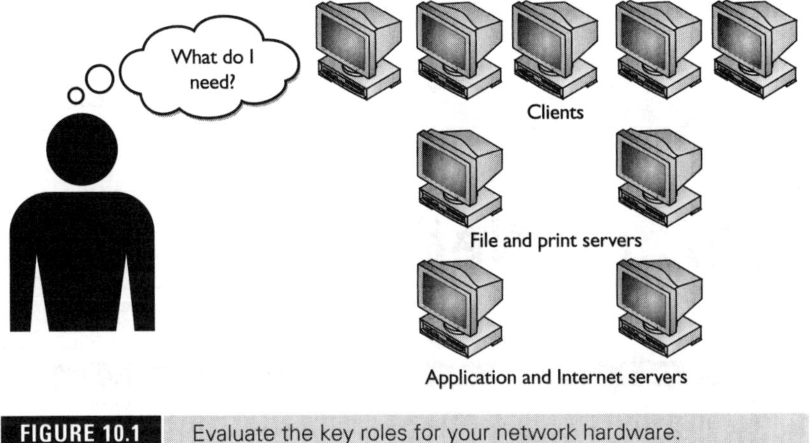

FIGURE 10.1 Evaluate the key roles for your network hardware.

Professional or Windows XP as their client operating system, although Linux clients, UNIX workstations, and thin clients (remember them from Chapter 8?) are also popular in some settings. The next main section in this chapter deals with client-related issues.

File and print servers, as the name implies, provide access to printers and stored data. In small environments that require little or no security, such as a home network, a single system frequently acts as both the client and server—a *peer-to-peer* network. In *server-based* networks, one or more systems act as dedicated file and print servers. A *dedicated server* does not function as a client—it exists to serve the needs of other systems. Because they can be physically isolated from the end users, dedicated servers can offer far greater security.

Application servers perform specific tasks or sets of tasks rather than just serving up stored files. Examples of application servers include web servers, e-mail servers, and database servers. Think about how a website such as www.whois.net operates. You type in a website address for which you want further information, and the site searches its database to find any matches and displays the results (see Figure 10.2). All the searching takes place on the server. The client simply displays the results.

Using an application server rather than performing actions on the client systems offers four key advantages. First, application servers make efficient use of network traffic. Rather than each client needing to download the entire database and perform its own search, the database stays on the server. Only a minimal amount of network bandwidth traverses the network. Second, only a single copy of the database exists, making maintaining and backing up the database a snap. Third, a single, very powerful server can provide access to a large database

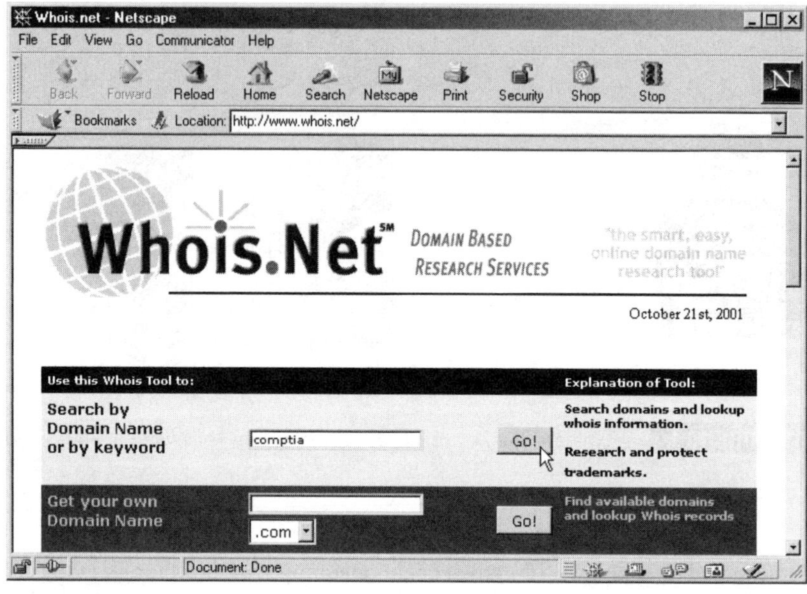

FIGURE 10.2 Searching www.whois.net for website information

for much less expensive, less powerful systems, thus reducing costs. Even a 386- or 486-based computer running a client application such as a web browser can access the database. Fourth, the server can control access to the database, providing different users with different levels of access.

Local Lingo

client/server Client/server has at least two distinct meanings. A *client/server network* has dedicated server machines and dedicated client machines. A *client/server application* performs some part of its processing on an application server rather than on the client systems.

Windows 2000 (and 2003) Server and Domain-Based Networking

Windows 2000 Server and Windows 2003 Server, Microsoft's main server products, offer all the features of Windows 2000 Professional and Windows XP, plus enhancements that optimize them to function as network server operating systems. Microsoft optimized the server versions so that they put a higher priority on serving requests over the network rather than on those of a user sitting at their keyboard.

Travel Assistance

For the sake of simplicity, from now on we will refer to both Windows 2000 Server and Windows 2003 Server as "Windows Server," unless we're discussing a feature specific to a particular version.

One key feature of a Microsoft's Windows network is *domain-based security.* Although it is possible to manage each server separately, servers can be grouped together (in a domain) and share a common security database that controls user access, configuration, and access to shared resources (folders and printers). With older operating systems (Novell NetWare 3.12, for example), a user needing to access more than one system would require a separate user account on each server. Maintaining multiple user accounts for each user created a huge burden on both administrators (who had to create and maintain all those accounts) and end users (who had to remember multiple user account names and passwords). Fortunately, some forgotten genius came up with the idea of a *single login,* which enables a user to log in once and access all their resources, regardless of the server on which a resource resides. Microsoft implements their single login through domains; Novell does the same through "trees."

In a domain, a group of special servers known as *domain controllers* store a common security database called the *Security Access Manager (SAM)* database. When a user logs in to the domain, they log into a domain controller that checks their username and password. When a user logs in successfully to the domain, the domain controller issues them an *access token,* the electronic equivalent of an ID badge. Whenever the user attempts to access a resource on any server on the domain, their computer automatically shows the server the access token (see Figure 10.3). Based on the access token, the server then decides whether to grant access.

Exam Tip

For Windows Servers, all computers within a domain share a common security database. Each user logs in once to access all their resources within the domain.

Novell NetWare

The continued use of older versions testifies to the power and stability of Novell NetWare. Many organizations upgrade their client software, but continue to use their existing NetWare 4.*x* and 5.*x* servers, following those ancient words of wisdom: "If it ain't broke, don't fix it." Network techs should familiarize themselves with three significant versions of NetWare: NetWare 4.*x*, NetWare 5.*x*, and NetWare 6.*x*.

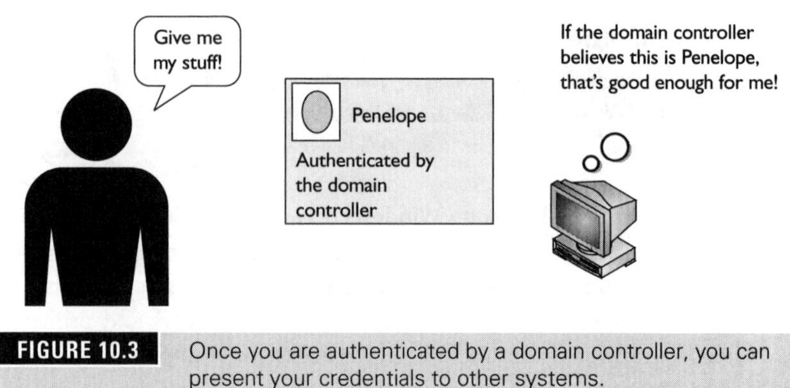

FIGURE 10.3 Once you are authenticated by a domain controller, you can present your credentials to other systems.

NetWare 3.*x* and the Bindery

NetWare 3.*x* offers solid file and print sharing capabilities using the IPX/SPX protocol suite, but lacks a centralized security database—each NetWare 3.*x* server maintains its own independent security database, called the *Bindery.* When a user logs in, the NetWare server compares the username and password to its Bindery database and then determines which resources it will share with the user. NetWare 3.*x* works best in small networks, and even though tools are available to synchronize user account information (such as passwords) between servers, general user administration is still very much done on a per-server basis; a user wishing to access resources on three different servers will require three separate user accounts and passwords (see Figure 10.4). Keeping account details (username and password) the same on each server simplifies things a bit for login purposes, but doesn't do much for the poor network supervisors. NetWare 3.*x*'s reliance on IPX/SPX also limits its use as more and more networks adopt TCP/IP as the protocol of choice.

Exam Tip

Although it *is* possible to add TCP/IP support to a NetWare 3.*x* server, this configuration is not common. For the purposes of the Network+ exam, assume that all NetWare 3.*x* servers use IPX/SPX as their sole networking protocol.

NetWare 4.*x* and NDS

NetWare 4.*x* built on the success of NetWare 3.*x* by adding two key features: Novell Directory Services (NDS) and TCP/IP encapsulation. *Novell Directory Services (NDS)* organizes all user and resource information in a database, referred to

FIGURE 10.4 NetWare 3.*x* servers maintain independent Bindery databases.

as the *NDS tree.* The NDS tree acts as a centralized security database, enabling users who "log into the directory" to access all their resources anywhere on the network. The general structure of NDS and the naming conventions used are based on an OSI standard called *X.500.*

NetWare 4.*x* also supports TCP/IP, allowing NetWare servers and clients to place IPX packets inside of TCP/IP packets, a process known as *encapsulation* (see Figure 10.5). NetWare's basic design assumes the use of IPX/SPX, and encapsulation enables Novell to use TCP/IP without massively redesigning the NOS. Encapsulation, however, degrades performance by adding an additional layer of protocol information to each packet.

Exam Tip

Windows servers enable users to log in once and access all their resources by logging into the *NT domain.* NetWare 4.*x* servers and above enable users to log in once and access all their resources by logging into the *NDS tree.*

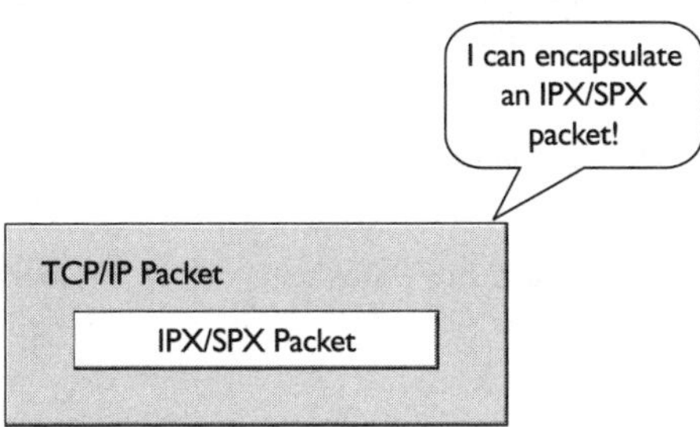

FIGURE 10.5 NetWare 4.*x* and TCP/IP encapsulation

NetWare 5.*x* and 6.*x*

NetWare 5.*x* (and 6.*x*) remove the need for TCP/IP encapsulation, enabling NetWare to run TCP/IP natively. *Native TCP/IP* means that NetWare 5.*x* no longer needs to use IPX/SPX at all (although it can for backward compatibility). Because NetWare 5.*x* can "speak" TCP/IP natively, it performs far more efficiently when using TCP/IP than NetWare 4.*x*. For NetWare 6.*x* servers, Novell uses the name "eDirectory" instead of NDS.

NetWare Summary For the Network+ exam, familiarize yourself with the protocols and security databases used by each version of NetWare, as shown in Table 10.1.

Microsoft Active Directory

Microsoft Active Directory (or Directory Services) is a new model for centralized server management and was introduced with Windows 2000 Server. Like NetWare Directory Services, it is based on the X.500 standard (an industry standard for directory services) and allows you to store information related to your entire network resources in a single database that's stored and updated (replicated) regularly on a number of designated servers. Active Directory includes backward support for NT domains and greatly simplifies the management of multiple servers (which was always the boast of Novell's NDS).

UNIX and Linux

UNIX, the mainstay of universities, scientific computing, and web servers, becomes more important for the average network tech in the trenches as the importance of the Internet continues to grow. Originally, the Internet consisted of a few UNIX-based systems at a few universities spread around the world. The basic Internet protocols (FTP, HTTP, DNS, ARP, and so forth) originated in the world of UNIX and were only later ported to other operating systems. UNIX comes in many flavors, but they generally share certain features. The flexibility of UNIX and the rise of open-source variants such as Linux and Free BSD make UNIX an NOS that network techs ignore at their own peril. From the network

TABLE 10.1 NetWare Security Database and Protocol

NetWare Version	Security Database	Protocol(s)
NetWare 3.*x*	Bindery	IPX/SPX
NetWare 4.*x*	NDS	IPX/SPX or TCP/IP
NetWare 5.*x*	NDS	IPX/SPX or TCP/IP

tech's point of view, all versions of UNIX look more alike than different, although occasionally you will find differences in command syntax that can keep you scratching your head if you originally learned the command you want to use on a different version of UNIX!

Exam Tip

The Network+ exam does not cover the differences between versions of UNIX.

Travel Assistance

A useful set of UNIX tutorials can be found at http://www.matchstick.com/unix/. For a useful "cheat sheet" of common Linux commands, download a copy of "The One Page Linux Manual" from http://homepage.powerup.com.au/~squadron/.

Sharing Files

UNIX systems can share files across a network in a variety of ways, including File Transfer Protocol (FTP—covered in Chapter 6), SAMBA (Chapter 5), and Network File System (NFS).

The *Network File System (NFS)* protocol enables an NFS client to treat files and directories on an NFS server as though they were located on the client system. NFS was originally developed for UNIX-to-UNIX file and directory access requirements, but it has since been implemented on many other platforms. Figure 10.6 shows how a UNIX directory called /data/sales/ can be "seen" on an NFS client PC. Windows-based machines don't come with NFS support as standard, but many third-party NFS client and server options are available. Although NFS is a useful way of accessing data and programs stored on "foreign" systems, it does not support file and record locking (essential features for multiuser database access) and so it is not suitable for every situation.

Web Applications

Although facing increasing competition from Windows servers, UNIX and Linux remain the servers of choice for providing basic Internet-based services such as web and e-mail. The March 2004 Netcraft survey shows Apache, the most common web server for UNIX- and Linux-based servers, with about 67 percent of the market and Microsoft Internet Information Services with about 20 percent. Adding to Apache's market share, Novell NetWare 6 installs the Apache web server by default.

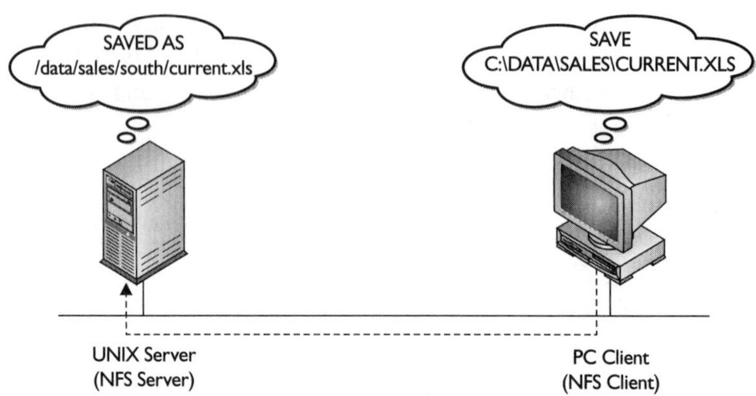

FIGURE 10.6 Accessing a UNIX-based file system using NFS

Travel Assistance

The Netcraft survey can be found at http://news.netcraft.com/archives/web_server_survey.html.

Open Source and Linux

Linux is an *open-source* operating system, meaning that anyone who purchases a copy receives full access to its *source code,* the building blocks of the operating system. Free access to the source code gives software developers tremendous power to modify the operating system to meet their needs, and has led to the rapid development of a wide variety of applications, including some of the most commonly used web and e-mail servers on the Internet—the Apache web server and the Sendmail e-mail server. In most cases, both the Linux operating system and Linux applications are available for free download on the Internet, although vendors such as Red Hat, SuSE, and Caldera charge for support services. For all intents and purposes, Linux is a full-featured clone of UNIX.

Travel Assistance

Your rights with a particular piece of open-source software vary depending on the license under which the software was released. For a thorough discussion of the various licenses and how they affect your rights to use open-source software, see http://www.opensource.org.

Networking Apple Computers

Although we've concentrated on the world of PC networking, we mustn't lose sight of the fact that other desktop systems are out there—and they, too, can be networked. As well as being known for their non-PC desktop computers, Apple Computer Inc. also developed their own networking protocol way back in the mid 1980s. AppleTalk (the current implementation, first seen in 1989, is known as "AppleTalk Phase II") can run over Ethernet, Token Ring, and Fiber Distributed Data Interface (FDDI) topologies as well as Apple's proprietary twisted-pair cabling system known as *LocalTalk* (bandwidth 230 Kbps). Access to Mac-based file and print services was performed using a protocol called AppleShare.

Apple systems can be connected to NetWare (NetWare Client for Mac), Windows (Windows NT Services for Macintosh), and Linux/UNIX servers (various solutions) either via an Ethernet or a LocalTalk NIC, but the latter is not so well supported these days. The ideal Mac connectivity solution is to use Ethernet and TCP/IP. You cannot run TCP/IP directly over LocalTalk, although it *is* possible to encapsulate TCP/IP packets in AppleTalk packets over LocalTalk (see Figure 10.7).

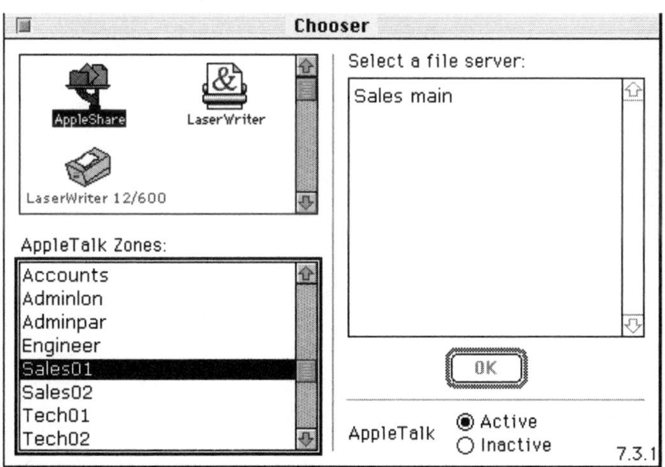

FIGURE 10.7 Navigating around an AppleTalk network

Objective 10.02 Network Clients

Microsoft products dominate the role of desktop clients—with built-in peer-to-peer networking functionality, too. Generally, all of Microsoft's desktop OS offerings provide similar network client functionality, with minor cosmetic differences between the ways that the network basics are set up.

Windows 9*x*

Microsoft Windows 95, 98, and Me (collectively known as Windows 9*x*) provide basic file and print sharing functions, but little security by themselves. A network tech can configure a Windows 9*x* system as simply a client, or as both a client and a server. As a server, however, Windows 9*x* uses share-level control by default, making it significantly less secure than more sophisticated server operating systems. Aside from its modest hardware requirements, Windows 9*x*'s key feature is its ability to connect to virtually any other kind of server, including Windows 9*x*, Windows NT, Novell NetWare, and UNIX.

Because Microsoft maintains a high degree of compatibility with their older network operating systems, their network client services enable a Windows 9*x* system to communicate with any of the following types of servers (client/server or peer-to-peer):

- Microsoft LAN Manager
- Windows for Workgroups
- Windows 95
- Windows 98
- Windows Me
- Windows NT 3.*x*
- Windows NT 4.*x*
- Windows 2000
- Windows 2003
- Windows XP

Windows 9*x* ships with Microsoft Client for NetWare Networks, which enables connectivity with Novell NetWare servers, but only using NWLink (Microsoft's IPX/SPX-compatible protocol). If you want to use TCP/IP, you need to install Novell's own Windows client kit, known as "Client 32" for short. You will also need to use Novell's client for full NetWare 4/5/6 compatibility because Microsoft's version does not recognize or work with NetWare Directory Services—it only supports Bindery mode. In general, Novell's client kits provide much more functionality than Microsoft's equivalents.

Travel Assistance

The latest Novell client kits can be found at http://www.novell.com/download/.

Windows NT Workstation

Windows NT Workstation offers the same user interface as Windows 95, but with greatly enhanced security and stability. A knowledgeable "power user" can often defeat most security measures on a Windows 9*x* machine by directly accessing the registry—the database that defines all settings, including security settings, on a Windows 9*x* system. Windows NT Workstation, in contrast, follows a more robust security model, and an able network administrator can prevent even power users from digging into the internals of the system. Windows NT Workstation also provides a more stable platform for running applications. Although applications can still lock up, Windows NT Workstation does a better job of protecting programs from each other—rarely will the failure of one program on an NT Workstation crash other programs.

Windows NT Workstation can also function effectively as a NetWare client. Microsoft provides its own NetWare client software, Client Services for NetWare (CSNW). As with Windows 9*x*'s Client for NetWare Networks, CSNW cannot connect to NetWare servers via TCP/IP and does not fully support NDS, so it's time to switch to Novell's Client 32 for Windows NT/2000.

Windows 2000/XP

Windows 2000/XP combines the friendliness (Plug and Play capabilities, good hardware auto-detection, snazzy interface, cozy slippers, and so forth) of Windows 9*x* with the robust core OS features of NT. Being the most recent high-tech client product from Microsoft, Windows 2000/XP incorporates all the latest security and connectivity features that may or may not be available as bolt-on functionality for 9*x* and NT, such as support for the latest encryption standards.

User Profiles and System Policies

Windows 9*x*, NT, and 2000/XP support the use of user profiles, which enhance both the usability and security of a network. *User profiles* are a collection of settings that correspond to a specific user account, and they allow each user to customize their working environment so that their wallpaper, desktop layout, and so forth remain consistent from session to session. Storing a user's profile on a network server (NT, NetWare, or other NOS) creates so-called "roaming" profiles that "follow" a user from desktop to desktop, so it doesn't really matter where they sit to work (this is ideal for so-called "hot-desking" environments). Profiles and system policies also allow network administrators to customize and restrict desktop settings, and many other Windows features (see Figure 10.8). An administrator can prevent users from running other programs, changing their desktop icons and wallpaper, and loading new programs.

User profiles and system policies offer both a consistent look and feel to the end user and control to the network administrator.

Exam Tip

The Network+ exam doesn't expect you to know *how* user profiles and policies are configured, just that they exist and what they do.

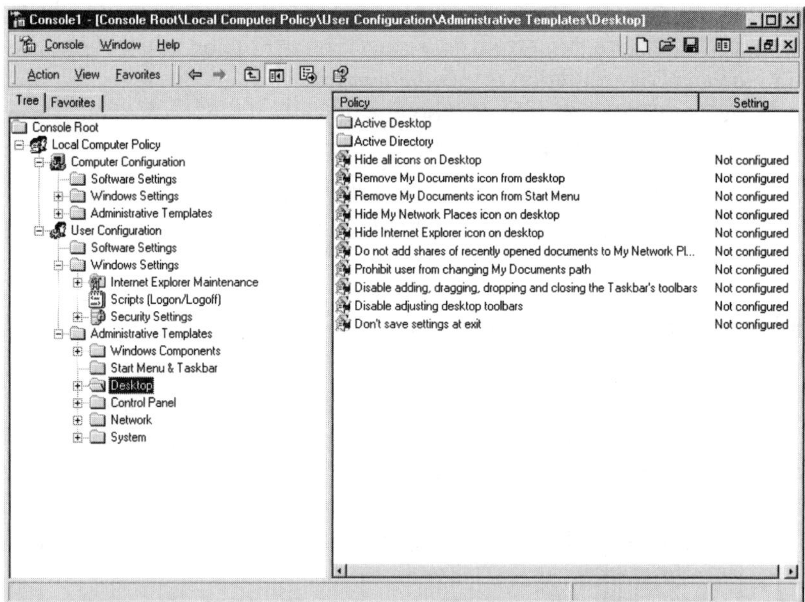

FIGURE 10.8 Configuring a user's desktop in Windows 2000

Maintaining the Network Infrastructure

The other key element of any network is its *infrastructure*. We've already covered the basics in previous chapters, so here's a consolidation of the key issues to consider when putting it all together.

Topology

The core of most business networks today is going to be based on a structured UTP system, but you may need to consider how legacy systems are going to connect into the system—you may need bridges or routers to integrate older cabling standards and other networking protocols, or you may need to make the decision to upgrade the older stuff to the new standard.

Always think ahead and plan your network infrastructure to cope with expansion (networks have a tendency to grow, rather than shrink!). Is it really worth saving such a small amount to get a 12-port hub when a 16- or 24-port is the same physical size and just a fraction more to purchase? Sure, we don't want to go mad and buy "top of the range" for everything, but going for the cheapest in all circumstances can be a false economy (and we haven't even mentioned build quality yet). Many a tech has been asked to hook up a couple new ports "right now" for the new starters and found themselves in among the spaghetti hanging out of the wiring cabinet desperately searching for someone (something!) they can disconnect to make room for the new guys! Oh, and if you *have* got such an untidy setup, why not plan an "out-of-hours tidy-up-and-document" session; it will sure help with future management and troubleshooting. On one site this actually helped identify the source of a previously untraceable network slowdown that was caused when the last hub in a rack was accidentally patched back to the first, creating a "ring" of hubs!

Documentation

Following the last chapter, you should know to have procedures in place to ensure that regular backups are made and that UPSs and backup power systems are tested regularly. Your life will also be made much easier if you document key activities that take place on the network—your maxim should be, "If in doubt, document it!"

Documentation is a broad category that encompasses not only the manuals and readme files from the manufacturer, but also your own documentation, such as network maps, change logs, and network history. You need to get and create this documentation, and then you need to find a way to store, manage, and update it as necessary.

Manufacturer's Data

The first category of documentation to hoard in your network library is the information you can get from the manufacturers—items such as the following:

- **Readme files** Often called README.TXT or README.DOC on setup CDs and diskettes.
- **Official software and hardware documentation, such as user manuals** These manuals often give in-depth installation instructions, frequently asked questions, and troubleshooting suggestions. These manuals also provide direction to more updated information, patches, or additional drivers.
- **The addresses of relevant websites** On websites, you can find searchable troubleshooting databases (often called "knowledge bases"). These databases are compiled based on the questions and problems that other customers have brought to the attention of the manufacturer. When the issue is resolved, it gets added to this database for your benefit.
- **The addresses of relevant newsgroups on Usenet** Usenet has many newsgroups that discuss specific types of hardware and software, as well as general hardware and networking topics. These groups are a good place to visit regularly, just to keep an eye on the current topics. They are also a good place to go when you have a problem—someone else may have already solved a similar one.

Travel Assistance

For all the Linux documentation that you could possibly need, visit the Linux Documentation Project at http://tldp.org/.

Read the Fine Manual

Although technical manuals can sometimes get a bad press, it *is* worth reading the documentation that comes with a new piece of software or hardware. The last situation you want to find yourself in is one where you are halfway through a product installation or upgrade and *then* you discover you need a specific update or additional item for *your* specific setup—look specifically for installation instructions and known bugs or incompatibilities.

After glancing through this provided documentation, many network administrators simply stick it in a pile and assume they can sort it out later. Unfortunately, when "later" comes, that same administrators are probably running around with their shirts on fire because the main e-mail server is down and they can't find the documentation for that server's NIC. It is best to organize your documentation by machine, or class of machine. If all your servers, for example, are built to the exact same specification, with the exact same components, you should keep a file for all the documentation for the server-class machines. When any server has even one piece of hardware that is not standard, that server should have its own file, with all the documentation for all its components. This allows you, when you are preparing for upgrades or doing troubleshooting, to take one binder or file folder and have all the information for that machine at your fingertips.

All Your Own Work

The list of documentation about your network that you should create yourself is even longer and broader reaching than the documentation you obtain from other sources. This documentation must accurately reflect the configuration of the hardware and software installed, as well as any changes that get made to it. Your documentation should have the following elements:

- Each piece of hardware and software has a variety of numbers associated with it, such as serial numbers, part numbers, and license numbers. It is important to keep a list of all the numbers associated with the hardware and software installed in each machine.
- Each of the machines in your environment was built at some point by somebody who put certain pieces of hardware and software into it. You should know what pieces of hardware and software are in the machines, when they were installed and configured, and by whom. This allows you to check back with that person for more information or assistance, if it becomes necessary. Look at Figure 10.9 for an example of a log that might give all the necessary details on a particular machine.
- The folder for each machine should also reflect each time one of the machines is changed in any way, including hardware and software upgrades, upgrades to BIOS or drivers, and changes to location.

B	C	D	E
Function and software	**Location/Phone**	**TCP/IP Settings**	**Harware**
PDC; Houston_WRT domain	Houston Server Room	IP=223.190.190.1	Standard Compaq Proliant 7000
OS = NT 4 Service Pack 3	713-999-9999	subnet = 255.255.255.0	inventory number SRVC7x01
Added SP 4 3/99		Gateway = 223.190.100.1	Video Card=S3 Verge DX
Added SP5 6/99			inventory number VCS301
			NIC=Intel 10/100
			inventory number NICI01

FIGURE 10.9 Sample log

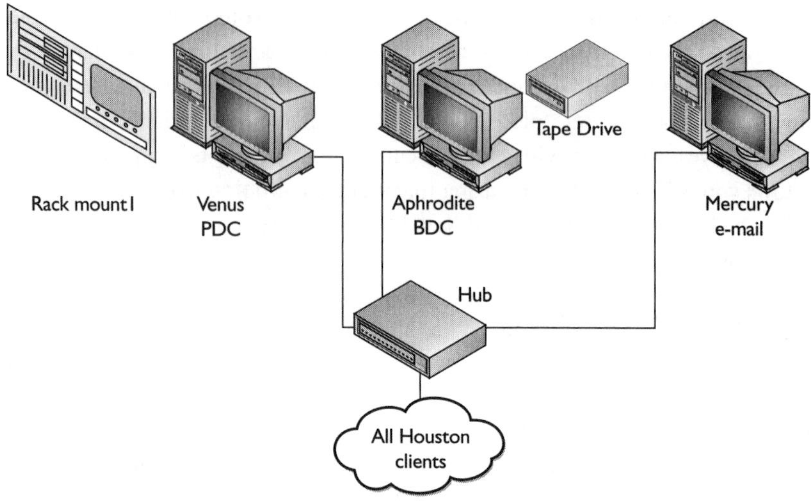

FIGURE 10.10 Sample Visio network diagram

- A network map, created with a program such as Visio, is often useful. Figure 10.10 shows an example of a network map created with Visio. This map would include the servers, workstations, printers and other peripherals, cables and cable closets, patch panels, hubs, routers, and any other elements of your network. This enables you to find the connections between problems as well as locate specific pieces of hardware.
- Each time a new procedure is created for installing, fixing, or configuring an element of your network, it must be documented and made available to anyone in your organization who might perform that task.
- Each time a new policy is set—for issues such as password length, login times, available storage space, or other issues—it must be documented.
- All domains, servers, or accounts that require an administrator's account should have a superadministrator account created and documented. This account information and password should not be available to most administrators. You might store it with the network manager or with other sensitive network documentation.
- Most network operating systems have the ability to configure groups and permissions or rights. You should document what users are members of which groups. Then, document which groups and users have which level of permissions or rights to which resources.

- Each network has mapped drives, servers that contain special data or have special functions, and other details. These details are important to document. New employees or consultants need this information when familiarizing themselves with your network.
- As you begin to create special configurations or batch files or to collect special drivers, these should be documented and backed up—what does that strange JOEBOB.BAT file do on the primary domain controller machine? Is it necessary? If you were a new network administrator just coming into an environment that had no documentation, you might be tempted either to run the batch file or to delete it. In one case, it might be a destructive program left by a disgruntled former administrator to delete your most important configuration files; in the other case, it might be the file that runs the nightly backup. Neither scenario bodes well for your stress level. If all the batch files were documented, however, you would know when each one could be run.

This list of suggested documentation for your network, although long, is just the tip of the iceberg. Each organization has elements of its network configuration that are unique—and these elements must be documented and available to the administrators, contractors, or consultants working on your systems.

Document Management

All the hours spent on documentation will be wasted if you allow elements of the network to be changed without updating the documentation. Similarly, no amount of documentation can help if the server that stores it all is the one machine that is irrevocably fried. Managing your documentation is as important as creating it—this consists of ensuring that changes made to the systems or networks are reflected in the documentation and that all the documentation is available when it is necessary.

First, you should ensure that all changes to machines get logged. Similar to the original log of how the machine was configured, the change log should include the who, when, what, and why information, as shown in Figure 10.11. This not only enables you to keep track of how your machines are currently configured, but it also ensures that you can return to the original configuration if necessary.

Next, you need to ensure that the documentation you've created, organized, and updated is available when you need it. Although it makes a great deal of sense to use a software-based knowledge management system for your documentation, make sure you can immediately put your hot little hands on at least one hard copy and a software backup of the documentation. This ensures that even if your network or the server that stores the information is unavailable, you have the information you need to troubleshoot that problem.

Change Log				
Name	**Added Software**	**Date/Who**	**Added Hardware**	**Date/Who**
Venus	NT Service Pack 4	3/1/99		
		John X. Tech		
	NT Service Pack 5	6/1/99		
		John X. Tech		
			Additional 10/100 NIC	John X. Tech
			inventory number NICI07	6/2/99

FIGURE 10.11 Sample change log

Objective 10.04 Planned Maintenance

Considering that your network infrastructure (media, servers, clients, and so forth) is vital to your business, it is important to treat it with respect. Upsetting the (sometimes) delicate balance between elements of the system (and we include the users in this!) is not a good idea, so any work that is likely to disrupt service—or even has the potential to do so—should be planned to occur after hours, or if that's not possible, at a time that's known to the users likely to be using the system during that period of time (see Figure 10.12). Planned maintenance includes the following events:

- Adding or removing network media or equipment
- Installing updates or patches on the servers
- Downloading software updates to client systems (known as a *software push*)
- Performing scheduled backups
- Performing diagnostics or testing on the network

FIGURE 10.12 Plan and announce scheduled maintenance.

Many a network tech has gotten away with pulling a cable out and quickly replugging it to perform a check or move a connection to another hub, and this leads to an atmosphere of complacency. It only takes that one time that you *do* bring down the whole network to make you realize how important it is to do things properly—it may be inconvenient to have to wait to perform what might seem to be a simple, quick repatching task, but it's the *professional* way to behave!

Software Updates and System Patches

Many network operating systems and other applications allow software updates and patches to be dynamically installed—sometimes without a need to reboot. Tempting as it might be to do an "invisible" update on your servers or for a particular application, these fixes should *always* be tested on a lab system that is not part of your production network before being released into the wild. Every serious network support team should have access to a lab area with test servers and client PCs where they can check for potentially unpleasant side effects. We've all heard the one about the software patch that fixes six problems and introduces four new ones!

Exam Tip

Software patches should be tested in a lab environment before live implementation.

Standard Builds and Self-Healing Systems

Using a fixed, basic configuration for your client PCs means you can reinstall systems easily from the network or CD, or just replace an entire hard disk with one holding a clean setup. This can save a considerable amount of time if you encounter a major problem with a machine—you can get it back to "square one" very quickly without having to install individual packages. A standard build also helps you test patches and updates because you know the target software environment very well. Software products are also available that take snapshots of client PCs at regular intervals so that they can be rolled back to pre-problem (pre-patch) times in the event a problem does occur. These systems are known as *self-healing*. Windows XP even includes support for "system restore points" right out of the box!

Objective 10.05

Viruses and Vulnerabilities

The greatest problem in today's sharing, networked computer society is the virus (see Figure 10.13). Viruses today can be executable files, Java or JavaScript applications, and macros that run in other applications (macro viruses currently account for about 80 percent of all viruses). These viruses can be transmitted in a variety of ways, including downloading documents from the Web, receiving viruses or infected documents via e-mail, or through more traditional means such as accidentally booting from an infected disk or running a Trojan horse (a program that claims to do something useful but actually contains a virus). The first step toward protecting your network from these unwanted critters is buying good network-based virus-protection software. For protection from downloaded viruses, you might also invest in a firewall that has the ability to screen out unwanted visitors. Firewalls can also be configured to block certain files or types of files from being downloaded. Although you probably would not want to block the download of all DOC or EXE files, you might block specific, known virus files.

A variety of companies, such as Network Associates, Symantec, Trend Micro, and Sophos, offer virus-protection suites to help protect your network. These software suites enable the scanning and cleaning of viruses on the servers and workstations in your network. You have two important tasks to make this work. First, buy and install the virus-protection software. Second, *make sure you keep it*

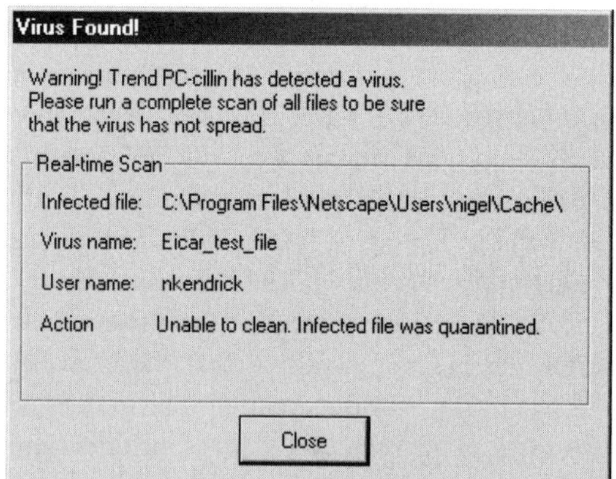

FIGURE 10.13 Detecting a (test) virus

updated. Most virus-protection software depends on often-updated files—usually called *data, definition,* or *signature files*—that search for and clean particular viruses. If you have good virus software but an out-of-date definition file, the newer viruses can have a field day in your systems. Check for new data files on a regular basis (once per week, but once a day is better) and have a predetermined method for making sure all the proper locations get updated (see Figure 10.14). This is the only way to protect your machines from infestation. The virus-protection suite is the best all-around method of protection for your network. It enables you to scan not only your servers, but also your workstations, and in some cases specific downloaded files and e-mail. The more complete the suite you buy, the more protected your network can be. Once again, don't forget to *test* all virus updates before letting them "go live"—even patches from well-respected antivirus companies have caused unexpected problems.

Exam Tip

Remember how important it is to update the virus definitions regularly.

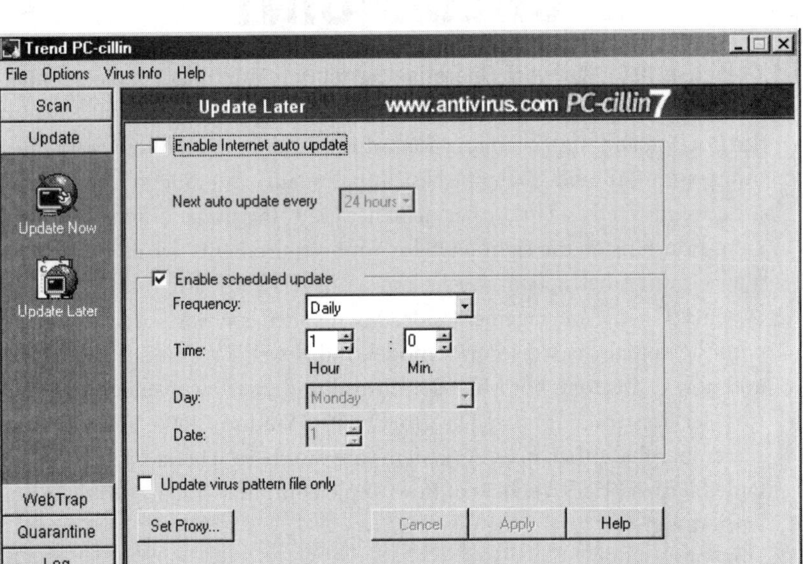

FIGURE 10.14 Scheduling virus-protection updates

Application Vulnerabilities

Although antivirus programs will help prevent malicious code from entering your systems, potential damage can also be caused by software vulnerabilities—unplanned program features that can be exploited to break systems or used as "back doors" to gain high-level access to systems and networks. Always keep an eye out for manufacturers' bulletins and announcements from advisory groups about the software you are using—and always test and implement security fixes as soon as possible.

Travel Assistance

Advisories about software-related vulnerabilities are published regularly by CERT (http://www.cert.org) and Security Focus (http://www.securityfocus.com/).

✔**Objective 10.01: Network Operating Systems** Your major choices for network operating systems include Windows NT/2000/2003, Novell NetWare 4.*x*./5.*x*/6.*x*, and the various versions of UNIX and Linux. All network operating systems provide the same basic functionality, but differ in the way they are administered and in the performance they offer under different working conditions. Install the right NOS for your requirements—if necessary, seek advice from other network techs and managers who have installed similar systems. On the management side, Microsoft has always been associated with the domain-based security model, and Novell with Bindery files, NDS, and now eDirectory, but Microsoft introduced their own version of Directory Services (called Active Directory) with Windows 2000. You must also remember that other, non-PC systems are out there. Therefore, this section ended with a brief overview of how Apple computer systems do their network thing.

✔**Objective 10.02: Network Clients** Microsoft dominates the client operating system world with their various flavors of Windows, but they do recognize that you may wish to connect to other systems and therefore provide client software for other environments, such as Novell NetWare. Generally, you will get better functionality by installing the client kits supplied by the NOS manufacturers ("Client 32" kits in the case of Novell NetWare). One delightful task a network tech can perform is to "lock down" a user's configuration so that they have fewer opportunities to mess with their system—in our case, this generally means using Microsoft's User Profiles and Systems policies features to curb their enthusiasm. Novell environments use Novell Zenworks for Desktops to lock down client workstations.

✔ **Objective 10.03: Maintaining the Network Infrastructure** One of the worst things that can happen is for a network to evolve; instead, it is better to document how the network works today and think ahead about how it will work in the future. No one likes managing documentation, let alone reading it, but *do* be a bookworm and show how much importance you place on getting things right. Ultimately, downtime due to lack of planning costs a business money (sometimes a *lot* of money), so don't take this responsibility lightly. Planning for expected system events, such as installing a new patch, should also be treated as a formal exercise: Test the patch in the lab area, schedule an update for a convenient moment, inform the users, establish contingencies to deal with unexpected results, and then install the patch, test it again, and "go live." Although this may sound like extra work, it's really just part of the job—it's unavoidable, but it is *not* unnecessary or time wasting.

✔ **Objective 10.04: Planned Maintenance** Planning ahead can prevent problems and also reduce downtime and inconvenience. All system changes or updates that *might* have an impact on the network or its users should be performed after hours, if possible, with plenty of warning and only after proper testing in an offline (lab) environment. Having a standard build for your client PCs will help you recover quickly from problems and when setting up new PCs. Self-healing software can save you considerable time when problems occur by rolling back machines to earlier (configuration) times.

✔ **Objective 10.05: Viruses and Vulnerabilities** Coping with potential virus attacks and software vulnerabilities is part of a network tech's implied job description. Do install a good antivirus package for your servers and clients. Do ensure that the virus definition files are updated regularly, and do remember to check the appropriate websites and newsgroups for virus bulletins and known vulnerabilities that could be exploited to disrupt your systems or to gain unauthorized access.

REVIEW QUESTIONS

1. What is the name of the security management system used by Microsoft Windows NT Server? (Select one answer.)
   - **A.** NTSEC
   - **B.** MDS
   - **C.** Peer-to-peer
   - **D.** Domain-based management
2. Which of the following are associated with user management with Novell NetWare? (Select all that apply.)
   - **A.** Bindery files
   - **B.** Active Directory
   - **C.** Domains
   - **D.** NDS trees
3. Which of the following protocols can be used for wide area connectivity and performance with a NetWare 5 server? (Choose all that apply.)
   - **A.** NetBEUI
   - **B.** IPX/SPX
   - **C.** TCP/IP
   - **D.** X.500
4. Which of the following can be used to share files between a UNIX system and a PC client? (Choose all that apply.)
   - **A.** NFS
   - **B.** DNS
   - **C.** FTP
   - **D.** SAMBA
5. What is the name of Apple's proprietary network cabling system? (Choose one answer.)
   - **A.** LocalTalk
   - **B.** LocalLink
   - **C.** AppleShare
   - **D.** AppleTalk

6. Which of the following can be used to allow John to see his customized desktop, regardless of which office computer he uses? (Choose one answer.)
   A. SAMBA
   B. Roaming profiles
   C. Policies
   D. Standard builds
7. Which of the following should be part of your network documentation? (Select all that apply.)
   A. Patches
   B. Drivers
   C. Network map
   D. Change log
8. Which of the following file types can be used to spread viruses? (Select one answer.)
   A. Program files
   B. Macros
   C. JavaScript
   D. All of the above
9. Novell's NDS and Microsoft's Active Directory are based on which standard? (Select one answer.)
   A. X.400
   B. X.500
   C. X.25
   D. None of the above
10. Which of the following security systems is used by NetWare 3.*x*? (Select one answer.)
    A. NDS
    B. Bindery
    C. Binary
    D. Active Binary

REVIEW ANSWERS

1. **D** Windows NT uses domain-based management.
2. **A D** NetWare 2.*x* and 3.*x* use Bindery files (A) and NetWare 4 onward use NDS (D).
3. **B C** NetWare 5 supports both IPX/SPX (B) and TCP/IP (C).
4. **A C D** DNS (B) is a name resolution protocol, but all the others can be used to transfer files between UNIX systems and other machines.
5. **A** Apple's proprietary cabling system is known as LocalTalk.
6. **B** Roaming profiles allow users' customized desktops to be loaded from a central location, whichever PC they use.
7. **C D** Your documentation should include a network map and a change log. Patches and drivers should be downloaded regularly from the supplier's website.
8. **D** All the file types listed can be used to spread viruses.
9. **B** NDS and Active Directory are based on X.500.
10. **B** NetWare 3.*x* uses Bindery-based security.

Troubleshooting Basics

ITINERARY

- **Objective 11.01** General Network Troubleshooting
- **Objective 11.02** Establishing a Baseline
- **Objective 11.03** Problem Analysis
- **Objective 11.04** Checking System Logs
- **Objective 11.05** Hardware Troubleshooting and Safety

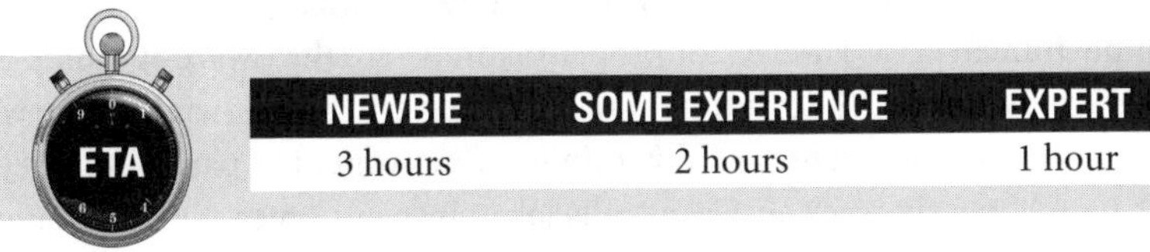

NEWBIE	SOME EXPERIENCE	EXPERT
3 hours	2 hours	1 hour

Back in Chapter 9 we taught you the facts of life. Really! Remember? No? OK, to save you flipping back, we'll go over it one more time. One day, when you least expect, it will hit you; out of the blue someone will come in to your life and utter those immortal words: "Something's wrong with the server." And as the phone rings to report the same problem for the fifteenth time, the words of Agent Smith from the film *The Matrix* will run through your mind: "Hear that, Mr. Anderson? That is the sound of inevitability."

Having good, methodical troubleshooting skills is essential for every network tech, but you must also be able to tell when things are "not right"—when the network's running slowly or the server's disk system seems to be a bit sluggish. You need a "nose" for the merest hint of a potential problem.

Objective 11.01 General Network Troubleshooting

Troubleshooting is not something that can be easily described in a nice neat list of ten easy steps. It is more of an art—an ability to be "one with the network" and have a feeling where the problems are hiding. The best troubleshooters are those who have a huge amount of knowledge about each of the elements of the network—hardware, software, connections, and so forth. These people can then synthesize all that knowledge into some good guesses about where to start looking for the problems. All these steps should serve to give you a theoretical idea of where to look and how to proceed with troubleshooting your own network. The theory, however, is easier to implement in real life if you have some examples to give you the feel of the art of troubleshooting.

Simple human error and lack of proper planning are the two root causes of local area network (LAN) downtime and inefficiencies. The following list shows the ten most common causes of downtime on networks (or part of the network), based on a six-week survey of calls taken by a customer support center, along with some simple tips that might have prevented the problems:

- **Misconfigured routers** Devices installed and configured incorrectly. You should take the time to plan your implementation and configuration of not only routers, but any network device or software. The time you save in the long run will be well worth the extra efforts in the planning stages.
- **Faulty Ethernet cards** Poor-quality cards that fail soon after installation, but take some time to detect. One of the best things you could do to

help prevent this kind of problem is to purchase name-brand network cards, or network cards that you or a person you know have had great experiences with. Another rule to follow when purchasing devices is to check the hardware compatibility list (HCL) for the operating system you are installing the hardware in. The HCL is a list published by Microsoft that comes with each operating system, and includes a list of devices that have been proven to work with the operating system already.

- **Broadcast storms** Caused by legacy applications on legacy servers, which should have been taken out of commission. Sometimes finding a new replacement to the legacy software or legacy hardware can save a lot of money in support cost over the long haul. Be sure to monitor network traffic for any devices or applications that pollute the network with an abundance of network broadcasts.
- **Unwanted protocols** Many networks suffer from having multiple protocols installed when only one or two may be needed. Because of the extra overhead involved, try to keep the number of protocols loaded to a minimum.
- **Poor switch allocation** LAN bottlenecks caused by too many devices being allocated to run through one overloaded switch.
- **Server overloading** Poor ongoing maintenance of file servers, causing slow spots on the network. Use the appropriate tools to monitor the health of the server and ensure that you are not placing too many responsibilities on one system. For example, if you have a server acting as your domain controller and file and print server, you would not want to place additional load on that system by making it your database server and e-mail server as well. Try to spread the roles of servers across many systems to keep the load on each system to a minimum.
- **Faulty devices** Fundamental faults with devices attached to the network, which can be difficult to detect initially. Creating your own in-house documentation should help support staff identify common device problems.
- **SNMP management tools** The design of the Simple Network Management Protocol (SNMP) is such that it can impact the performance of the devices being managed and add to the traffic burden on the network.
- **Rogue equipment** Unauthorized connection of illegitimate or inappropriate devices to the network. For example, Bob wishes to

learn a little more about DHCP, so he builds his own DHCP server during lunch hour, not realizing that this DHCP server is giving out faulty IP addresses to clients looking for one. This could cause a lot of headaches on the network because support staff will be troubleshooting why clients can't access network resources. Clients will not be able to access network resources because they have received an inappropriate IP address from an unauthorized DHCP server.

- **Power outage** The total failure of power supplies to networked devices. Ensure that you have backup power sources for all your critical systems.

The art of network troubleshooting can be a fun, frolicsome, and usually frustrating skill to gain. By applying a good troubleshooting methodology and constantly increasing your knowledge of networks, you can develop into a great troubleshooting artist. This takes time, naturally, but stick with it. Learn new stuff, document problems and fixes, talk to other network techs about similar problems, and read related troubleshooting websites, such as http://www.microsoft.com/technet/support/default.mspx (the Microsoft TechNet support site). All these factors can make your life much easier when crunch time comes and a network disaster occurs—and a network disaster *will* happen. When it does, you want to make sure you are well prepared.

Troubleshooting Connectivity Problems

You will be placed in a wealth of different troubleshooting scenarios as a network tech. This section identifies some of the most common network connectivity problems as well as the steps to take to troubleshoot these problems and help you identify their potential cause.

I Can't Surf the Web. Why Not?

It's 7:45 A.M. and you have just managed to sit down at your desk with your Tim Horton's coffee cup still half full. Sean, a user on your network, calls and asks why there is no Internet access this morning. You start your browser and manage to navigate a number of websites with no problem. You tell Sean that you will be right over.

In Chapter 6 you learned a number of utilities for network troubleshooting—you are now going to put them to the test! When you arrive at Sean's desk, you sit down to start your troubleshooting. As a first step you are curious to know whether he has an IP address assigned to his system. To find this out, you use the IPCONFIG utility (winipcfg.exe if you are using Windows 9*x* systems). As shown in Figure 11.1, IPCONFIG without any switches will show you Sean's IP address, subnet mask, and default gateway. From a troubleshooting standpoint, you should be looking at these numbers to make sure they are valid for your network. For example, looking at the configuration in Figure 11.1, you can see that the subnet mask is 255.255.255.0. You learned in Chapter 6 that if there is a 255 in the subnet mask, the corresponding octet in the IP address is part of the network ID. In this example, you need to ensure that all hosts on the network (including Sean's computer) have the same first three octets—which is 192.168.1.*x*. With this configuration, each host believes it is on the 192.168.1.*x* network. If Sean's system was configured with a different network ID (say, 192.168.4.*x*), that would be a reason why he could not communicate on the network—his system believes it is part of a different network and would try to use a router for communication with any LAN devices.

Let's assume that the IP address and subnet mask are correct for your network—your next focus should be the default gateway entry displayed in the IPCONFIG output. You learned in Chapter 6 that the default gateway is the address of the router. The router is the device on the network that is responsible for sending all data *off* the network. (Remember, if you are communicating with a local machine, your system does not use a router. It sends the data directly to the other machine.) The point here is that Sean has called you because he is having trouble browsing the Internet, and to browse the Internet, Sean's computer would have to send and receive all data through the default gateway (the router). When troubleshooting the default gateway, the first thing to do is to look at the address and ask yourself, "Is that the address of our router?" If it is not, you have found the reason why Sean cannot surf the Web. If the address is correct, another reason for not being able to browse the Internet could be that the router is down. We discussed the PING command in Chapter 6; we will now use it to verify that the router is up and running. Looking at Figure 11.1, you can see that Sean's default gateway is 192.168.1.1. To verify that the router is up and running, type the following in a command prompt (Figure 11.2 shows the output of a PING command):

```
PING 192.168.1.1
```

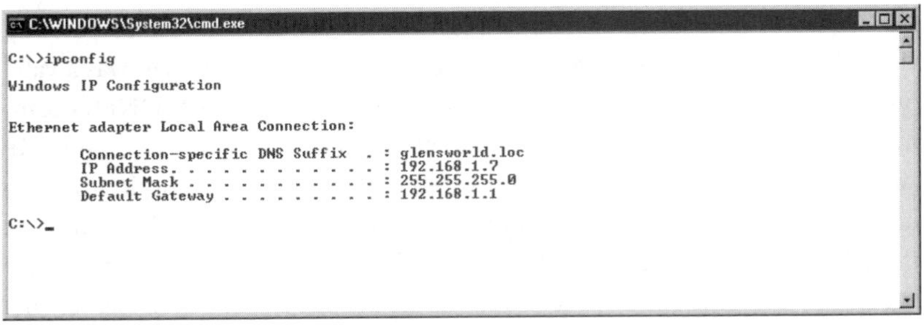

```
C:\WINDOWS\System32\cmd.exe

C:\>ipconfig

Windows IP Configuration

Ethernet adapter Local Area Connection:

        Connection-specific DNS Suffix  . : glensworld.loc
        IP Address. . . . . . . . . . . . : 192.168.1.7
        Subnet Mask . . . . . . . . . . . : 255.255.255.0
        Default Gateway . . . . . . . . . : 192.168.1.1

C:\>_
```

FIGURE 11.1 Looking at TCP/IP settings with IPCONFIG

```
C:\WINDOWS\System32\cmd.exe
C:\>ping 192.168.1.1

Pinging 192.168.1.1 with 32 bytes of data:

Reply from 192.168.1.1: bytes=32 time=1ms TTL=150
Reply from 192.168.1.1: bytes=32 time<1ms TTL=150
Reply from 192.168.1.1: bytes=32 time<1ms TTL=150
Reply from 192.168.1.1: bytes=32 time<1ms TTL=150

Ping statistics for 192.168.1.1:
    Packets: Sent = 4, Received = 4, Lost = 0 (0% loss),
Approximate round trip times in milli-seconds:
    Minimum = 0ms, Maximum = 1ms, Average = 0ms

C:\>_
```

FIGURE 11.2 Testing connectivity with the PING utility

Notice after the four replies come back that there is a summary section summarizing how many messages were sent and how many replies were received. If you do not get replies from the IP address of the default gateway, you know that the reason Sean cannot browse the Internet is because the router is down. Normally, if the router is the problem, it would mean that all users on the network could not browse the Internet, and because you were able to navigate from your own computer earlier, this was a long shot—but one worth checking.

Travel Advisory

When using the PING utility to ping systems on remote networks, be aware that the network administrators of the remote networks may configure their firewalls to block the PING packets (ICMP traffic). Keep this in mind when troubleshooting because there may be nothing wrong with your system or the remote system, just that the PING packet has been blocked. If this happens, try to ping a few different remote systems.

IPCONFIG /ALL Before leaving the IPCONFIG utility, let's look at a different scenario. Going back to when you used IPCONFIG on Sean's system and were looking to see if his system had an IP address, subnet mask, and default gateway, we said that you were looking to see if the IP address that Sean had was a valid one for your network. What if it is not a valid address? The IPCONFIG command supports the /ALL switch to display additional information, such as the IP address of the DHCP server that gave you the IP address. If you notice that you have an invalid address on a system your first question should be, "How did I get this address?" or "Who gave me this address?" Then you should figure out where the DHCP server is (in this scenario, it is an unauthorized DHCP server that someone studying for an exam has built, and the problem is that the rogue server is dishing out bogus addresses to the network) and start troubleshooting the server. Figure 11.3 displays the output of the IPCONFIG /ALL command. Notice that the IP address of 192.168.1.3 is the system that gave you the IP address (the DHCP server). It is also worth noting that the /ALL switch displays your lease information (how long the client machine has the IP address).

Now that you have the IP address of the server that has given you your TCP/IP configuration, you are extremely curious as to what the name of that system is. Most of us in network administration roles know the names of the systems on the network, or at least the servers. How can you find out the computer name (a.k.a., the NetBIOS name) of a system when you have the IP address? In Chapter 6 you learned of a utility called NBTSTAT (NetBIOS over TCP/IP STATistics). We are now going to put it to good use!

Microsoft operating systems make heavy use of computer names, and they register these names in what is known as a *name table* (stored in memory of each machine). You may use the NBTSTAT utility to query the name table of a remote system if you know its IP address (and we have an IP address we are curious to query—192.168.1.3). The syntax to query a remote name table is

```
NBTSTAT -A <ip address>
```

Exam Tip

Be sure to review the NBTSTAT command and its switches by typing **NBTSTAT /?** in a command prompt. You will be tested on the output of some of the different switches.

Figure 11.4 displays the output of querying the name table of the rogue DHCP server. Notice that that there are a few entries called "WIN2003," and also

```
C:\WINDOWS\System32\cmd.exe

C:\>ipconfig /all

Windows IP Configuration

        Host Name . . . . . . . . . . . . : lap-xppro
        Primary Dns Suffix  . . . . . . . :
        Node Type . . . . . . . . . . . . : Unknown
        IP Routing Enabled. . . . . . . . : No
        WINS Proxy Enabled. . . . . . . . : No

Ethernet adapter Local Area Connection:

        Connection-specific DNS Suffix  . : glensworld.loc
        Description . . . . . . . . . . . : Accton EN2242 Series MiniPCI Fast Ethernet Adapter
        Physical Address. . . . . . . . . : 00-D0-59-32-86-35
        Dhcp Enabled. . . . . . . . . . . : Yes
        Autoconfiguration Enabled . . . . : Yes
        IP Address. . . . . . . . . . . . : 192.168.1.7
        Subnet Mask . . . . . . . . . . . : 255.255.255.0
        Default Gateway . . . . . . . . . : 192.168.1.1
        DHCP Server . . . . . . . . . . . : 192.168.1.3
        DNS Servers . . . . . . . . . . . : 192.168.1.3
        Lease Obtained. . . . . . . . . . : Sunday, March 14, 2004 10:08:43 AM
        Lease Expires . . . . . . . . . . : Thursday, March 18, 2004 10:08:43 AM

C:\>
```

FIGURE 11.3 Viewing additional IP information with IPCONFIG /ALL

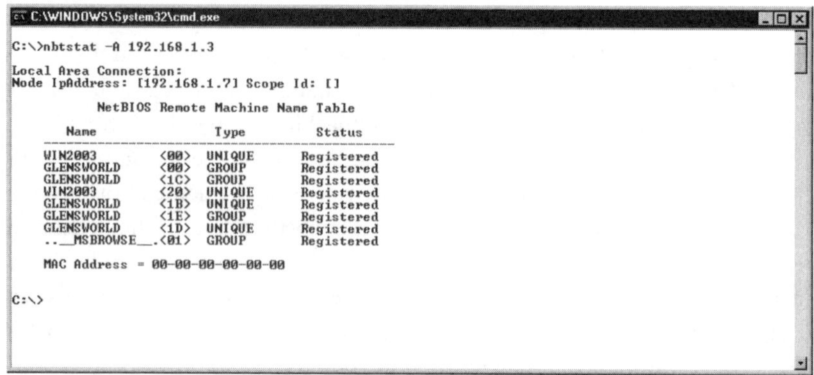

FIGURE 11.4 Displaying the NetBIOS name table of a remote system

notice that these entries have codes after the names such as <00> and <20>. These codes are called *NetBIOS name suffixes* and are appended to the computer names automatically. The important point is that each code represents a different service running on that computer. For example, <00> is the workstation service and <20> is the server service. Bottom line: The name that has a <00> and <20> with it is the computer name of the 192.168.1.3 address.

Travel Assistance

For more information on the NetBIOS name suffixes and the meaning of each suffix code, see Microsoft Knowledgebase article 163409 or visit http://support.microsoft.com/default.aspx?scid=http://support.microsoft.com:80/support/kb/articles/Q163/4/09.asp&NoWebContent=1.

If Sean's system did receive an invalid IP address from a rogue DHCP server on the network, you will need to renew the address once you remove the invalid server. To renew the address, you will type the following command in a command prompt:

```
IPCONFIG /RENEW
```

Let's summarize some of the steps and utilities we have used to help us troubleshoot in this scenario:

- **Step 1** When troubleshooting network connectivity or network problems, the first thing you need to know is whether the system you are troubleshooting is configured correctly. On a TCP/IP network, you use IPCONFIG or IPCONFIG /ALL to give you that information.

- **Step 2** Once you verify the configuration, you will move on by trying to communicate with another system on the network by using the PING utility. This will let you know if you can communicate on the network.
- **Step 3** Once you have verified you can communicate on the network, you will then try to ping the router. If the router is down, it would prevent your network clients and servers from being able to communicate with resources on different networks.
- **Step 4** After verifying the router is working, you will then ping a system on a different network, such as a resource on the WAN in a remote office or a system on the Internet. This will verify that you can communicate through the router to other networks.

Why Is My IP Address 169.254.46.57?

One of the things that newer operating systems (Windows 98/Me/2000/2003/XP) are taking advantage of is a feature called *Automatic Private IP Addressing (APIPA)*. An APIPA address always starts with 169.254.*x.y*. By using APIPA, if a client on the network is looking for an IP address and there is no DHCP server on the wire to satisfy the request, the client will randomly pick an address from the 169.254.*x.y* network range (see Figure 11.5).

As a network tech, you need to understand why this system cannot get on the Internet, and it's possible that APIPA may be responsible. The first thing you will notice is that the IP range is not the range of your network. You saw earlier that Sean's system was configured with a 192.168.1.*x* number. So this means that this

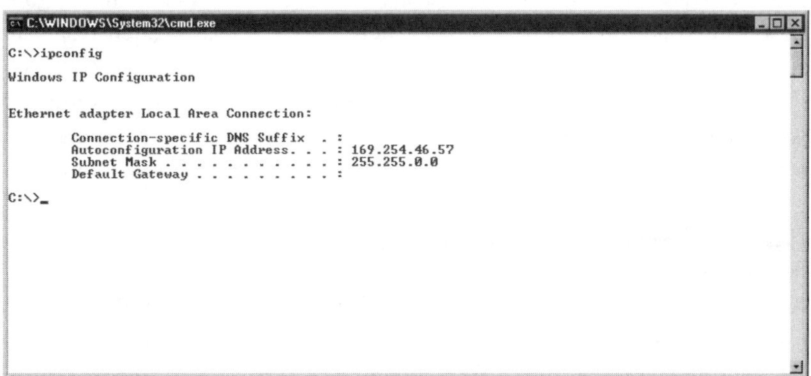

FIGURE 11.5 Identifying a system with an APIPA address

client (the one with the 169.254.*x*.*y* address) will be unable to communicate with any system on the network with a valid IP address. This is because the IP at the client looks at its own address and then compares it to the address of the remote system and says, "Does that guy exist on my network?" The answer is no in our example because the network IDs are different.

When the network IDs are different, the sending computer will try to forward the data off your network by passing the data to the default gateway, if it's configured. And that is our other problem with APIPA. Looking at Figure 11.5, you can see that the machine with an APIPA address is not configured with a default gateway. This means that this client will only be able to communicate with other hosts on this network that are misconfigured the same way.

The question is how did this machine get that incorrect address? The answer is that it is a feature of the operating system. When there is no DHCP server on the network, the client configures itself for an address. The problem in this scenario could be a connection problem with the client, or the DHCP server could be missing. Check the physical connections on the client first and then try to renew the address by typing the following in a command prompt:

```
IPCONFIG /RENEW
```

You should be able to identify whether this is a server-related problem or client-related problem by checking another client on the network. Renew another workstation's address and see if it can receive a valid address from the DHCP server. If the problem is server related, double-check the physical connections on the server and then check the DHCP server settings. Verify that there is a DHCP scope built (a *scope* is a group of addresses the server is allowed to give out), that the scope is active (making the scope *active* means that the server can use that scope—a deactivated scope will not be used even though it exists), and that there are still available addresses in the configured scope. To summarize this scenario, if you notice that a system has an APIPA address, you should check the physical connections and then try to renew the IP address. If you receive another APIPA address, it probably means that there is something wrong with the DHCP server—and the DHCP server should receive your focus.

Name Resolution Problems

A large number of networking problems occur because of what we call "name resolution" problems. I don't know too many people who browse the Internet by using IP addresses; we typically use addresses such as www.osborne.com. When you're using a name like this, there has to be some method of converting it to an IP address—and this conversion is name resolution!

The reason this is an important troubleshooting topic is because when Sean calls you up and says "I don't have Internet access," what is probably happening is he is typing in a friendly address such as www.osborne.com and getting an error because the name cannot be converted to an IP address—you just have to figure out why.

You learned in Chapter 6 that there are two types of names used in networking environments today—a NetBIOS name (computer name) and the fully qualified domain name (FQDN). An FQDN is the style name we use in Internet applications, and it looks something like www.osborne.com, whereas a NetBIOS name looks something like SERVER1.

The first step when troubleshooting name resolution problems is to ask yourself, "What type of name am I using?" For example, let's assume that Sean calls you over to his desk because he is having trouble starting Microsoft Outlook. You check out the settings in Outlook and notice that Outlook is trying to connect to an Exchange server called EXCHANGE1. EXCHANGE1 looks like a NetBIOS name, not an FQDN, so you would troubleshoot name resolution of a NetBIOS name versus troubleshooting ways to resolve an FQDN.

Let's take a look at troubleshooting name resolution on each name type.

I Can't Seem to Connect to \\WIN2003. Why Not? You have a file and print server on the network that Sean is trying to connect to. This server is named WIN2003. Looking at this name style, the first thing that pops into your head is that it is a NetBIOS name. As you learned in Chapter 6, NetBIOS names are converted to IP addresses usually by a WINS (Windows Internet Name Service) server, or through a text file called LMHOSTS located on each computer. Be aware, however, that NetBIOS names are also resolved through broadcast when there is not a WINS server present.

The first thing you should do when running into communication problems is go to a command prompt and ping the server by its name. By doing that, you are getting out of the application you are using and going to a lower level, a simple command prompt. If you get a response when pinging the computer name, you know that the NetBIOS name is converting to an IP address successfully. Name resolution is not the problem, and you no longer need to troubleshoot name resolution.

If you do not get a response when you ping the computer name, and get an error that says "unknown host WIN2003," you are in a scenario where the computer name is not being resolved to an IP address. The next thing you should do is try to ping the IP address of the machine (in this case, WIN2003). The idea here is that if you can ping the IP address but not the computer name, you are sure the problem is with name resolution and not that the server is down. Let's assume that you did get a response from pinging the IP address.

Now that you have identified that there is a name resolution problem, you need to think about where things are going wrong. The first question you should ask yourself is, "Does the network have a WINS server?" You can find out if the client is pointing to a WINS server with IPCONFIG /ALL. When viewing all your TCP/IP settings, you should see an entry for a WINS server if you are using one. If you see that you are pointing to a WINS server, the next thing you want to do is verify that the WINS server is up and running. To do this, you ping the IP address of that WINS server. Let's assume that there was no response. You now know what the cause of the problem is: The WINS server is down.

Let's assume you are not using a WINS server in your environment. As mentioned earlier, if you are not using a WINS server, the names are resolved through broadcast. When you try to connect to a system, your computer yells out on the wire, "Whoever has this computer name, I need your IP address." This is sent to all systems on the network, and the system that has that computer name responds with its IP address. The trick here is that because the names are being resolved by broadcast, and typically broadcasts do not cross routers, this scenario only works well on a small LAN. Any large network will require the use of a WINS server, or you could start using the dreaded LMHOSTS file (which is located on each system). Using the LMHOSTS file would be difficult to manage. In a large Microsoft network, because Microsoft has been so dependant on computer names, you will want to use a WINS server. Note that with Windows 2000 networks and above, Microsoft has been moving away from WINS and using DNS as their preferred name resolution tool.

I Can't Seem to Reach ftp://ftp1.ourcompany.com. Why Not? In this next scenario, you have Sean calling you (again) saying that he is having trouble connecting to a site (or server) named ftp1.ourcompany.com. Notice that Sean is not using a computer name to connect to this resource but rather a fully qualified domain name (FQDN). Either a DNS server converts FQDNs to IP addresses, or a text file called HOSTS does.

You troubleshoot this scenario the same way that you troubleshoot the computer name scenario. The first thing you should do is try to ping the address from a command prompt. If you get a response, you know that there is no problem with the name being converted to an IP address. If you don't get a response, you start suspecting that name resolution is the problem. Let's assume you did not get a response—you should then ping the IP address of the system you are trying to communicate with. If you get a response, you know the system is running and there are name resolution problems; if you don't get a response, you know that the server, or site, is down.

If you get a response from pinging the IP address but don't get a response when pinging the FQDN, the first thing you should verify is that the client is pointing to a DNS server. As you learned in Chapter 6, DNS is used to resolve FQDNs to IP addresses. You use IPCONFIG /ALL to display your TCP/IP settings and see if the client is pointing to a DNS server.

If the client is pointing to a DNS server, you should then ping the IP address of the DNS server. This will verify whether the DNS server is up and running. If you do not get a response from pinging the IP address of the DNS server, you know that the DNS server is down and that this is the problem. Also, if the DNS server is down, you should notice that a number of clients are affected by the same problem, and you move your focus over to fixing the server.

Exam Tip

DNS servers are used to convert an FQDN (www.osborne.com) to an IP address, whereas WINS is used to convert NetBIOS names (\\server1) to an IP address.

How Can I Tell If Someone Has Planted a Trojan on My System?

Troubleshooting network problems is not always related to improper IP address configuration or name resolution problems. You will also hit problems when a computer has been attacked by a virus or a malicious program. This section will help you identify if an attacker has planted a malicious program on your system.

A *Trojan* is a program that is malicious and disguises itself as doing something other than what it is really doing. For example, an attacker may trick you through an e-mail to run a program called update.exe, stating that it upgrades holes in the operating system. When you run the program, what it really does is open up a port on your computer so that the attacker can come in at a later time.

The question is, how can you monitor what ports your system is listening on? In Chapter 6 you learned of the NETSTAT utility. This utility can display important networking information, such as all the connections and listening ports, show the process ID of each connection (which you can then use to go into Task Manager and end the process that is allowing connections), and display the routing table in Windows.

Using the NETSTAT –a command, as shown in Figure 11.6, you can view who is connected to your system and on what port. The first column in the

```
C:\WINDOWS\System32\cmd.exe

C:\Documents and Settings\gclarke>netstat -a

Active Connections

  Proto  Local Address          Foreign Address        State
  TCP    lap-xppro:smtp         lap-xppro:0            LISTENING
  TCP    lap-xppro:http         lap-xppro:0            LISTENING
  TCP    lap-xppro:epmap        lap-xppro:0            LISTENING
  TCP    lap-xppro:https        lap-xppro:0            LISTENING
  TCP    lap-xppro:microsoft-ds  lap-xppro:0            LISTENING
  TCP    lap-xppro:1025         lap-xppro:0            LISTENING
  TCP    lap-xppro:1027         lap-xppro:0            LISTENING
  TCP    lap-xppro:1032         lap-xppro:0            LISTENING
  TCP    lap-xppro:1038         lap-xppro:0            LISTENING
  TCP    lap-xppro:1041         lap-xppro:0            LISTENING
  TCP    lap-xppro:1047         lap-xppro:0            LISTENING
  TCP    lap-xppro:5000         lap-xppro:0            LISTENING
  TCP    lap-xppro:ms-sql-s     lap-xppro:0            LISTENING
  TCP    lap-xppro:http         win2003.glensworld.loc:33679  ESTABLISHED
  TCP    lap-xppro:netbios-ssn  lap-xppro:0            LISTENING
  TCP    lap-xppro:1036         lap-xppro:0            LISTENING
  TCP    lap-xppro:1036         win2003.glensworld.loc:netbios-ssn  ESTABLISHED
  TCP    lap-xppro:1047         win2003.glensworld.loc:3389  ESTABLISHED
  TCP    lap-xppro:ms-sql-s     lap-xppro:0            LISTENING
  TCP    lap-xppro:15819        lap-xppro:0            LISTENING
  UDP    lap-xppro:epmap        *:*
  UDP    lap-xppro:microsoft-ds  *:*
  UDP    lap-xppro:isakmp       *:*
  UDP    lap-xppro:1026         *:*
  UDP    lap-xppro:1028         *:*
  UDP    lap-xppro:1033         *:*
  UDP    lap-xppro:1037         *:*
```

FIGURE 11.6 Viewing connections with NETSTAT

figure shows what protocol is being used (either TCP or UDP), the second column shows which port of yours (local address) someone has hit, the third column shows who has connected to your system (foreign address), and the fourth column shows whether or not someone has established a connection or if your system is in a listening state (that is, is waiting for a connection) on that port.

You can see in Figure 11.6 that the fourteenth entry in the list is an HTTP connection on the local system (named XP-PRO). What we don't see from this is that your local port for this HTTP connection is 80. Microsoft displays "http" instead of 80 for readability purposes so that you know it is the web server someone is connected to. You can also see on that entry that a foreign machine is connected to port 80 named win2003, and it is using its 33679 port (that is, the port of that person's web browser hitting your web server).

So, NETSTAT –a is a great tool for monitoring which applications are listening for connections (this is how you can monitor for Trojans on your system, because the Trojans allow the attacker to connect at a later time by placing a port into a listening state) and also for monitoring who is connected to your system.

Exam Tip

Be sure to review all the switches of NETSTAT by typing **NETSTAT /?** in a command prompt. You will be tested on the output of the different switches on the Network+ exam.

Objective 11.02 Establishing a Baseline

The best way to know when a problem is brewing is to know how things perform when all's well with the system. You need to establish a baseline—a static picture of your network and servers when they are working correctly. One of the common tools used to create a baseline is the Performance Monitor utility that comes with Windows NT, relabeled the Performance console in Windows 2000/XP/2003 (but you can also create baselines using most network management utilities).

Performance Console

Administrators use the Performance console, also known as PerfMon, to view the behavior of hardware and other resources on NT/2000/XP machines, either locally or remotely. The Performance console has a snap-in called System Monitor that can monitor both real-time and historical data about the performance of your systems. To access the Performance Monitor applet on Windows NT 4.0, choose Start | Programs | Administrative Tools | Performance Monitor. In Windows 2000/2003/XP machines, choose Start | Programs | Administrative Tools | Performance.

Once you access the Performance console, select System Monitor on the left (we use System Monitor to display data, but you will need to configure it to display the data you care about). The process of configuring System Monitor requires you to understand the concept of objects, counters, and views. An *object* in System Monitor relates directly to the component of your system that you want to monitor, such as the processor or memory. Each object has different measurable aspects, called *counters*. Counters, in other words, are the portions of an object that you want to track. For example, you decide that you wish to measure the processor object; the processor object has a number of different counters, such as % Processor Time, % User Time, and % Privilege Time. You select the counters you wish to monitor of a given object at any given time. As you decide which object(s) to monitor in your system, you then select one or multiple counters for each object.

System Monitor can display selected counter information in a variety of views, with each view displaying your captured data in different ways. For example, you may view your data as a line graph with the View Graph button on the toolbar (see Figure 11-7), you may view the captured data as bar charts with the View Histogram button, and finally you may view the numeric data by choosing the View Report button on the toolbar.

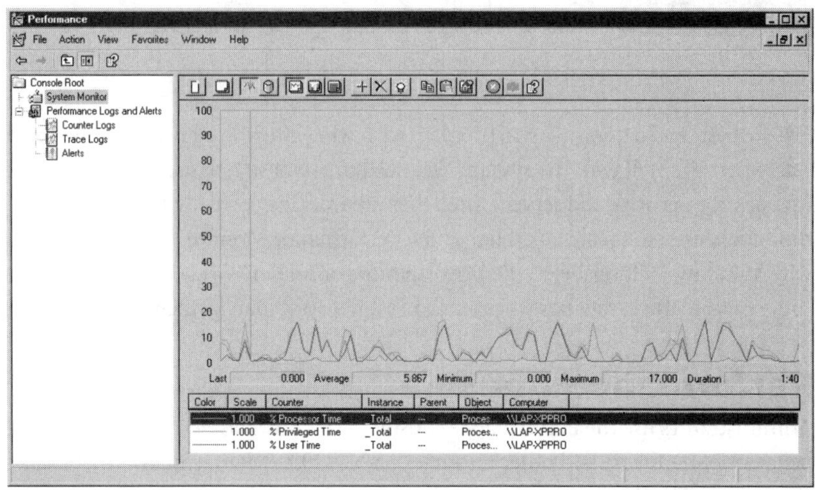

FIGURE 11.7 Looking at System Monitor

Creating a Baseline

When creating a baseline, you store data about your systems to a file that can be reviewed at a later time with System Monitor. To actually store the data, we use a different feature of the Performance console called Counter Logs. Counter Logs will allow you to select components of the system to monitor, but instead of displaying the data live on the screen, it stores the information in a "log" file that can be viewed later in System Monitor. This is our baseline feature! To compare the health of your system today with what it is in three months, you would store its data in a file that can be opened at a later time, allowing you to compare the data.

To create a baseline, go to Performance Logs and Alerts, right-click Counter Logs, and choose New Log Settings (see Figure 11.8). You will then be asked for a name for the log as it appears in the Performance console. Use a meaningful name, such as PostSQLInstallation, so that you have an idea of when you created the log. (You actually will have a date and time with the file, but it is much easier to say, "The last application we installed on the server was SQL Server. How did that affect the performance of the server?") After typing a meaningful name, click OK.

You are then presented with the properties of your new Counter Log, and you can select which counters (characteristics of an object) you wish to monitor (see Figure 11.9). Notice the filename that the log data is being written to at the top of this dialog box. Once you add a counter, you will be able to select the time interval for the system to sample the data. If you want to monitor the system

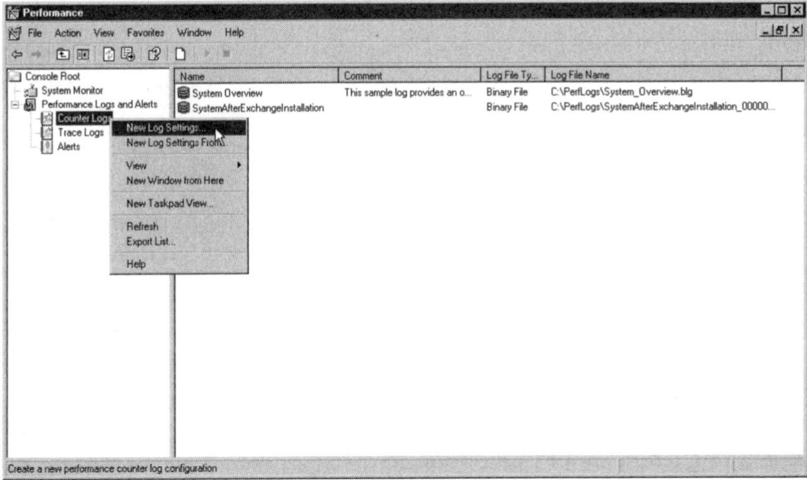

FIGURE 11.8 Creating a baseline with Counter Logs in Windows 2000/XP

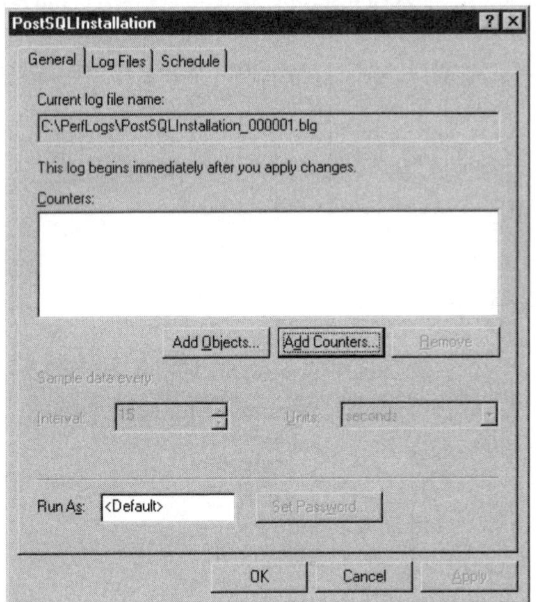

FIGURE 11.9 Viewing Counter Log settings

health for a few days, you may set a high interval of every 30 minutes or every hour. Notice that the default is every 15 seconds; if you use the default, you may log too much data if logging over a long period of time. Also, the more frequent you log information, the more load you put on the server.

Let's add a few counters by clicking the Add Counter button. In the Add Counters dialog box (see Figure 11.10), you may select to monitor the local machine or choose to monitor a remote machine by specifying its computer name. Although it is often easiest to monitor a machine locally, it is often more accurate to monitor the machine remotely because of the load the process of monitoring places on a computer. Performance Console running on a machine uses a certain amount of resources to take the measurements and to display the data graphically. Especially when you troubleshoot issues with disk performance, memory and paging, or processor use, you should not corrupt your results by monitoring locally. You may, however, have to monitor a system locally if you cannot access that system over the network.

After selecting which computer you will use to monitor on, you then choose which object you wish to measure by selecting the object from the Performance Object drop-down list. Some of the important objects to look at are Processor, Memory, Logicaldisk, Physicaldisk, and System. Let's select the Processor object and then choose from the list of counters % Processor Time (which is what percentage of the processor is being used at this time). After selecting the counter,

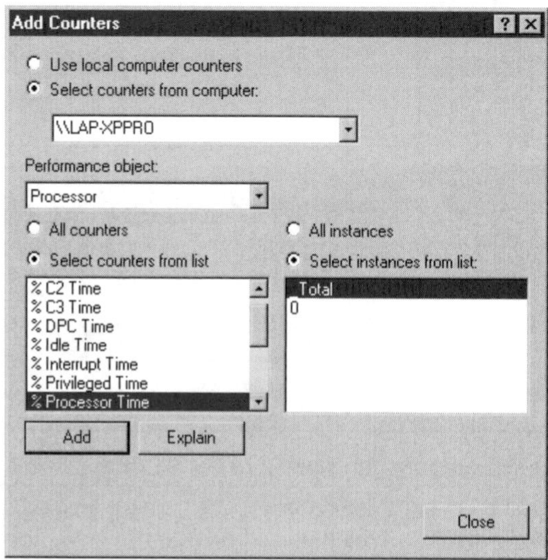

FIGURE 11.10 Selecting which counters to monitor

you then choose the instance. If you had two processors you would have two instances: instance 0 and instance 1. You can choose which processor you wish to monitor by selecting either instance 0 or 1, or you could choose to monitor them collectively by selecting the total instance. After you select the total instance, you then click the Add button to add the counter to your log. After you select all the counters you wish to add, you then click the Close button and you are sent back to the Log Settings dialog box. Click OK to create the log file.

In Windows 2000/XP, the counter log is started right away, which means that it is sampling data based on the interval you selected and recording that to a file. You can tell whether you are actively writing to the log because the icon for Log is green instead red. When you are done logging your data, you can right-click the log and choose Stop (see Figure 11.11).

Reviewing a Baseline

To view your Counter Log graphically like when you monitor live data with System Monitor, you will need to go to System Monitor and click the View Log Data button on the toolbar (normally View Current Activity is selected). When you select to view log data, you will then need to select the source file for the data to display. Make sure the log files option is selected and then click Add to add your log file to the view (see Figure 11.12). You will need to find the Counter Log file you created earlier (the default location is c:\perflogs). Once you find the file, select it and click Open and then click OK to leave the System Monitor properties dialog box.

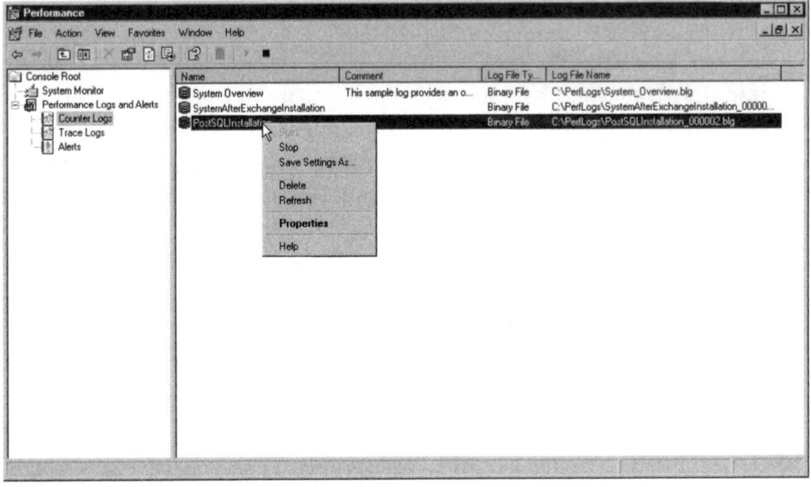

FIGURE 11.11 Stopping a Counter Log

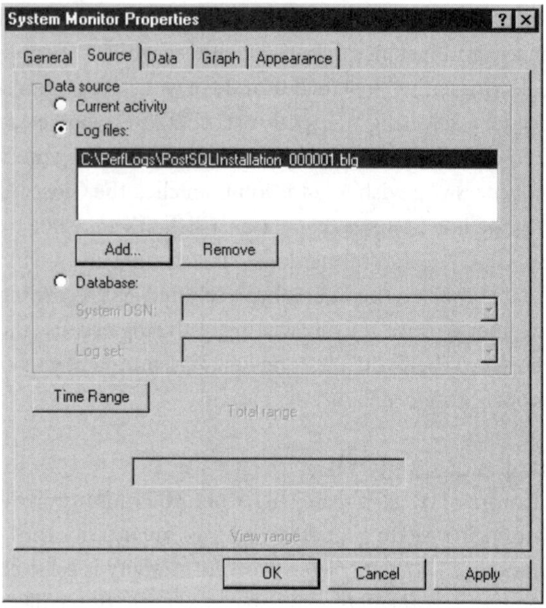

FIGURE 11.12 Selecting a Counter Log file to display in System Monitor

After you select the log you wish to display the data from, you then need to select which counters (of the recorded ones) you wish to view. You will now add counters the way you have in the past when using System Monitor to view live data, the difference being you will notice that you only have the counters available that were recorded in the Counter Log file.

The benefit of having this Counter Log file that you can reference at any point in time is that you have a baseline to compare to when you suspect that your system is running slower. The question you need answered is, What part of the computer is getting the performance hit? The process, memory, or disk? You will need to compare your current activity with your baseline to get the answer.

Network Monitor

Whereas the Performance Console tool allows you to monitor the health of the system, Network Monitor (a Microsoft tool) is a tool that allows you to monitor network traffic. Network Monitor (see Figure 11.13) is an example of a packet sniffer, or LAN analyzer, and helps diagnose problems with communication over the network.

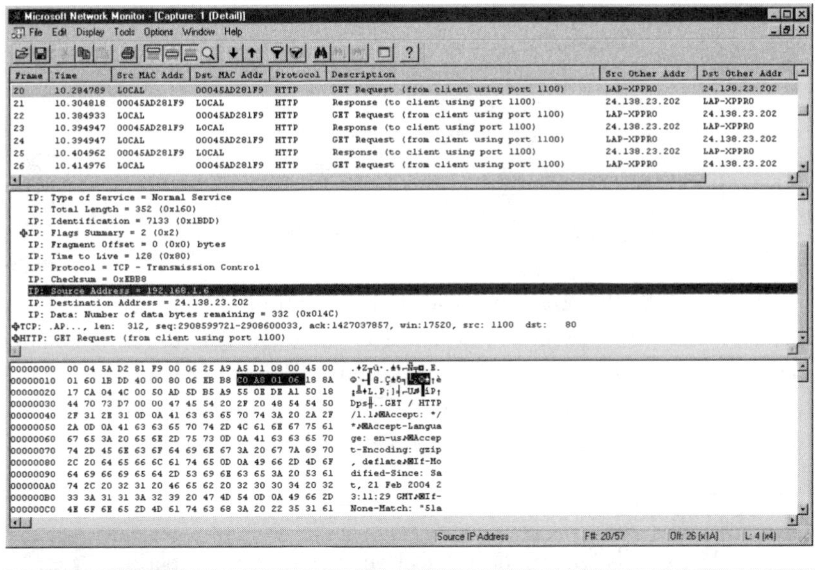

FIGURE 11.13 Looking at Network Monitor

For example, let's say that you are responsible for installing a new sales application on each computer found in the Sales department. This application, after installed, will connect to a special application server in the back room running the server part of the sales application. You install the server and client parts without a hitch! You start up the client application on Sean's computer, but it is having trouble connecting to the server portion of the application. (By the way, Sean is starting to get annoyed because it seems to be him who's always having the bad luck on the network—I think he is losing faith in us IT people!)

You know nothing about this application, and you have followed the installation instructions—what can you do? One of the first things you can do is run Network Monitor and see what port on the server the client is trying to connect to (maybe the server port is configured incorrectly). This is the type of thing that Network Monitor is good at doing—monitoring traffic and displaying the contents of a discussion between two systems.

You can install Network Monitor on a Windows NT server, Windows 2000 server, or Windows 2003 server through Add/Remove Programs. When in Add/Remove Programs, go to Add/Remove Windows Components and select the Management and Monitoring Tools and then click the Details button. When in the Details screen, select Network Monitor Tools.

Travel Advisory

The version of Network Monitor that comes with the Server versions of the operating systems only allows you to capture data being sent through the network card of the system doing the monitoring. You will not be able to analyze traffic on the entire network segment. System Management Server comes with a version of Network Monitor that enables you to monitor the entire network segment.

Once you have the program installed, start it from the Administrative Tools menu. Then, once the program has loaded, click the Start Capture button on the toolbar. This will start to record network traffic. While recording, generate the type of traffic that you wish to analyze and then you can stop recording by clicking the Stop and View Capture button. Now start analyzing your network traffic!

Exam Tip

You will need to be aware of the fact that Network Monitor is a tool used to monitor and troubleshoot network traffic. The details of the captured data are beyond the scope of the Network+ exam.

NetWare Monitor

On a NetWare server, most of the critical information you might need to see and document to establish your baseline can be obtained by loading the Monitor application (see Figure 11.14) on the server itself. Novell calls a program that runs on the server in this way a *NetWare Loadable Module,* or *NLM,* and you issue the command LOAD MONITOR at the server's console prompt to start the program.

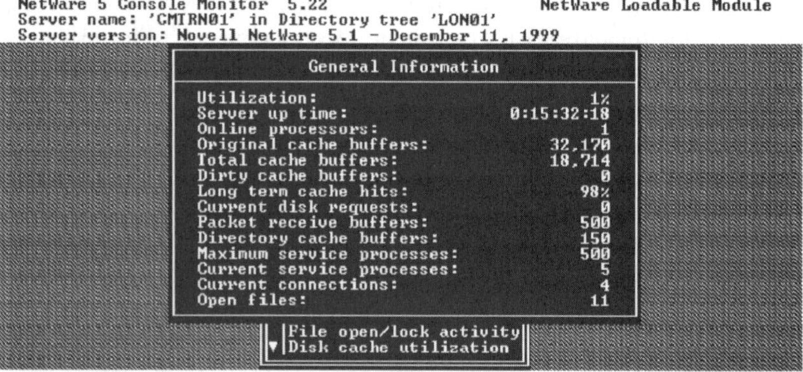

FIGURE 11.14 NetWare 5 Monitor general information screen

The Monitor NLM can display a wide range of information, from memory usage to individual statistics about the NICs installed in the server. Many system managers leave Monitor running all the time so that they can keep an eye on things; it can also be used to disconnect users from the server and see which files they are accessing!

Exam Tip

Be sure to know the difference between Network Monitor and NetWare Monitor. It could be a trick question!

Objective 11.03 Problem Analysis

All the planning and documenting we discussed in Chapter 10 comes in handy when the network (or something on it) stops working like it should—you now need to go from planning and prevention mode to troubleshooting mode. When you move into troubleshooting mode, your purpose is to figure out what the problem really is. This can be challenging, as you can imagine, when a user calls you complaining that he or she cannot log onto the server. This symptom could be traced to a variety of causes, including (but not limited to) user error, a broken or unplugged cable, a server crash, or an incorrect protocol configuration. The trick is to figure out which one. This requires a troubleshooting model or method that helps you to keep your mind open while ruling out things that are obviously not causing your problem. With this troubleshooting model, it also helps to know which tools to use to diagnose problems. A variety of both software and hardware tools can aid in ruling out your wild guesses.

Troubleshooting Model

No matter how complex and fancy we decide to make it, any troubleshooting model can be broken down into simple steps. Having a sequence of steps to follow makes the entire troubleshooting process simpler and easier because we have a clear set of goals to achieve in a specific sequence. The most important steps are the first three that help us to narrow down the cause of a problem to a specific item. These steps carry so much weight because when you figure out what's wrong, you've probably also figured out how to fix the problem and how to prevent it from happening in the future. The basics of any troubleshooting model should include the following steps:

- Establish the symptoms.
- Identify the affected area.
- Establish what has changed that might have caused the problem.
- Identify the most probable cause.
- Implement a solution.
- Test the solution.
- Recognize the potential effects of the solution.
- Document the solution.

Establish the Symptoms

If you are working directly on the affected system and not relying on someone over the telephone to guide you, establishing the symptoms will come down to your observation of what is (or isn't) happening. Over the telephone, you will need to ask questions based on what the user is telling you. These questions can be *closed ended*—to which there can only be a "yes" or "no" type answer, such as "Can you see a light on the front of the monitor"—or they can be *open ended,* such as "Tell me what you see on the screen." The type of question you use at any instant will depend on the information you need and the abilities of the user—if, for example, the user seems to be technically oriented, you might be able to ask more closed-ended questions because they will know what you are talking about. If, on the other hand, they need a little encouragement, open-ended questions will allow them to explain what is going on in their own words.

Identify the Affected Area

One of the first steps in trying to determine the cause of a problem is to understand the extent of the problem; find out if the problem is specific to one user or if it's networkwide. Sometimes, this entails trying the task yourself—from a user's machine and from your own machine.

For example, if a user is experiencing problems logging into the network, you might need to go to that user's machine and try to use their username to log in. This lets you determine if the problem is a user error of some kind as well as enables you to see the symptoms of the problem yourself. Next, you probably want to try logging in with your own username from that machine or try having the user log in from another machine. In some cases, you can ask other users in the area if they are experiencing the same problem—this helps you determine if the problem is affecting more than one user. Depending on the size of your network, find out if the problem is occurring in only one part of your company or across the entire network. What does all this tell you? Essentially, it tells you how big the problem is. If nobody in an entire remote office can log in, you may be able to assume that the problem is the network link or router connecting that office to the rest of the corporate network. If nobody in any office can log in, you may be able to assume that the server is down or not accepting logins. If only that one user in that one location can't log in, it may be a problem with that user, that machine, or that user's account.

Exam Tip

Eliminating variables is one of the first tools in your arsenal of diagnostic techniques.

Establish What Has Changed

After determining the extent of a problem, the next step requires eliminating all the extra variables—all the other possible causes of the problem. If you have determined that the problem is specific to that user on that machine, you have already learned a great deal. First, you have learned that it is not a user account problem, because you tested that user's ability to log in from another machine. This means that the user knows the credentials they should be supplying, so unless Cap Locks is enabled on their system, they would be able to log in. By having other users try the task, you have also eliminated the possibility that the server is down.

Ask Isolating Questions

The goal of this substep is to isolate the problem to a specific item (hardware, software, user, and so forth) or to identify what has changed that might have caused the problem. You may not have to ask many questions before the problem is isolated, or it might take some time and involve further work "behind the scenes." Isolating questions are designed to "home in" on the likely cause of the problem. Here are some examples:

- "Tell me what the system was doing when the problem occurred."
- "Has anything been changed on the system recently?"
- "Has the system been moved recently?"
- "When was the last time that task was performed?"

Notice the way we've tactfully avoided the word "you," as in "Have *you* changed anything on the system recently?" This avoids any implied blame on the part of the user and makes the whole troubleshooting process more friendly.

Some isolating questions might be asked "internally" by you to yourself, such as "Was that machine involved in the software push last night?" or "Didn't a tech visit that machine this morning?" As you can see, these questions can only be answered if *your* documentation is up to scratch. Sometimes, isolating a problem may require you to check system and hardware logs (such as those stored by some routers and other network devices), so make sure you know how to do this.

While working through the process of determining the cause of a problem, you will need to use many tools. Some of these tools, as mentioned earlier, are difficult to quantify–such as asking questions, referring to your network baselines and documentation, and synthesizing all your network knowledge. Other tools are easier to describe—these are software and hardware tools that enable you to gain more information about your network. Some of the tools that fall into this category have been described already, and others are covered in Chapter 12—the trick is in knowing how to apply these tools in solving your network problems.

Identify the Most Probable Cause

This one comes down to experience (or good use of the support tools at your disposal, such as your knowledgebase); you need to decide from the *possible* causes which one is the most *probable*—we're trying to ensure that the solution you subsequently choose fixes the problem the first time. This may not always happen, but in any event, you don't want to spend a whole day "stabbing in the dark." However, you want to take your time and logically think about reasons why this problem could have happened. A lot of times it may be easier to draw a diagram to help identify causes of the problem, especially when dealing with connectivity problems.

Implement a Solution

Once you think you have isolated the cause of the problem, you should decide what you think is the best way to fix it and then try your solution. This may be advice over the phone to a user, a replacement part, or a software patch. All the way through this step, document what you are trying and try one likely solution at a time—there's no point installing several patches at once, because this doesn't tell you specifically which patch fixed the problem; similarly, there's no point in replacing several items of hardware (such as a hard disk and its controller cable) at the same time, because this won't tell you which part (or parts) actually failed.

Although it may take longer to be methodical, it will save you work the next time, or perhaps allow you to pinpoint what needs to be done to stop the problem from reoccurring at all, thus reducing future call volume to your support team—and that's got to be worth the effort!

Test the Solution

This is the bit everybody hates. Once you think you have fixed a problem, try to re-create the problem and implement the solution again to see if it consistently fixes the problem. If the problem hasn't gone away after implementing the solution the second time, you know you've not finished the job at hand. Many techs want to slide away quietly when everything seems to be fine, but it doesn't impress your customer when the problem starts up again 30 seconds after you've left the building—and who wants to make another two-hour car trip the next day to "fix" the same problem?

Recognize the Potential Effects of the Solution

The other thing to watch for when testing your solution is to make sure that the solution you have implemented does not have a negative effect on other parts of the system or network. You want to be a network tech who worries about the big picture and not just the current problem. Nothing will diminish your credibility more than implementing a solution and walking away, while in the meantime your solution has caused three other problems.

When *you* have changed something on the system—think about the wider repercussions of what you have done. If you've replaced a faulty NIC in a server, will the fact that the MAC address has changed (remember, it's built into the NIC) affect anything else, such as logon security controls or your network management and inventory software? If you have installed a patch on a client PC, will this change the default protocol or any other default settings that may affect other functionality? If you have changed a user's security settings, will this affect their ability to access other network resources? Partly, you are still testing the solution to make sure it works properly, but you are also making yourself think about the effects of *your* work on the system as a whole.

Document the Solution

It is *vital* that you document the problem, symptoms, and solutions to all support calls for two main reasons. First, your support database becomes a knowledgebase for future reference, allowing everyone on the support team to learn how to identify new problems as they arise and know how to deal with them quickly, and without having to duplicate someone else's research efforts. Second, the documentation allows you to track problem trends and anticipate future workload, or even to identify where a particular brand or model of an item such as a printer or a NIC seems to be more unreliable (or is causing you more work) than others. Don't skip this step—it *really* is essential!

Exam Tip

It is important for the Network+ exam to remember these problem analysis steps!

Objective 11.04 Checking System Logs

Most network operating systems and modern client systems maintain their own log files, and it is important to check these logs on a regular basis—once a day is a good idea, especially for servers. Checking the logs achieves two things: It can tell you *why* a certain problem has occurred, and it can alert you to a problem that may get worse if not treated—for example, a log file can alert you to "timeout errors" from a hard disk that's having problems reading or writing data—*before* it becomes another blip on the bathtub curve!

Especially with a fault-tolerant server, examining the system logs regularly is vital because some component failures will be logged but, because the system has redundant items, the server may still run as if nothing has happened. It's both good and bad to discover that one of your mirrored drives actually failed several weeks ago without anyone noticing—good that the system kept running, bad that no one realized that a disk replacement was needed to maintain full fault tolerance.

Travel Advisory

Some systems allow for the enabling of *verbose* logging, which is the logging of more information than normal logging to help troubleshoot system problems. Verbose logging is typically disabled by default because the amount of information being logged could slow system performance.

The Windows Event Viewer

The Windows Event Viewer (NT/2000/XP/2003) displays any errors or problems that have occurred on your system. For example, if a user repeatedly failed at their logon, this can be recorded in the appropriate log in the Event Viewer tool. That information could be the clue you need to help troubleshoot the cause of a problem such as a user being locked out, either because they forgot their password or because someone has been trying to hack into that account. The three main logs managed by Event Viewer (see Figure 11.15) are as follows:

- **The System log** This tracks three main types of events: information (noncritical system events), warnings (events that might need checking), and errors (software or hardware component failures). Typically you will find errors dealing with device drivers failing to load or services failing to start.
- **The Security log** This tracks security events based on auditing settings found in the security policy—these events include successful or unsuccessful login attempts, files accessed, and resources used. This log can be especially useful when someone can't access a network resource, or when you wish to audit tasks performed by your administrative team.
- **The Application log** This log tracks events for network services or applications running on your server, such as SQL Server or Exchange Server. When these applications have information to report, instead of cluttering the System log (used for operating system events) they write their events to the Application log.

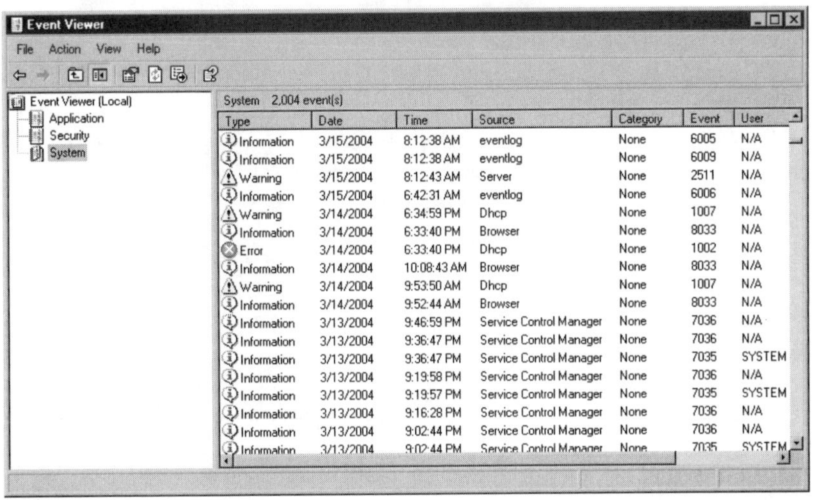

FIGURE 11.15 Looking at Windows Event Viewer

After selecting a log (either System, Security, or Application), you will see the different event messages that have been written to the logs. To view the details of the event (see Figure 11.16), such as a description of what the problem is, you simply double-click the event.

When viewing the event details, you can see a lot of important information you can use when troubleshooting. You can see the date and time that the event was recorded; you can see the type of event (whether it is a warning, error, or information type event) and then a description of the event, which should help you troubleshoot your problem. There is also an event ID that you could use to search Microsoft TechNet for additional information.

Exam Tip

Windows Event Viewer is used to monitor the system for errors such as device drivers failing to load and services failing to start.

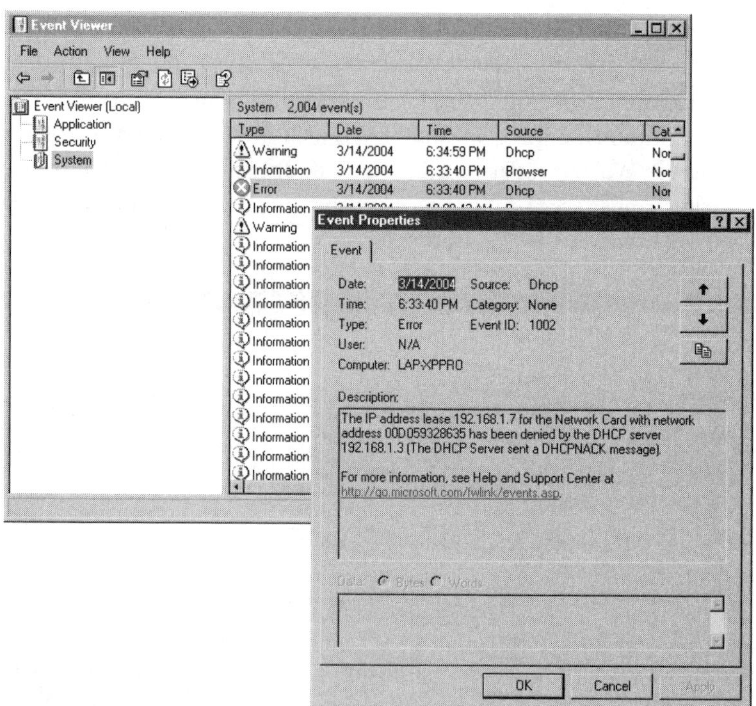

FIGURE 11.16 Viewing details of an event message in the System log

Novell NetWare Server Error Log

The General Error log on a NetWare server is called SYS$LOG.ERR and can be found in the \SYSTEM folder on the main (SYS) volume. Although the file is in plain-text format and can be viewed in any editor you want to use, it is easily accessed through menus in the main system administration tools—NWADMIN and ConsoleOne.

NetWare gives each event in the error log a *severity* number from 0 to 6 (0 to 5 on older versions of NetWare) that indicates how serious the logged event might be—a severity of 0 is an informational message. A severity of 3+ is usually worth immediate investigation. Figure 11.17 shows the error logged when a NetWare server needs more RAM fitted.

The Locus and Class numbers attempt to isolate the error to a specific function of the server; Locus 19, Class 2 indicates a problem with the cache memory (19) that is a temporary issue (2)—the last bit means that something hasn't actually broken, but needs attention all the same.

Exam Tip

Remember what logs are available on Windows systems and NetWare servers, and that they should be inspected regularly. Do not worry about the specifics of how the logs are formatted.

Equipment Logs

As well as servers, a great deal of networking equipment (hubs, routers, and so forth) maintain their own logs, and these can generally be checked using several methods—the most common being the following:

- **SNMP** The Simple Network Management Protocol. This allows you to retrieve status and logged information using an SNMP-compatible management program such as HP OpenView, Sun NetManage, Novell's Zenworks for Servers, and IBM NetView. Using a management program can automate the process of checking devices. It also allows

```
23-10-99   4:16:34 am:    SERVER-4.11-2324
   Severity = 5  Locus = 19  Class = 2
   Cache memory allocator out of available memory.
```

FIGURE 11.17 A NetWare error log entry

error conditions and alarm thresholds to be defined, and alerts can be sent to on-duty techs via e-mail, pager, and cell phone. This type of access to a device (via the LAN) is known as *in-band management.*

- **Terminal** Some devices have a built-in serial port to which a terminal (or a PC running something like HyperTerminal) can be connected. It is useful for when the network's not working properly and you need to check the device—but it's not so flexible for general checking, because you have to visit the device. This type of access to a device (not using the LAN) is known as *out-of-band management.*
- **Web interface** This is a popular way of accessing devices across the network for setup and management because all that is needed is a web browser rather than (possibly) an expensive SNMP management tool (see Figure 11.18).

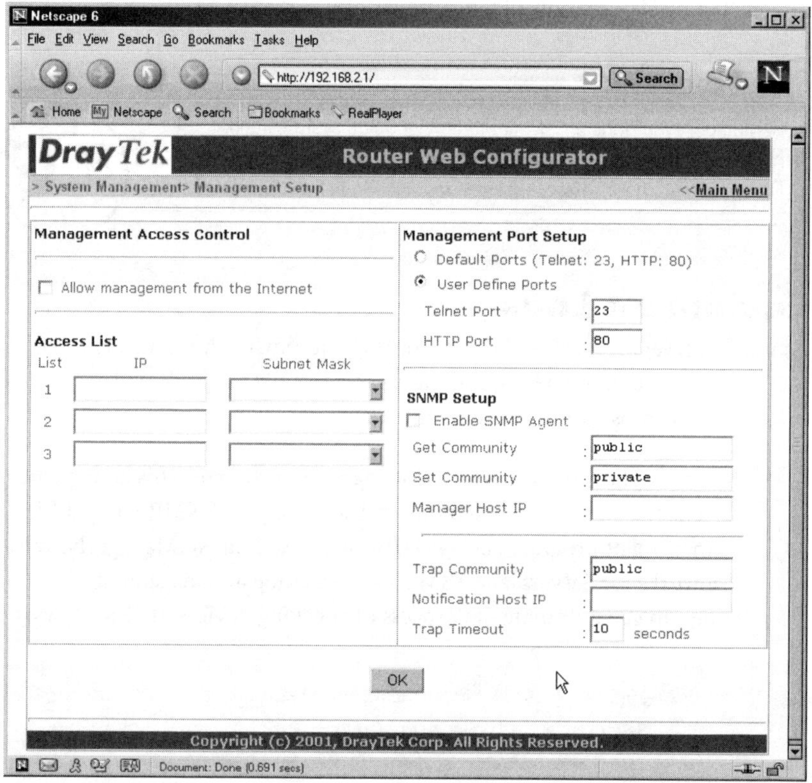

FIGURE 11.18 Setting up in-band management on an ISDN router via its web interface

Hardware Troubleshooting and Safety

One of the troubleshooting techniques used for hardware is testing by substitution—once you think you have identified a faulty item, you replace it and see whether your diagnosis is correct. You might also want to remove a hardware component and replace it to make sure that it is seated properly, or to clean its connectors. The simple premise that must be understood when ripping apart pieces of hardware (sorry… performing diagnostic substitution!) is that you only do such things *if you know what you are doing*. Prodding haphazardly around an expensive server with a screwdriver can be costly to both the equipment and yourself. The Network+ exam doesn't expect you to have an in-depth knowledge of service techniques (that's the job of the A+ certification), but it's not a bad idea to understand the basics:

- *Electricity is dangerous.* Shut down, switch off, and disconnect all power leads before even thinking about opening up a computer or any other piece of equipment—it's the thing to do before you do *anything* else. Electrical safety is paramount; your life is precious to you, your friends, colleagues, and family, so look after it. PC power supplies and monitors are especially dangerous because they can hold a high-voltage electrical charge for some time after they have been switched off. Leave these items to the professionals.
- *Electronic components don't like static electricity.* Watch out for electrostatic discharge (ESD)—also known as *static electricity.* Always use proper grounding techniques when working inside the PC. Try to use a grounding strap. If a grounding strap is not available, touch the power supply before working on the PC to discharge yourself (see Figure 11.19).

Many replacement parts will come in shiny, gray bags that are made from a material that protects the contents from ESD. Keep the parts inside the bags until you need them—and store spare parts in the right packaging, too.

FIGURE 11.19 Touching the power supply

✔ **Objective 11.01: General Network Troubleshooting** Troubleshooting is a mix of knowledge, intuition, and common sense. The knowledge bit we can help you with to a degree, but you only gain the *right* kind of knowledge by working "out in the field" and speaking to your peers, making use of their experience and learning from their (and your) mistakes. When troubleshooting network connectivity, use IPCONFIG to display your configuration, use PING to see if you can communicate with another computer, and be aware of name resolution problems.

✔ **Objective 11.02: Establishing a Baseline** You can sometimes only tell when things are not as they should be because you *know* how the system should work under normal circumstances. This makes it important to establish a *baseline*—a documented, static picture of your network and servers working correctly. For NT/2000/2003 servers, the Performance Console is one tool that you can use to monitor real-time and historical data. On a

NetWare server, you can see most of the server's operational parameters through the Monitor application that's run on the server (it's classed as a NetWare Loadable Module, or NLM).

✔ **Objective 11.03: Problem Analysis** It is important to approach any troubleshooting in a methodical way—what needs to be done to solve a specific problem will vary according to the nature of the problem, but the general chronology of how things must happen is reasonably generic: establish the symptoms, isolate the cause of the problem (identify the affected area), establish what has changed that might have caused the problem, identify the most probable cause, implement a solution, test the solution, recognize the potential effects of the solution, and document the solution.

✔ **Objective 11.04: Checking System Logs** Don't forget that a server can tell you a lot about what's going on (or going wrong) if you take a look at its logs. The logs can also be used to preempt some problems and stop them from becoming reality. As well as being troubleshooting tools, the logs help you manage the health of your server before something nasty happens, so checking them should be a standard operating procedure.

✔ **Objective 11.05: Hardware Troubleshooting and Safety** Before *any* hardware troubleshooting is attempted, make *sure* you know what you are doing—electricity can kill, so check and double-check that the equipment you are planning to open is completely isolated from the power source before starting work. Electronic components (memory, hard disks, NICs, and so forth) can be damaged by incorrect handling procedures because they are sensitive to static electricity, so always use the proper service tools (a wrist strap and ground cord) and take the necessary steps to minimize the potential to zap your expensive kit.

REVIEW QUESTIONS

1. Which of the following help to identify some problems before they occur? (Select all that apply.)
   - **A.** Establishing a baseline
   - **B.** Checking system logs daily
   - **C.** Testing solutions thoroughly
   - **D.** Using isolating questions

2. Which of the following is not part of the troubleshooting model? (Select one answer.)
   - **A.** Identify the most probable cause.
   - **B.** Test the solution.
   - **C.** Establish a baseline.
   - **D.** Establish the symptoms.
3. Susan cannot log on to the network. Which of the following would be the best question to ask first? (Select one answer.)
   - **A.** "Tell me exactly what happens when you try to log on."
   - **B.** "Is anyone else nearby having problems logging on?"
   - **C.** "What protocols are installed?"
   - **D.** "What operating system are you using?"
4. Which of the following commands or programs could be used to establish a baseline? (Select all that apply.)
   - **A.** NETSTAT
   - **B.** MONITOR.NLM
   - **C.** PFMON
   - **D.** PerfMon
5. Which of the following are closed-ended questions? (Select all that apply.)
   - **A.** "Has anything been changed on the system recently?"
   - **B.** "Can you see a power light on the monitor?"
   - **C.** "What lights can you see on the monitor?"
   - **D.** "Tell me what happens when you move the mouse."
6. Which of the following programs can be used to view the error logs on a NetWare Server? (Select all that apply.)
   - **A.** Notepad
   - **B.** Event Viewer
   - **C.** NWADMIN
   - **D.** SEVERITY
7. Which of the following programs can be used to view the error logs on a Windows 2000/2003 server? (Select all that apply.)
   - **A.** Event Viewer
   - **B.** PerfMon
   - **C.** APPLOG
   - **D.** MONITOR.NLM

8. Which of the following steps should be first in a troubleshooting model? (Select one answer.)
   - **A.** Isolate the cause of the problem.
   - **B.** Establish what has changed that might have caused the problem.
   - **C.** Establish the symptoms.
   - **D.** Recognize the potential effects of the problem.
9. What is the first step to be taken before installing a new NIC in a server? (Select one answer.)
   - **A.** Clear the error logs.
   - **B.** Remove the NIC from its packaging.
   - **C.** Fill in the guarantee/warranty card.
   - **D.** Shut down and isolate the server from its power source.
10. Kevin in Marketing cannot log in to his company's TCP/IP network. What should you do to identify the scope of the problem? (Select one answer.)
    - **A.** Ping Kevin's workstation.
    - **B.** Check whether other users in Kevin's area can log in.
    - **C.** Check whether users in other offices can log in.
    - **D.** Ask Kevin to run WINIPCFG.
11. You notice that your system is running slowly and you suspect that someone has planted a program on your system and is using that program to get unauthorized access. What command and switch could you use to troubleshoot this?
    - **A.** IPCONFIG /ALL
    - **B.** NETSTAT –r
    - **C.** NBTSTAT –A
    - **D.** NETSTAT –a
12. You are having trouble connecting to http://www.microsoft.com and you suspect that the name is not being resolved to an IP address. What tool is used to convert this name to an IP address?
    - **A.** WINS
    - **B.** DNS
    - **C.** LMHOSTS
    - **D.** PING
13. You are looking at your web server log files and you notice that a machine on your network with the IP address 192.168.3.2 has been sending a

number of invalid requests to the web server. You would like to track down whose computer this is on your network. What command would you use?

A. PING 192.168.3.2

B. NETSTAT –r

C. NBTSTAT –A 192.168.3.2

D. NETSTAT –a 192.168.3.2

14. Bob is having trouble connecting to the network. You visit his desktop and view his TCP/IP settings with an IPCONFIG command. You notice that he has an IP address of 169.254.34.56. Why can't Bob connect to network resources?

A. He is missing a default gateway entry.

B. He has an APIPA address.

C. He is not running the correct protocol.

D. His system is not running the right client software.

15. You wish to analyze the health of your server over a three-day period of users actively using the server. Which feature of Windows 2000/2003/XP would you use?

A. Counter Logs

B. System Monitor

C. Network Monitor

D. NETSTAT

REVIEW ANSWERS

1. **A** **B** Establishing a baseline (A) gives you a standard by which network operation can be compared to at any time. Checking system logs daily (B) will help you identify events that could become issues at a later time.
2. **C** Establishing a baseline is not part of the troubleshooting model—it's a separate activity that should come before you have any problems.
3. **A** The first step in the troubleshooting process is to establish the symptoms.
4. **B** **D** Monitor (B) will help you establish baselines for a NetWare server. PerfMon (D) will do the same for NT/2000 servers.

5. **A B** Closed-ended questions can usually only be answered with either "yes" or "no."

6. **A C** NetWare error logs can be viewed using the administration utility (C), but because they are in pure text you can also open them with Notepad (A).

7. **A** The Event Viewer is used to view the logs on any Windows NT–based operating system.

8. **C** Establishing the symptoms is the first step of the troubleshooting process.

9. **D** Always shut down and isolate equipment from its power source before attempting any form of internal activity.

10. **B** Checking whether other users in Kevin's area can log in will identify the immediate scope of the problem. Choice C would come next, just to make sure it's not a networkwide problem, and then you might ping his machine (A) to see if it can be "seen" from your location.

11. **D** Using NETSTAT –a, you can view the TCP and UDP connections and listening ports on your system. Choice A is incorrect because IPCONFIG will only display your TCP/IP information and shows nothing about connections. Choice B shows the routing table of your system and shows nothing about connections or listening ports. Choice C displays the NetBIOS name table of a remote system and has nothing to do with this scenario.

12. **B** Because this is an example of a fully qualified domain name, we will use DNS to resolve it to an IP address. Choices A and C are methods that will resolve NetBIOS names to IP addresses, and choice D is used to verify that a system is up and running and has nothing to do with this scenario.

13. **C** The NBTSTAT command with the –A switch is used to view the remote name table on a computer when you supply the command with an IP address. This is a great way to find out what someone's computer name is when you know the IP address. Choice A is incorrect because the PING utility just tells you whether the system is up and running. Choice B is incorrect because it displays your routing table, and choice D is incorrect because you don't supply the NETSTAT command an IP address. NETSTAT –a will display connection information.

14. **B** Bob has an APIPA address. A feature of Windows operating systems is that if a client cannot contact a DHCP server, they randomly choose an address from the 169.254.*x*.*y* network range. The likely problem is that the DHCP server was not available at the time the client requested an address.

15. **A** Counter Logs are used to record performance data to a file so that you can review the data at a later time with System Monitor. Choice B is considered incorrect (although you still need to use System Monitor at a later time) because you need a Counter Log of three days' worth of data first. Choice C is used to monitor network traffic and bandwidth (not server health), and choice D is used to view network connections.

CHAPTER 12

Configuring and Troubleshooting Hardware and Software

ITINERARY

- **Objective 12.01** Troubleshoot Network Media
- **Objective 12.02** Configure and Troubleshoot Software
- **Objective 12.03** Configure Hardware
- **Objective 12.04** Install NICs and Modems
- **Objective 12.05** Troubleshoot NICs and Modems
- **Objective 12.06** Basic PC Connector Types

NEWBIE	SOME EXPERIENCE	EXPERT
3 hours	2 hours	1 hour

Previous chapters have given you insight into many aspects of networking and network technologies. Here's where you bring some of that knowledge together and apply it to some specific hardware and software configuration and troubleshooting issues. Bear in mind that the best way to learn about this kind of thing is to actually do it; CompTIA states that the Network+ exam is suitable for persons with at least nine months of experience in the field. You can learn most of what you need from a book (such as this one!), but it's the practical experience that counts when you're out there faced with a dead server and an IT manager pacing up and down outside the computer room door!

Troubleshoot Network Media

Symptoms of network media faults can range from the inability of a single client to connect to the network to the failure of an entire system. The topology of your network determines the extent of a problem caused by a single failure and how you troubleshoot media-related problems. On a bus-based network, a single cable break will shut down the entire segment, but with a UTP-based star-bus topology, a cable fault may affect only one client, unless it's the cable between two hubs or to a server. Also, with a star topology you may have a single point of failure if the hub breaks down.

Media faults can generally be categorized as follows:

- Cable breaks
- Cable shorts
- Incorrect wiring to connectors
- Badly fitted or damaged connectors
- Incorrect or overlong cables or segments
- Cables located near sources of interference
- Environmental effects (heat, cold, water, and so on)

Most network cable installers carry an arsenal of tools to help them install and test new structured cabling systems. These tools range from inexpensive crimpers (the tools that put the connectors on the ends of the cables) and punch-down tools (the tools that push UTP wiring into the connectors on wall plates, or into punch-down connectors on patch panels like those shown in Figure 12.1) to

FIGURE 12.1 Punch-down connectors on the back of a patch panel

multi-thousand-dollar cabling testers that plug into two ends of a cable. The higher-end testers provide acres of detailed information to ensure that the electrical properties of a cable pass a battery of EIA/TIA standards. These tools are indispensable to the folks who install cable, and most of them require significant training to use and to understand.

Visual Indications of Problems

Apart from the obvious—a completely severed cable, for instance—look for help from indicator lights on NICs and hubs. A broken coax Ethernet segment will often cause the collision light on a hub to stay on permanently, and there may also be a partition light to indicate that a faulty segment has been isolated from the rest of the LAN. Broken UTP cables tend to cause LINK lights on NICs and hubs to turn off. Using these visual indicators is important because inspecting connectors on cables for signs of damage is not always easy because the fault may be internal to the connector; testing by substitution is an easier option.

Travel Advisory

Some network techs tie a knot at one end of a known faulty cable, as close to the connector as possible. This ensures that the cable doesn't get placed back with good cable stock. Even if it does, it will be easy to see that the cable shouldn't be used.

Testing Equipment

Because bad versus good cables and working versus faulty network topologies have specific, measurable characteristics, test equipment can often save a great deal of time when you're looking for faults, especially when you have narrowed the problem down to a specification issue, such as an overlong segment or poorly installed UTP cabling that's laid too close to a power cable. These types of faults do not generate any physical symptoms, and they can be found only by performing a range of tests. The most common types of test equipment are described here.

Simple Test Meters (Multimeters)

A multimeter, shown in Figure 12.2, can be used to test a cable or bus segment for open or short circuits by testing an electrical characteristic called *resistance,* measured in *ohms.* A good cable will have close to zero resistance (zero ohms) between its ends (pin 1 to pin 1 on a UTP cable, or core to core on a piece of coax). A faulty or broken cable will show a higher than normal resistance—anything above a few ohms to infinity, which is written as ∞.

You might remember that a bus-based network needs to be terminated at either end for correct operation. These terminators have a resistance of 50 ohms, and when they are placed correctly as a pair, their effective resistance is seen as half this value. So if you use a multimeter to probe a good segment of coax (at the NIC connector on a T-piece), you should get a reading of around 25 ohms, plus the resistance of the cabling (see Figure 12.3). The reading may be a few ohms higher on a very long run of cable. If you see a higher value, say above 50 ohms, then you have a break in one direction or another along the bus (see Figure 12.4). A reading of lower than 25 ohms indicates a short circuit somewhere.

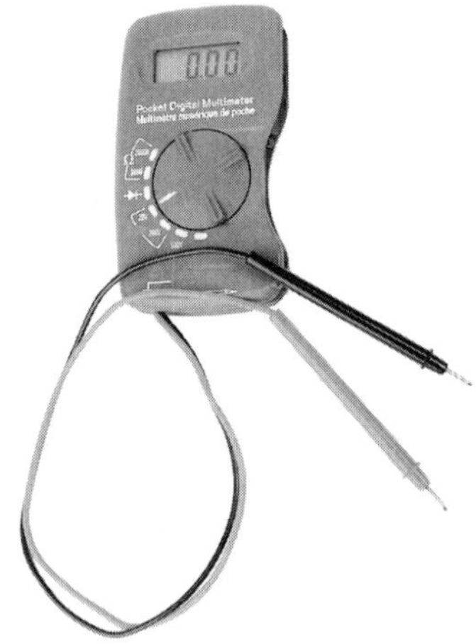

FIGURE 12.2 A simple multimeter

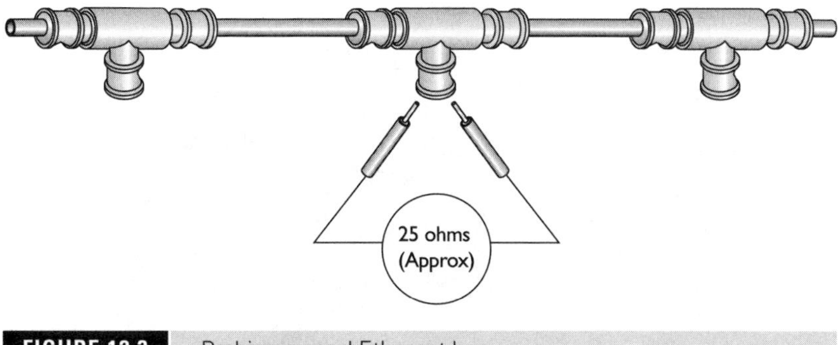

FIGURE 12.3 Probing a good Ethernet bus

Tone Locators

Even in the best of networks, labels fall off ports and outlets, mystery cables disappear behind walls, and new cable runs are added. To help you figure out which end belongs to a cable when you are working with a stack of cables, you can use tone locators. A *toner* is a generic term for two separate devices that are used together: a tone generator and a tone probe. These two devices are often referred to as *Fox and Hound,* the brand name of a popular toner made by Triplett Corporation. The tone generator connects to a cable with alligator clips, tiny hooks, or a network jack, and sends an electrical signal along the wire at a certain frequency. A tone probe emits a sound if it comes close to the cable to which the tone generator is connected (see Figure 12.5).

To trace a cable, the tone generator is connected to the cable, and the tone probe is moved next to all the possible cables. The tone probe then makes a sound when it is next to the right cable. More advanced toners include phone jacks, enabling the person manipulating the tone generator to communicate with the person manipulating the tone probe: "Jim, move the tone generator to

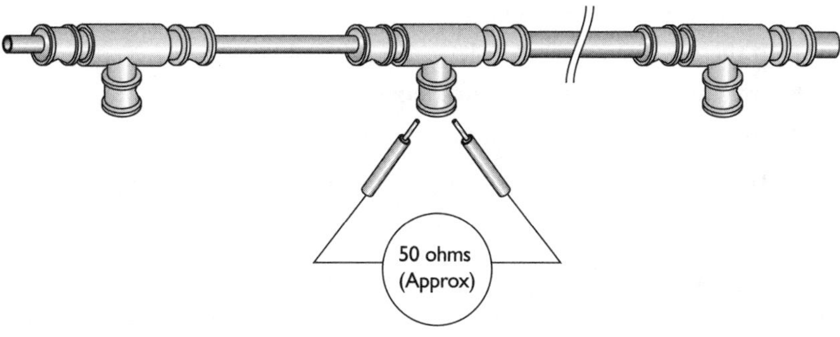

FIGURE 12.4 Probing a broken Ethernet bus

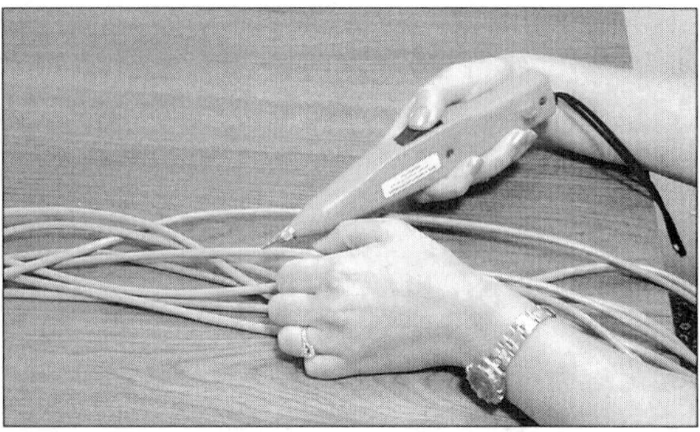

FIGURE 12.5 A tone locator in use

the next port!" Some toners have one probe working with multiple generators. Each generator emits a different frequency, and the probe emits a different sound for each frequency. Good toners cost around U.S.$75. Bad toners can cost less than U.S.$25, but usually don't work very well. If you want to support a network, you'll need to own a toner.

Together, a good, medium-priced cable tester and a good toner are the most important tools used by folks who support, but don't install, networks. Be sure to add a few extra batteries—avoid the frustration of sitting on the top of a ladder holding a cable tester or toner that has just run out of juice!

Cable Testers

As the name implies, cable testers test cables. But before we can talk about cable testers, we have to determine what makes a cable bad. When troubleshooting cables, ask yourself the following questions:

- How long is this cable (is it over its rated length)?
- Are any of the wires broken?
- If there is a break, where is it?
- Are any of the wires shorted together?
- Are any of the wires not in the correct order?
- Is there too much electrical or radio interference from external components?

Cable testers are designed to answer some or all of these questions, depending on the amount of money you are willing to pay. The low end of the cable-tester market consists of devices that test only for broken wires; these testers are often called *continuity testers.* Some cheap testers will also test for improperly wired cables, such as having the wires in a different order at either end, or they may test for shorts in the cable (see Figure 12.6).

These cheap testers usually require you to insert both ends of the cable into the tester. That can be a little bit tough if the cable is already installed in the wall! A number of testers come in two parts so that you can connect the tester to a cable in the wiring room, while taking the other part of the tester to the wall jack (located elsewhere) for that cable.

Medium-priced testers add the ability to tell you the length of the cables by switching the mode of the tester to what is usually known as the "length" mode. They also tell you where a break or short is located in a cable. These are generically called *Time Domain Reflectometers,* or *TDRs* (see Figure 12.7).

The medium-priced testers will have a small loopback device that gets inserted into the far end of the cable, enabling the tester to work with installed cables. This is the type of tester that you want. With a basic unit, you can plug in both ends of a patch lead, and the tester will check for correct wiring and open or short circuits. If you are testing a wall port, you generally fit a loopback plug into the socket at the other end to complete the circuit and enable testing.

Exam Tip

Most UTP wiring schemes specify a maximum segment length of 100 meters, whereas Thinnet has a maximum length of 185m, and Thicknet has a maximum distance of 500m.

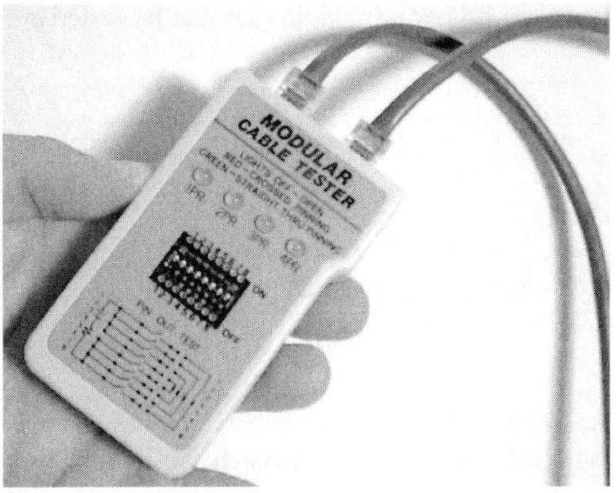

FIGURE 12.6 A simple cable tester

FIGURE 12.7 Time Domain Reflectometer (TDR)

A combination of troubleshooting methodology and test equipment will enable you to determine whether a particular cable is bad. In most troubleshooting situations, you will use other clues to determine whether you have a hardware or software problem. In the "I can't log on" scenario, for example, if you have determined that everyone else in the area can log on, and that this user can log on from another location, you have narrowed the problem to either a configuration or hardware issue. If all network activity is broken (that is, if nothing is available in Network Neighborhood, or you can't ping the default gateway), you may choose to test cables connecting the PC to the server. This is not the only option, but it is one variable that can be tested and eliminated.

Travel Advisory

When troubleshooting network problems, don't forget to check the simple stuff first—you can save yourself a lot of time. For example, check to make sure that cables are physically connected, or verify that the printer is online before checking more complicated solutions.

Protocol Analyzers

Things are getting a bit heavy when you reach for a protocol analyzer because this means that you're checking out your network at a very fundamental level by analyzing individual data packets on the network. Software-based protocol or network analyzers (also called *packet sniffers*) include applications such as the Network Monitor (NetMon) provided with Windows NT/2000/XP. Use these tools when unexplained slowdowns occur on your network, to help you determine which machines are possibly sending rogue or malformed packets. A protocol analyzer enables you to determine whether there is a broadcast storm (or just too much broadcasting in general) or whether you have a faulty NIC installed in a machine that is flooding the network with malformed packets. Protocol analyzers can serve many purposes; in addition to identifying faulty hardware, they can help determine whether there's any faulty software on the network that might be sending out dodgy data, and sometimes they can even help trace intermittent faults, such as cabling problems (though other, simpler diagnostic steps can usually be taken first, employing some of the troubleshooting methods and tools discussed earlier).

Configure and Troubleshoot Software

Throughout the book, you have read about software tools that can be used when configuring your network and that can also be applied to troubleshooting. Because most of these have been described elsewhere in this book, this section presents just a review of the basic purpose of these tools and the circumstances under which they may be used.

I Can't See Anything in Network Neighborhood!

When a user is completely cut off from the network, the problem is usually limited to that user's workstation or network connection. When Suzy Tech gets a call from Johnny saying that his Windows 2000 machine is on, but he can't log in and he can't see any other machines on the company's TCP/IP network, Suzy goes to Johnny's office to run some tests. The first test that Suzy runs is a PING command on an external machine. She doesn't expect this to work, but she tests just to be certain. Next, she tries to ping Johnny's machine by using either PING Localhost or PING 127.0.0.1. Using PING 127.0.0.1 is a way of testing that the software stack for TCP/IP has been loaded properly; if it has not, the user will be unable to communicate on the network. So, when the ping of the local machine does not work, as shown in the next example, Suzy guesses that the problem is in the TCP/IP configuration.

```
C:\>PING 127.0.0.1
Unable to contact IP driver, error code 2
```

To view the machine's TCP/IP configuration, Suzy uses IPCONFIG (see the example that follows), and this command tells her that there's something wrong with the machine's setup. After checking the network configuration, she notices that the only protocol installed is NetBEUI (needed for a couple of systems not running TCP/IP). Suzy installs TCP/IP, and Johnny is now able to connect to the network.

```
C:\>IPCONFIG
Windows 2000 IP Configuration
Error: TCP/IP is not running on this system
```

Exam Tip

To view the TCP/IP configuration of a Windows 9*x* machine, use WINIPCFG. To view the TCP/IP configuration of a UNIX/Linux system, use IFCONFIG. For NetWare servers, use the CONFIG command.

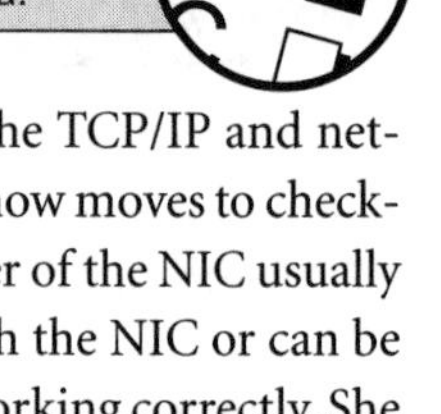

If Suzy's PING 127.0.0.1 works, she must assume that the TCP/IP and networking configuration of Johnny's machine is correct. She now moves to checking hardware, using a network card utility (the manufacturer of the NIC usually has a diagnostic utility that exists on the CD that came with the NIC or can be downloaded from the Web) to verify that the NIC itself is working correctly. She uses a cable tester to verify that the cable from Johnny's workstation is working correctly. When the cable tester shows that the cable is bad, she replaces the cable between Johnny's workstation and the patch panel and is able to connect.

I Can't Get to This Website!

Reaching external websites requires that a variety of components be configured correctly. Some of these components are within your company's internal control; many of them are not. When Fatima calls and tells Suzy Tech that she cannot reach http://www.comptia.org, Suzy's first step is to try to reach that site herself. In this case, Suzy is also unable to get a response from the Comptia.org site. One of her next steps is to try to ping the site, first by name and then by IP address. She gets no response by name, but she does get a normal response when she tries to ping the site by IP address (see the example that follows). As you saw in Chapter 11, this immediately indicates to her that the problem lies with name resolution (in this case, DNS).

```
C:\>PING 216.119.103.72

Pinging 216.119.103.72 with 32 bytes of data:
Reply from 216.119.103.72: bytes=32 time=28ms TTL=105
Reply from 216.119.103.72: bytes=32 time=27ms TTL=105
```

```
Reply from 216.119.103.72: bytes=32 time=27ms TTL=105
Reply from 216.119.103.72: bytes=32 time=26ms TTL=105
Ping statistics for 216.119.103.72:
    Packets: Sent = 4, Received = 4, Lost = 0 (0% loss),
Approximate round trip times in milli-seconds:
    Minimum = 26ms, Maximum =  28ms, Average =  27ms
```

Travel Advisory

Be aware that Windows 2000/XP/2003 systems store DNS responses in memory (called *DNS Resolver Cache*), including negative responses, which are responses that say "Nope, there is no record here by that name." This is important because if the name becomes available in DNS, your system will be unaware because it will continue to use the answer in cache until it times out. When troubleshooting, you may flush the DNS cache by issuing IPCONFIG /FLUSHDNS.

If Suzy is unable to ping with either the IP or host name, she might consider two things. First, if her company uses a firewall or proxy server to reach the Internet, she would want to ping that machine. This is usually the same IP address as the default gateway's TCP/IP setting. If Suzy can successfully ping her default gateway, the problem is almost certainly not something she or her company has any control over. To verify this, Suzy should attempt to reach some other external sites, both by pinging and by using a browser. If she can reach other sites successfully, the problem is most likely with the Comptia.org site or gateway.

Travel Advisory

A number of companies block the PING request at the firewall so that it cannot reach their web server. They do this for a couple of reasons. The first reason is because if the site is a popular site and there is a large number of PING requests sent, the web server is kept busy sending responses to the PING requests, essentially slowing down the website because the server is already busy. The other reason is from a security point of view. When an attacker is building a profile of what systems are running on a network, they use a PING sweep program that pings all the IP addresses in a network range. By not allowing the PING requests through their firewall, the company can keep their systems from responding to those requests, so the attacker does not know whether those systems exist.

If pinging the website by DNS name and IP address proves unsuccessful, but pinging the network's default gateway is successful, Suzy can also try using the TRACEROUTE (TRACERT) program to check the routing of data between the local network and www.comptia.org. If a routing problem exists anywhere along the line, TRACERT will indicate a timeout error at that router hop.

Travel Advisory

Be aware that TRACERT uses ICMP, and ICMP traffic is typically blocked at firewalls—this may cause TRACERT to timeout. For a set of troubleshooting tools that includes tools to look up a website's IP address, visit http://www.samspade.org.

Our Web Server Is Sluggish!

A slow response from a server can be related to a variety of factors. Usually, however, the culprit is either a connection to the server or the server itself. When Wanda, who is working at home, calls and tells Suzy Tech that she's getting a very slow response from their company's website, Suzy leaps into action. She tries to reach the offending server and is immediately connected, which indicates that it may be a connectivity problem for that user. She asks Wanda to try a TRACERT command from her workstation to the slow server. This reveals to Suzy that the slowdown happens at one of the intermediate steps that Wanda connects through. This problem is out of Suzy's hands, unless she can offer a direct dial-up option for Wanda.

If Suzy finds that she cannot reach the offending server quickly when she tries from her workstation, however, then the problem may lie with the server itself. Suzy checks the Change Log for the web server, to see if anyone has changed anything recently. If she finds that, say, a new antivirus component was recently added, she should check the vendor's website to make sure that there are no known problems or patches for that piece of software. She would also use the Performance Console to compare the server's current responses to the baseline that she has. This would help her determine that the bottleneck is related to excessive paging, indicating that the server may need more physical memory, or maybe that the % CPU usage is continuously greater than the value of 80%, which indicates that an upgrade is needed.

The web server may be sluggish because too many request are being sent to the website; maybe Suzy's company did not foresee the popularity of the site and did not plan for number of hits it would receive. In this case, it is possible that two web servers are needed and the load of the requests can be split between the two servers (this is called *load balancing*).

General Software Configuration Issues

One simple trick of the trade when you are experiencing networking problems that you can't quite pin down is to ensure that you are using the latest drivers and modules for every piece of hardware and software possibly (and sometimes not possibly!) related to the problem. For example, if you cannot pin down why a machine is running slowly, visit the website of the NIC manufacturer and see whether a more recent driver is available for the card. Check out whether newer disk and display drivers are available for your OS. Bear in mind that, if you're running Windows 98, for example, the drivers supplied on the original CD will be several years old. Remember, too, that newer drivers may fix the current problem, but they may also introduce new ones, so always be prepared to go backward and reinstall older drivers. Make sure you either make a backup before you install the new drivers, or check that you have a copy of the old ones on a CD or floppy disk. Don't just keep a copy in a network folder—if you have network problems, how are you going to get at them?

Travel Advisory

A useful jumping-off point for getting new drivers for almost anything is www.drivershq.com.

Objective 12.03 Configure Hardware

A desktop computer or server contains a lot of hardware—lots to go wrong! Obviously, the Network+ exam's focus is on networking, so that might lead you to think that all you have to worry about is the NIC. That would be a big mistake! Sure, the NIC may develop a fault, and you may need to confirm this by running the diagnostics software that came with it (you *did* buy a decent NIC that came with such stuff, didn't you?), but your troubleshooting skills also need to cover *installing* NICs—along with tape units, CD-ROM drives, new hard disks, modems, and so on. The Network+ exam doesn't assume that you're a super tech or that you know the ins and outs of everything hardware related—that's the focus of the A+ exam—but it pays off in real life (and for the exam) to know the basics. This section contains all you need to know, in super-condensed format.

Travel Advisory

For a list of devices supported by your operating system, check the operating system hardware compatibility list (HCL), usually found on the operating system CD or Microsoft's website.

Configuring System Resources

Modems and NICs require system resources to function properly. Don't worry about how to set these resources at this point; just be aware that they exist.

System resources is a term (now part of the tech vernacular) that describes four totally different PC elements: IRQs, I/O addresses, DMA channels, and memory addresses.

IRQs

Interrupt requests (IRQs) are used by devices to tell the CPU that they need some attention. This approach is more efficient than having the CPU check every device one by one. Virtually every device in the PC uses an IRQ. Certainly, a NIC will require an IRQ, and so will a modem if it plugs straight into the PC's expansion bus; if it's plugged into a serial port, the IRQ is taken care of.

A standard PC has 16 numbered IRQs, but many of these are already taken up by devices such as the hard drives and floppy drive. Table 12.1 lists all the IRQs and the devices that use them.

As you can see, realistically, a PC has only a few spare interrupts that can be used for a NIC and other plug-in devices. The most likely candidates are 10, 11, 5 (unless you have a second printer port fitted), and 2/9. IRQ 12 may be available if you have your mouse plugged into a serial port *and* you disable the onboard (PS/2 style) mouse interface; this is usually an option in the PC's setup program.

TABLE 12.1 PC IRQ Assignments

IRQ	Default Function	Available?
IRQ 0	System timer	No
IRQ 1	Keyboard	No
IRQ 2/9	Open for use	Yes
IRQ 3	COM2	Yes
IRQ 4	COM1	Yes
IRQ 5	LPT2 (if fitted)	Maybe
IRQ 6	Floppy drive	No
IRQ 7	LPT1	No
IRQ 8	Real-time clock	No
IRQ 10	Open for use	Yes
IRQ 11	Open for use	Yes
IRQ 12	Mouse port	Maybe
IRQ 13	Math coprocessor	No
IRQ 14	Primary hard drive controller	No
IRQ 15	Secondary hard drive controller	No

Just in case you're wondering, IRQ 2 and IRQ 9 are tied together. It's an historic thing, and they're called the *cascaded* interrupts. Don't worry too much about this, but you might like to know that they're free for use by NICs and other hardware, although they don't work too well under some circumstances. Most techs treat them as available only as a last resort.

Windows 9*x*, 2000, XP, and Windows Server 2003 support a feature known as the *Plug and Play (PnP)* configuration environment. PnP is a system that avoids the hassle of manually configuring all four system resources for NICs and other plug-in cards, by having the PC and the operating system work out everything for themselves. The best line to take is that if an exam scenario raises the possibility of any resources being accidentally shared between devices, this sharing is likely to cause problems: either the PC will crash or the NIC (or whatever is clashing) won't work properly.

Exam Tip

The golden rule for the Network+ exam is that interrupts cannot be shared between devices. For example, if you have a tape streamer in a server with its expansion card configured to use IRQ 10, you wouldn't try to use this IRQ for a NIC.

If PnP is so great, you might be wondering why we're even discussing system resources. Three issues require network technicians to have a thorough understanding of resources. First, and perhaps most shocking, PnP does not always work perfectly and occasionally requires a little manual configuration. Second, millions of older devices came out before PnP. These *legacy* devices require you to understand system resources in detail. Third, and possibly most important, the Network+ exam tests you on system resources. Know your resources!

Exam Tip

You will not need to memorize the IRQs of all devices; just be sure of what the IRQs of popular ports are, such as COM1, COM2, LPT1, and LPT2.

I/O Addresses

The second system resource is the *I/O address,* or *port address.* Every device in the PC has an I/O address, or a range of them. Whereas the IRQ is used to send a signal to the processor that a device needs attention, the I/O address is the mechanism used to send data to the processor, or have the processor send data to the device. I/O addresses are specified by four-digit hexadecimal numbers. Here are a few examples of common PC I/O addresses:

- **0060** Keyboard
- **01F0** Primary hard drive controller
- **03F0** Floppy drive controller

There are dozens of other I/O addresses in use or allocated to other devices and, just like with IRQs, some I/O address ranges are free for expansion cards. The golden rule remains the same: You can't have two devices sharing I/O addresses.

DMA Channels

If an add-in card (or internal device) supports *Direct Memory Access (DMA)*, it can access memory directly instead of requesting it from the CPU. Some NICs, sound cards, and disk controllers support DMA, but most internal modems don't. Many years ago, DMA was a popular method for speeding up devices that required constant access to memory. A PC has eight DMA channels, as listed in Table 12.2.

Exam Tip

Be aware that DMA is a system resource and that a NIC may need to have a DMA assigned when it is installed.

DMA channels should be treated exactly like IRQs and I/O addresses: no two devices should ever share a DMA channel.

TABLE 12.2 DMA Channels

DMA Channel	Default Function	Available?
DMA 0/4	System	No
DMA 1	Open for use	Yes
DMA 2	Floppy drive	No
DMA 3	Open for use	Yes
DMA 5	Open for use	Yes
DMA 6	Open for use	Yes
DMA 7	Open for use	Yes

Memory Addresses

The fourth and last system resource is the *memory address*. Some NICs (and various other add-ins) require a range of RAM to be set aside for their own use. This is defined by memory addresses, which are generally specified in pairs as the start and end locations for the allocated RAM. Here's an example:

```
000A0000-000AFFFF
```

Often the leading zeroes are omitted. For this reason, you might find the preceding example abbreviated as follows:

```
A0000-AFFFF
```

The numbers are written in the ever-popular hexadecimal (base 16) notation, and—guess what?—having two devices competing for the same memory area is a no-go.

Assigning Resources

When IBM designed its PC, it defined industry-standard combinations of system resources for many of the built-in devices and functions. The Network+ exam doesn't expect you to know *all* these resource allocations, but you *might* get a question or two about the serial (COM) and parallel printer (LPT) ports, so memorizing Table 12.3 is a good idea.

External modems often plug into an existing COM port (there are a few parallel port modems, and USB modems are becoming increasingly popular), such as COM1 or COM2, so an external modem will effectively use one of the I/O and IRQ pairs associated with the port it is plugged into. Internal modems will be configured to use a COM port and use the resources of that COM port.

You will need to remember that devices cannot share resources. So if you have a device using COM1, you will be unable to have a different device use COM3, because they use the same IRQ. If, for example, you have a mouse connected to

TABLE 12.3 Common Port Settings

Port Name	I/O Address	IRQ
COM1	03F8	4
COM2	02F8	3
COM3	03E8	4
COM4	02E8	3
LPT1	0378	7
LPT2	0278	5

COM1 (address 03F8, IRQ 4), you should avoid configuring an internal modem to COM3 (address 03E8, IRQ 4). The best option here would be to configure the modem to use either COM2 or COM4. If your PC has a built-in COM2 (most PCs these days have two serial ports), you could possibly disable it using the PC's CMOS setup program. If you *do* configure an internal modem so that it shares an interrupt with another serial device, chances are that one of the devices will fail to work, if not both. The best way to troubleshoot these types of problems is to draw out your current setup on a piece of paper so that you can visualize where the conflict is.

Remember that there are four system resources—I/O addresses, IRQs, DMAs, and memory addresses—and that all NICs and modems will require an I/O address and an IRQ; a network card may also need a DMA channel or a memory address.

Plug and Play Resource Assignment

If the computer system's BIOS, PnP cards/devices, and operating system are all PnP, assigning system resources is automatic (hooray!). The system will boot, recognize the PnP device, and load the driver. If the operating system does not have the driver, it may prompt for the driver disk (see Figure 12.8). The rest is automatic, although you will probably need to reboot.

Manual Resource Assignment

If the card is non-PnP, you still have more work to do. You need to set the resources on the card using the utility that came with the CD-ROM or floppy disk for the card. The configuration of the resources is typically burned into an EEPROM chip on the card after you choose to save the settings. These utilities are almost always DOS programs. Figure 12.9 shows a typical utility.

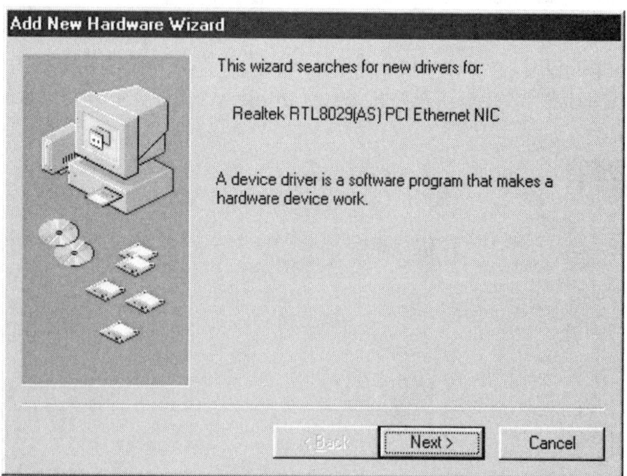

FIGURE 12.8 Plug and Play helping to configure a NIC

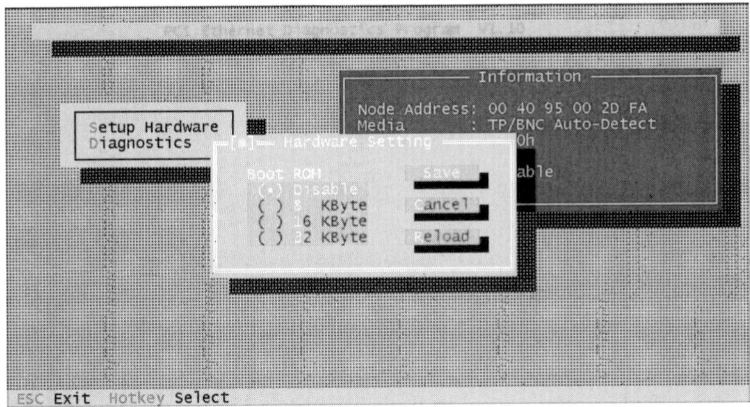

FIGURE 12.9 NIC configuration utility

Objective 12.04 Install NICs and Modems

Installing a device in a PC is a three-step procedure: First, you must physically install it. Second, you (or PnP) must assign it unused system resources. Third, you (or PnP) must install the proper drivers.

Physical Connections

First, plug in the card. One thing is for sure: If you don't plug the NIC or modem into the computer, it just isn't going to work! Fortunately, physically inserting the modem or NIC into the PC is the easiest part of the job. If the card is not PnP, however, you must determine the available system resources and then determine how to set the resources before you install the card. The best way to determine available unused resources is with a third-party utility such as Touchstone's CheckIt. If you are installing a card on a Windows 9*x* system or on Windows 2000/XP, use the Device Manager to determine open resources by clicking the Computer icon, as shown in Figure 12.10.

After settling on the open resources you want to use, determine how to set those resources for your non-PnP card. Today, this is normally done with a special software utility on the driver disk, but with older cards this is done through tiny jumpers on the card that place a shorting link (sometimes called a *strap*) over a pair of pins to complete an electrical circuit and set a corresponding configuration, such as a specific IRQ (see Figure 12.11).

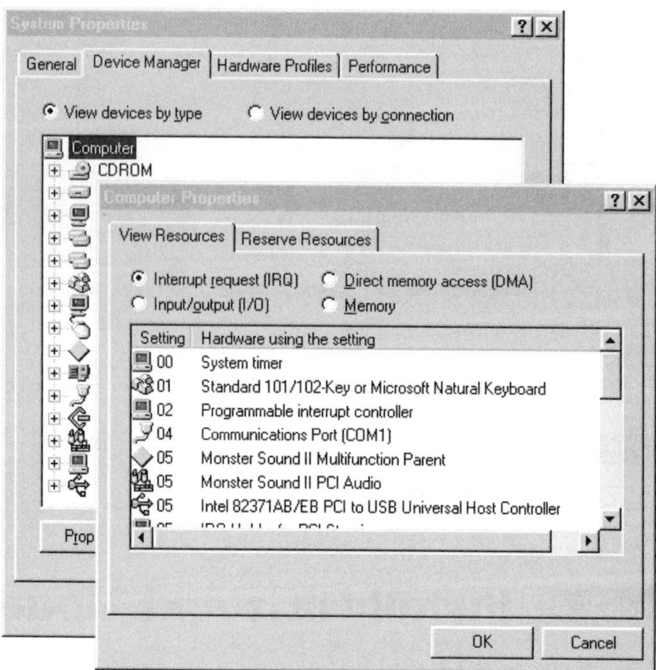

FIGURE 12.10 Windows 9*x* Device Manager

FIGURE 12.11 An old network card that uses jumpers for configuration

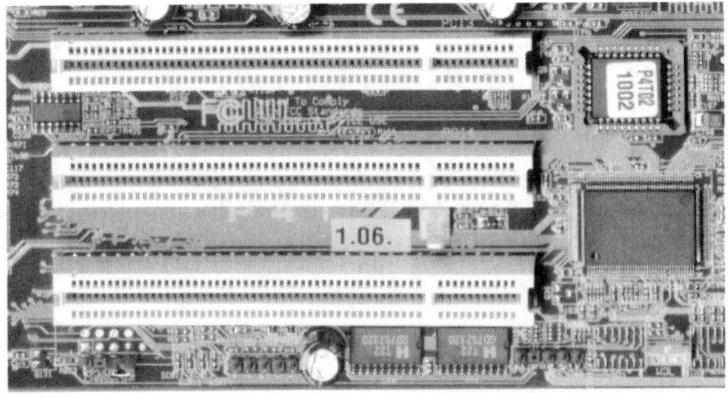

FIGURE 12.12 PCI slots

Most PCs today have two types of expansion slots. The first, and most common, of the two expansion slots is the Peripheral Component Interconnect (PCI) type (see Figure 12.12). These are 32-bit, fast, PnP-compatible expansion slots; virtually all new NICs sold today are of the PCI type, and it's most likely what you will see in the real world.

Still present in older systems (from 286 computers to Pentium systems) are the old Industry Standard Architecture (ISA) slots (see Figure 12.13). These slots date back to the old 80286-powered IBM AT computer and have not changed at all since then. They are 16-bit and very slow, running at 8 MHz. Some modern PCs still have a few of these old ISA expansion slots to support, or hold, any existing ISA cards that your organization might have.

Once you have connected the device and configured its resources, it is time to install the driver. The driver may be installed either automatically through Plug and Play, as long as the operating system has a driver for the device, or when the system is booted after the device has been physically connected. If prompted for the driver, simply supply the manufacturer's CD for that device. If the manufacturer did not supply a CD for the driver, you will need to visit their website to download a current driver.

FIGURE 12.13 ISA slots

Troubleshoot NICs and Modems

If a PC can't access the network, it's prudent to look in the back and be sure that the cleaning person didn't accidentally unplug the network cable during the night.

Don't laugh! When a network problem arises, especially a problem with a networked PC that ran well previously, the first thing to check (depending on the symptom) is whether it is plugged in. There have been too many situations where some fancy-pants, overly certified network guru doesn't have the common sense to check such basic things as whether the LINK light is on!

Troubleshooting NICs

If you do feel that the NIC may be faulty, reach for a copy of its driver disk. Every (decent) NIC's driver disk has a handy utility to perform diagnostics on the card and verify that it is functional; sometimes it's the same utility used to set system resources—just a different command. Poke around on the driver disk and find it. Like the configuration utility, the testing utilities are usually DOS programs. Figure 12.14 shows an example of a diagnostic program in action.

The NIC diagnostics may help you pinpoint the problem, but if the card has a blown transceiver (the bit that carries data between the network media and the NIC itself), the NIC's card-checking diagnostics may not pick this up. Knowing this, most NIC diagnostics include a test-the-network diagnostic function that makes the card send or receive test packets. You usually need another identical NIC in another system running the same diagnostic function to do this test.

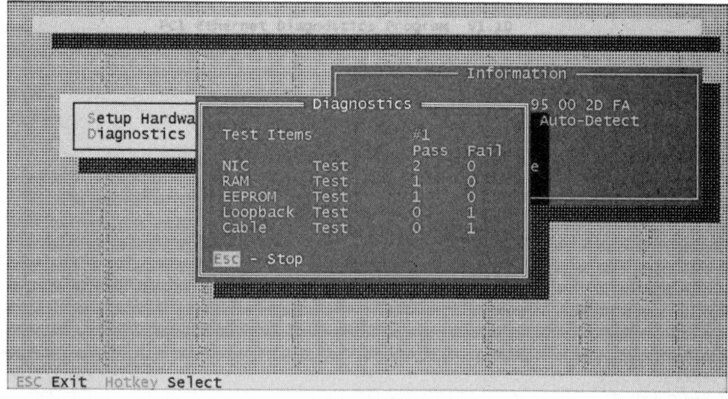

FIGURE 12.14 NIC diagnostics in action

Another device that is often used to confirm that a NIC is functioning correctly is a hardware loopback device. This device usually plugs directly into the NIC and bounces back any transmitted test packets so they can be picked up and verified by the diagnostics software.

If you really have exhausted all possibilities and still believe that the NIC is faulty, the next thing to do is to test by substitution, but be careful to ensure that the replacement NIC is 100-percent identical to the suspect one. If you're not sure, or if it's definitively not the same, you will have to remove the existing NIC drivers and install ones for the replacement card.

Troubleshooting Modems

Modems rarely have a diagnostic disk, but all versions of Windows 9*x*, Me, and 2000 have a basic communications check built into the Modem applet in the Control Panel. This function attempts to send some basic commands to the modem and then displays the responses. The responses will vary from modem to modem, but if you *do* get something back, at least you know that your PC seems to be connected correctly to the unit and can communicate with the modem.

You can also use the Windows HyperTerminal program to talk directly to your modem; simply configure the program to communicate with the Direct to Comx option and specify the COM port to which the modem is connected or configured. You can then pretend that you are Dial-up Networking and send your modem command strings that should elicit a response. A typical test sequence works like this:

Action	Description/Notes
Configure HyperTerminal and connect to your modem.	Besides choosing the Direct to Comx option, don't forget to specify the COM port.
When the terminal screen appears, press ENTER a couple times.	This allows the modem to sense your connection speed.
Type **ATE1V1** and press ENTER.	This command ensures that your modem echoes commands back to the screen so you can see what you are doing. You may have to blind type this if command echoing is currently off.
Type **AT** and press ENTER.	If you are communicating with a modem, it should respond with OK.
Type **ATDT** followed by valid phone number—maybe your cell phone number or a nearby internal extension (for example, **ATDT5551234567**).	If your phone system uses pulse dialing instead of tone dialing, use **ATDP**. If you need to dial 0 or 9 for an outside line, add this with a comma before your telephone number (for example, **ATDT9,5551234567**).
If your phone rings, press ENTER to cancel the call.	See the next sequence if your phone doesn't ring.

The preceding sequence should ring your phone (press ENTER to cancel the call; you don't have to pick up), or you will see one of the following responses:

Response	Diagnosis
BUSY	Check the phone you are calling. Maybe the cell phone network is busy. Try again.
NO DIALTONE	The modem can't sense a dial tone. Check the modem phone lead and/or plug a real phone into the outlet to check that it's live.
NO ANSWER	Did your phone ring? If not, try again. If you are calling your cell phone, maybe your call went through to your messaging service. Are you in a service area? Does the modem's phone line have a bar on cell phone numbers? You may need to find a local number or extension to call.

The response should give you a basic indication of the state of the modem (see Figure 12.15).

Sometimes a fault occurs because the internal interface between the modem and the phone line gets fried by an electrical surge down the line caused by an electrical storm. In this case, your PC can communicate with the modem, but the modem will never see the phone line again, so all you get is NO DIALTONE. If you verify that the modem itself is faulty, it's usually cheaper to replace it than to have it repaired, unless it's covered by a warranty.

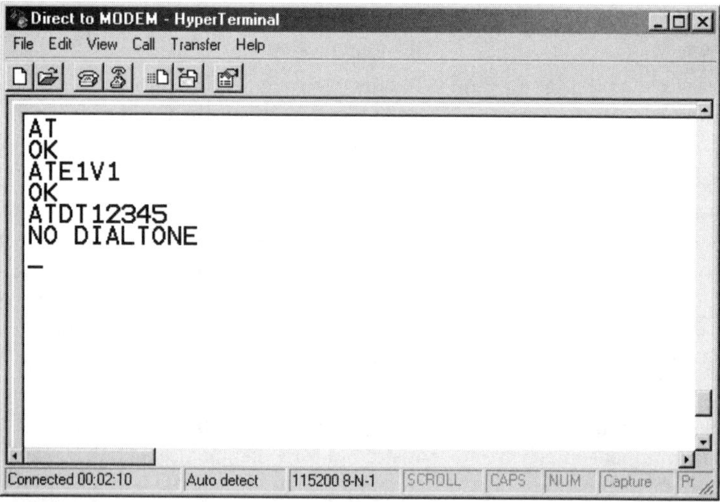

FIGURE 12.15 Having a chat with a modem

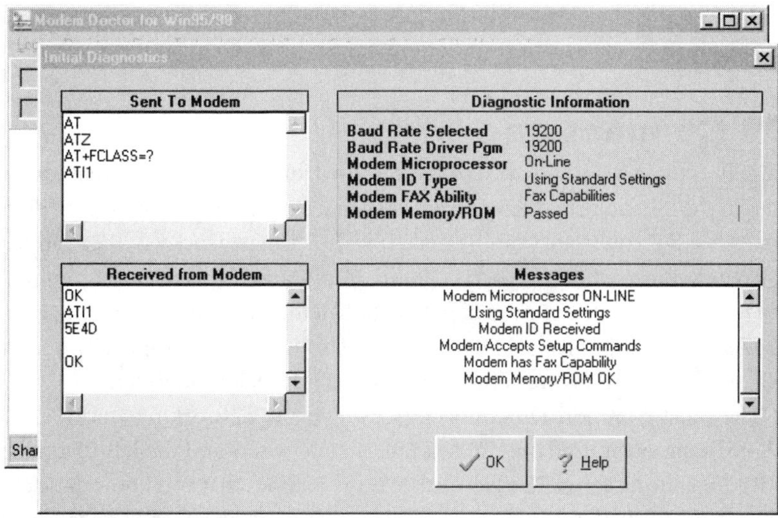

FIGURE 12.16 Modem Doctor

To simplify modem checking, you could also use the popular shareware application Modem Doctor, written by Hank Volpe. Modem Doctor comes in a DOS and a Windows version and is the best modem tester available (see Figure 12.16).

Basic PC Connector Types

Most external modems connect to the PC through an available serial port, and almost all PCs come with two serial ports—often with male 9-pin connectors (sometimes called *DB-9M connectors*) or a male 25-pin connector (sometimes called *DB-25M*). It's important to know what connector types you are likely to see on a PC, especially because some are used for several different purposes. Also, if you plug the wrong thing into the wrong port, you may do some damage!

Exam Tip

The Network+ exam does test on connectors! You have to know which ones are used for what purpose.

Because the Network+ exam throws in the odd connector-based question, here's an overview of what you need to know.

DB Connectors

DB connectors are the D-shaped connectors used for hundreds of different connections in the PC and networking world. DB connectors come in a number of different forms. DB connectors can be male (pins) or female (sockets), they can have different numbers of pins or sockets (9-pin, 15-pin, and 25-pin are most common), and they usually have two rows of pins, although there are a few exceptions. Figure 12.17 shows a 25-pin female DB connector. This is called, appropriately, a *female DB-25* or a *DB-25F.* Figure 12.18 shows a DB-25M (male) connector.

The most common DB connectors used in the networking world are the DB-15F connector used on 10Base5 Ethernet networks and the DB-9F used on older Token Ring cards. The Network+ exam assumes that you know these connectors as well as the standard connectors used on the back of PCs (see Figure 12.19), such as the DB-25F (for parallel ports) and the DB-9M or DB-25M (for serial ports).

Be aware that the multifunction aspect of DB connectors can lead to confusion because totally different devices could use the exact same DB connector. For example, 10Base5 NICs, joysticks, and Musical Instrument Digital Interface (MIDI) cards (a digital interface for musical instruments and other equipment), all use the DB-15F connector. If you see a DB-25F, it might be a parallel port or a *SCSI (Small Computer System Interface)* connector (see "SCSI Connectors," later in this chapter).

How can you tell the function of one of these connectors? The trick is, first, to remember that DB-25F and DB-15F connectors are widely used in the IT world for various ports and interfaces, so it's never safe to think, "Ah, a DB-25F—must be a parallel port!" Second, know the functions of the various connectors on each expansion card. For instance, almost every PC has a sound card, and that

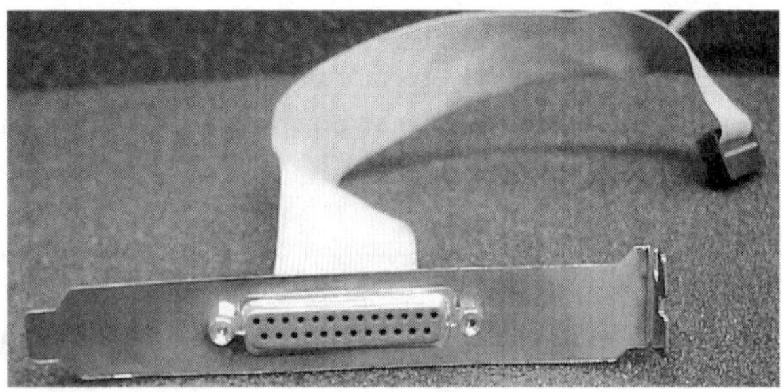

FIGURE 12.17 DB-25F connector

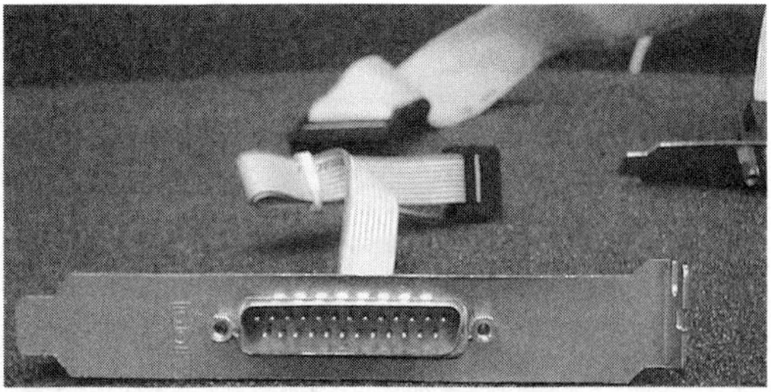

FIGURE 12.18 DB-25M connector

sound card will have a DB-15F connector for a joystick or MIDI port, as well as microphone and speaker connections. Figure 12.20 shows a typical sound card with a DB-15F connector and audio jacks. If you can identify the card, you also know the DB type! Figure 12.21 shows a 10Base5 card. Will a 10Base5 card have speaker connections? Of course not! If you know the functions of the NIC card's connections, it takes little more than some common sense to determine which connector is which. Finally, use a process of elimination based on the cards/connectors you can identify on the back of the PC.

Centronics Connectors

Another connector to watch for is the Centronics connector. This is not a DB connector, but it tends to get lumped in with DB when techs discuss connectors. Centronics connectors are the D-shaped connectors on the backs of printers. They do not have true pins. Instead, they use a single blade that contains some number of flat tabs that make the connection. Although Centronics connectors do not truly have pins, the term *pins* is still used with these connectors to reflect the number of tabs. Centronics connectors come in both female and male

FIGURE 12.19 Serial and parallel ports on the back of a PC

FIGURE 12.20 Sound card connectors with audio jacks and a DB-15F connector for a joystick or MIDI device

versions, and in only two common sizes: the famous 36-pin Centronics connector on the backs of printers, and the increasingly rare 50-pin connector used with SCSI devices. Figure 12.22 shows the female 36-pin Centronics printer connector.

SCSI Connectors

Fortunately, the Network+ exam isn't interested in your ability to configure SCSI. However, the exam does demand that you know the many connections unique to SCSI devices. No other one class of devices has as many connections as SCSI. SCSI has been in existence for a long time and has gone through four distinct standard upgrades, plus many variations within each standard over the years.

FIGURE 12.21 10Base5 card with a DB-15F AUI port

FIGURE 12.22 36-pin Centronics printer connector

SCSI devices can be either external (outside the PC) or internal (inside the PC). This gives SCSI drives an advantage over EIDE drives. There are two types of internal SCSI connections. Both of these connections are inserted into a ribbon cable, just as with EIDE: the 50-pin *narrow* connection and 68-pin *wide* SCSI. Figure 12.23 shows a typical 50-pin narrow connection with a ribbon cable attached.

The oldest external SCSI connector is a 50-pin Centronics connector (see Figure 12.24). Although it is dated, a large number of SCSI devices still use this connector. It looks like a slightly longer version of the printer Centronics connector.

Many older host adapters use a DB-25F connector. This SCSI connector is identical to that for a PC parallel port; however, if you plug your printer into the SCSI port (or a SCSI device into the printer), it definitely will not work, and in some cases you may damage something!

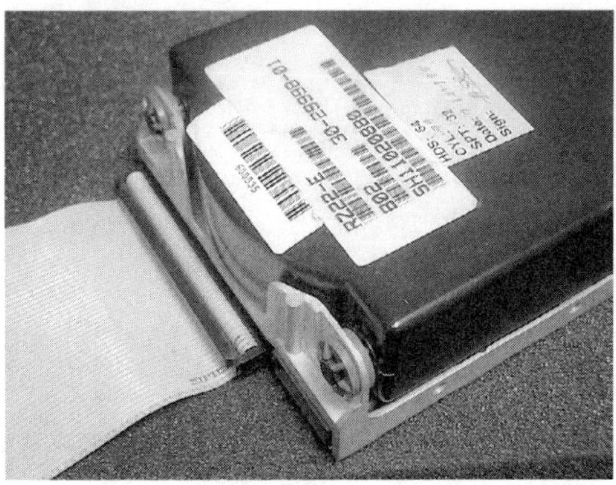

FIGURE 12.23 50-pin narrow SCSI connection

FIGURE 12.24 50-pin SCSI Centronics connector

Most modern SCSI devices now come with special, SCSI-only, high-density DB connectors. High-density DB connectors look like regular DBs at first, but they have much thinner and more densely packed pins. High-density DB connectors come in 50-pin and 68-pin versions. The 50-pin version is much more common (Figure 12.25).

Make sure you know all the different connector types, even those that are not used for network connections. The Network+ exam writers love to make up questions that include bizarre combinations, such as DB-36M, in an effort to catch those who don't know their connectors. DB and Centronics connectors are very common and can have multifunction aspects that provide the basis for some absolutely excellent (or tricky, depending how you look at it) questions, which you will get wrong if you are not comfortable with connectors.

FIGURE 12.25 High-density DB-50 connector

✔**Objective 12.01: Troubleshoot Network Media** Experience counts when troubleshooting anything, and this is true for networks as well. Knowing the typical faults and their symptoms within the framework of the network topology in use will help you pinpoint a fault quickly. A number of tools are available to help you fix problems, from simple hand tools to expensive Time Domain Reflectometers (TDRs), but it's your knowledge that helps you decide what tools to use and when. Your knowledge also determines whether you can make meaningful use of test results. At the simplest level, the basic tools will help you reconnect or fix a faulty cable. When things get heavy, TDRs and protocol analyzers can help you fix the most obscure problems.

✔**Objective 12.02: Configure and Troubleshoot Software** The simplest, and often the most effective, software tools are the freebies that come with the various operating systems. You can do a lot with PING and TRACERT (and the rest) to diagnose network problems. Many common faults are protocol related; if you don't have the right protocols installed, or if they are misconfigured, then you are not going to see all systems (or maybe anything) on your network. Once again, start simple and look for the obvious, rather than dashing straight into super-tech mode.

✔**Objective 12.03: Configure Hardware** The key to getting hardware working correctly is ensuring that it is allocated nonconflicting resources. Today, Plug and Play should make this a much easier task, but there's still some legacy hardware out there that doesn't support it. Knowing how to set IRQs, I/O addresses, DMA channels, and memory addresses manually is essential. Knowing what resources are already in use is also important.

✔**Objective 12.04: Install NICs and Modems** Knowing each step in the installation process will help you get things right. You should also be aware of the different expansion bus technologies (PCI and ISA being the main two) and the importance of ensuring that the NIC or (internal) modem you're about to install matches the available slot(s).

✔**Objective 12.05: Troubleshoot NICs and Modems** I never get tired of saying that a methodical approach to troubleshooting pays dividends. (Hey, did you see that? I've just said it again!) Looking for obvious symptoms of faults is a good start: Check NIC LINK lights and look for broken or disconnected modem phone line cables first, rather than suspecting some deeply technical problem. The problem may well turn out to be not so simple after all, but check the basics first and use the (free) diagnostic tools at your disposal, such as the software that came with the NIC and the testing features built into most modern versions of Windows.

✔ **Objective 12.06: Basic PC Connector Types** If you have been working in a technical environment for any length of time, you will surely know what plugs in where, but you may not always know what all the connectors are called. Knowing your DB-9F connectors from your Centronics 36 connectors will help when you read information and instructions. It will also add up to Network+ exam points.

REVIEW QUESTIONS

1. Which of the following tools can identify a cabling fault due to an overlong segment? (Select all that apply.)
   - **A.** Multimeter
   - **B.** TDR
   - **C.** Tone locator
   - **D.** Punch-down tool
2. Isabel suspects that electrical interference is affecting a segment of network cabling. What should she do first to test her diagnosis? (Select one answer.)
   - **A.** Use a TDR.
   - **B.** Use a protocol analyzer.
   - **C.** Install a length of optical fiber.
   - **D.** Reroute the media.
3. Which of the following commands will specifically confirm that TCP/IP has not been installed correctly on a client PC running Windows 98? (Select all that apply.)
   - **A.** ATDT 123
   - **B.** PING 127.0.0.1
   - **C.** IFCONFIG
   - **D.** NBTSTAT
4. Which of the following commands will display the TCP/IP configuration of a system running UNIX/Linux? (Select one answer.)
   - **A.** WINIPCFG
   - **B.** PING 127.0.0.1

C. IFCONFIG

D. IPSTAT

5. Stella complains that her modem won't make a connection. What would be the best first step in the troubleshooting process? (Select one answer.)

A. Ask Stella what exactly happens when she tries to use the modem.

B. Run HyperTerminal and issue the command AT and press ENTER.

C. Replace the phone cord.

D. Check the phone line.

6. John can connect to the local Internet server using its IP address, but not using its URL (www.acmeintra01.com). What is the most likely cause? (Select one answer.)

A. The server is down.

B. WINS is not configured properly.

C. The default gateway is faulty.

D. DNS services are not available, or DNS has not been set up properly on John's PC.

7. Which of the following configurations is used by COM1? (Select one answer.)

A. Port 02F8, IRQ 4

B. Port 03F8, IRQ 3

C. Port 03F8, IRQ 4

D. Port 0378, IRQ 3

8. Which of the following configurations is used by LPT2? (Select one answer.)

A. Port 0278, IRQ 5

B. Port 0378, IRQ 7

C. Port 02F8, IRQ 5

D. Port 0278, IRQ 7

9. Which of the following connectors are *not* used for a SCSI port? (Select all that apply.)

A. Centronics 50-pin

B. DB-25F

C. DB-9M

D. High-density DB-36

10. Which of the following systems resources are *not* generally used by an internal modem? (Select all that apply.)
    - A. IRQ.
    - B. I/O address.
    - C. Memory address.
    - D. All the above are used.

REVIEW ANSWERS

1. **B** From the list, only a TDR will accurately determine segment length. A multimeter (A) will be able to measure resistance, but this measure cannot really be translated into length.
2. **D** Keep it simple. Move the affected cable and see what happens. If this doesn't work, then it's time to think about a protocol analyzer.
3. **B** Only the PING command will check whether the local TCP/IP configuration is working. IFCONFIG (C) is a UNIX command, and the question addresses Windows 98. ATDT (A) is a modem command, and NBTSTAT (D) is a command to troubleshoot NetBIOS names on the network.
4. **C** IFCONFIG is the command that displays TCP/IP configuration information on a UNIX/Linux system. WINIPCFG (A) is a command to use on Windows 9*x*.
5. **A** Good methodology says that you should identify the symptoms first.
6. **D** You know that John can connect to the server, so he's communicating over the network, thus ruling out A and C. Since John is communicating with a web server via its URL, it's not a NetBIOS name problem, so B is irrelevant (WINS resolves NetBIOS names and has nothing to do with URLs).
7. **C** COM1 uses port 03F8 and IRQ 4.
8. **A** LPT2 uses port 0278 and IRQ 5.
9. **C** **D** SCSI ports can use Centronics 50-pin connectors (A) or DB-25F connectors (B), among others. The high-density connector used is also a 50-pin connector, not a 36-pin connector (D).
10. **C** Internal modems don't need memory address resources.

About the CD-ROM

Mike Meyers' Certification Passport CD-ROM Instructions

The CD-ROM included with this book comes complete with MasterExam and the electronic version of the book. The software is easy to install on any Windows 98/NT/2000/XP computer and must be installed to access the MasterExam feature. You may, however, browse the electronic book directly from the CD without installation. To register for a second bonus MasterExam, simply click the Online Training link on the Main Page and follow the directions to the free online registration.

System Requirements

Software requires Windows 98 or higher and Internet Explorer 5.0 or above and 20 MB of hard disk space for full installation. The Electronic book requires Adobe Acrobat Reader.

Installing and Running MasterExam

If your computer CD-ROM drive is configured to auto run, the CD-ROM will automatically start up upon inserting the disk. From the opening screen, you may install MasterExam by selecting the *MasterExam* link. This will begin the installation process and create a program group named "LearnKey." To run MasterExam, use START | PROGRAMS |LEARNKEY. If the auto run feature did not launch your CD, browse to the CD and click the "LaunchTraining.exe" icon.

MasterExam

MasterExam provides you with a simulation of the actual exam. The number of questions, the type of questions, and the time allowed are intended to be an accurate representation of the exam environment. You have the option to take an open book exam, including hints, references, and answers, a closed book exam, or the timed MasterExam simulation. When you launch MasterExam, a digital clock display will appear in the upper left-hand corner of your screen. The clock will continue to count down to zero unless you choose to end the exam before the time expires.

Electronic Book

The entire contents of this book are provided in PDF. Adobe's Acrobat Reader has been included on the CD.

Help

A help file is provided through the Help button on the main page in the lower-left-hand corner. Individual help features are also available through MasterExam.

Removing Installation(s)

MasterExam is installed to your hard drive. For *best* results when removing the program, use the START | PROGRAMS |LEARNKEY|UNINSTALL options to remove MasterExam.

LearnKey Technical Support

For technical problems with the software (installation, operation, removing installations), and for questions regarding the online bonus exam registration, please visit www.learnkey.com or e-mail techsupport@learnkey.com.

Content Support

For questions regarding the technical content of the electronic book or MasterExam, please visit www.osborne.com or e-mail customer.service@mcgraw-hill.com. For customers outside the 50 United States, e-mail international_cs@mcgraw-hill.com.

Career Flight Path

Network+ Certification generally serves as the follow-up to the immensely popular A+ Certification and is an important cornerstone for any number of career flight paths. Many IT companies see Network+ Certification as the foundation for networking expertise. After Network+, you have a number of certification options, depending on the types or specific brands of network hardware you choose to support. Look at these four in particular:

- CompTIA Server+ Certification
- Microsoft Certified Professional Certifications
- Novell NetWare Certifications
- Cisco Certifications

CompTIA Server+ Certification

Server+ Certification offers a more in-depth testing of your knowledge of PC and server-specific hardware and operating systems. If you plan to follow the path of the high-end hardware tech, Server+ is a good next step—and Server+ is a natural lead-in to Cisco certifications (see the section that follows).

Microsoft Certified Professional Certifications

Microsoft NT, 2000, XP, and 2003 operating systems control a huge portion of all installed networks, and those networks need qualified support people to make them run. Microsoft offers a series of certifications for networking professionals that naturally follow the CompTIA certifications. Microsoft offers a whole slew of tracks and exams, but here's what I suggest. First, take one of the two networking system exams required and one client operating system exam. Any one gives you the first certification, Microsoft Certified Professional (MCP).

Once you've taken one of the two networking system exams, take the other one, because if you've followed the path I've suggested, you're well on your way to attaining the Microsoft Certified Systems Administrator (MCSA) certification.

To become an MCSA, you need to pass three exams and one elective. The cool part is that you can substitute A+/Network+ or A+/Server+ for that elective exam. You're almost there already!

Finally, if you want to stay the course, Microsoft's ever-popular Microsoft Certified Systems Engineer (MCSE) certification holds a lot of clout for those looking to work in the networking field. The MCSE consists of seven exams—six core and one elective—of which you'll already have at least three. Check out Microsoft's Learning and Certification website at http://www.microsoft.com/ for details.

Novell NetWare Certifications

Novell NetWare may not be the powerhouse it once was, but a huge installed base of NetWare networks is still out there! The surge of techs toward Microsoft certifications has created a bit of a shortage of good NetWare certified techs. The Certified NetWare Engineer (CNE) is the certification to go for if you want to get into NetWare networks. Novell has a number of tracks. You can check out Novell's certification website at http://www.novell.com/ for more details.

Cisco Certifications

Let's face it: Cisco routers pretty much run the Internet, not to mention most of the world's intranets. Cisco provides three levels of certification for folks who want to show their skills at handling Cisco products. Nearly everyone interested in Cisco certification starts with the Certified Cisco Network Associate (CCNA). The CCNA can be taken as one or two exams and is a darn easy way to slap the word *Cisco* on your resume! After the CCNA, you should consider the Certified Cisco Networking Professional (CCNP) certification. See the Cisco certification website at http://www.cisco.com/.

Index

B

C

D

I

J

K

L

M

O

Q

R

U

V

W

X

INTERNATIONAL CONTACT INFORMATION

AUSTRALIA
McGraw-Hill Book Company
Australia Pty. Ltd.
TEL +61-2-9900-1800
FAX +61-2-9878-8881
http://www.mcgraw-hill.com.au
books-it_sydney@mcgraw-hill.com

CANADA
McGraw-Hill Ryerson Ltd.
TEL +905-430-5000
FAX +905-430-5020
http://www.mcgraw-hill.ca

GREECE, MIDDLE EAST, & AFRICA (Excluding South Africa)
McGraw-Hill Hellas
TEL +30-210-6560-990
TEL +30-210-6560-993
TEL +30-210-6560-994
FAX +30-210-6545-525

MEXICO (Also serving Latin America)
McGraw-Hill Interamericana Editores
S.A. de C.V.
TEL +525-1500-5108
FAX +525-117-1589
http://www.mcgraw-hill.com.mx
carlos_ruiz@mcgraw-hill.com

SINGAPORE (Serving Asia)
McGraw-Hill Book Company
TEL +65-6863-1580
FAX +65-6862-3354
http://www.mcgraw-hill.com.sg
mghasia@mcgraw-hill.com

SOUTH AFRICA
McGraw-Hill South Africa
TEL +27-11-622-7512
FAX +27-11-622-9045
robyn_swanepoel@mcgraw-hill.com

SPAIN
McGraw-Hill/
Interamericana de España, S.A.U.
TEL +34-91-180-3000
FAX +34-91-372-8513
http://www.mcgraw-hill.es
professional@mcgraw-hill.es

UNITED KINGDOM, NORTHERN, EASTERN, & CENTRAL EUROPE
McGraw-Hill Education Europe
TEL +44-1-628-502500
FAX +44-1-628-770224
http://www.mcgraw-hill.co.uk
emea_queries@mcgraw-hill.com

ALL OTHER INQUIRIES Contact:
McGraw-Hill/Osborne
TEL +1-510-420-7700
FAX +1-510-420-7703
http://www.osborne.com
omg_international@mcgraw-hill.com

LICENSE AGREEMENT

THIS PRODUCT (THE "PRODUCT") CONTAINS PROPRIETARY SOFTWARE, DATA AND INFORMATION (INCLUDING DOCUMENTATION) OWNED BY THE McGRAW-HILL COMPANIES, INC. ("McGRAW-HILL") AND ITS LICENSORS. YOUR RIGHT TO USE THE PRODUCT IS GOVERNED BY THE TERMS AND CONDITIONS OF THIS AGREEMENT.

LICENSE: Throughout this License Agreement, "you" shall mean either the individual or the entity whose agent opens this package. You are granted a non-exclusive and non-transferable license to use the Product subject to the following terms:
(i) If you have licensed a single user version of the Product, the Product may only be used on a single computer (i.e., a single CPU). If you licensed and paid the fee applicable to a local area network or wide area network version of the Product, you are subject to the terms of the following subparagraph (ii).
(ii) If you have licensed a local area network version, you may use the Product on unlimited workstations located in one single building selected by you that is served by such local area network. If you have licensed a wide area network version, you may use the Product on unlimited workstations located in multiple buildings on the same site selected by you that is served by such wide area network; provided, however, that any building will not be considered located in the same site if it is more than five (5) miles away from any building included i such site. In addition, you may only use a local area or wide area network version of the Product on one single server. If you wish to use the Product on more than one server, you must obtain written authorization from McGraw-Hill and pay additional fees.
(iii) You may make one copy of the Product for back-up purposes only and you must maintain an accurate record as to the location of the back-up at all times.

COPYRIGHT; RESTRICTIONS ON USE AND TRANSFER: All rights (including copyright) in and to the Product are owned by McGraw-Hill and its licensors. You are the owner of the enclosed disc on which the Product is recorded. You may not use, copy, decompile disassemble, reverse engineer, modify, reproduce, create derivative works, transmit, distribute, sublicense, store in a database or retrieval system of any kind, rent or transfer the Product, or any portion thereof, in any form or by any means (including electronically or otherwise) except as expressly provided for in this License Agreement. You must reproduce the copyright notices, trademark notices, legends and logo of McGraw-Hill and its licensors that appear on the Product on the back-up copy of the Product which you are permitted to make hereunder All rights in the Product not expressly granted herein are reserved by McGraw-Hill and its licensors.

TERM: This License Agreement is effective until terminated. It will terminate if you fail to comply with any term or condition of this License Agreement. Upon termination, you are obligated to return to McGraw-Hill the Product together with all copies thereof and to purge all copies of the Product included in any and all servers and computer facilities.

DISCLAIMER OF WARRANTY: THE PRODUCT AND THE BACK-UP COPY ARE LICENSED "AS IS." McGRAW-HILL, ITS LICENSORS AND THE AUTHORS MAKE NO WARRANTIES, EXPRESS OR IMPLIED, AS TO THE RESULTS TO BE OBTAINED BY ANY PERSON OR ENTITY FROM USE OF THE PRODUCT, ANY INFORMATION OR DATA INCLUDED THEREIN AND/OR ANY TECHNICAL SUPPORT SERVICES PROVIDED HEREUNDER, IF ANY ("TECHNICAL SUPPORT SERVICES"). McGRAW-HILL, ITS LICENSORS AND THE AUTHORS MAKE NO EXPRESS OR IMPLIED WARRANTIES OF MERCHANTABILITY OR FITNESS FOR A PARTICULAR PURPOSE OR USE WITH RESPECT TO THE PRODUCT. McGRAW-HILL, ITS LICENSORS, AND THE AUTHORS MAKE NO GUARANTEE THAT YOU WILL PASS ANY CERTIFICATION EXAM WHATSOEVER BY USING THIS PRODUCT. NEITHER McGRAW-HILL, ANY OF ITS LICENSORS NC THE AUTHORS WARRANT THAT THE FUNCTIONS CONTAINED IN THE PRODUCT WILL MEET YOUR REQUIREMENTS C THAT THE OPERATION OF THE PRODUCT WILL BE UNINTERRUPTED OR ERROR FREE. YOU ASSUME THE ENTIRE RISK WITH RESPECT TO THE QUALITY AND PERFORMANCE OF THE PRODUCT.

LIMITED WARRANTY FOR DISC: To the original licensee only, McGraw-Hill warrants that the enclosed disc on which the Product is recorded is free from defects in materials and workmanship under normal use and service for a period of ninety (90) days from the date of purchase. In the event of a defect in the disc covered by the foregoing warranty, McGraw-Hill will replace the disc.

LIMITATION OF LIABILITY: NEITHER McGRAW-HILL, ITS LICENSORS NOR THE AUTHORS SHALL BE LIABLE FOR ANY INDIRECT, SPECIAL OR CONSEQUENTIAL DAMAGES, SUCH AS BUT NOT LIMITED TO, LOSS OF ANTICIPATED PROFITS OR BENEFITS, RESULTING FROM THE USE OR INABILITY TO USE THE PRODUCT EVEN IF ANY OF THEM HAS BEEN ADVISED OF THE POSSIBILITY OF SUCH DAMAGES. THIS LIMITATION OF LIABILITY SHALL APPLY TO ANY CLAIM OR CAUSE WHATSOEVER WHETHER SUCH CLAIM OR CAUSE ARISES IN CONTRACT, TORT, OR OTHERWISE. Some states do not allow the exclusion or limitation of indirect, special or consequential damages, so the above limitation may not apply to you.

U.S. GOVERNMENT RESTRICTED RIGHTS: Any software included in the Product is provided with restricted rights subject to subparagraphs (c), (1) and (2) of the Commercial Computer Software-Restricted Rights clause at 48 C.F.R. 52.227-19. The terms of this Agreement applicable to the use of the data in the Product are those under which the data are generally made available to the general public by McGraw-Hill. Except as provided herein, no reproduction, use, or disclosure rights are granted with respect to the data included in the Product and no right to modify or create derivative works from any such data is hereby granted.

GENERAL: This License Agreement constitutes the entire agreement between the parties relating to the Product. The terms of any Purcha Order shall have no effect on the terms of this License Agreement. Failure of McGraw-Hill to insist at any time on strict compliance with this License Agreement shall not constitute a waiver of any rights under this License Agreement. This License Agreement shall be construe and governed in accordance with the laws of the State of New York. If any provision of this License Agreement is held to be contrary to la that provision will be enforced to the maximum extent permissible and the remaining provisions will remain in full force and effect.